... century
...nadian - Biography.

LEACOCK

A BIOGRAPHY
Albert & Theresa Moritz

First published in 1985 by Stoddart Publishing
A Division of General Publishing Co. Limited
30 Lesmill Road
Toronto, Ontario
M3B 2T6

CANADIAN CATALOGUING IN PUBLICATION DATA

Moritz, A.F.
Leacock, a biography

Includes bibliographical references.
ISBN 0-7737-2027-8.

1. Leacock, Stephen, 1869-1944 - Biography.
2. Authors, Canadian (English) - 20th century -
Biography.* 3. Humorists, Canadian - Biography.
I. Moritz, Theresa. II. Title.

PS8523.E22Z77 1985   C818'.5209   C85-098147-6
PR9199.2.L42Z77 1985

Cover Design: NewtonFrank

Cover Painting
Portrait of Stephen Leacock
by Edwin Holgate
Courtesy of the National Gallery
of Canada

Typesetting by Jay Tee Graphics Ltd.
Printed and bound in Canada

Contents

To
Professor Louis H. Belden
and
Mrs. Jean Belden

Chapter One

We Have With Us To-night

STEPHEN Butler Leacock often was asked about the art of writing humor. While maintaining that humor was no business for amateurs, he willingly discussed his methods. Like a magician urging the audience to examine his apparatus for making a lovely lady disappear, Leacock told his questioners just exactly how his trick was done. First, write down the ideas as soon as they come. Sometimes an idea could be a bit slow in forming, true, but writing it down was never difficult. The key to getting ideas, Leacock said, was a clear head, such as a person could obtain from sleeping outdoors (in all weathers) and rising at five o'clock in the morning. At least, that was how he did it.

There is no evidence that the Leacock technique gained many disciples or created a flock of student humorists who followed in the master's footsteps, but there is considerable evidence that it worked for him. If he couldn't teach people how to be funny, Leacock was certainly funny himself. And, after all, he wasn't a teacher of writing. He was a professor of political economy.

It was humor that made Leacock well-known during his life-time — his books were bestsellers for more than thirty years — and his legacy of humorous sketches, parodies and essays keeps interest in him alive forty years after his death. His gift for writing "humorous articles," as he termed his creations, made his life remarkable. It was remarkable for the sheer volume of work he produced (he had almost thirty humor collections to his credit) and for the rewards this work brought him, financial and otherwise. More remarkable still is that Leacock's career as a humorist was, for him, a second career that really did not begin until he was forty. When *Literary Lapses*, his first book of humor, was published in 1910, Leacock was in his tenth year as professor of political economy at McGill University in Montreal. He had already published a

1

very successful economics textbook and had toured the world as an expert in British imperial politics and economic issues.

The combination of humor and a professorship in economics prompted many witticisms over the years, but not from Leacock. He did not insist that every novice funny-man must begin with a doctorate in the theory of values, as he himself had done. But neither did he ever suggest, by word or action, that he regretted having undertaken his university work, or that he regarded it only as a stepping stone to becoming a professional writer. On the contrary, he continued in his post at McGill until the age of sixty-five, when he found himself forced to retire, much against his will. He referred to himself as the victim of the university's mandatory retirement rule; he had been "Mc-Guillotined."

The question that should be put to Leacock, then, is not simply how to make people laugh, but how to make people laugh and teach other people economics, all in the same lifetime. Leacock was, in addition, a family man deeply involved with his mother, brothers, sisters, nieces and nephews, as well as with his own household of wife and son. He was fond of the company of his fellow teachers and the students of McGill and his many friends, those at the University Club in Montreal and the many others, such as Robert Benchley, gained in the course of his writing career and his deep involvement in public affairs. Writing and teaching, for Leacock, meant engagement with living political and economic issues. Writing also led him into his career as a public figure and popular speaker, not always in the role of a humorist and entertainer, but often as an authority on economics and politics.

Leacock's humor makes generous use of his own experiences. He often writes in a narrative voice that the audience is invited to identify as Leacock's own, although the comprehension and capability of this narrator change from piece to piece. Undoubtedly, readers of Leacock feel they know him and would like to know him better. Canadian editor and essayist Peter McArthur said that a Leacock biographer would have an easy time of it, because all that needed to be done was to arrange the information Leacock himself had provided in his articles. Hovering on the edge of his delightful improbabilities is the question: did this, or something quite like it, really happen? Leacock asks his readers to believe that the things that occur in his writings are very close to the things that occur in life — in Stephen Leacock's life, to be specific. His humor — perhaps all humor — depends very much on this sense that reality is actually being described, and that the exaggerations and fictionalizing white lies only serve to throw the truth into sharper relief. Without the real presence of Leacock in his work, we would not feel that a living man was revealing his foibles and our own, and his laughter would not give us the strong sense that all is well, despite human faults and failings. This is the vision and gift of Leacock's humor at its best, and it raises the question of how much of real life, especially Leacock's own life, is in the Leacock opus. The answer can only come from a search for the circumstances of Leacock's life as it can be reconstructed from sources independent of his work. Then comparisons between what he himself wrote and what we can determine did happen reveal the extent to which Leacock invented his world and the extent to which he simply reshaped the oddities that happened to come to him. The search is worth the effort; as remarkable as Leacock's life might seem from his own accounts, it was in many ways even more memorable for the things he did not put into his writings but left a part of his private experience.

Leacock had published ten successful books of humor when, on 14 September, 1921, he sailed from New York on the *Metagama* with his wife, Beatrix, and young son, Stephen Junior, bound for Liverpool, England and his first professional speaking tour. Christy & Moore Agents Limited provided him with first-class passage as part of their service during the three-month engagement Leacock had agreed to undertake at the agency's invitation. It was a glittering time of screen stars, royal personages, influential political commentators and society ladies turned novelists: the transatlantic commerce in celebrities was brisk. H.G. Wells was in Washington for a world disarmament conference. Margot Asquith was giving out exclusive photographs and interviews to Montreal and Toronto newspapers as part of her promotional tour for her first book, an international bestseller. Leacock arrived in London at the same time as Charlie Chaplin and just days ahead of the movie dream couple, Douglas Fairbanks and Mary Pickford. In such a heady atmosphere, Leacock traveled inconspicuously. He seemed simply a busy professor taking an unusual break in his routine as an opportunity for a family holiday, much as he had done in 1907 when, on behalf of the Cecil Rhodes Trust Fund, he had made his only other international speaking tour. On that occasion he appeared as an expert on British imperial economic and political policies. He had visited England in 1907 and had been well-received, even spending a weekend with Rudyard Kipling at the author's country house. But the 1907 trip had not prepared him for the treatment he would receive now that he was a widely read humorist. The morning after his arrival in London, he found himself surrounded by reporters eager for interviews. British readers evidently hoped to hear about Leacock as much as they looked forward to hearing from him. He was, to his surprise, a celebrity.

Back at home in Canada, the newspapers reported that "it looks as though Stephen Leacock may become as much an idol with the middle class in England as Charlie Chaplin is with the populace. Chaplin gives the impression of hiding from his admirers but since Leacock's arrival on Sunday interviews with him abound." Leacock was winning the British over by declaring that "he would rather have written *Alice in Wonderland* than the *Encyclopaedia Britannica*." The London *Morning Post* article that described his arrival, which was of sufficient interest to be reprinted in New York, identified Leacock as a worthy successor to Mark Twain (who had died in 1910) in the role of ambassador of humor from America to England. In fact, he was even more welcome than Twain because of the special quality of his Canadian humor. "His fantastical ideas are often in the nature of American hyperbole — but they are developed in English fashion as a rule, in a quiet and close-knit narrative which has none of the exuberance of the typical American humorist." The *Morning Post* reminded its readers that before publishing a humor collection, Leacock had achieved wide popularity in England through reprintings of his early magazine pieces, such as "Boarding House Geometry." The interviewer speculated that, far from hindering the humorist, a background in political economy provided the right touch of unlikeliness to mark Leacock out as a memorable character. "No doubt, Mr. Leacock owes something to the fact that he himself is an incarnation of the incongruous, being Professor of Economics at McGill University, whose humor is taken more seriously than his political economy — more seriously, we repeat."

The most enthusiastic of many prominent interviews appeared in the London *Times* on 27 September, 1921. It is worth examining in some detail because it gives a strong impression of Leacock, and also because Leacock himself put it to a good use in creating a running tongue-in-cheek skirmish with the London press that lasted through much of his tour. The *Times* interviewer, writing under the headline "A Master of Satire," reported:

> Mr. Leacock is a burly man in a light tweed suit; the sort of man it is hard to imagine wearing anything but a light tweed suit. He has a broad, strong face, with a wide forehead, half-covered by masses of low-growing hair and a thick moustache over a well-set mouth. Take him feature by feature and he might remind you of Thomas Carlyle.

With his eyes "twinkling," Leacock talked "in the most impartial manner of the beauties of economics and laughter."

Leacock proved something of a problem at first because, against all the laws of celebrity status, he didn't seem to want to talk about himself:

> It was not so easy to persuade Mr. Leacock to let the public into the mysteries of his craft or to talk about himself at all. First, there was a substantial barrier to be crawled over and under and around. That barrier was O. Henry.
>
> Every reader of Mr. Leacock must be aware that he adores the stories of O. Henry on this side of idolatry. He has been blamed by stern critics for extravagance of worship. "I don't care," he says. "I stand by every word I've written of that magician." There happened to be in the company a man who had known O. Henry personally and this man was obliged to stand and deliver. All that O. Henry had ever done and said in his presence, what O. Henry had earned and where he had spent his money, why O. Henry was shy and whence he had drawn his inspiration — this and much

also to similar purpose had to be debated and threshed out, accompanied by recollections of this plot and that, with zealous eulogy, before Mr. Leacock would condescend to realize that he himself was also a writer and an interesting person.

Was Leacock's reticence due to zeal for O. Henry, or to a failure to realize his own importance, or to native modesty? It is tempting to think that Leacock, besieged by questioners probing the secrets of his personal life and his professional successes, indulged in a bit of leg-pulling by displaying an "extravagant" interest in the private doings of another writer. Once he got started, though, he was willing to unburden himself. He said that "political economy had saved him from being considered merely a 'funny man'" and reminisced about his early disappointments in trying to publish a collection of humor. He said his manuscript was returned with the explanation that "humor was dangerous." According to the *Times*, it was his brother George who discovered a publisher for him. "Reading the rejected 'trifles', he observed fraternally, 'Oh hell, these are good,' and sent them into safe and profitable harbourage." The rest of the story of *Literary Lapses* can wait for its proper place; it is enough to say here that Leacock's brother George was in truth a key figure in launching the first book, although the publisher's rejection slip really had said that, "humor was too uncertain," suggesting that the danger posed by the humor, in their admittedly shortsighted eyes, was financial failure. Ten years later, Leacock had published his ten books with another company and was contentedly giving out the secrets of his success: early rising, sleeping outdoors, getting the idea down fast, and so on.

He also reminisced to the *Times*, in appropriately humorous fashion, about his teaching days in an Ontario grammar school:

Fathers and mothers too — you know how tiresome they can make themselves by interfering with the school master? I remember a man who used to check his son's lessons. Once, opening the boy's exercise book, I came on a note, "How is it that after being with you three months Robert knows no Latin?" Under this note I wrote another: "Probably his ignorance is hereditary." Another boy was helped by his relatives; I went over his Latin prose with him and pointing to one sentence said, "I don't agree with your grandmother's view of the dative," and to another, "Your grandmother fails in her declensions." The treatment was effectual.

There was much more of the same, all positive, all witty, and all excellent advance publicity for Stephen Leacock's lecture tour.

Like a true showman, Leacock left them begging for more. The tour did not begin in London. Instead, his first engagement, on 4 October, was held in the Yorkshire city of Thirsk; Leacock or his agents preferred to take the show out of town before attempting the capital. However, Leacock was not idle between the opening in Thirsk and his first scheduled appearance in London, on 17 October. On the contrary, the Sunday before he was due to speak in London, Leacock published in a London paper his own account of being interviewed.

I pass over the fact that being interviewed for five hours is a fatiguing process. I lay no claim to exemption for that. But to that no doubt was due the singular discrepancies as to my physical appearance which I detected in the London papers.

The young man who interviewed me immediately after breakfast described me as "a brisk, energetic man, still on the right side of forty, with energy in every movement."

The lady who wrote me up at 11:30 reported that my hair was turning grey, and that there was a "peculiar langour" in my manner.

And at the end the boy who took me over at a quarter to two said, "The old gentleman sank wearily upon a chair in the hotel lounge. His hair is almost white."

The trouble is that I had not understood that London reporters are supposed to look at a man's personal appearance. In America we never bother with that. We simply describe him as a "dynamo." For some reason or other it always pleases everybody to be called a "dynamo," and the readers at least with us like to read about people who are "dynamos," and hardly care for anything else.

In the case of very old men we sometimes call them "battle horses" or "extinct volcanoes," but beyond these three classes we hardly venture on description. So I was misled. I had expected that the reporter would say: "As soon as Mr. Leacock came across the floor we felt we were in the presence of a 'dynamo' (or an 'extinct battle horse' as the case may be)." Otherwise I would have kept up those energetic movements all the morning. But they fatigue me, and I did not think them necessary. But I let that pass.

Leacock said without "any spirit of elation or boastfulness" that he had been interviewed eighteen times in all and that, from the question of his appearance right through to the question about the relative merits of American and French drama, he had felt off balance.

With this article, Leacock moved from celebrity guest to a participant deeply embroiled in the heady give-and-take of London letters. His jests at his supposed unfamiliarity with the methods of the British press poke gentle fun at the whole process of "selling oneself." Leacock holds no brief for the methods of American newspaper people, whom he portrays as jingoistic promoters of their individual cities, looking only for some controversial or complimentary remark to hang on each distinguished visitor's well-known name. At the same time, he calls into question the reliability of the reporting process, even when undertaken so high-mindedly as the British presumably did it. He questions just what a reporter can hope to see: will it really be everything, will it even be true? He himself changed during a day of interviewing, and it was precisely the interviewing that did it. Leacock also implies a distinction between what he was prepared to give his interviewers and what the interviewers were attempting to get from him. He preferred to spin yarns of his own choosing and reveal himself in that way rather than to provide direct answers to questions about his personal life or to be treated as an enigma suitable for dissection. He did not have a scandal to hide, but he prized his private life and wished to keep it separate from the public attention that inevitably followed from his success as a humorist. His article enabled him to enter his own opinions about how impressions should and should not be gathered and won him fresh headlines only the weekend before his London opening.

It also drew some ill-natured words from the humor magazine *Punch*. *Punch*'s 12 October number carried a brief paragraph about Leacock's claims on the quantity of his interviews. It seems he said he had been interviewed eighteen times, sixteen times by men and four by women. *Punch* replied, "We are not saying it in any spirit of superiority, but we make it twenty." Considering the form of the remark, and its source, we may suspect that Leacock intended a slight on his female interviewers. At any rate, he did not change its wording or offer any explanation when he later republished his newspaper piece in the book he wrote about his trip, *My Discovery of England* (1922). More important, though, was another article in the same issue of *Punch* by Ernest Jenkins entitled, "Mr. Stephen Leacock, An Interview Gone Wrong." Jenkins, offering a mock apology for his failure to provide a thorough physical description of Leacock, explained:

> I called one morning soon after Mr. Leacock's arrival in this coun-try. I made full notes as to his eyes, their position, quality, flash-point, and colour. I took particulars of his hair, its shade, density, specific gravity and cube root. With callipers and tape-measure I arrived at the area in square millimetres of his jaw. I also made a rough sketch of the suit he was wearing and took a sample for chemical analysis. But on opening my evening paper I discovered that most of this, if not all, had been done by another interviewer.

Undoubtedly, Jenkins was mocking the *Times* as well as Leacock's protestations. But he went on to recount some of the questions he had put to Leacock — on subjects of literature and economics, the British press and political celebrities — and suggested an inadequacy in the answers he received. He con-cluded with a stab at the humorist's discussion of his special subject:

> And finally, when I asked him for a few hints as to how to write humorous sketches, he responded with great readiness and fluen-cy, yet without giving me any real encouragement to believe that now I knew exactly how to do it. At this point I concluded my enterprise, made a courteous bow — and took my leave — a little disillusioned.

Leacock, it seems, had not impressed everyone equally with his ability to be funny and to describe how to be funny. But he had certainly established himself as a name to contend with and argue over — and all without once speaking publicly in London. It was an auspicious beginning.

In the fall of 1921, Leacock was fifty-one; he would turn fifty-two on 30 December, just after his tour ended. To modern eyes, that might seem rather late in life to become a celebrity in demand worldwide. But Leacock was heir to a tradition that brought revered novelists, like Charles Dickens, to the lecture stage late in their writing years. He had first lectured extensively as a humorist during World War I, to raise money for the Belgian Relief Fund. But despite a growing number of engagements, both in Canada and the United States, until the spring of 1921 Leacock never contemplated any change from his annual routine of winters in Montreal and summers in Orillia, Ontario. The invitation from Christy & Moore prompted him to request leave from the principal of McGill, his old friend and former student, Arthur Currie, formerly chief of the Canadian Corps during World War I. Not since the 1907 Rhodes tour had Leacock been absent from the university during the academic year. Currie agreed to approach the board of trustees for the leave, which was granted during the summer. Leacock planned a tour of fifty appearances from early October to late December; he would go to England, Scotland and Cardiff, Wales. Britain was a small country by American standards, as Leacock himself was quick to point out, but to crisscross it as he did for fully three months from Bournemouth to Aberdeen, with several stints of daily appearances, was a stern task. For the most part, his wife and young son remained in London at 58 Romney Street, Westminster, while Leacock traveled alone to meet the various audiences and chairmen arranged for him.

The test may have been arduous, but Leacock was so much a match for it that he added several other engagements to his regular speaking schedule and managed a busy social life as well. We should remember that the Leacock of 1921, although fifty-one, was the hearty, energetic figure of the *Times* interview. (That interview was doubtless given at an early-morning hour.) Some of the most famous pictures and portraits of Leacock date from his final years, when he lived primarily in Orillia and presented the aspect captured, for instance, in Yousef Karsh's photographs of 1939: a gray-haired, stoop-shouldered, wrinkled but smiling country sage. In 1921, Leacock's thick, unruly mop of hair was brown touched with gray; his face, though lined, was full of color, and the contour of his jaw was firm and square. His most striking feature was his eyes, gray-blue and (as the *Times* said) always twinkling, the kind of eyes that promise candor and inspire confidence. His lips turned easily into a smile. He did not always wear tweeds, but his well-tailored clothes somehow came to every occasion rumpled and a little the worse for wear. His ties wouldn't stay tied but always seemed to be inching loose so as to give him freer rein to look about and speak easily. He was of middle height and carried his compact body erectly, although with a slight stoop at the shoulder. His voice, trained by years of teaching and storytelling at home and in his club, was deep and full, with an educated accent. His laughter, "a laugh a humorist would be proud of," according to the *Times*, sounded frequently when he spoke on the stage. Although it suited his own sense of a proper comic manner, Leacock said that his laughing on stage sometimes aroused resentment. He recalled one disgruntled listener who objected: "Well, I will say . . . you certainly do seem to enjoy your own fun," to which Leacock replied, "If I didn't, Madam, who would?"

The answer was that thousands would, and did. Leacock said later that so many people came to hear him during the British tour that he calculated his earnings worked out to about thirteen cents a person, but he admitted that the crowds had been consistently excellent. In his famous essay, "We Have With Us To-night," from *My Discovery of England*, he makes light of his treatment on this trip, of the horrors he endured at the hands of confused, self-important or dues-seeking chairmen. But on 17 October, the night of his first engagement in London, Leacock had at the Aeolian Hall a chairman who must have pleased him with the warmth and good humor of his introduction. Sir Owen Seaman, editor of *Punch*, taking as his theme the special qualities of Leacock's Canadian humor, praised its appeal for the British. "Now Mr. Leacock's humor is British by heredity, but he has caught something of the spirit of American humour by force of association. . . . His humour contains all that is best in the humour of both hemispheres." Seaman said ruefully of the Americans, "When we fail to appreciate their humour, they say we are too dull and effete to understand it, and when they do not appreciate ours they say we haven't got any." Leacock was safe on both counts. Events proved that he appreciated the humor of the British and the British appreciated his, to the point that he could honestly conclude that "all the good old jokes about the lack of humour in the British people are a pure myth."

Leacock offered a selection of four speeches on the tour: "Frenzied Fiction," "Drama As I See It," "Laugh with Leacock" and "Literature at its Lightest." The latter two were compilations of passages from previously published work. The first two, which proved the most popular, were lighthearted essays on the foibles and foolishnesses of contemporary popular stories and plays. Readers can find three "Frenzied Fiction" lectures in a book published late in Leacock's career, *Here Are My Lectures* (1938). Leacock had used the title "Frenzied Fiction" for a number of stage appearances during World War I; thus, he had three different lectures under that name for publication in 1937. Formally, they are similar to many lectures Leacock wrote in the pattern that is found in "The Snoopopath; or, Fifty Stories in One," in which he says, "This particular study in the follies of literature is no so much a story as an essay." The essays were illustrated not with samples from the works of other authors but with Leacock's own outrageous parodies of fashions in literature and drama. The flavor of his speeches can be found in one of his most popular pieces, "The Great Detective," closely based on one of the "Frenzied Fiction" lectures. It begins, "I propose tonight, ladies and gentlemen, to deal with murder. There are only two subjects that appeal nowadays to the general public, murder and sex; and, for people of culture, sex-murder." It was a style in which Leacock retained the delightful touches of pure fancy and of parody familiar from the *Nonsense Novels* and *Behind the Beyond*, yet emerged as a speaking voice in his own right, personally directing his jests, displaying his insights, controlling the audience's reactions to literature, all in a narrative voice that was apparently to be identified as that of the real-life Stephen Leacock. It was the "magnifying-glass method," as the London *Spectator* called it, the technique of holding life up to a view so clear that it became clearly foolish. It suited Leacock's stage manner, which was more that of the witty raconteur than of the performer. Some commentators have said that Leacock modeled his stage manner, with its ease and informality, on his classroom technique, although Leacock's former students have been unanimous over the years in maintaining that he rarely seasoned his lectures on political economy with jokes.

The 1921 lecture tour was an important event for the development of Leacock's writing, as well as for the impetus it gave to his prominence as a public figure and celebrity. In fact, there is a link between the increasingly personal and direct tone of his humor from the twenties on and his awareness that he had become a respected man, one who was known and listened to. For some years prior to his triumph in England, his work had been showing a tendency to move away from the fictional approach of *Sunshine Sketches of a Little Town* or the pure, impersonal parody of *Nonsense Novels*. Increasingly he had begun to write in the first person, in a voice that seemed to be offered to the reader as his own. He had already used this technique at times to develop a humorous fictional narrator, as in his famous "My Financial Career." As his career progressed, however, it seemed that Leacock was creating — or projecting — a narrator-character who was very close to himself or to what he would like to be. It is this side of Leacock's writing that received a boost from his British tour. His book about the tour, *My Discovery of England*, contains many pieces, including the famous "Oxford As I See It," in which the voice that speaks is clearly intended to be Leacock's own. The brilliant wit is subordinated to a sage's quite serious teaching on the nature and proper methods of education. This aspect of Leacock, which grew in importance in the last twenty-five years of his life, links him to the great tradition of author as wise man and social adviser. Leacock thus joined the ranks of public figures and social reformers such as Mark Twain, George Bernard Shaw, G.K. Chesterton, H.G. Wells, George Orwell and many more writers who defined the age as much through their opinions as through their creative works.

Leacock's tour began with a speech in Thirsk, Yorkshire on 4 October and ended in Bournemouth, Hampshire on 23 December. In eighty days, Leacock gave fifty scheduled speeches; the busiest period of the tour began early in November after a triumphant series of London engagements.

Following his 17 October speech, the one introduced by Seaman, Leacock took the stage three more times in London and on each occasion was presented by a distinguished journalist: on 19 October by J.A. Spender, editor of the *Westminster Gazette*; on 20 October by Sir Campbell Stuart, editor of the *Times*; and on 21 October by J. St. Loe Strachey, editor of the *Spectator*. During the next seventeen days, Leacock took two breaks, one for three days and the other for four, while speaking in the middle and southern sections of England, from Shrewsbury on the Welsh border to Folkestone near Dover. He made his single visit to Wales — an appearance in Cardiff — on 7 November. For the rest of November he was scarcely free for more than one day at a time. During this period he made a lengthy foray into Scotland with appearances at Glasgow, Edinburgh and Aberdeen. A return to the London area early in December was followed by a brief swing through Scotland and northern England and then south again for the conclusion of the tour.

His recollections of the tour lectures — described in two of the essays from *My Discovery of England*, "We Have With Us To-night" and "Do the English Have a Sense of Humour?" — present two different sides of his experience. "We Have With Us To-night," despite acknowledging his warm reception during the tour, emphasizes the doubtful pleasures of being a public speaker, with often hilarious complaints about misintroductions, unfortunate circumstances and unforseen complications. Once he was introduced as a criminal.

> Witness this (word for word) introduction that was used against me by a clerical chairman in a quiet spot in the south of England:
> "Not so long ago, ladies and gentlemen," said the vicar, "we used to send out to Canada various classes of our community to help build up that country. We sent out our laborers, we sent out our scholars and professors. Indeed, we even sent out our criminals. And now," with a wave of his hand towards me, "they are coming back."

On the other hand, Leacock said frequently that he found his audiences, like his interviewers, eager and appreciative. If they had any faults, it was only that they hoped to hear something from him and not simply to look at a famous person. In "Do the English Have a Sense of Humour?", he said this was perhaps the most significant difference between his audiences in North America and in Britain.

Being a celebrity meant that Leacock was sought out by celebrities. Postwar England was rich in writers whose work appeared in newspapers, magazines and pamphlets as well as in books. Many of them were frequently seen on the lecture stage. Leacock met John Galsworthy, Hugh Walpole, Arnold Bennett, Dean Inge and Sir Gilbert Parker. He discussed the nature of humor with G.K. Chesterton, after a game of billiards. Chesterton joined the on-lookers at the Oxford and Cambridge Club, where Leacock was engaged in the game with an old friend from Montreal, W.E. Gladstone Murray. Afterwards, Leacock and Chesterton talked privately; according to Murray, Leacock felt that this conversation "helped to crystallize my conception of humor as, perhaps, the highest product of civilization." Actor Cyril Maude took Leacock to Westminster to meet playwright J.M. Barrie, then sixty-one, whose *Peter Pan* was enjoying a revival in London. Their encounter was a command performance conducted in the eccentric style Barrie demanded: he reclined on a sofa in a darkened apartment and his guests were ushered in to amuse him. The unlikely pair — the langorous Barrie and the energetic Leacock — found common ground in O. Henry. Years later, Leacock wrote an account of the visit as a memorial to Barrie, whom he remembered as one of the few people in England at the time who had read O. Henry and "was crazy over his stories." Leacock was able to supply Barrie with firsthand information about O. Henry's life thanks to accounts of O. Henry's acquaintances, perhaps including the one he discovered at his press conference. Barrie was reluctant, in the end, to let Leacock go.

The circumstance of O. Henry's name cropping up on the tour is not as much by chance as it might seem at this distance in time. O. Henry's death in 1910 had signaled a new admiration for his works in America and in England, an interest they had not enjoyed during the writer's life. In 1916, Leacock wrote a strong defense of O. Henry. He attacked those critics who found fault with O. Henry for publishing some inferior material, which they said he must have done for money. While sympathizing with the personal pressures that might cause an artist to succumb to financial necessity and publish poor work, Leacock criticized commentators who would dismiss the good works of a contemporary author because of a few bad pieces and would allow a classic author praise on the basis of his greatest efforts. He eulogized O. Henry as an author very little swayed by the modern machinery of syndicates and press services. Interestingly, Leacock's praise of O. Henry came at a time when Leacock was being criticized for writing too fast, and charged with doing so for the sake of earnings. In writing about O. Henry and the private tragedy of want and neglect that lay behind the production of his stories, Leacock showed a keen understanding of the difference between good writing and commercial success. Either tardy or early financial rewards always put great pressure on the writer. Leacock found himself having to deal with the opposite of O. Henry's experience: fame and financial rewards came to him if not early in his life, then at least relatively early in his writing career. One of the most tantalizing questions about Leacock's work is the impact this success had on the type of writing he chose to pursue.

Leacock took short busman's holidays on the tour by visiting several universities. He had a special text, "The Economic Man," intended for such serious occasions. One of his most satisfying stops was at Oxford, where he had spoken during his 1907 Rhodes Trust visit to England. It was a rare family outing: his wife and son went along to stay at the famed Mitre Inn. After addressing the Oxford Union, Leacock was also entertained at a breakfast by former McGill students. These events formed the basis for one of Leacock's most famous essays, "Oxford As I See It," a very serious praise of education at the British university sprinkled generously with flashes of wit. As Leacock's career continued, the theme of quality education would engage him more and more. Much of his basic concern that education be tailored to individual students, rather than made into a wholesome commodity, is expressed clearly in the Oxford report. A visit to the London School of Economics gave him another opportunity to stir up controversy. On 12 December, he was the guest speaker at the inaugural meeting of London's Canadian Club. He was introduced by Sir Gilbert Parker, a transplanted Canadian living in London, whose novels of Canadian adventure were bestsellers. Leacock used the occasion to make some much-appreciated jokes about a recent Liberal election victory back home. Turning to British politics, he said that complaints about income tax, common at the time of his visit, failed to take into account the heavier burden of hidden and indirect taxes borne by citizens of other countries. Leacock maintained that the Britons were, in fact, well off with respect to taxation. This brought a storm of letters against him in the press, which Leacock invited the School of Economics students to answer on his behalf if they agreed with his remarks. The students complied with the request readily, and in gratitude he treated them to lunch during a return visit to London.

One of the most remarkable performances during the tour was Leacock's speech on 8 December at the London Society. An account in the *Times* places the speech in the third person but still reproduces clearly the flavor of Leacock's remarks. Just as he turned the tables on his interviewers with his article on being interviewed, so here Leacock turned the tables on English impression-gatherers in America by giving his impressions of England — and some impressions on forming impressions.

He came here a raw Canadian; he was now a cooked Londoner. He had nothing but admiration for his hosts' fellow islanders who crossed the Atlantic to pick up impressions like huckleberries on the other side. As far as he knew, Mr. H.G. Wells had outdistanced all rivals in that art, by having formed 2,758 impressions in a fortnight, or at the rate of four and one-half per second! (Laughter) Personally he could only pick up impressions somewhat laboriously, although he had sold them before he landed in this country. (Laughter) He had been told that among the first places which he must see in London were the Tower, in which there was the most marvellous collection of instruments of torture in the world, and the British Museum, with its most extraordinary collection of Egyptian writings; but he had become a sophisticated Londoner in that he had not seen those places, although he had seen the splendid spectacle entitled *Cairo*. (Laughter) Among the monuments of London, one which he could not too much admire represented Sir

17

Wilfrid Lawson drinking tea. When he and some Americans were told that it represented the first prohibitionist all that they wanted was that there should be placed beside it in equal majesty a statue of the last prohibitionist.

Complaining of his troubles in gaining impressions about the workings of British government, Leacock made this report on the House of Commons:

He would describe the situation of the luncheon-room, the tea-room and the bar but of the actual chambers, not a good deal. He would explain that the legislative chamber was very little used, because at the present time legislation was not conducted there but elsewhere as, for example, in the home of Mr. Lloyd George, or in Ireland, or in any other convenient spot and then at the earliest convenient moment the members were summoned together to hear the latest thing in legislation and were expected to cheer or groan or, if they chose, to do both. (Laughter)

Despite ribbing those who "form impressions," Leacock proved in this speech and on other occasions that he was confident in his own ability to gather these saleable commodities.

Leacock's book about his trip, *My Discovery of England*, enjoyed considerable popularity and critical success on its publication in the fall of 1922. It went through several printings both in the United States and England. (It was not as popular in Canada, where a second impression was never made from the first edition.) Reviews were generally enthusiastic, although some dissenting voices were also heard. The Boston *Transcript* said it was "bright with the humor which bubbles irrepressibly from the writings of this Canadian 'Mark Twain'." In England, he was called "not only amusing but shrewd" in his analysis of English politics and press. His friend Robert Benchley filed a favorable notice in the New York *Tribune*. A glowing report came from New York's *Outlook* magazine: "Mr. Leacock's humor has never been more enjoyable than in this book. He contrives to touch up the foibles and follies of English and Americans alike, and without giving offense in either direction. Capital reading!" Negative judgments complained that the book's "blithe conception" was not uniformly realized. In the *Nation*, Lawton Mackall wrote, "Philosopher, pedagogue, political economist that he is, the responsibility of being unflaggingly rollicksome becomes at times almost an anxious duty." Over the years, *My Discovery of England* has lost favor among Leacock's humor collections. Although two of its pieces, "Oxford As I See It" and "We Have With Us To-night," are among his most frequently anthologized articles, the book as a whole is judged to be less successful than his earlier books, including *Literary Lapses, Nonsense Novels* and *Sunshine Sketches*

Leaving to one side the question of the book's merits, it must be admitted that it was produced with a speed rivaling H.G. Wells' record as cited by Leacock to the London Society. The manuscript of the book was at the publisher's in March, but that fact scarcely indicates the rapidity with which Leacock was working. As we have seen already, at least two of the pieces were prepared and presented during the trip itself. A third was published in *Outlook* in February of 1922; this was Leacock's answer to the question, "Do the English Have a Sense of Humour?". Several other sections were published in *Harper's* early in 1922. Although the crowds in Britain had enjoyed his impressions and magazines were eager for the pieces, Leacock found that his publisher was not so enthused. A Dodd, Mead and Company editor reported, "I must confess to a feeling of disappointment that it is not actually fiction." Is *My Discovery of England*, especially from what we know now of its manner of preparation, a sign of one critic's claim that Leacock's ambition to be "an imaginative writer" had faded after 1915? Or was he, whatever his ambitions, succumbing to a desire for money, or fame, so that he wrote too quickly or too carelessly?

As Leacock said in speaking of O. Henry, perhaps an artist should be judged by his best work because all artists have, at one time or another, produced something of doubtful quality. From that perspective, *My Discovery of England* contains enough of Leacock's best work that it might be sufficient to put aside all questions of deterioration in his craftsmanship. In addition, *My Discovery of England* was undertaken as a humorous, highly individual response to a particular event; it required Leacock to speak in his own voice in a form "more like an essay than a story." In writing "Parisian Pastimes" for *Behind the Beyond* (1916), Leacock used a similar approach to discuss the objects of travel and how to travel. The special circumstances of the London trip also encouraged him to make the attempt of speaking as a recognized author responding to his established audience. The danger that such a course held for Leacock was not that he would cease to be funny, or even that he would not longer write fictions. The excellence of Leacock's control of parodies and sketches did not of necessity require that he move solely in the direction of sustained narrative. Rather, the danger he faced was that he would be led to expect that his own individualized manner of treatment — a humane, informed and always humorous approach — would guarantee success no matter what the subject. Even in *My Discovery of England*, there are occasions when his jokes, however sound, seem insufficient because of the breadth of subject he seeks to handle with a witticism.

The tour came to an end in Bournemouth, Hampshire, on 23 December. He spent Christmas and New Year's in London, and then took his family to Paris, where he spent some time helping prepare French translations of his work. The Leacocks sailed for home from Le Havre on 14 January, 1922. Leacock wrote to Christy & Moore that he had enjoyed the tour. That year, lecture fees from the tour boosted his annual income to more than twenty thousand dollars for the first time. Despite his success, however, Leacock did not choose to follow up his new-found fame. He never again interrupted his McGill routine to mount a lecture tour on the same scale. After his Bournemouth engagement, Leacock told a *Times* correspondent that he did not expect to return.

> As far as I know, it is not very likely that I shall ever have the opportunity to be free from my college work to come back again, but I leave with very great regret. I have met with such extraordinary kindness, and such generous appreciation from the audiences who have heard me all over England and Scotland that the experience is one which I shall long cherish. I am afraid that when I go back to Canada, and say how I have been treated, it will let loose upon these shores, a flood of Canadian humorists and economists. I hope, for my sake, that they will be treated as I have been treated. From my experience here, I am convinced that all

the good old jokes about the lack of humour in the British people are a pure myth. I have made during the last three months a very handsome livelihood out of the British sense of humour and I am properly grateful for it.

With an ingenuousness worthy of Jack Benny, Leacock admits to those who pay him to be funny that he is making a good living from them; out of deference to their sensibilities he will even give this information in the form of a jest at his own expense (the only expense he had to meet in the whole transaction, after all). Full of impressions he planned to sell in the form of *My Discovery of England*, Leacock said his grateful goodbyes.

The Bournemouth *Times* correspondent said that Leacock made his last appearance in his home county of Hampshire, which he had left at the age of six. Some of Leacock's friends and colleagues made much of the humorist's British birth in praising his special brand of transatlantic humor. But in writing *My Discovery of England*, Leacock said very little about his feelings on returning for only the third time in more than forty years to his home country, and for the first time in all those years to his home county. Years later, however, Leacock told a story about visiting Hampshire in 1921. He described a car trip with E.V. Lucas, a writer for *Punch*, whose humorous work Leacock very much admired. The trip was urged on Leacock by Lucas because there were special souvenirs of cricket, Lucas's favorite sport, at Bury Lodge, near Hambledon Village; Bury Lodge was the ancestral home of the Butlers, the family of Leacock's mother, Agnes. Leacock relates that Lucas was much more impressed by the ancient cricket scores kept in Bury Lodge than by any sentimental associations the place held for his companion. He jokes, too, that he approached the village pub expecting a warm scene in honor of "the return of the native," but got scarcely a nod of interest. Even in a work intended as autobiography, Leacock presents this single account of his visit in terms that more conceal than reveal his sensations at a complex event.

He had returned a successful man, a sought-after man, to his home county after an absence of more than forty years. England was a homeland to which he openly acknowledged an enormous debt. He was proud of his inheritance as an English-man and was a strong supporter of Canada's place within the British empire. At the same time, England meant memories of his childhood, which had not been always pleasant. Leacock's pride of country was shadowed by the questionable family heritage of his father, a son shipped out repeatedly to the colonies by an impatient father. Birth in England was more or less an accident for Leacock. (Some of his brothers and sisters were born in South Africa, others in Canada.) Was Leacock proud of what he had made of himself, proud to lay claim to his national heritage because of his success in overcoming the limitations of his childhood situation? Or was he sorry to remember the hard times and embarrassment of his early years? The trip to England had brought Stephen Butler Leacock, the successful Montreal economist and humorist, face to face with his earliest, troubled days.

Chapter Two

My Victorian Boyhood

STEPHEN Butler Leacock was born in the village of Swanmore, Hampshire, England on 30 December, 1869, in the middle year of Queen Victoria's reign. He was a child of the mid-Victorian period, of imperial England at its height. As he grew, his mind and his writing never ceased to look back to Victorian England and to draw energy from a complex attitude towards it. That attitude was made up of idealization, criticism and measured respect. The year of Leacock's birth, now five generations behind us, might seem remote, lying, as it does, at the heart of a period the twentieth century charges with false attitudes, dogmatism and hypocrisy. And yet, the year 1869 remains in many respects curiously familiar, part of a nostalgically remembered time that led directly to our own.

Leacock came into the world on England's quiet southern coast at a time long before flight or atomic power. But many of the developments that shaped the modern world — steam, industrialization, the railway — were already in full play. In 1869 the first modern wars, the American Civil War and the Crimean War, were recently concluded, and the Franco-Prussian War was about to begin. Leacock admired two authors above all others and produced biographies of both, Mark Twain and Charles Dickens. Twain had begun his writing life in 1865, and Charles Dickens, although still vigorously working and publishing, would die in 1870. Leacock's exact contemporaries were people who, like himself, were nurtured by the nineteenth century and, in adulthood, helped to shape a very different era: Neville Chamberlain, Mohandas Gandhi and André Gide were all born in 1869. Many of the great inventions of the industrial period had occurred earlier, but the year of Leacock's birth produced several that affected day-to-day life in ways that are still felt. The electric washing machine was developed in 1869, as were margarine and celluloid. Although the first widespread use of celluloid was as a replacement for linen in the manufacture of men's detachable shirt collars, a garment long vanished, the material found a permanent and honorable place in modern history by making motion-picture film possible.

The country in which Leacock was born was as important to him as the period. Although he lived in England for only six years, he always treasured the fact of his English birth. He was the product of a marriage that had united two established families, and Leacock could properly claim, as he did throughout his life, to be a direct heir of a cultured English tradition and an active, educated, middle-class form of participation in the country's history and institutions. For Leacock in his adulthood, these institutions were embodied, however, as much in the empire as in England herself; the empire formed a living link to the mother country for Englishmen in colonies or former colonies. As a Canadian for sixty-eight of his seventy-four years, Leacock lived in the empire — later the Commonwealth — for most of his life, and always affirmed that he would not have changed his Canadian manner of being English even for the opportunity to return to England. Somewhat like Saint Paul, who, as a Christian, retained his sense of the privilege of Roman citizenship, Leacock felt that the mere fact of having been born an Englishman was a gift any person would wish to possess.

Ironically, it was little more than an accident that he received this birthright. Had family plans progressed as intended, he would not have been born in Swanmore but in southern Africa or in Canada or even in the United States. From the earliest days of their marriage, Leacock's parents were required by his father's family to look outside England for a permanent home. Leacock's father experimented with farming ventures in the British colony of Natal, South Africa, and in Kansas (each home was intended to be permanent) before the move to Canada was made in 1876. Swanmore was only a brief station in the wandering existence of the family during Leacock's first six years.

Located about eleven miles south of Winchester, the village of Swanmore has grown considerably since the Leacocks lived there. The cottage in which Stephen was born, in a second-story bedroom under thatched eaves, is still standing near the center of town, and a historical marker memorializes the writer's birth. In 1869 the cottage was three centuries old, according to its present owners; although far from luxurious, it was a comfortable and respectable accommodation for the small family, not by any means the tenement the Leacocks would inhabit later in Porchester, just before their emigration to Canada. When writing late in life of his childhood, Leacock commented that Porchester, his family's residence during his last two years in England, and not Swanmore, was the site of his only clear English memories. It is evident that the Swanmore home did not occupy an important place in Leacock family memories. It is seldom referred to, and Leacock, for much of his life, incorrectly identified his birthplace not as Swanmore, Hampshire, but as the village of Swanmore near Ryde on the Isle of Wight, where his paternal grandfather and great-grandmother had homes.

Stephen was the third child of Walter Peter and Agnes Emma (Butler) Leacock, and was born just two days before his parents' third wedding anniversary. Agnes and Peter were married on 1 January, 1867 in a ceremony attended only by two witnesses and the officiating minister, the Reverend J.L. Macdonald, at All Saints Church near Paddington Station in London. Their engagement and wedding were kept secret from both families until after the ceremony took place. It seems likely that the secret romance included a sexual liaison that resulted in pregnancy; the couple's first son was born in Natal just seven months after the wedding. Peter was seventeen, about to turn eighteen, and Agnes was twenty-two but would celebrate a birthday in just seven days. They had known one another in childhood; Agnes's family had connections to the Isle of Wight and vacationed near the Leacock family home of Oak Hill. But the secret engagement dated from the summer of 1866, when they met again after several years during which Agnes had not spent her summers in the area.

Peter, born on 15 January 1849, was a younger son of Thomas Murdock Leacock. Thomas was the son of John Leacock, who had grown wealthy from the family wine business in Madeira and had purchased the Oak Hill estate. The

25

founder of the Leacock line, according to a family history, had shipped out from England many years before as a cabin boy and had made a fortune in the wine trade, by managing vineyards and by exporting wine to England. Although the Leacock wine business continued to flourish in Madeira as late as Stephen Leacock's lifetime, his great-grandfather John retired from it to take up the life of a country gentleman on the Isle of Wight, ending the active involvement of this branch of the family in trade. In nineteenth-century English society, Leacock's family was not nobility or even landed gentry, having been at Oak Hill a bare three generations by the 1860s. Nevertheless the Leacocks were an important and established part of the community. Thomas had directed his two oldest sons, Peter's elder brothers John and Charlie, to careers as officers in the Royal Navy. Thomas planned to send Peter, who had shown no special distinction in education or ambition, to the colonies. Leacock often referred scornfully to his grandfather's determination to settle his children away from the Isle of Wight, but the provision for younger sons in wealthy families often took the form, for gifted and troublesome children alike, of the purchase of land abroad, in the hope that money would buy more abroad and provide a better future than was available in Britain. Thomas provided in much the same way for another younger son, E.P. (later memorialized by Stephen Leacock in "My Remarkable Uncle"). Although Thomas showed generosity in buying a farm for Peter, he did not approve the secret marriage. Peter and Agnes were not welcome at Oak Hill before they left for their farm in Africa, and Thomas showed an unsympathetic determination to provide for Peter only outside of Britain after the farm had failed and the couple had returned within a year to England.

Peter's bride, Agnes Emma Butler, was born on 4 January, 1845, the youngest child of the Reverend Stephen Butler (for whom Stephen Butler Leacock was named) and Caroline Linton Palmer. Both of Agnes's parents had been married and widowed and each had several children by the earlier unions; Agnes had a half-brother who received a Victoria Cross for heroic service in the Indian Mutiny of 1857. The Reverend Stephen Butler was a Hampshire man who had the living of Soberton, where Agnes was born. However, Stephen Butler and Caroline Palmer were married on the Isle of Wight, in the bride's home parish. There the young Caroline had been a friend of a Mrs. Young, who was the paternal grandmother of Peter Leacock and who had a home, Westridge, not far from Thomas Murdock Leacock's Oak Hill.

Agnes's early life was marred by tragedies that left her an orphan by the age of eleven. Her mother died when she was only five and her father six years later. These six years seem to have been difficult ones for the Reverend Butler, a distinguished clergyman who at this time held the living of Holy Trinity Church in Southampton. After his wife's death he suffered nervous attacks and generally failing health. He was at least once carried from his pulpit in the throes of what seems to have been an epileptic seizure. In early childhood, Agnes suffered a concussion from a fall which affected her health throughout her life. Despite such adversities, she was well cared for and educated by attentive relations on both sides of her family. On her mother's side, Agnes was the niece of three distinguished university educators: Herbert Bradley, dean of Merton College, Oxford University; Granville Bradley, headmaster at Marlborough; and Andrew Bradley, classics master at Liverpool College. Through her father's mother, Agnes was descended from Sir Henry Lushington. The Butlers had been established for more than one hundred fifty years in their home, Bury Lodge, at Hambledon Downs, Hampshire.

Despite the loss of her parents, Agnes remembered her childhood as a happy time. She lived with the family of her uncle, the Reverend Thomas Butler, first at a cottage near Bury Lodge and later, following the death of her grandfather, at the Lodge itself. Agnes was educated at private boarding schools and at a fashionable London finishing school. She was an accomplished young woman whose active life included church work and watercolor painting. In short, her background and upbringing were the conventional ones that, in the nineteenth century, produced the polished wife of a gentleman. Everything suggests that, at the age of twenty-two, there were two possible courses before her: marriage at her social station or spinsterhood. A formal marriage settlement, written after the wedding, reveals that Agnes brought to the marriage four thousand pounds' worth of investments that had been made for her by her family and from which she drew a small income.

The few details of the courtship of Agnes Butler and Peter Leacock that are now known come from an account of her early life that Agnes wrote much later, in Canada, at the request of her children. According to Agnes, another of her uncles, the Reverend Charles Butler, took her to the Isle of Wight in the summer of 1866. She relates that Peter, who was fond of sailing, came in the evenings in his own boat to Seaview, where she and her Uncle Charles were staying. She would slip out to meet Peter, and they went out on the water together in Peter's blue boat. The couple spent the days together at Oak Hill and went to visit Peter's relations, the Youngs, at Westridge. Agnes' sister, Kate, was visiting in England briefly from her home in Calcutta, and Agnes spent much of the fall with her at Portsmouth. Peter met her frequently there. In mid-December Agnes planned a trip to London to visit other family members for Christmas. Peter followed soon after and they were married. Agnes wrote:

> I can never think of it without sorrow and shame for deceiving my kind good uncles. It was Uncle Charles I was staying with — he went to the station and took my return ticket to Waterloo Bridge for me little thinking I was going to meet Peter and be married to him. They had nothing against his character, but he was not quite eighteen and a Roman Catholic and going to the Colonies. They had not then decided where.

After the wedding, the couple took rooms in Burand Street, Russell Square. Their colonial destination having been chosen by Peter's father, they bought tickets for Natal. The Butler family refused to allow any visits from Peter, and not only because of the secret marriage. The staunch Anglican churchmen of the family had been disappointed in the Leacocks years before when Peter's mother converted to Roman Catholicism and had all her children baptized in that religion. Agnes' father had been the godfather of Peter's brother, Charles, in his Anglican baptism. Although there is little sign that Peter actively practiced the Roman Catholic religion, his conversion, nevertheless, was a barrier for Agnes' relations. In March, 1867 Agnes and Peter took ship on the S.S. *Burton*

Hatter for their first venture as colonial farmers. They were both good sailors and enjoyed the trip until the final week, which was spent in sight of the Bluff of Natal in repeated, fruitless attempts to land. Their farm, near Pietermauritzburg, was a developed property. A land agent was there upon their arrival to show them around. They saw a comfortable house and farm buildings, facilities for raising livestock, and one hundred fifty acres given over to the growing of corn. The Leacocks entered South Africa before the discoveries of precious metals and gems that made it a goal of economic adventurers later in the century; at the time, it was known in England as a place admirably suited to lucrative farming. Early in the century the British government had conducted studies of the relative merits of southern Africa and Canada as destinations for emigrants, and had decided entirely in favor of Africa because of the milder, more familiar climate and the country's more settled way of life. Agnes left an account of the family's journey to Pietermauritzburg and the thirty-mile trek to the farm. She portrays it as a genteel expedition, an exercise in civilized dabbling at "roughing it." She traveled with an Irish maid, and she recalled how her retriever ran alongside and harried the native bearers who transported the family's heavy luggage. The community they found was reminiscent of home, even to the extent of being embroiled in a dispute over Anglican church matters, precipitated by the famous African Bishop Colenso's questioning of the literal interpretation of the Old Testament. This seemed a promising beginning, but when economic hardship resulted from the destruction of the first crop by locusts, the couple quickly decided that the farm was untenable. They returned home at once, Agnes complaining of the discomforts of the climate. The one tangible thing they carried back from the trip was their first son, Thomas James, born on 14 July, 1867.

During the next seven years, Agnes and Peter Leacock were reduced to a lower social and economic level than they had known prior to their wedding, or than they had apparently expected to maintain in Africa. They were not welcome to their families, and they spent no more carefree summers devoted wholly to boating and other leisure pursuits on the Isle of Wight or in Hampshire country seats. Instead, they moved often and to ever smaller homes. Stephen Leacock later remembered that, of the six children his mother brought with her to Canada in 1876, only two had been born in the same place.

Although the African farm failed, Thomas Murdock Leacock persisted in directing Peter towards an overseas farming career; he made it clear that this was the only future he would help to finance. On Stephen's birth certificate, Peter listed his occupation as "asphalt contractor." This line of work, to whatever extent Peter pursued it, did not render him independent of his father and thus able to remain in England. His principal occupation at this time was to study farming in fulfillment of his father's demand that he should prepare himself for another trip abroad. For Agnes, the early years of married life represented a dismaying change from her childhood and adolescence as the niece of a cultured, well-to-do clergyman. In reduced circumstances she followed her husband to a series of small towns including Swanmore, Shoreham-by-Sea (in Sussex) and Porchester, the only English home Stephen remembered. Her work as a mother increased almost every year. After Thomas James, the son born in Africa, there followed Arthur Murdock (born on 29 July, 1868) and then, at Swanmore, Stephen. He was baptized on 23 January, 1870 at the Anglican church of Saint Barnabas, which stands on a hill near the cathedral city of Winchester. Grace Pierpoint, a friend of Agnes from her London finishing school, was Stephen's godmother.

Agnes found herself unwelcome to her husband's family and ostracized by most of her own family. She was able to visit Bury Lodge, but had to do so alone, without her husband or children. The Reverend Charles Butler was one family member who did not cut her off; he apparently remained on cordial terms with her. Although Leacock later wrote sarcastically that Agnes and her children had been settled in Porchester, opposite Portsmouth, so they would not be able to visit Thomas Leacock while waiting for Peter to take them to America, the town had another advantage for Agnes: her uncle Charles was serving there. Leacock recalled hearing him preach and visiting with him in Porchester. In 1873 or early 1874, Peter had been sent by his father to a new farm in

Kansas. He was supposed to prepare the land for his family, which now included Charles John Gladstone (Charlie), born 6 December, 1871 and Agnes Arabella (Missie), born 15 March, 1873. Stephen wrote his father to announce the birth of another new baby, Edward Peter (Teddy), on 6 January, 1875:

Porchester
Ja

✽ My dear Dadda
    I thank you for the book. Jim has a young Xtmas [sic] tree We have got a new Baby he was born on the 6th We very often go in to Fareham

Your affec son
Stephen

Soon after, Peter returned with the news that the farm in Kansas had been destroyed by grasshoppers. With very little delay, his father sent him out again, this time to Ontario.

Leacock recalled his English years in later writings, but unfortunately this is one of the periods of his life about which he has little to say. He had clear memories of only his last two years in England. What he does record of this time comes largely in autobiographical rather than humorous writings, but nonetheless it brings out his instinct for highlighting incongruous details and embroidering upon certain facts, and so he does not provide anything like a detailed narrative. His major account of this period comes in the early pages of his unfinished autobiography, the four completed chapters of which were posthumously published as *The Boy I Left Behind Me* (1946). For this book he drew upon an earlier essay, "Migration in English Literature," which he had published in *My Remarkable Uncle* (1942). He also alluded to his years in England in the title story of this volume, a story about his uncle E.P.'s experiences in Canada. One of the most interesting features of all this material is Leacock's changing interpretation of his father. Leacock displays an increasing tendency to blame his father for not accepting family responsibilities or dealing effectively with the conditions of his life. In 1912 Leacock wrote a brief autobiographical sketch as an introduction to *Sunshine Sketches of a Little Town*; there he passed off the family's move to Canada in a joke: "My parents migrated to Canada in 1876, and I decided to go with them." In his stories about his uncle E.P., who drew his father into disastrous Canadian land speculations, Leacock spoke of Peter as a simple man, well-intentioned but ill-suited for business and practical affairs. But *The Boy I Left Behind Me* casts doubt on Peter's willingness to do what was necessary to support his family. Leacock glanced skeptically at the locusts of Africa and the grasshoppers of Kansas and implied that he exonerated them from full responsibility in the failure of Peter's pre-Canadian farming ventures. He characterized his father's "study" of farming in Hampshire as a series of beer-drinking bouts with local agriculturalists — and even at this, Leacock says, his father was bested.

Leacock's assessment of his English childhood in *The Boy I Left Behind Me*, insofar as any clear opinion emerges from his string of anecdotes and jests, can only be termed cheerful in comparison with his family's actual situation. His writings on his childhood place special emphasis on the historic associations of his family's residences, in part because he could supply the deficiencies of his memory from such material, but also to avoid a too-direct recounting of his early years. For example, in describing his parents' brief African episode, he gives most of his attention to Bishop Colenso, known as an author of mathematical textbooks, whose liberal theology had so enraged members of the southern African Anglican community that some of them had been refusing, during the Leacocks' residence there, to have their children baptized by him. Leacock's oldest brother was one of the infants involved in this controversy. Another example is the Butler ancestral home, Bury Lodge. Speaking of his mother's family seat, Leacock mentioned only its close associations with the history of the game of cricket. His account of Porchester is a mixture of personal reminiscence and information that would be suitable for a tourist guidebook or history, although the account is filled with Leacock's living sense of the past: the street in which Dickens was born, Nelson's flagship swinging at anchor in the harbor and an ancient church restored by Queen Anne, where his "uncle" Charles (Agnes's uncle) served. He has very limited memories of the large extended families that existed in England on both his maternal and paternal sides, and from which his parents were obviously excluded. In the passage on Bury Lodge, he recalled only one childhood visit to Hambledon Downs. He wrote with great learning and interest of a present given to him during a visit to the Isle of Wight by his grandfather, Thomas Murdock Leacock — a fragment of wood from the American frigate *Chesapeake*, captured by the British in 1813, whose timbers Leacock made a personal point of researching to their eventual destinations. He traced many of the best beams to a corn mill in Wickham, near Porchester, and found the mill still operating during his 1921 British tour. But the visit on which he received his present, which he treasured to the end of his life, was also the single trip to his grandfather's home that he records. In general, his description of the relations between his family and his grandfather displays a wry bitterness that stands out from an otherwise bantering account of this troubled period.

Thomas Murdock Leacock received a considerable portion of the space Leacock devoted to his English childhood. Thomas was identified as the motive force behind the family's compulsion to find a livelihood in farming. His grandfather, Leacock said, had apparently concluded that the Isle of Wight was not big enough for both himself and his children. Even the present of the wood fragment was given to young Stephen apparently in celebration of the knowledge that his family was finally about to leave England for good. Leacock portrayed Thomas as a man who was content to live in leisure and to provide for his children only a push in the direction of working to support themselves. He pointed out that the Leacocks for three generations — those of Peter in his youth, Thomas, and Leacock's great-grandfather John — had lived off accumulated wealth. Thomas had contributed nothing new to the family inheritance. Leacock commented that by the time of his own generation, the inheritance had been exhausted.

Leacock's fondest reminiscences of England were of the town of Porchester. He lived there for two years, until the spring following his sixth birthday, and had his earliest few months of formal education at a private school in Porchester that his two older brothers also attended. The only lesson he remembered from the school was his first instruction in geography. The teacher held up a map and led the children in a chorus, "The top of the map is always the north, the bottom south, the right-hand east, the left-hand west!" Leacock was tempted to ask whether the top might be the north only because the teacher held it that way, but feared to because of the teacher's ruler.

What Leacock gratefully remembered about Porchester and the Portsmouth area was, first of all, the depth of English history that it held in its buildings and associations, and second, the typical if somewhat fairytale-like Englishness, redolent of Gilbert-and-Sullivan fantasy, that he recalled in it. Porchester was named for Porchester Castle (the word "Porchester" meaning "port castle"), and in Leacock's day was a tiny settlement on the west shore of Portsmouth harbor. In the neighborhood was Paul's Grove where, according to ancient and apocryphal legend, Saint Paul had preached to the Britons. The castle itself, a huge, turreted rectangle, was mainly of Norman construction but had been built upon an earlier Roman fortification. Inside the castle precincts, the Normans had, in the twelfth century, built the Priory Church of Saint Mary in the Close, restored after fire damage through the munificence of Queen Anne. This was the church of Stephen's "uncle" Charles, where the family attended Sunday services. Stephen remembered Charles Butler's satisfaction that Porchester was unaffected by new religious movements, that no one there attended church revival meetings or suffered sudden conversions but "got religion" gradually during "eighty years of sleepy Sundays." As a child, Leacock had been aware of the symbolic presence of Nelson's flagship *Victory*, which had been retired to Portsmouth harbor, but it was only later, probably, that he realized how close chance had placed him to Charles Dickens's birthplace, for he did not read his first Dickens book, *Pickwick Papers*, until he was living in Canada. In 1921 he revisited the house his family had occupied in Porchester, and to his adult eyes it was a poor place. He found pathos in the tiny hallway his mother had called a parlor and the cupboard she had "had the nerve" to term a breakfast room. He attributed this emotion, however, not to shame at his parents' poverty but to the fact that he himself had become accustomed to ease and comfortable surroundings.

Leacock left Porchester in 1876 and was not to return to England, even on a short visit, for many years. If he continued to reflect on his English heritage and its roots in these mid-Victorian years on the southern coast, this was largely due to the care with which his mother later nourished and protected these roots. When he looked back to England, he could see in Porchester a legacy that was transmitted to him through the Victorian era but went much farther back, to the medieval, Norman, Roman and legendary pre-Roman history of the nation. Perhaps this is a source of the strong and poetic sense of history Leacock possessed. He felt that the English heritage was his by right of his intuitive understanding, his great and informed interest, and his concern to make it a living part of himself and of the present. Although it has been said that he can be understood as a Victorian, it is surely untrue that he was "Victorian" in the common sense of the term. Quite the contrary: Leacock was an opponent of dogmatism, prudery and hypocrisy. His strong belief in his right to the English heritage later made him a critic of its shortcomings, especially the institutions of heredity that had threatened to cut him off from his cultural birthright and all the unmeaning conservatism and self-righteousness that buttressed such abuses.

Leacock's lifelong feeling that English and Victorian values had to be revised to save their true meaning and make this available to all inevitably recalls both the life and work of Charles Dickens. Leacock's Porchester school stood on a rise that looked down into the street where Dickens had been born, in 1812, at 1 Mile End Terrace (today 393 Commercial Road, Portsea, the Dickens Museum), and to which the novelist had returned in 1838 while touring the Portsmouth area to research *Nicholas Nickleby* (1838 to 1839). Leacock shared with Dickens the passionate belief that English tradition must be reformed to preserve, refine and democratize its advantages, and both writers spent in the Porchester locale some of the bittersweet early years that imbued them with a deep love of their heritage and a realization of how insecure their possession of it might be. Like Dickens, Leacock looked back to a childhood that had promised but finally had not delivered an entrée into an English society that, to the child, had appeared a golden land of love and peace. This early sense of a cultivated, emotionally harmonious and stable existence, free of necessity, was all the more poignant because it was never fully possessed by the child, although he thought he had glimpsed its possibility — and even its reality, for others. Dickens and Leacock both display a vital element of bitterness over the social circumstances that made this life impossible for them; and even when, as adults, they knew this ideal world had never existed, it remained in them as the vision of what human society might be like. Each writer distributes responsibility for childhood pain to certain evil features of society and to the weaknesses of the grownups who had charge of him. To some extent, Victorian England remained for Leacock a symbol of much that is good in the normal life to which human beings aspire. But he realized that the Victorian world was inexorably receding into the past as people embraced other ideals and goals, just as in his childhood it had receded into the distance due to the mysterious failures of his parents and the injustices of the society around him.

One respect in which Leacock was very different from Charles Dickens was in his opinion of Canada. Dickens did not react any better to the Province of Canada than he did to the United States when he visited them on his celebrated trip of 1842. His initial enthusiasm for America as a country with a new approach to social virtues was quickly dissipated by what he saw, and in Canada he reacted particularly against a strain of rabid Toryism that was anathema to his reformist temper. Leacock came of age in the vastly different Canada of half a century later, and was always proud to be a Canadian. The decision to come to Canada was made by — or for — Agnes and Peter Leacock in the mid-1870s, almost immediately after Peter's return from Kansas. His father bought Peter a one-hundred-acre farm in Ontario near Lake Simcoe. Peter went to this property early in 1876, leaving Agnes to prepare the six children for a voyage across the Atlantic. Years later, Leacock remembered that his mother cried at the thought of leaving England, and it is probable that she knew, despite her earlier retreat to England from Africa and her husband's from Kansas, there would be no coming back from Canada. The trip was final, and Agnes and her children found their permanent home in Canada.

Their journey began in Liverpool on a ship of the Allan Line, the *Sarmatian*, a vessel that combined steam and sail and that so impressed the young Leacock that he carefully followed its subsequent career until it was broken up after World War I. For Stephen and the other five children, the departure was high adventure. When the *S.S. Sarmatian* sailed in May of 1876, Canada was in its ninth year as a dominion. Leacock had been born just two years after Confederation, which had united the colonies of New Brunswick, Nova Scotia and Canada (divided to form Ontario and Quebec) into the Dominion of Canada, a self-governing nation. In 1869, the year of his birth, the young country had met one of its first serious challenges: Louis Riel and Métis (prairie-dwelling descendants of French and Indian intermarriage) opposed westward expansion in the Red River Rebellion near the site of present-day Winnipeg. By 1876 Canada had grown until it reached from sea to sea by adding to the original four provinces three new ones, Prince Edward Island, Manitoba and British Columbia, as well as the vast Northwest Territories. The first Dominion census (1871) counted 3,689,257 inhabitants, but immigration was increasing this number rapidly; by 1891 the population had grown to 4,833,239. The great majority of the immigrants at this time came from Great Britain; they became the country's soldiers, lawyers, engineers, storekeepers, politicians, professionals, journalists, educators and laborers. Canada's first prime minister, Sir John A. Macdonald (1815 to 1891), had arrived in Canada years before Confederation as the young son of an impoverished immigrant, in much the same way as Leacock arrived in 1876.

Leacock's voyage was uneventful. He later wrote of the stirring sensation of the departure and of the last sight of the cliffs of Dover. But his chief recollection was of his first glimpse of Canada, the Gaspé coast, and of the striking contrast its bright, rocky harshness made with the verdurous softness of the English shore. Perhaps this memory remained with him because it foretold what lay immediately ahead: as difficult as his early childhood in England had been, his first years in Canada were to be much more so.

Chapter Three

The Struggle to Make Us Gentlemen

STEPHEN Leacock was born an Englishman, but he grew up in Canada. The separation between the old country and the new was not absolute; letters, money and even a remarkable uncle found their way from England to the Leacock farm north of Toronto, Ontario near the village of Sutton, which was on the shore of Lake Simcoe. Although the neighbors were not always English enough to suit Agnes Leacock, Ontario was, in its institutions and population, among the areas of Canada most loyal to the British homeland. It was a new life whose course was determined in large measure by the family's roots in England. The farm had been chosen from England, and money from England made education available to the Leacock children. Stephen's brilliance as a student soon set him apart from his brothers and sisters. From 1876, when he arrived in Canada, until 1887, when he graduated as "head boy" from Toronto's prestigious private boys' school, Upper Canada College, Stephen developed from one among thousands of British immigrant children to an individual distinguished for his promise. Schooling, which was clearly to his taste, held out to him one possible route of escape from the limiting prospects his parents could provide for him. In 1887, he was just one year younger than his father had been when marriage to Agnes set him on the wavering course he pursued throughout life. At seventeen, Stephen seemed much more a man of promise than his father had been. But at the very time when he had earned the right to an independent future, he was faced with the question of caring for his mother and eight brothers and sisters left alone on a debt-ridden farm by his father, who abandoned them, after numerous brief separations and difficult times together, within months of Stephen's high-school graduation.

This period on the farm and in high school — so dramatic in itself and so important in Stephen's development — inspired some of the most vivid of his later writings. *The Boy I Left Behind Me* provides more information about these years than about his first six years in England, although it takes the form of a string of memorable incidents and colorful reflections rather than a complete story. Once Leacock's accounts are weighed for their literary intentions, they provide an invaluable supplement to the little that is known from independent sources about the essentially secret years he lived on the farm near Lake Simcoe. On another level, of course, the literary component of Leacock's autobiography is the most important feature of the work, offering a rich embodiment of his assessment, many years afterward, of the way in which a difficult childhood had entered and enriched his later life. Like his explicitly autobiographical writings, Leacock's humor draws on experiences on the farm and at high school much more frequently than it draws on the years in England. His use of his life in Canada begins with pieces in his first published book, *Literary Lapses* (1910), and extends through *My Remarkable Uncle* (1942). As Leacock glanced back, these first eleven years in Canada were memorable for two things: first, his unhappiness with life on the farm and his determination to escape; and, second, his great love of learning, both the studies he began at home under his mother's direction and his years at Upper Canada College, with all its accoutrements of English tradition, refinement and masculine camaraderie. It was a period of personal success achieved despite difficult family circumstances, but at its end, Stephen found himself called upon to surrender his awakening ambition and assume responsibility for his mother and his brothers and sisters, whose situation had worsened dramatically in his years away at school.

The Leacock farm lay on a rise of ground four miles south of Lake Simcoe. The nearest sizable community was Sutton; the Leacocks lived closest to the tiny settlement of Egypt in the Township of Georgina. Agnes and the six children began their Canadian journey at Montreal, where the S.S. *Sarmatian* docked in May of 1876; they transferred to a river steamer for the trip to Toronto and passed Kingston on Victoria Day. A train took them from Toronto to Newmarket, thirty miles north and at that time the nearest railhead to the south shore of Lake Simcoe, another thirty miles away. Peter and a hired hand met the family at the railway station and packed them and their belongings into two horse-drawn wagons to make the rough, hours-long trek to the farm over dirt tracks and on corduroy roads through cedar swamps. According to Leacock, the family's first impressions of the neighborhood were far from favorable. Peter told the children crowded on the bucking wagon that the narrow dirt road through empty fields was their road, and Egypt their village. Even the modest home Agnes and the children had shared in Porchester made these new surroundings seem dismal and forbidding. They had left behind the quiet charms of a traditional English town overlooking one of the world's busiest harbors for a straggling village of taverns and one general store. The village was the only relief from miles of swamp. The farm dismayed them further. Agnes said nothing at the time, but she later told Stephen that her first sight of the home in which she expected to spend the rest of her life had broken her heart.

Today, the trip from Toronto to the farmstead can be accomplished in a pleasant drive of little more than an hour. Egypt is now only a crossroads, marked by a sign and one building dating from the turn of the century, a former school that is now the Egypt Women's Institute. There is no Leacock shrine either at the village or at the farm; in fact, few but local people know where the family once lived. However, the Lake Simcoe region is rich in carefully preserved memories of the humorist. Four miles north of Egypt, on York Regional Road 18, is Sibbald Point, where Stephen Leacock is buried in the family plot at Saint George the Martyr's Anglican Church, on a scenic bluff overlooking the lake. On the opposite, northern shore of Lake Simcoe is Orillia, where the Leacock Memorial Home stands at Old Brewery Bay, on the site chosen by Leacock in 1908 for his summer home. Although the Leacocks had difficulty adjusting to the new farm, they took root in the Lake Simcoe region as they had failed to do in all of the other locales they sampled. Agnes lived on the farm or in towns around Lake Simcoe for the rest of her life. Many of her children, including Stephen, visited the region regularly or lived there during their adult years. Leacock's attachment to the region was not based, however, on any childhood love of the farm. On the contrary, his years there filled him with an abiding desire to escape.

The site of Peter Leacock's hundred-acre farm is now the west half of Lot 6, Concession 4, in the Township of Georgina; it stretches north of Concession Road 4 about three hundred yards west of the road's intersection with York Regional Road 18, known locally as the "Egypt sideroad." A rough tractor trail leads north from Concession Road 4 to the northern boundary of the farm, which is situated on a rise that provides a panoramic view to the south of fertile farmlands dotted with houses and barns. On this rise stood the buildings of the Leacock farm; here, as in Africa, Peter Leacock came not to an undeveloped tract of land but to an established farm. The buildings included a house, which was enlarged considerably soon after the family's arrival. The original house was constructed of logs covered with clapboard; the addition was made of frame lumber and lath and plaster, and proved much colder than the rest of the building. During Leacock's lifetime, the original portion of the building was removed, which came as a surprise to family members when they made a nostalgic pilgrimage to the site in the 1940s. Other farm buildings included three log barns, two of them running east and west and the other running north and south between their western edges, so that the three buildings formed a U. The farm's facilities were completed by a large implement shed and outhouse with an attached smokehouse. None of the buildings is now standing on the site. The last of them, the house, burned down on 25 February, 1960. The land is still under cultivation, but the owner lives some miles distant.

Peter worked the farm with the help of a hired hand named Tommy, a Yorkshireman whose own farm in Ontario had failed. They grew wheat and other grains; the farm included grazing land for cattle, a market garden and a yard for chickens and pigs. The cash crop was wheat. During the depression that hit Ontario during the 1870s, wheat rarely returned a profit and bankruptcies were common. Leacock remembered only one year in which the farm did not work at a loss. In the first years, the children helped in the many jobs to be done, and by the time Stephen left for Upper Canada College, he had gained a thorough, and most unwelcome, knowledge of the demanding routine of the farm.

The family lived in virtual isolation. Their nearest neighbor was almost a mile away, the roads were poor, and bad weather often made travel altogether impossible. Sutton was only four miles away but the trip took at least an hour by wagon, involving as it did many hills and stretches of difficult road. The boys were accustomed to walking behind the wagon to rest the horse on the inclines and to lighten the load on the declines. Although conditions isolated the Leacocks, they were also separated from their neighbors by Agnes' determination to keep the children away from influences she considered dangerous. At risk, in particular, were the children's manners and accents, according to Leacock. All of the nearby families but one were considered undesirable. The Leacock children were taken out of the local Georgina Township school, which was located on or very near the site of the present Egypt Women's Institute. The school was built in 1900 to replace one that had burned down in the 1890s. This earlier structure was the school the older Leacock children attended for some time, and where Stephen studied for a little more than a year before Agnes became dissatisfied with it. In part, the problem was that, during the winter months, the trip was often too difficult, but more important for Agnes was the loss of habits of speech and dress that the children retained from England. The Leacock children were not allowed to go barefoot; it was "a question of caste and thistles," Leacock said. Agnes largely succeeded in her efforts: Leacock maintained his British intonation throughout life. The one important break in the isolation was the weekly trip to Saint George Church. The children contrived to make this into a pleasure excursion as well as a religious observance by meeting with friends to swim, boat or skate.

The isolation of life on the farm was perhaps the dominant impression Stephen carried away from his late childhood and early adolescence. His writings refer to it again and again. The farm, he said, was located in a "lost corner of Ontario." The railway did not reach Sutton until 1879, and Stephen did not see a train for three years between his first arrival in Canada and the gala opening of the Sutton station. The technologies that allow for personal communication over distances — the telephone and radio, above all — still lay in the future. In fact, Alexander Graham Bell patented his invention the year the Leacocks immigrated. Ontario was the scene for some pioneering firsts in telephone technology — the first long-distance call, for example, in 1878 — but home service was still some years away. There was as yet no hint that the automobile would replace the horse and buggy. The population of the district was sparse and far-flung; to travel one of the monotonous farm roads at night was to pass through miles of darkness broken only by an occasional glimpse of a kerosene lamp from the window of a distant farm house. There was a silence, Leacock recalled, that no city dweller could imagine. The years from 1876 to 1882 were for him "a six-year unbroken sentence." It was not loneliness or drudgery that Stephen feared on the farm. He was afraid also of being unable to choose a different life for himself.

Into this family solitude, in the fall of 1878, burst Peter's younger brother, Edward Philip, Stephen's "Remarkable Uncle." E.P., as he was called, was two years younger than Peter and was being provided for, much as Peter had been, with financing intended to settle him in the colonies. He was on his way to the Canadian west, drawn by tales of the fortune to be made in real estate in the rapidly opening province of Manitoba. A rail route through the United States was already open, and John A. Macdonald, campaigning for his return to the office of prime minister that fall, promised that soon there would be an all-Canadian railway from coast to coast. Immigrants were going to the prairies, and the hard times in Ontario drove many settlers off their failing or bankrupt farms in hopes of better times farther west. The children were in awe of their dashing bachelor uncle, fresh from a tour of the Mediterranean and bright with anecdotes of his distinguished friends. E.P. remained at the farm long enough to become involved in the national election. He was Conservative and an expert at barroom canvassing, where he used his name-dropping acquaintance with the English aristocracy to flatter local farmers and tradesmen into Conservatism. Extending his efforts to the speaking platform in Toronto as well as in the Lake Simcoe district, E.P. stayed in Ontario long enough to return Macdonald to power and then moved west. He wanted Peter to follow him.

From the beginning, life on the farm clearly did not suit Stephen's father; accustomed as he had become to long, if pointless, trips in distant parts, he found the promise of quick wealth in the west far more attractive than the uncertain fortunes available to him in Ontario. It is difficult to date with precision Peter's departure for Manitoba, but it probably came sometime in mid-1880 or in 1881. Leacock wrote in *The Boy I Left Behind Me* that he had been mistaken in earlier sketches when he said Peter left with E.P. Maymee Douglas Leacock was born on 24 November, 1880. Before he left, Peter auctioned off some farm equipment and machinery. His two older brothers, when they started classes at Upper Canada College in November, 1881, gave their father's profession as farmer, while Stephen's registration form from 1882 listed Peter as a real-estate agent in Winnipeg. It seems likely that he could not have left before 1880; on the other hand, he arrived in Manitoba while the boom in real estate was still underway, and its collapse came in 1882. When Peter left, nine children remained behind with Agnes: the six she had brought from England, and Maymee, George (born 1 March, 1877) and Caroline (born 16 August, 1878). Peter promised that soon the struggle to make ends meet would be over because he would make a fortune in the west.

E.P. never disappeared altogether from Stephen's life, nor did he lose the aura of personal charm that had first endeared him to Peter's children when he visited the farm. Although Leacock made it clear that his uncle's business ventures bordered on the fraudulent, he respected E.P. for his essential kindliness and unfailing zest for life. Leacock never blamed his uncle for starting Peter toward the west, although the move proved to be disastrous. The blame for Peter's failure lay altogether with him — at best with his simplicity, and at worst with his irresponsibility. Even without E.P., Peter might well have been drawn, as so many Ontario farmers were, to try his luck in Manitoba. E.P. remained if not a particularly lucrative source of help at least a fairly constant one for the Leacock children for many years. Stephen's oldest brother, Jim, went into business with him, and Dick went west to be with him before joining the North-West Mounted Police. E.P. did Stephen an important good turn in the early 1890s by helping find a teacher to take over Stephen's post at Uxbridge High School so Stephen could accept a better position.

With Peter absent, life for the family revolved primarily around the children. Agnes's love of her Victorian and English heritage manifested itself in the negative campaign to keep the children from backwoods habits and also in her determination to provide them with a good education. Stephen more than any other of the children took up from her this respect for learning and for the English tradition in which the particular form of education he received was rooted. After withdrawing the children from Georgina Township School, Agnes first tried to give them lessons herself. Armed with an excellent education and a trunkload of textbooks she had brought with her from England, she nevertheless found the job impossible. As Leacock explained, "But it was no good, we wouldn't pay attention, we knew it was only mother." With the practiced eye of a long-time student and teacher, he laid the fault to the books she brought as well as to her methods. The books, including Slater's *Chronology*, Peter Parley's *Greece and Rome* and Bishop Colenso's *Arithmetic*, reduced learning to tricks and rote responses to leading questions. Stephen remembered with much greater approval his mother's fondness for literature; she introduced him to the novels of Walter Scott, Daniel Defoe, Charles Dickens and Mark Twain at an early age. *Pickwick Papers* was a particular favorite, but *Tom Sawyer*, sent to the family soon after its 1876 publication in the United States, was not a success with him.

Determined to keep the children out of the local school, Agnes appealed to Thomas Murdock Leacock, who provided money to hire a tutor. Private education as a prelude to high school or university was still a common practice in Great Britain; there are frequent allusions to it, especially among the children of impoverished but well-educated clergymen, for example. Tutors were not completely unknown in Ontario, but they were much more common in the homes of rich, well-established families than in farmhouses like the Leacocks'; Joseph Scriven, the author of the hymn, "What a Friend We

Have in Jesus," had worked for many years in the Rice Lake district as tutor to the children of a retired naval officer, Captain Robert L. Pengelly. Agnes found a tutor in the Sutton area, a university student, Harry Park, who was unable to finish his training because he had run out of money. Establishing a schoolroom in the Leacock house, Park organized a class of five children, including the four oldest boys — Jim, Dick, Stephen and Charlie — and their oldest sister, Missie. Park recognized Stephen as the best student of the group, and he returned the favor by remembering Park's training as the best he had ever received. At eleven, Leacock reported, he was an excellent speller and sound calculator in mathematics and possessed a solid preparation in literature, history and geography. Park ran his class with strict discipline, despite its location in a busy household; in fact, his watch overruled the claims of the kitchen clock. All his life, Leacock preached a theory of education that emphasized individual encouragement of the gifted rather than limited programs geared to the abilities of the average child. It seems likely that fond memories of the early success with Park were important in his conviction that educators needed to care as much for the special needs of the brilliant student as they did for the needs of the majority.

Stephen continued as Park's student for about three years, and Park remained a fixture in the Leacock home for some time after the three older boys went on to Upper Canada College. During this same period, Agnes made some other changes in the family routine. Beginning in 1880, the family moved to the shore of Lake Simcoe during the summer months; at first, their "summer cottage" was a dilapidated former rectory for which Agnes paid a yearly rent of eight dollars. The older boys had to stay on the farm much of the time during the summer to work while their father was away. This was undoubtedly the period in which Stephen got his practical education in farm work, which led him to a thorough dislike of the fields, the animals and even the garden — his responsibility. Despite the financial worries that must have become greater and more apparent as the boys grew older, Leacock dated his love of the Lake Simcoe region from his late childhood, when he was able to travel more freely off the farm to join his brothers and sisters and their friends in games, and especially activities on the water. Swimming, skating and boating drew him to the lake year-round. The winter weather that had been a barrier to the children's freedom became an opportunity for special fun. But it was Lake Simcoe especially that charmed him. "Here the blue of the deeper water rivals that of the Aegean; the sunlight flashes back in lighter colour from the sandbar on the shoals; the passing clouds of summer throw moving shadows as over a ripening field, and the mimic gales that play over the surface send curling caps of foam as white as ever broke under the bow of the Aegean galley." The boys built rafts, which sometimes were caught in the changeable weather on the lake and had to be towed to shore. Leacock often chuckled about the troubles a novice had in sailing Lake Simcoe, but then he studied the lake throughout his life and made it a part of his personal history.

Several pieces of Leacock's work look back fondly on the era in which he lived on a farm, but he always retained the conviction that farm life was not for him. He often honored and celebrated the virtues he found in rural people and the way of life he felt had in many ways been replaced by something worse in the agricultural communities he observed as an adult. He admired his tutor's devotion to learning, which flowered and perhaps was even intensified in its unpromising setting. During the 1930s, Leacock wrote a warm tribute to the Sutton village doctor, Charles Noble, whom he remembered as supporting whole families not only in healing but in the aftermath of injury or death. As an adult, Leacock faulted his teachers for not awakening in him an enthusiasm for the history of the area in which he was growing up. Just as his love for England was fueled by the historical associations he was taught to recognize in the streets and churches he knew, so he felt a love of Canada would follow from a sympathetic realization that, although different from Europe, North America held its own romantic past to be discovered by each new generation. He remembered a settler's grave hidden in an overgrown patch of bush on the Leacock farm; this was history, just as surely as a cathedral or monument of Europe represented history.

In *The Boy I Left Behind Me*, Leacock displayed his enthusiasm for the historical associations of Lake Simcoe by providing the sort of information he wished had been made available to him as a child. Sandwiched between Lake Simcoe and Georgian Bay was the home of the Huron Indians, the Huronia of the seventeenth century, which was a principal target for the activity of missionary Jesuits until the Hurons' enemies, the Iroquois, forced the French to abandon the region in 1649. There was virtually no European settlement in present-day Ontario until after the Napoleonic Wars, although England had begun efforts to create a colony in the region before 1800 under the direction of Colonel John Graves Simcoe. In a manner of speaking, the farm at Sutton was only one generation away from the wilderness; Leacock remembered bonfires from the summer of their arrival that cleared out the last of the primeval cedars and oaks remaining from the first wave of homesteading. Still, if it was a frontier, it was not the sort of frontier prairie children knew in the same period. Although he went to Toronto rarely before his teens, Stephen lived only a brief train ride from the city. He grew to feel, in later life, that all too much of what he had known as a child had been sacrificed for the sake of replacements of doubtful value. Above all, as so many social commentators do to good effect, he used the simpler pattern of life he had known as a child as a foil for the frenzy, hypocrisy and vanity he wished to attack in the world he saw around him. He regretted, for example, that boat traffic on Lake Simcoe had been destroyed by the coming of the railroad. Although trains effectively connected the town with the outside world, they also eliminated a form of transportation that was a delight to the eye, a charming mode of travel and one that best suited the needs of the small communities surrounding the lake.

Still, it was easier for Leacock to see the Lake Simcoe area in this kindly light from a distance. He dated his appreciation of the farm to his arrival at Upper Canada College, where his desire for an education was at first overshadowed by a severe case of homesickness. His ability to overcome his desire to return home became for him a proof of the school's virtues: it had helped him to endure the first shock of separation from his family and set him on a path of independent effort. The break from home was not absolute in 1882, when Stephen began at Upper Canada College. During his first year there, he roomed with his two older brothers, and during the school year of 1883 to 1884 Agnes rented a house in Toronto where all three boys lived, attending the school as day students. Still, despite the close family ties that still linked him to home during the Upper Canada College years, Leacock's emphasis on the break with family he had to endure when he first arrived at school underscores what school meant for him: the personal responsibility to excel in the school subjects he preferred to farming in hopes that he might not have to be limited to the farm for the rest of his life.

From 1882 until 1887 Stephen's life was centered on Upper Canada College. Although he spent vacations and summers on the family farm or at the cottage, he identified himself increasingly with the city of Toronto, which remained his home for more than ten years after his graduation from Upper Canada College; he returned to the school as a master of languages in 1889. The period of his life that drew to a close in 1882 was one that always impressed him as difficult, unhappy and disadvantaged. Although he softened this charge against frontier farming and against his parents, in particular, in many ways — making the dislike a matter of personal taste, pointing out many redeeming features of his childhood, and so on — he did not regret his determination to leave the farm or apologize for his distaste for farm work. Many readers of Leacock's work have questioned either the correctness of his evaluation of his childhood circumstances or the rightness of his attitude towards life on the farm. It may seem difficult to reconstruct the context of Leacock's experience to judge the relative comfort or hardship his circumstances posed; Leacock's own remembrances usually date from the very end of his life, more than sixty years away from the events themselves. On the other hand, it is clearly true that the family farm failed, that Peter provided little if any significant income before he left and none after and that the course of Leacock's life after high school demonstrated that he had exhausted the sources of financial assistance that had given him the one significant luxury of his childhood, his education. In sum, it seems that the Leacock farm, its house and outbuildings were not exceptionally poor by the standards of the place and time. On the other hand, Leacock vividly recreated the burden of labor that these standard conditions involved for all who endured them. Other portraits of the time differ more in the sentiment of acceptance or pride than they do in the estimate of the work required to run such a family farm.

Leacock identified himself in his autobiographical writings as one of a generation of Canadians whose early lives were spent on the farm and who gained from the experience a common ambition to get off it as soon as possible. Many of the distinguished politicians, professionals, educators, engineers and scientists who were Leacock's contemporaries put farms behind them to pursue education and achievements that would, have remained beyond their reach had they surrendered to what often seemed the necessity to remain in rural occupations. The pattern that Leacock exemplified is one familiar from the biographies of Canadian authors. The drive for education and urban experience leads them away from the family homestead and community, and only rarely do they mingle their adult lives with the actual rigor of maintaining a working farm. Of course, not every writer who grew up on a farm disliked the experience. Nellie McClung, novelist and women's rights activist, cherished fond memories of her farm childhood while nevertheless choosing, and never regretting, to leave the farm to get an education. Born in 1873 near Chatsworth, Ontario, less than one hundred miles from the Leacock farm, McClung was an almost exact contemporary of Stephen Leacock. Poor soil and uncertain markets drove her family, the Mooneys, off their Ontario farm. They were a part of the same push west that took E.P. to Manitoba; the Mooneys settled on land near the Souris River at its fork with the Assiniboine, about sixty miles from Brandon, Manitoba. Even now, long after the period in which most Canadians grew up on a farm, let alone a frontier farm, many authors still trace their roots to isolated farming communities: Sinclair Ross, Earle Birney, Rudy Wiebe and Robert Kroetsch, among others. Many authors who came from rural or small-town Canada were not farm children but the offspring of professional people: doctors, clergymen, journalists and the like. For them, education was a family expectation and seemed inevitable, but for farm children like Leacock there was no such inevitability of education in their future. On the contrary, it seemed that these children were destined to a life of farming or some other closely related rural occupation, usually in their native region. Where a child did obtain education, the credit often belonged, as in Leacock's case, to one determined parent who preserved a love of learning and a conviction of the future it could provide. Such parents not only instilled a love for education but persisted in providing means and encouraging a child to go away to school, even when it meant the certain loss of a child, including potential earning power, to the rest of the family. Perhaps, in part, Leacock's impatience with the farm reflects a lesson learned from his mother in childhood, her fear that the lonely Ontario acres would prove an inescapable prison to her sons and daughters.

Even Leacock's return to the Lake Simcoe area as an adult has been offered as proof that his childhood experiences on the farm were more pleasant than he pictured them, or that he learned he had been wrong to judge them so harshly. On this, however, Leacock deserves the final word.

> You had your choice! Stay there and turn into a hick, get out and be a great man. But the strange thing is that they all come back. They leave the old farm as boys so gladly, so happy to get away from its dull routine, its meaningless sunrise and sunset, its empty fresh winds over its fields, the silence of the bush — to get away into the clatter and effort of life, into the crowd. Then as the years go by they come to realize that at a city desk and in a city apartment they never see the sunrise and the sunset, have forgotten what the sky looks like at night and where the Great Dipper is, and find nothing in the angry gusts of wind or the stifling heat of the city streets that corresponds to the wind over the empty fields . . . so they go back, or they think they do, back to the old farm. Only they rebuild it, not with an axe but with an architect. They make it a great country mansion with flag-stoned piazzas, and festooned pergolas — and it isn't the old farm any more. You can't have it both ways.

Wryly picking his way between sentimentality and pomposity, Leacock admitted freely that much was lost in leaving a life on the land. But he still insisted that his choice had been right and necessary. He himself became one of those who returned by building a large, comfortable house, and indulging in small-scale, gentlemanly farming at a loss that he made up out of his other earnings. He began, though, with little more than a tent and a bit of lakefront, and always maintained that he wished to return to nature and to Simcoe County, but never to the old farm.

The choice of Upper Canada College for the education of the Leacock boys was in some measure a matter of necessity. It was the nearest secondary school to the farm. In 1881, when Stephen's two older brothers began attending classes, Toronto was a single convenient train trip away from Sutton. Of course, it was not the only high school in the province, or even the only prestigious one. In Port Hope, for example, there was the Anglican-founded Trinity College School, from which not too many years before had graduated the poet Archibald Lampman. Leacock wrote that it was strictly necessity that had determined the choice of Upper Canada College. On the other hand, Upper Canada College in the 1880s was at the height of its prestige and offered an admirable opportunity for Agnes to further her ambition to bring up her sons as gentlemen. The school had been founded in 1829 as a private boys' school by Sir John Colborne, then lieutenant-governor of the Province of Upper Canada (later Ontario). Associated with the University of Toronto, which was chartered in 1827 as an Anglican college but secularized in 1849, Upper Canada College was a training ground for college-bound young men; other secondary schools in the province were associated with other colleges — Trinity College School with Trinity College in Toronto, for example. Upper Canada College stood on King Street near the intersection with Simcoe Street. The grounds formed a pleasant green preserve near the bustle of wharves and warehouses along Toronto's lakefront. The buildings were of brick and designed in a heavy, severe style that Leacock compared to a penitentiary or an asylum, although he approved heartily of their interior arrangements of dormitories, classrooms and study halls. Upper Canada College later moved, during Leacock's tenure as a teacher, from King Street to its present grounds on Lonsdale Avenue facing south down Avenue Road towards the Toronto lakefront. The school stands, as it did when Leacock taught there, on spacious grounds removed from city traffic. In 1882, when he first enrolled, there were approximately one hundred students; to-day, the school has nine hundred students in grades one through thirteen. Through his life, Leacock's humor often illuminated the clash between new problems and old values, between outmoded institutions and fresh ideas; rarely does his wit come closer to his personal circumstances than in his analysis of the concept of the "gentleman." Impressed from childhood reading by the specifically American principle that all men are created equal, he could not help but notice that his mother was setting him a course that was intended to secure for him his birthright as a gentleman. His survey of Ontario history in *The Boy I Left Behind Me* emphasized the efforts made by early provincial officials to transplant English class consciousness and lifestyle to the Canadian backwoods. Leacock showed that his uncle E.P. could touch a love of title and nobility in every farmer and tradesman, and that his mother maintained strict discipline among her servants: the lowest maid was "as low and humble as even an English Earl could wish it." While poking fun at the incongruity of these transplanted manners, Leacock did not divorce himself altogether from the traditions he found among the conservative residents of Ontario. He seemed to realize that, in some ways, he had benefited from his mother's conviction that a better life was due him because he was a gentleman. He wished to argue that the better life should be available to all, or to all those whose merits could win it for them, but he could not forget that a sense of preserving traditional values, even as it applied to granting certain people special privileges due to birth or associations, had played a fundamental part in his own life.

Upper Canada College was to Leacock something of a sore point in this regard. He looked back fondly on the years he spent there and the education he received; he was proud of his record and delighted to recall that Upper Canada College boys were pointed out in the streets as people who commanded special interest and respect. In *The Boy I Left Behind Me*, he portrayed the school as remarkable for its freedom from all taint of class distinction. Yet only two years earlier he published *My Remarkable Uncle*, which included a sprightly essay, "The Struggle to Make Us Gentlemen," that poked determined fun at Upper Canada College's efforts to be "a

53

school of gentlemen." The first time he heard the phrase as a junior student, he recalled, he was impressed with the seeming impossibility of meeting the high standard demanded. Over the years, however, the word "gentleman" began to be tarnished by the doubtful examples of gentlemanliness the school could offer in its "old boys" and by an incident Leacock recorded from his own experience. In order to complete a form, a teacher asked Stephen for his father's occupation. Stephen replied that his father did nothing, at which the teacher promptly wrote down the occupation as "gentleman." What Leacock meant was that his father "was probably to be found along on King Street having a Tom-and-Jerry in the Dog and Duck, or at Clancey's — but whether to call that his occupation was a nice question." The article concluded by asserting that the school had failed to make him into a gentleman, yet a joking list of a gentleman's qualifications, provided in the same piece, seems in many respects a description of Leacock himself.

> No gentleman cares to talk about himself; no gentleman talks about money, or about his family, or about his illness, about the inside of his body or about his soul. Does a gentleman swear? Oh, certainly; but, remember, no gentleman would ever swear at a servant — only at his own friends. In point of language a gentleman is not called upon to have any particular choice of words. But he must, absolutely must, have a trained avoidance of them. Any one who says, "them there," and "which is yourn" and "them ain'ts his'n" is not a gentleman.

Was Upper Canada College a "school for gentlemen"? Was Leacock, one of its best students, one of its best "gentlemen"? Perhaps, as in his nostalgia for the farm, Leacock wished to have the best of all he had experienced without being touched by undesirable elements. It would have been ungrateful to deny the gifts of education and distinction, but he did not wish to be regarded as someone who relied on being a "gentleman," born to claim things he had not worked to earn.

Stephen's school years were an exciting time in Canada and in Toronto. Toronto was a rapidly growing city whose business district stretched almost a mile up Yonge Street from the lakefront; the city's tree-shaded residential districts were beginning to fill the rolling hills to the north. It was the western-most major center in the country; the prairies were still unsettled. In 1881, the year before Stephen started school, work began in earnest on the Canadian Pacific Railway, and the last spike was driven in in 1885 at Craigellachie, British Columbia. The North-West Rebellion of 1885 stirred Toronto — as had the Red River Rebellion in 1869 (both led by Louis Riel) — with calls for swift action against the prairie Métis and their leaders. The 1880s began with the composition of the national anthem, "O Canada," the establishment of the Royal Canadian Academy of Arts and the Royal Society of Canada. In Toronto, George Brown, a Father of Confederation and politically active founder of the *Globe* newspaper, was shot in his office by a dismissed employee and died days later in his home not many blocks from Upper Canada College. Visiting dignitaries like Matthew Arnold found Toronto quite different from the muddy, distressing town earlier visitors from abroad had reported it to be. There was increasing cultural activity in the city. The *Globe* published an around-the-world diary by a woman reporter, Sara Jeannette Duncan. Politics and literature were discussed in the city's new magazines, including Goldwin Smith's controversial *The Week*. Vainly hoping to support herself by magazine work, Ontario poet Isabella Valancy Crawford had settled in Toronto and published in 1884 *Old Spookses' Pass, Malcolm's Katie, and Other Poems* while living on John Street at King, the same area in which Agnes Leacock rented a house to be near her three sons at school. In the same year, railway builder Sir Sandford Fleming, long-time Toronto resident, saw his system of international time zones adopted around the world; travel by rail had made long-distance trips possible in short enough periods that a method for organizing time-keeping on a global scale became necessary.

This was the city Stephen Leacock came to in February, 1882, to begin classes at Upper Canada College. Just turned twelve, he barely had time to start missing his home before illness forced his removal from the school. He returned to the farm with his mother and spent the next several months recuperating and studying Latin, to begin again with the regular school session in the fall of 1882. It was his first real introduction to the life he would learn to enjoy during the next five years. He remembered the younger boys were spared the hazing that was a notorious part of life at English public schools. The boys were all equally short of pocket money, and none the worse for it. Stephen soon adapted to dormitory life, which he found one of the most rewarding parts of his high-school years; it provided him with a chance to share his entire day — sports, classes, studies and leisure — with other students. Sports were a special delight, especially cricket, although he never excelled at it. Years later, he looked back to 1882 and remembered attending lectures and debates given by University of Toronto students, a tame pleasure by later standards, perhaps, but for that time, he said, a most exciting event: as an upperclassman, he became an active participant in the debating society of Upper Canada College. He finished his first year with excellent grades, especially in Latin and English literature.

In 1883 Agnes made an unexpected decision: she rented the farm to a neighbor. Leaving her younger children at Egypt in the care of Harry Park, she moved to Toronto, where she rented a house on John Street. Leacock attributed the decision to a "casual legacy" from England, which, he regretted to say, his mother chose to spend rather than invest. Perhaps she was seriously considering the possibility of moving the family off the farm altogether, on the strength of Peter's speculations in the west or the hope of continued money from England. Family tradition recalls the house on John Street as one shared by Agnes and Peter, with the younger children also present. Leacock indicated in *The Boy I Left Behind Me* that the trip west had not kept his father or uncle away from Ontario entirely. He remembered seeing E.P. ushering around his business partners from Winnipeg. Although the move to town made use of extra income, it might have been intended also as an economy measure. Stephen and Dick became day-students rather than boarders. Jim left school and went west to find work; it is possible that he made the trip with his father. On 28 June, 1884, Stephen wrote Peter news of the family's summer holiday plans, including a train trip to Sutton that had a difficult beginning. "The little ones all started for the lake this afternoon; they went this morning, but they missed the train," Stephen wrote. "Mother wants me to tell you that it was not the children's fault that they missed the morning train, as they were all up at half past four, in fact they hardly slept at all, and their trunk had been packed about a week before." Stephen also mentioned his mother's condition following the birth on 28 May of the tenth Leacock child, Rosamond Mary (Dot). "Mother was out in the yard for the first time yesterday and had the pleasures of beating me in a game of croquet." Although Stephen was devoted to his mother, he quite likely regretted rather than welcomed her move to the city. For him, school life revolved around the camaraderie of the boarding-school students; day students at Upper Canada College, he noted regretfully, were forced to leave before sports activities, scheduled for late afternoon when classes were over, began for the day.

Whatever hopes had accompanied the move, the experiment ended after just one year. Agnes returned to the farm, Stephen returned to the dormitory and his brother Dick went west to find work. Stephen continued to win high marks in all his subjects and became more active in student activities. He was chairman of the football club and one of the editors of the school newspaper, *The College Times*, during the 1886 to 1887 school year. The first signed article Leacock ever published, called "The Vision of Mirza (New Edition)," was published on 7 April, 1887 in *The College Times*. Its postscript has the rhythm of Leacock's humorous delivery:

> I have since made inquiries as to who my friend the genius was. I only succeeded, however, in finding that he is in the sixth form; but as there are so many geniuses in the sixth, the information has not enabled me to discover his identity. I have heard that a price of ten demerits has been set on his head.

In his last year at school, Stephen reached the top of his class, winning all the individual subject prizes and the award for "general proficiency." Leacock reflected on this achievement, one he took great pride in, and characteristically found something in it to fault. Recalling his dislike for the formula questions and answers he met in his mother's old textbooks on the farm, he lamented that the pursuit of top marks had led him to put passing tests ahead of serious study. "History for me just turned into an underlined book of which I knew by heart all the underlined tags, headings, and dates."

In the summer of 1887, Stephen Leacock graduated as head boy of Upper Canada College. He had already taken his matriculation examinations for the University of Toronto and received excellent marks. His chosen future was to go on to college, with no specific course of study or career yet in view but only the desire to pursue the schooling in which he had already shown great distinction. At the time he was making these plans, however, and taking pride in his honors, he realized that university might be impossible. The sources of money available to him in the past were gone; his grandfather did not provide for education beyond high school. His brothers had set a family pattern by going to work; in 1885, Dick went west to join the North-West Mounted Police. Stephen could expect little, if any, help from his parents. During 1885, Peter returned to Ontario from Winnipeg; the collapse of the Manitoba land boom had left him bankrupt and discouraged. Chafing at the unaccustomed restriction of life on the farm after years in a boom town, Peter now took no pains to conceal his drinking from the children. He would not work the farm, which had gone increasingly into debt. A crisis finally came within a few months of Stephen's graduation. A niece of Stephen's, Elizabeth Kimball, presented a tragic history of confrontation in her reminiscences of the family, *The Man in the Panama Hat.* Elizabeth was the daughter of the youngest Leacock child, Daisy, who was born in September of 1886. Elizabeth said that her grandmother, Agnes, had been forced to carry Daisy out of the house to escape Peter who, in a drunken rage, had attempted to harm Agnes with a knife. Stephen rescued his mother and baby sister from the bitter cold, according to Elizabeth, and drove them to a neighbor's house, where they remained for several days, until Stephen forced his father to leave the farm. Other family members have placed Peter's final departure in the summer of 1887, when Stephen was seventeen, and they have agreed with Leacock's account that his father unexpectedly announced that he would leave before he was forced to go. Whatever the precise timing of the event, which Leacock did not describe in *The Boy I Left Behind Me,* family traditions seem agreed on one thing: Stephen, the oldest brother at home although only seventeen, confronted his father at the Sutton railway station and threatened to kill him if he ever returned.

Peter never returned, although Agnes always spoke of herself as "separated" from her husband. The family must have felt great relief that a growing threat of physical danger was removed. At the same time, the situation Peter left behind was a grim one. For Stephen, in particular, it was a sad contrast between his personal hopes and the enormous responsibility of the farm, his mother and eight younger brothers and sisters to care for. It has sometimes been said that Leacock's childhood left him insecure and, therefore, overly concerned about earning money. On this view, he was prevented from doing the best literary work he might have accomplished because he was content to follow editorial directives that promised him greater financial returns. However, in 1887, when he was faced with a choice between continuing his education and searching for a career that would assure him of an income, he stubbornly pursued education. He pursued it although it drove him to undertake ten years of high-school teaching, a job he did not like and did not consider himself suited for, in order to have employment he could combine with university studies. During these years, he did not seem inclined to think much about what he most wanted to be; rather, he emphasized those things, like farm work or high-school teaching, that would not satisfy him. What he wanted, at the price of considerable sacrifice, was an education, an education that held for him, even in the face of doubts about finishing it, a hope for the future he would not let slip away.

Chapter Four

Education Eating Up Life

I N JUNE 1887, Stephen Leacock graduated from Upper Canada College as its leading student; two years later he was back as a junior master in modern languages. As a student he had loved the school and as a teacher he remained there for ten years, but Leacock took the position out of necessity rather than choice. To the end of his life he maintained that he had disliked the work of high-school teaching from his first day to his last. Perhaps the edge of his dislike never dulled because he recalled how he had preserved, throughout the decade, an eager determination to find a career that suited him better. He filled his hours away from teaching with study and writing, and if these efforts were not at first clearly planned and directed, they eventually did free him forever from high-school teaching. The necessity of his family at Sutton forced him to look for work soon after his own high-school graduation, and it was another sort of family necessity — his plans to marry, formed in 1898 — that finally spurred him to set himself free of the routine he had endured against his will.

Leacock was seventeen when he graduated from Upper Canada College and twenty-nine when he resigned from the school's faculty. This represents a period of life in which most men who will be successful are well-launched on the training and career to which they will devote their mature years, but for Leacock the time was passed primarily in a sort of prolongation of his adolescence. Still circumscribed by the needs of his mother and brothers and sisters, just as he had been in his farm years, Leacock continued to fret under the routine of a high-school life, which held less and less charm for him. Yet, despite the lingering of his youth's constraints, this period was also a coming of age. He did not begin degree work in the subjects that were to be his specialties at McGill University — economics and political science — but he did set himself an ambitious course of private study in them. Most important, he began selling humorous pieces to newspapers and magazines. Although he abandoned publication of humor almost completely for more than ten years after resigning from the Upper Canada College staff, the work he published during the 1890s formed the bulk of his first collection, *Literary Lapses*, which established his reputation as a popular writer. There was thus a rich productivity in the life he pursued outside the classroom, even if this was not evident to some who viewed him as a man relatively contented in a high-school teaching career. While working to make, on his own terms, the changes he wanted in his life, he had the satisfaction of seeing that his sacrifices bore fruit in an increasingly comfortable life for his mother and family — a life he shared during his summer vacations at Lake Simcoe.

This is the least documented of all periods in Leacock's life. His autobiographical account, *The Boy I Left Behind Me*, breaks off shortly after 1889, and the witness of external sources — reminiscences, press accounts — does not begin in earnest until his arrival at McGill in 1901. To fill in the intervening years there are brief anecdotes told by a few friends, and there is what can be deduced from Leacock's writings of the time and the considerable amount of writing about education and teaching he did throughout his career. For the most part, then, the key decisions of his life are made out of our sight during this period when he began to write humor, study economics and consider university teaching as his permanent career. Leacock's own explanation, in *The Boy I Left Behind Me*, of why he took up and then abandoned high-school teaching is that it was initially attractive because it gave a comparatively high starting salary, which he needed if he was to support himself, help his mother and pay his university costs. But as years passed, salary increases did not match the income that might be available to him in other professions. Towards the end of the 1890s, if not earlier, he was clearly considering marriage, and at the very end of the decade he became engaged — such planning also may have compelled him to seek a better position. On this consideration, he wrote,

Every career should look forward to marriage as a thing that can in due course and time be accepted with all that it brings in the way of children and a home, without the pinching and semi-poverty that reduces it to a status not good enough to rank with that of other professions. . . . The trouble with our school-teaching in Canada is that up to now it does not offer these things.

Although never really satisfied with the salary he received as a professor, he received from that job benefits of status and opportunity to speak and publish. Other factors producing restlessness when he was teaching high school may have been boredom with the routine of high-school teaching and an increasing sense that the subjects he was teaching, the disciplines he had chosen as his own, were useless, not relevant to the living problems and concerns of the day. It may always remain something of a mystery why this brilliant student and teacher of languages and literature decided in mid-career to switch to economics and political science, but part of the explanation must lie in the fact that these were the booming "social sciences" of the time. Their direct applicability to the running of a nation and the world — as well as to the teaching of those setting out for leadership — might have seemed certain to him. Finally, he might already have been hoping for success as a popular writer, but writing — a way to increase status and prosperity — was suddenly cut off by events in 1897.

Leacock's long search for a suitable career and way of life was always affected by the routines and pressures of his days as a teacher and student of language. For only one year after his high-school graduation he was free of teaching duties. Despite the upheaval at home caused by his father's departure, Stephen enrolled in the University of Toronto in November 1887. In June he had taken the matriculation (compulsory entrance) examinations for the university and his scores were excellent, placing him among the ten highest-ranked applicants in all but one subject. On the strength of this performance he was offered a one-hundred-dollar scholarship. According to his account in *The Boy I Left Behind Me*, there was nothing substantial on which to base a hope that he would be able to complete his degree. Family finances were stretched to the limit to pay for even one year of education. On the other hand, he mentions no plan to attend university on a part-time basis, a possibility he would have known at first hand from the example of his tutor, Harry Park. Rather, he says specifically that a review of finances at the end of his first year showed there simply was no money with which to go on. Perhaps the departure of Peter Leacock had not at first seemed so definitive a break with the Leacock family in England as it appeared a year later; Agnes may have hoped that financial support from her father-in-law, which had seen Stephen through Upper Canada College, would continue if Stephen had a successful year at university.

He did have a remarkable year, ranking very high in all but one of his six subjects; the exception was mathematics, at which he was in the second rather than the first class of students. He was enrolled at University College, a non-denominational liberal-arts college among the University of Toronto's many religious affiliated colleges, including Trinity, Victoria, St. Michael's and Wycliffe, where he roomed. Records are lost for student activities in the year of Leacock's entrance, 1887. All that can be said is that he took freshman courses with very high marks and that, due to his marks and the excellence of the Upper Canada College program he had accomplished so successfully, he was entitled to enter the university the following year as a junior rather than a sophomore. Leacock himself referred to this achievement as "taking two years in one," which he really did not do in the sense of performing a double class load. But the effect was the same: the university credited him with two years.

This outstanding performance was not enough to enable Leacock to continue his studies. No help came from England, and at home he found that no help could be expected from his two brothers at work in the west. The oldest, Jim, was a courthouse clerk in Winnipeg, and Dick belonged to the North-West Mounted Police. Neither of them had any money to spare. His mother's income for a month during this period, Leacock later calculated, was perhaps eighty dollars. She had to support the eight children at home, ranging in age from infancy to sixteen. Until Stephen was able to begin helping her, Agnes got along by drifting into debt, and she clearly could spare nothing towards a university education. At eighteen, a year after his success at Upper Canada College, Stephen found that he could not continue, as his more well-to-do friends would, directly through university and into a profession. He would have to work first. Leacock often joked that education seemed to separate people from life rather than suit them to it. He later said of his own education to this point that it had equipped him for only one job: to pass education on to others. Clearly, this was only a quip: it was with pride that he took the work he was suited for and developed its advantages. Now, as at other times during his life, he displayed the determination to strike a balance between what he wanted for himself and what seemed to be demanded of him.

In the late nineteenth century, Ontario elementary-school teachers were trained at "normal schools" (teachers' colleges), but the growing number of high schools in the province had created a need for special programs of instruction to qualify people who did not have a bachelor's degree as high-school instructors. Only a few years before Leacock entered the profession, a procedure had been established at several Ontario high schools whereby students with some college qualifications could gain a special high-school teaching certification by completing a thirteen-week program of studies in education, including student teaching, observation of classroom techniques and readings in education theory. In September 1888, Leacock was accepted as one of six men and women student teachers to begin a three-month preparation of this type at Strathroy Collegiate Institute in Strathroy, a small town near London, Ontario. The few months at Strathroy were the first independent life Leacock had ever known. The year at the University of Toronto had been, by comparison, a close continuation of an established routine of travel between Sutton and Toronto; he simply moved from an Upper Canada College dormitory to a Wycliffe College dormitory and, just as at Upper Canada College, he followed a demanding schedule emphasizing study of classical and modern languages. Strathroy marked the definitive break with this old life. The trip there was the first railway journey he had made, outside the familiar trip between Sutton and Toronto, and he had his belongings packed in a simple wicker suitcase. At Strathroy, Leacock made the acquaintance of boarding-house life. From the first the battle was joined. He spent only one afternoon in his first boarding house. He stopped in his room briefly before dinner to write a note to his mother, in which he complained of conditions in the establishment. Leaving it on his desk, he went down to the community dinner, where the landlady shortly afterward joined the boarders and told Leacock that if he did not like the house, he should not stay. He was evicted and spent the night in another house, which he found little different from the first. "Boarding House Geometry," one of his earliest published humor pieces, was based on these early days in Strathroy and the many rooming houses in which he later stayed during his first years as a master at Upper Canada College.

In Strathroy the boarding houses were more troublesome to Leacock than were his studies. After success in a demanding academic program at the University of Toronto, he was comfortable in the new routine of observation and giving classes. The program soon grew tedious, but in retrospect it seemed praiseworthy to Leacock, the veteran professor, because he had been required to spend only three months at it, while student teachers a short while later had to devote a full year of their university education to practice teaching. The program qualified him as a teacher of English, French, German, Latin and Greek, and he was highly recommended by the Strathroy principal, James Wetherell, who administered the course. For Leacock, the most memorable event in the program occurred when he was called on by Wetherell to take over a demonstration class in English that the principal had begun. Leacock, the high-school humorist, continued the lecture in a voice and manner so exactly like Wetherell's that the students were delighted and the principal himself was moved to comment on the performance afterward. "I admire your brains more than your manners," he told Leacock, whom the words stung sharply enough for him to remember through the years and record in his autobiography. He credited them with giving him an important insight into humor, that kindness should be a basic part of its message or it is valueless. Nor did the incident rest in Leacock's memory alone. When he introduced himself many years later to a newly appointed principal of McGill University, General Sir Arthur Currie, Currie replied that he remembered Leacock well from Strathroy Collegiate Institute, where Currie had been a scholar in 1888, as the student teacher who had so brilliantly mimicked Wetherell.

The Strathroy program was arranged to coincide with the fall school term, so newly certified student teachers could start to seek work in January. Leacock began his search with little to go on, although some jobs were advertised; he lost one of them, at Bishop Ridley College, to a future principal of the University of Toronto, H.J. Cody. But an old friend quickly came to his aid with an offer of a position at a school less than twenty miles from the Leacock family farm. In 1889 Stephen's former tutor, Harry Park, was principal of Uxbridge High School and he offered a post there as language master at a salary of seven hundred dollars per year. Leacock accepted immediately. His high-school teaching years began in a town of fifteen hundred inhabitants, in a new brick school building. In comparison to Sutton, Uxbridge was large but still quiet and comfortable ("dull but unaware of it," Leacock said). As it turned out, he only taught there a few months. In June, with his contract for the coming fall signed, he went to spend the summer with his mother at Sutton, setting a pattern for all the summers of his high-school teaching years; for the next ten years he participated each summer in the busy social life of the cottage communities around lakes Simcoe and Couchiching, where his mother and family lived. But then in the fall, shortly after classes at Uxbridge began, he received an offer to teach in another rural community, Napanee. Napanee offered two hundred dollars more than Uxbridge. Although Leacock wished to go to Napanee and asked to be let out of his contract, the Uxbridge trustees refused. In *The Boy I Left Behind Me*, Leacock states that their action was contrary to the general practice followed at the time with school teachers; because of generally poor salaries and expectations, they were free to follow any advancement that presented itself. He was held to the contract and stayed, but soon afterwards another opportunity arose, this time for no more money but at a better school, Upper Canada College, where he was offered a position as a junior language master. This would mean not only employment but also the chance to continue his university studies in Toronto. The trustees again refused him, but this time he asked for a meeting. Encouraged by the surprise of one trustee's support, he requested a week in which to find a replacement. Many years later, in 1936, Leacock received a reminder of this incident when one of the Uxbridge trustees wrote to him in response to an article on education that he had published in *Maclean's*. Former trustee F.N. Raines, by 1936 an elderly lawyer in Vancouver, was still incensed over Leacock's view of the matter, which had been briefly recounted in the magazine piece. Said Raines, "I am one of the 'merry fellows' you mention as trustees of the High School who refused to let you go when you were a teacher under Dr. Park as principal." Raines objected to Leacock's implication that the trustees had not let him go: they had done so when he received his Upper Canada College offer, but his previous, Napanee, offer had come in mid-term, when finding another teacher would have been too difficult for the school. He criticized Leacock for complaining of his yearly salary of $700 — Raines himself had taught one year at $350 during an earlier period. In 1943, when writing *The Boy I Left Behind Me*, Leacock pointed out that the salary of teachers in the 1880s and 1890s, when he himself had been of primary school age, had been $300 or $400. Leacock carefully wrote back to Raines, giving his side of an event that still impressed him after the passage of forty-six years. He mentioned the Napanee offer and then recalled:

Later I was offered a job at Upper Canada College and they let me go provided I would get a substitute which I did. I appealed to the men in person and they were going to refuse when Mr. Brittain said with great emphasis let the boy go you can't expect to keep a boy like that in Uxbridge. All my life I have appreciated the warmth and kindliness of what he said and that's why I remember it.

Leacock's departure was not totally due to his own efforts. His uncle, E.P., helped him locate a language master able to take his post and to satisfy the trustees. It is at this moment that Leacock's reminiscences in *The Boy I Left Behind Me* end with the feeling words, "I was free."

"Free" in a comparative sense. Free to work during the days at a job he increasingly disliked and to attend university in the evenings, while continuing the regular monetary contributions to his family that he had begun to make from Uxbridge and that added to the difficulty of his attempt to save money for his own future education. Nonetheless, he was back in Toronto and had gotten around the problem that had troubled him in Uxbridge — the possibility that he would not be able to earn enough in teaching to give up the work and return to school. He began teaching at Upper Canada College and simultaneously attending the University of Toronto as a junior in the fall of 1889.

How did the Leacock of this period perform in his Upper Canada College classroom? According to his supervisors, he was one of the best teachers the school had ever had. There is little testimony from his high-school students about his teaching of language. B.K. Sandwell, later a prominent literary man and one of Leacock's best friends, once recalled that "he always had something good to say," but also qualified his praise with the comment that Leacock was not interested in teaching for its own sake but only to earn money for his education. Leacock himself claimed to have no difficulty either in following the prescribed procedures for language teaching or in maintaining classroom discipline. The secret, he said, was never to give the students a moment to doubt your authority: begin speaking at once, speak on the subject and command their attention. He counseled against attempting to engage students' affection through humor or sympathy, and maintained that good classroom order would inevitably follow from these principles as it had for him. To understand his frequent professions of dislike for teaching, it is necessary to look beyond the idea that he found himself to be a failure at it.

Perhaps he at first paid little attention to his teaching itself because he was busy attempting to finish his bachelor-of-arts degree. He lived, as did many undergraduates at the time, in boarding houses — seventeen of them, he claimed, in his search for one that suited him. During his first year at Upper Canada College, he taught until three o'clock and then spent what time he could in university classes. Class attendance was not then compulsory at the university: this made it possible for him to enroll in the requisite junior-year program towards an honors degree in modern languages even though his work might frequently prevent him from attending lectures. The honors degree also gave him more latitude to choose his courses than a regular pass degree would have done; many of his classmates assumed, because of the emphasis he put on classics in his program, that he was taking a degree in classical rather than modern languages. At the end of his junior year he again placed very high in all his subjects and won a special award for studies in German.

In addition to his teaching and studies, Leacock devoted himself to caring for his family on the Egypt farm. He conducted sight-seeing excursions to Toronto for the younger children frequently and was always home for the holidays. His youngest sister, Daisy, particularly remembered him as the inspiration for Christmas celebrations:

> I don't remember Stephen being at the farm much in the summer, although he spent most of the holidays there. But in the winter, and especially at Christmas, I remember very clearly, he used to bring Dot and me wonderful toys "from town" (Toronto). He loved Christmas, and in later years he would have us hang up pillow slips instead of stockings. "Stockings aren't half big enough," he'd say. If the pillow slips were only half full we never noticed. It was the excitement, Christmas morning, of diving into them to see what we'd get.
>
> I do remember one Christmas at the farm. Dot was six and I was four. Stephen got Dot skates and after breakfast we went down to the pond. (Our farm was inland, away from either Lake Simcoe or the Black River.) Stephen took a kitchen chair and had Dot push it about to learn how to skate, which she did in no time at all. Every Christmas we got new hand sleighs, and we would try them out as soon as we were dressed, and while we lived on the farm we would go sleigh-riding across the south fields which sloped away from the house.

Daisy's reference to her age places this holiday in 1890, during Leacock's second year at Upper Canada College and his senior year at the University of Toronto. Just turned twenty-one, he still had a fondness for childhood amusements; Daisy remembers that the boys, led by Stephen, borrowed the new sleds to build ice boats for sailing on Lake Simcoe.

During his senior year, doubtless encouraged by the ease with which he had balanced his studies and teaching, Leacock began to be involved in extra-curricular activities, especially in the university newspaper, *The Varsity* and the debating society. He was co-editor of *The Varsity* for several months and was remembered in accounts of student dinners and dances as a good speaker. However, these additions to the schedule finally proved too demanding. He resigned his co-editorship early in 1891, and even found himself in the position of accepting help from his University of Toronto Italian teacher, who took over some of his Upper Canada College classes so Leacock would have time to study for his final examinations. Even so, his performance on them was much below the standard of his junior year. The difficulties he was experiencing, and the ingenuity he used to overcome them, are suggested by the story of how he came to take a third-class mark in ethnology as one of his final grades. With his roommate G. Howard Ferguson (a future premier of Ontario), Leacock was studying frantically for the upcoming examination in algebra, a subject in which he always had done poorly. Leacock fortuitously came across a university regulation that entitled him to substitute, even at that late date, another subject. He struck upon the idea of taking the examination in ethnology, for he believed the subject would require only reading of the textbook. Leacock and Ferguson made the substitution. Their poor showing in ethnology, based on instantly acquired knowledge, came as a relief.

That was the end of his university career in Toronto. The sheltered social and intellectual oasis that the university provided for many of its students had not been available to Leacock, but at least he received his degree, and with it a promotion and salary increase at Upper Canada College. Soon he was also appointed housemaster, in charge of a dormitory; this reduced his living expenses, provided an addition to his salary and ended his running skirmish with boarding-house proprietors by giving him living quarters at the school. He lived as close neighbor to a fellow classmate from his days as a high-school student, Pelham Edgar, who had returned to Upper Canada College to teach English. Edgar later became an influential historian and critic of Canadian literature and a professor at the University of Toronto's Victoria College. He remembered the Leacock of this period as a man who seemed unambitious and unconcerned about the future. Many of the school's best faculty members were rising young scholars who went on to university posts in Canada and the United States; this was the sort of ambition then entertained by Edgar himself. Although Leacock was professedly saving money to further his education, Edgar remembered him as someone whose talents seemingly could have been put to better use. Leacock, at least on the surface, did not share this worry. By the summer of 1894 it seemed he was becoming positively frivolous. According to family tradition, he fell in love with a young woman whose mother took her to Colorado for a tuberculosis cure. Leacock went off in pursuit and, being refused permission to see her, remained at the foot of the mountain where her sanatorium was located. When her mother finally relented, it was Leacock's turn to grow cold. The family hymn-sing to which he was invited sent him back to Toronto immediately. Equally unsuccessful were some sentimental stories written soon after this episode. These were his first writings submitted for publication, and all were returned without encouragement from publishers in New York.

Despite Edgar's testimony that Leacock seemed unconcerned that his talents might be going to waste at Upper Canada College, Edgar is also the source for the information that Leacock, about 1894, began reading economics and political science in his spare time. Leacock was famous in later life as an early riser, often using the hours before the family breakfast for his commercial writing. At Upper Canada College he rose early and devoted his morning to study; he liked to compare himself to the English philosopher John Stuart Mill, who spent hours studying in the early mornings before going to work in a trading-company office. Edgar, trying to help his friend, introduced Leacock to James Mavor, a professor of history at the University of Toronto and an expert in what were then the very new academic disciplines of economics and political science. For some reason that has not been recorded, Mavor took a strong dislike to Leacock and declined to direct his independent studies. Nothing daunted by this discouragement, Leacock continued to pursue his interests as an informal, self-directed activity. He was encouraged and helped in his studies by the arrival at Upper Canada College of another young man with interests similar to his own. Edward (later Sir Edward) Peacock, two years younger than Leacock, joined the teaching staff in 1895; before Leacock had left the school for the University of Chicago, his new friend had already written and published *Trusts, Combines and Monopolies* (1898). Peacock, who made his later career in Great Britain, became as famous and influential a financier as Leacock was an economist, and the two men remained in close contact until Leacock's death. Peacock left Upper Canada College in 1902 to join the Dominion Securities Corporation. It moved him to London in 1907, and there he rose to become director of several companies in at least four different countries; among his directorships were ones in the Canadian Pacific Railway and the Bank of England. Peacock's presence at Upper Canada College and other factors surely confirmed Leacock's choice of economics as a field of study, but this in no way damaged his natural genius for humor, or his ambition to develop his humorous ideas for publication. Edgar remembered Leacock in these years as a great storyteller. He would call on Edgar and his wife at their quarters in the married-teachers' section of the Upper Canada College buildings, especially on Sundays after church, and entertain them with anecdotes. It was on such occasions that Leacock presented ideas that took form as some of his first published sketches, including "My Financial Career" and "Boarding House Geometry." He professed to have composed them in church during the sermons, which provided one of the quieter times during the week for him.

At Upper Canada College, Leacock began to express a strong independence from even a social adherence to religious practice. There is a story that one Sunday he offered to help another master, charged with taking the Methodist students to church, by taking them there himself rather than attending Anglican services. "You know it's all the same to me," he said. Later, the conscientious young master was shocked to find Leacock in his rooms: Leacock explained that he had gathered the boys but then found that another master was actually planning to go to the Methodist service. Leacock passed the charge along and took the chance to miss church altogether. Principal George Parkin wrote in his diary at this time about a disturbing meeting he had attended with several of his young faculty members; he found them uninterested in maintaining the school's traditional policy of mandatory church attendance. Parkin worried that perhaps he should not take the disagreement lightly. He doubted he should continue at the school if his teachers did not share his conviction that religious faith and practice were the fundamental principles underlying the building of character the school attempted with its students. Parkin did not mention Leacock by name, but Leacock's infractions in this area are well documented. Parkin makes a clear link between religious practice and conservative moral traditions which Leacock, for all the fact that he shared such traditions, did not make in his own case.

The pleasant academic community of Upper Canada College was shaken in 1895 by the wholesale firing of the staff. The college had been severely affected by losses in endowment that followed upon the reorganization of the University of Toronto in 1891; the Province of Ontario was now directing to the reorganized university moneys previously given to Upper Canada College. The loss of income occasioned a search for new trustees and new funding, and led to much adverse criticism of the principal. A new principal, George (later Sir George) Parkin, came to Upper Canada College with a record of distinguished service from the College School in Fredericton, New Brunswick, where he had done much to direct and encourage two of Canada's earliest important writers, the poets Bliss Carman and Sir Charles G.D. Roberts. Parkin rehired many of the Upper Canada College teachers who had been fired, including Leacock, and, despite a certain reserve of personality that made him stand back from some of the personal eccentricities of his language master, eventually proved a strong promoter of Leacock's gifts. But the shakeup convinced Pelham Edgar that he should leave the school and begin the doctoral-degree program he had been planning.

Leacock stayed on and soon was deeply involved in another activity that, judging by the productivity he achieved, must have taxed him as much as teaching and studying had. Beginning with a single article in 1894, Leacock went on, between

1895 and 1897, to publish several humor pieces annually, most of them in New York publications. By his own account, before 1894 he had been placing very slight items — paragraph-long jokes or comments on current events — regularly. But his career as a humorist is usually considered to have begun on 11 April, 1895 with the appearance of one of his most enduringly popular pieces, "My Financial Career," in the New York periodical of the time called *Life* (not the modern magazine of this name or its immediate predecessor).

It was a period of great comic creativity. Mark Twain's career flourished as Leacock grew up in the obscurity of the Lake Simcoe farming region, and continued until the year *Literary Lapses* was published. Whereas Twain's finest work had been done in his novels, Leacock was already proving to be best at brief, occasional essays and sketches that combined invented and autobiographical elements. In some cases his work was close to fiction, in others to nonfiction. Leacock was preparing to become the chief continuer of the great nineteenth-century tradition of American humor and the man who helped to transform it into the modern form it assumed not only in his own hands but in those of the writers who rose to prominence in the decades following his own earliest popularity: Don Marquis, Franklin P. Adams, Dorothy Parker, Robert Benchley, S.J. Perlman, Christopher Morley, H. Allen Smith, James Thurber and others. American humor, based on character (and often dialect as well) presented in brief sketches or stories, is generally traced to Washington Irving and to the Major Jack Downing stories of Seba Smith that began to appear in the 1830s. This tradition received its major impetus before Mark Twain from a Canadian, the Nova Scotia judge Thomas Chandler Haliburton, who gained international fame with his stories of Sam Slick, the shrewd Yankee clock peddler, the first volume of which appeared in 1836. Haliburton, one of the early nineteenth century's most popular authors, did at least as much as any other individual writer to establish humor, expressed primarily through brief sketches collected in volumes, as a separate and appreciated literary genre in its own right. In the 1890s, American sketch humorists of character and dialect included not only Twain but Bret Harte, Artemus Ward and George Ade. Leacock was not American, however much he was attracted to American writers and features of American life and thought. Like his forerunner Haliburton, he was, as a Canadian, not only able but compelled to look both to the United States and to Great Britain. If his earliest sketches (such as "My Financial Career" and "Boarding House Geometry") seemed quintessentially American in their presentation of contemporary vicissitudes through character, his later and more characteristic essays combined the American directness and colloquial quality with an urbanity and easy sense of culture that American writers seldom displayed, perhaps seldom sought. This is one of the factors that placed him and keeps him among the very few great international humorists, able to cross the boundaries of taste not only between North America and Great Britain but between speakers of English and speakers of many other languages.

In the mid-1890s, when his essays first began to appear, the New York periodicals that carried them were filled with the humorous work of American writers such as Mark Twain, Bret Harte and O. Henry, and many London-based Englishmen, such as J.M. Barrie, the novelist George Gissing (*Diary of a Nobody*), and perhaps the most famous, then, of all living British humorists, Jerome K. Jerome, author of *Three Men in a Boat*. Jerome, who produced many magazine pieces later collected in volumes such as *Idle Thoughts of an Idle Fellow*, bears the closest resemblance to Leacock, in style and form, of any of the enduring humorists of the nineteenth century on either side of the Atlantic. Both write in a light, colloquial, generally nonacerbic vein, and both can present the ridiculous minutiae of daily life and popular culture in delightfully sharp detail. Both resemble, and indeed helped to father, the modern humorous columnist who complains of changing fashions in food or transportation or social custom. Even their most elaborately expanded sketches can be traced to a starting point in the sort of ephemeral incongruity that is the province of the columnist. What distinguishes both Jerome and Leacock from many other humorists is the ability to see in such detail a reflection of the very nature of modern life and bring to the point a wide-ranging breadth and ingenuity of thought and expression.

Most of the humorists of the time lived near the source of their income; that is, in London or New York. The uncertainty of a living based on the sale of free-lance pieces had turned many of the period's aspiring authors (Jerome K. Jerome is a good example) into staff writers and editors for popular magazines. For those who had to leave home and family to live in a literary center, as Leacock would have had to do, the compensations were the chance of a livelihood and access to the writing community that existed in the cities. Jerome's London friends included, among others, Arthur Conan Doyle, J.M. Barrie and Bret Harte, by century's end living out his life as a dandified old-west curiosity in the London literary world. In the New York–Boston area lived such writers as Twain and William Dean Howells; a large number of popular magazines hungry for material formed a powerful magnet for hopeful writers.

Many Canadians found the attraction of the literary centers impossible to resist. Some who left their homeland behind around the turn of the century proved to be internationally popular authors: the novelist Sara Jeannette Duncan, for instance, who, during Leacock's high-school days, had been a Toronto *Globe* columnist and had praised his writing in *The College Times*; and Sir Gilbert Parker, who wrote highly regarded historical novels about French Canada and served eighteen years in the British Parliament after settling in London in 1890 as a rising journalist. Bliss Carman, a native of Fredericton, worked for many years as an editor in New York, became one of the most popular "American" poets of the early twentieth century and edited the first *Oxford Book of American Verse*. His first cousin Sir Charles G.D. Roberts followed a similar path, as did the naturalist and popular author Ernest Thompson Seton; Roberts, a poet and fiction writer, and Seton are together credited with creating the animal story, a form that grew out of their Canadian experience but was presented to the world through their efforts in the New York literary marketplace.

However, there were other Canadian writers who, without leaving home, found their principal audiences in the United States and Great Britain. The Ontario-born Presbyterian minister Charles Gordon wrote, under the pen name "Ralph

Connor," a long series of highly popular and very moral tales of western adventure and expansion, which were much praised — as Leacock too would later be — by Theodore Roosevelt. In 1893 a world bestseller came from Nova-Scotia-born novelist Margaret Marshall Saunders; her *Beautiful Joe* was based upon Canadian experiences but was set in the United States and achieved its greatest sales there, although the author lived most of her life in Canada.

Leacock was one of those who did not move to New York or London to find better markets or to participate in the busy literary life of an important publishing center. His opportunities in Toronto were very limited. Apart from Edgar's appreciative listening, Leacock was almost entirely without the excitement and support of a literary community. During the decade he placed only a few pieces in the important magazines of the day, and even this slight participation was at long range. Meanwhile, in the city where he lived what cultural excitement there was came largely from imported books and ideas and visiting celebrities.

The connection he had with New York was a friend who was instrumental in enabling him to publish in magazines located in the city without having to move to it. Peter McArthur, later famous in his own right as a Canadian humorist called "the sage of Ekfrid," was a native of Ontario and a near contemporary of Leacock's — he attended the Strathroy teacher-preparation program the year before Leacock did, and was at the University of Toronto during one of Leacock's years there. In 1892, after working for Toronto newspapers, McArthur went to New York to try free-lancing. He was working at *Life* magazine when "My Financial Career" was accepted, but, more important, he was editor of *Truth*, another New York magazine, from 1895 through 1897. During this period Leacock placed more than twenty pieces with *Truth*; these represent the bulk of the work that he is known to have published in magazines in those three years. Without McArthur's help, Leacock might have had much more difficulty in publishing his work in New York. As it was, he became a fairly regular contributor to at least one major magazine and so could be sure of a source of income and a prominent forum for his work. McArthur's importance in the transactions is indicated by the fact that in 1897, when he left *Truth*, Leacock's contributions there ended, and hence his overall rate of publication dropped dramatically.

Most of these early pieces were collected in *Literary Lapses*, Leacock's first book of humor, which did not appear until 1910. There is some question whether he was already, in the 1890s, considering a writing career based on this material. If so, was it the failure, or at least the uncertainty, of his earliest attempt at such a career that convinced him to stake his future on university teaching? Apparently he was not prepared to emigrate to a publishing center, nor does he seem to have been attracted to journalism, a profession commonly used at the time as a step towards other types of writing success, especially by those who specialized in the type of occasional prose Leacock was producing. Certainly, other factors besides fear of financial failure entered into his choice. His tastes and the education he had pursued marked him out for a level of participation in cultural and intellectual traditions beyond the ephemera of the popular press. His long-time service, willingly undertaken, to his mother and family perhaps made him reluctant to take a gamble that might have lessened his earning power and would surely have taken him, now the head of family, far away. Since he so disliked high-school teaching, it may appear contradictory that he chose teaching at a higher level as a life's work. However, he always directed his criticisms not against teaching itself but against the general treatment and perception of high-school teachers: the pay was too low and the acknowledgment from society too little, especially in view of the importance of education. Although he would eventually complain about university salaries too, a professorship kept him in the field of education, which he deeply respected, while providing many of the things he found lacking in high-school teaching. He was able to earn acceptance as an important voice in society, and he was relied upon by a much broader and more influential community to provide insight into social and political issues. The emphasis that, later in life, he laid on the students who had gone on from his classroom to be generals and statesmen suggests that he honestly hoped for a chance to make a definite and influential contribution to society through his teaching, and would not be content with less. He wanted to teach, but not on a level at which it seemed his efforts were largely being wasted.

Leacock had begun to feel that his field, languages, cut him off from the type of influence he wanted to exercise through his teaching. Languages, along with philosophy and history, had formed the core of a liberal education for centuries. When language study was expanded to include modern languages, the methods of instruction followed the pattern established for classical languages, emphasizing grammar and translation from literary and other texts. Leacock complained that he was never taught to speak French or expected to teach his students to speak the language. Throughout his life he wrote vigorously about the need, especially in a bilingual country such as Canada, to form a program of language teaching that would make acquired languages genuinely useful to the student. Despite his advanced and prophetic sense of the direction language teaching should take, Leacock did not set out to reform the field. He felt that language study, even if correctly conducted, was not what he wanted. He needed a subject that would enable him to feel a direct connection between his expertise and his teaching, on one hand, and, on the other, the contemporary world beyond the classroom and the campus. Eventually he decided that his best route lay through private study of economics, to lead later to an advanced degree.

In the meantime he maintained his high-school-teaching routine. It left his summers free, and throughout the 1890s he spent his vacations with his mother and younger siblings in the Lake Simcoe area. Leacock had moved them off the farm in 1892, shortly after he had settled in Toronto. Agnes realized nothing from her ownership of the land and probably did not cover the debts she had accumulated since her husband's departure. After leaving the farm, Agnes apparently resided with her younger children in a large house called "Rotherwood" that was part of the estate of the Sibbalds, one of the Sutton region's principal pioneering families, which in the late 1830s had been led to Canada by Mrs. Susan Sibbald. The Leacock and Sibbald families were close, and the Leacocks received encouragement and help from their well-established friends. "Rotherwood" is now gone, but its site was not far east of St. George Church; the large area east of the church that comprised the Sibbald grounds is now Sibbald Point Provincial Park. In 1895 Agnes moved to Orillia, and later she lived with her younger daughters in Beaverton, on the east shore of the lake; this town remained the home of Carrie Leacock (Mrs. Jan Ulrichsen), who became the mother of Leacock's beloved niece and secretary of the 1930s, Barbara Ulrichsen. Afterwards, Agnes again lived on the Sibbald estate, in "The Grange," a white stucco house that was her home during the 1910s; it is, for instance, the address at which she received the news of the birth of Leacock's son in 1915. Finally, Agnes's daughter Dot built her an attractive, somewhat eccentric house in the village of Sutton West, about four miles west of the Sibbald estate, and there she lived during the last two decades of her life; for the summers she had the permanent let of a cottage owned by Jack Sibbald and located just outside the estate, near St. George Church. These movements bespeak improved fortunes that enabled Agnes to experiment in an attempt to find attractive living conditions. She did not stay at Orillia or Beaverton: clearly she preferred the south shore of Lake Simcoe, where the Sibbalds and other friends were located. In the 1890s Agnes was not yet permanently settled here, but she was at last free of the worries of the farm. With her children growing up around her and more money coming to her from her older sons, she provided a household that was a relaxing change for Stephen during his summer months. Perhaps she had found little to recommend in the life of the Lake Simcoe area farmers in the 1870s, but in the 1890s she was living in a pleasant and leisurely manner reminiscent of her childhood days in Hampshire and on the Isle of Wight. Toronto businessmen were increasingly establishing summer homes for their families around Lake Simcoe, and Leacock was not only a part of his own family circle but a well-remembered member of the local summer-season sporting and social society, its tennis and cricket clubs, its summer cruises, dances and parties. He was an enthusiastic organizer of events: cricket matches, lake excursions, outings in his own small boat. Perhaps if he had not had this diverting and flattering society, he would have left school teaching sooner.

Leacock as he was during his social summers during the 1890s at Lake Simcoe can be glimpsed in stories that have been handed down from his local acquaintances and from a few of his intimate friends who continued to know him for many years. These stories portray him as a good singer, an avid sailor and a careless dresser. Curiously, a large number of them disparage his sporting skills. Pelham Edgar, Leacock's Upper Canada College colleague, was a Lake Simcoe vacationer during these years — his father had a summer home there, and Edgar remembered many gatherings at which Leacock was present. In a memoir written at the time of Leacock's death, Edgar mentioned that his friend, despite his professed enthusiasm for cricket, had not been a good player. He had not been on the school team (Edgar had). Edgar also remembered Leacock as not much of a sailor. In later years, when Leacock had become famous, stories multiplied about the Lake Simcoe fish that always succeeded in escaping from the master teller of fish stories. In many instances, however, there are other stories that directly contradict these and that insist — especially in regard to sailing — upon Leacock's skill and therefore, presumably, upon the right he had to speak on such subjects. It bears remembering that Leacock was perhaps the leader of all those who would notice and later recall the sorrowful limitations in his own performances as a sportsman. There is no doubt that he could laugh at himself, and in such a way as to make others join in and remember the fun. Some of the stories seem almost as if he wrote them, as if they are self-deprecating sketches spoken by the voice we hear in his published work: it seems probable that Leacock was to some extent already creating his humorous personality and voice in life as well as in his earliest published essays and stories. Another factor may also have contributed to the undoubted exaggerations of his sporting incompetence in some of the anecdotes from the period. Leacock, for all his love of sport, maintained an irreverent attitude towards the self-professed expert at any activity, regarding such proficiency as mostly complacency and self-delusion. This view, frequent in his writings and perhaps expressed just as pointedly in life, must have stung many of those who took great pride in their prowess at cricket or boating, especially since it came from a young wit who never ceased to compete with them and to mock the idea that a "star" merited any special respect or standing.

Lady Matilda Edgar, Pelham Edgar's mother, provides one glimpse of the summertime Leacock of 1889. In August, writing to Pelham from her summer place at Lake Simcoe, she mentions that a family member

> drove over to Sutton to get supplies & took his dinner with Stephen Leacock who is camping out with his uncle at Jackson's Point. He says Stephen looks a different fellow, altogether strong and well set up. So the year away from study has done him good. He has been teaching at Uxbridge.

The Sibbald estate was located near Jackson's Point, which is opposite Georgina Island and is one of the main points on the south Lake Simcoe shore. The uncle in question is certainly E.P., who had just been helping Leacock locate a replacement teacher for himself at Uxbridge High School, so that he could take up the post he had been offered at Upper Canada College. A friend of Leacock's from the 1890s, Robert B. Pattison, states that during this period, while Agnes lived at "Rotherwood" on the Sibbald grounds, the Leacocks — presumably Stephen and one or more of his brothers — spent one or two summers at a nearby log house called "The Parsonage," and that E.P. was then living in a tent in the immediate area. Incidents recalled by Pattison throw much light on Leacock and the summer idyll that he and his family had made for themselves at Lake Simcoe and were to maintain and renew each year until age and death slowly brought it to an end in the 1930s. Once when playing tennis at Rotherwood, Leacock interrupted his game with the score at thirty-forty to find a piece of paper: the answer to a geometry problem he was puzzling over had come to him during the game. Just before the match, he had been translating Vergil fluently and studying both Greek and geometry by reading Euclid in the original. "The Parsonage" held the many prize books the former Head Boy had won at Upper Canada College. At tennis, Leacock was skillful enough to give practice to his friend Maud Osborne, a noted Canadian champion in the sport. He helped organize and played in cricket matches pitting Lake Simcoe area teams and communities against each other. Above all, sailing and fishing were his sports, and much of his socializing took place around them. A ship breakfast he once gave on his boat, "Pilot," forecast many dinners he would later organize at his home at Orillia, Old Brewery Bay: like them, it began in plans of elaborate formality but gradually, under the pressure of events, turned into an episode of good-natured foraging. The ship breakfast was to be at "seven sharp;" it got under way at eleven. The main course was announced as fresh-caught Lake Simcoe fish, but the fish did not comply with Leacock's hopes. The guests decided to have bacon and eggs instead, but found they had to settle for bread and butter, which Leacock had laid in "to be on the safe side." He did have milk, dubbed "cream," for the coffee — but there was no coffee. The canard that Leacock was a poor sailor may have originated in the fact that he *was*, at times, a foolhardy one, carried away by high spirits and humor. He once decided to shinny up the mast of his small boat. When he was half way up, his weight capsized the vessel, spilling himself and his passengers into the lake. This was not the only such mischance he caused. In fact, he developed a habitual joke for these occasions: while he floundered in the water, he would shout out, "And the last thing seen of the unfortunate sailors, they were clinging desperately to the torn rigging." On the other hand, when occasion called for it, he exhibited both skill and daring on the often dangerous waters of Lake Simcoe. One night a strong storm stranded his yachting party on a small island near Georgina Island. He himself sailed to shore and back to the island, through violent wind and waves and in the dark, to bring food and blankets.

It was at Lake Simcoe, during the summer of 1898 or 1899, that Leacock met his future wife, Beatrix Hamilton. The encounter took place at a tennis outing held on the estate of her grandmother, which was near Orillia. Beatrix's mother, Mrs. Robert Hamilton, was the sister of one of Toronto's richest men, the eccentric millionaire Sir Henry Pellatt. It was Pellatt who built the largest castle in North America, Casa Loma, among the most extravagant of all the white elephants raised in North America by pre-Depression dreams; it remains today, looming on a bluff overlooking downtown Toronto, one of the city's best-known landmarks and tourist attractions. Through Beatrix's grandfather, the first Henry Pellatt, father of Sir Henry, the entire family had good financial expectations, although the son's extravagance largely gutted the estate that had been originally built up through banking and stock investments. Beatrix lived the comfortable, leisured life of a daughter of well-to-do North Americans of the period; her father, Robert Hamilton, was an investment broker and a colonel in an army regiment. After his earlier, perhaps apocryphal pursuit of the hymn-singing sanatorium patient, Leacock seems to have chosen the sort of girl Victorian mothers are supposed to have hoped their sons would choose: someone well-known to local society and of good family and comfortable means. Beatrix was, however, somewhat out of the ordinary. She took the drama classes and voice study that would have been acceptable as a hobby in a young lady of her standing, but demanded a chance to go on the stage. Immediately after her summer romance with Leacock, which moved very quickly to his proposal and her acceptance, she set out from home for a year of study and stage work in New York. Although to go on the stage was a conventional dream for society girls at the end of the nineteenth century, very few of them actually made the attempt. More unconventional still than her stage career was her decision to marry Leacock, who — whatever his charms and abilities around the social circuit — was just a high-school teacher already at the limit of his salary potential and the apex of his community standing, with no family money or position to give promise of an improved future.

In his tenth year at Upper Canada College, Leacock had reached the highest level available to him without an advanced degree. Language study, which he might have pursued in Toronto, now held little interest for him; at any rate, most Canadian scholars of the era were obtaining their doctorates in England or, very occasionally, in the United States. Even if he had gone on in his own field with the aim of returning to high-school teaching, promotion would have meant an administrative post, and he preferred the classroom to administration of the student body and curriculum and the public relations and promotional duties that fell to a principal. His own principal, George Parkin, who admired Leacock as a scholar and later as a public speaker, had reservations about his suitability for high-school work, especially administration; Parkin thought him a likely candidate for success as a university professor.

In 1899 the pressures on Leacock to change his life were increasing in intensity. He was free from worry over his mother and younger brothers and sisters and was filled with determination to have a family of his own. He had nurtured, throughout his busy Upper Canada College years, two important interests: the writing of humor and studies in economics as a key to the vital realities of the contemporary world. Although humor had supplied a steady stream of small successes, by 1899 Leacock's New York connection was gone and he was publishing much less than he had two years earlier. The example of many other writers would have shown him that a passable income from writing, and the satisfaction and recognition that went with worthwhile publications, required service in the literary capitals of London or New York — nor was the income certain even for those who lived there. Instead, he chose to pursue his other interest, the study of economics, towards a university teaching career and to put aside humor altogether while pursuing his degree, a new profession and the financial security he wanted to provide for the family he and Beatrix would begin.

Chapter Five

Has Economics Gone to Seed?

I N THE FALL of 1899, Stephen Leacock, twenty-nine and engaged to be married, a veteran of more than ten years of high-school teaching, left his long-time home in Toronto to study economics at the University of Chicago. In a life that blended extraordinary success and a very conservative approach to change, studying at Chicago was the most surprising thing Leacock ever did. The nineteenth century had its journalist humorists, its musical-comedy humorists, even its Oxford-mathematician humorists. Leacock was the economics-professor humorist; he never gave up his demanding university schedule to pursue singlemindedly his international success, when it came, as a writer of comic essays and sketches. His decision to study economics as a life work and to undertake a doctoral program at the University of Chicago is the first proof that Leacock had determined to commit himself to a career of serious intellectual endeavor as teacher and writer. For lovers of his humor, especially for those Canadian critics who have been disappointed that Leacock did not produce the great Canadian novel, his interest in economics has been difficult to accept. There is the temptation to think that Leacock either did not understand his own gifts or that he was not courageous enough to pursue the difficult life of an artist. By 1899, however, Leacock had not been publishing humor for two years. If his decisions at the time were due only to fear of taking a risk, then he should not have gone to Chicago. His first year cost what savings he had accumulated from the years at Upper Canada College and required a loan as well, yet he went. Thus, he did not fear to take a risk; at most, he might be charged with taking the wrong risk, but that is to assume that his studies in economics were only a hindrance to his humor. An examination of the crucial years between his move to Chicago and the publication of *Literary Lapses* will show that the opposite is true. Leacock was attracted to university life for many reasons beyond his interest in economics and political science, and there is every evidence that he felt richly repaid for the risk he took to make a place for himself there. He found a subject that he trusted was important enough that his opinions, through his students, could influence the future of his country. He was involved in a community of thinkers whose ideas and achievements encouraged and challenged his own efforts. Humor writing began for Leacock as an experiment and a hobby, but it reached its maturity as only one of many types of writing that reflected his deep involvement in the issues of his time. Economics was one subject among many others, including literature, social issues and history, about which he began to write regularly once he was established at McGill University. He put aside humor to win a position of social importance, and once that position was securely his, he turned again to the development of his art with renewed creativity.

But still the question remains: what was it that convinced Leacock to study economics? The problem is an important one not only because of the possible battle between the claims of economics and humor, but also because it has been said that Leacock was a poor economist. Some former students have denigrated his performance in this field with which he is most identified; colleagues, too, at various times openly criticized his work in economics, as did certain writers and reviewers who opposed him in the controversies of the day. Professor James Mavor of the University of Toronto had declined to help Leacock with his studies, and Leacock was, after all, the honors student who preferred to risk his grade average on a subject he had never studied rather than face an algebra test. Why did he study economics if he was not equipped in mathematics?

Most of Leacock's readers today are neither economists nor students of the history of that complex subject, and are doubtless more interested in him as a humorist than as an economist, a good one or not. He cannot be regarded as a man who has influenced profoundly, through his teaching or his political and economic thought, the direction of Canada's development or the development of other countries where his writing circulated. The judgment against him is far from unanimous; the only recent commentator upon Leacock's social criticism regards him as a sound and insightful commentator on his age and regrets that, in the end, his humorous writings effectively drowned interest in his serious work. Specific challenges to the quality of his teaching and writing in economics will be considered as they arise. But in general it can be said that an examination of Leacock's career reveals a more than competent economist with strongly held, often controversially forward-looking views. He was interested in the practical and humane application of economic ideas, rather than in theory, although he deeply respected economic theoreticians for their vital work. His own approach, though, led him to argue his ideas uncompromisingly before the largest audience his powers of literary style could command. He sought influence and gained it, with the general reading public but more especially with Canadian and British governments and business leaders. He advocated social welfare programs and a type of mixed economy that would restrain free enterprise while avoiding socialist elements: such ideas were far in advance of any that Canadian politicians of the 1920s and 1930s were willing or able to implement. They also placed Leacock to one side of Canada's fledgling socialist movement, strongly represented at McGill and in his own department. The result of his aggressive stance was that Leacock's work was often discussed, often praised, but often rejected, too. His opponents, especially those writing in Canadian newspapers with a very conservative view of the economy, would sometimes try to disparage rather than criticize his work; it was they who repeated the feeble witticism that this or that piece of Leacockian economics belonged with his humor. Unfortunately, some later writers — concerned only with Leacock's humor, and in love with the image of a homespun philosopher with interesting foibles — have created a false impression by emphasizing attacks on Leacock the economist, especially those attacks that make good stories. Disputes are inevitable in any prominent academic's career. Leacock's spanned thirty-five tumultuous years of change — World War I, the twenties, the Great Depression, the resurgence of German nationalism, among many other events — and corresponding change in volatile fields like economics. The best economists of the day,

Leacock among them, sought to match these historical events with new theories and judgments. There is much at stake, even for someone interested only in understanding Leacock's university career as a background to his humor, in evaluating Leacock's worth as an economist. Was Leacock, that most common-sensical of men, so hopelessly blind on this one point that he could not see his failings as an economist? The short answer is that he knew his own abilities, and he made his work in economics an integral part of his career, one that has a close relationship to all his other writing.

Economics as a separate field, distinct from history or philosophy, was only about a century old when Leacock began his informal studies at Upper Canada College. There were certainly influential works on wealth, trade, labor and so on dating back to the Greeks, but the modern study began properly with Adam Smith, who published his *The Wealth of Nations* in 1776. Economics, or "political economy" as it was usually called in the nineteenth century, was gradually being introduced to college classrooms at the very end of the 1800s. It was a social science, that is, an outgrowth of moral philosophy under the traditional university curriculum and linked to ethics or history in theory and in presentation. A university might decide to separate economics from the philosophy or history department, but the subject rarely became a department by itself, separate from other social sciences. At McGill, for example, Leacock was hired to teach in the newly formed department of economics and political science; in fact, he gave the school's first political-science course. Established universities looking to staff a department in the new field turned to history or philosophy departments for their experts. Professor James Mavor at the University of Toronto was a historian. In his book *Elements of Political Science*, Leacock puts in a word about the difficulties of keeping the fields altogether separate:

Political science stands also in close relation to political economy. ... Inasmuch as the production and distribution of material wealth is very largely conditioned by the existing form of government and the institutional basis of economic life, the study of political economy is brought into an intimate relation with that of political science.

In a footnote, he adds:

> The ambiguous relation in which the terms "political science" and "political economy" stand to one another is rendered still more confusing by the divergent usages of leading American universities. At Harvard "Economics" is a subdivision of the department of "History and Political Science." At Yale both "Economics" and "Politics" appear under the departmental title of "Social Sciences." At Chicago "Political Economy" and "Political Science" constitute separate departments.

Many of the persons quick to speak disparagingly of Leacock as an economist speak highly of him as a political scientist, yet it is clear that in Leacock's own department at McGill, and during his training at the University of Chicago, the division between the two fields was not as complete as it has since become. The differences that have grown up between Leacock's and modern perceptions of his field are not limited, however, to the more careful distinction we make between economics and political science. For Leacock, for the classic authors in the two fields and for Leacock's teachers, the social sciences were an outgrowth of history and ethics, not of statistics or, more generally, of the scientific method as it has come to be applied to the study of society, especially the economy, in the twentieth century. Leacock's insistence upon ethical and humane values in economics over analysis and theory marked him as — in one respect — a member of the old guard. It was this that accounted for most of the criticism against him from academic opponents.

Leacock had always enjoyed the study of history and performed very well in history classes on the high-school and university levels. This helps account for his decision to explore economics, but the era in which he lived undoubtedly gave him special encouragement. Leacock rejected language teaching because he feared that in its contemporary form it had little relevance for his students. Economics and political science were fields growing up in direct response to the explosive social changes brought about by the Industrial Revolution.

To some who sat in his classroom in the 1930s, Leacock did not seem a forward-looking economist, but he entered the field for forward-looking reasons and in a progressive fashion: he was drawn to it because it was relevant to contemporary problems. He decided to take his degree in the United States rather than in Great Britain, and he chose the University of Chicago largely on the strength of a very revolutionary teacher, Thorstein Veblen. The American-born son of Norwegian immigrants, Veblen (1857 to 1929) published his first major book, *The Theory of the Leisure Class*, in 1899, the same year Leacock decided to attend the University of Chicago, where Veblen had been teaching since 1896. Leacock may have read the book before he went to Chicago or he may have known of it through reviews; and he may have known of Veblen himself through the economist's publications in journals of the social sciences. Whether the book made Leacock determined to go to Chicago, *The Theory of the Leisure Class* became an influential text for Leacock's later thought and is echoed strongly both in his economic writing (*The Unsolved Riddle of Social Justice,* for example) and in his humor (*Arcadian Adventures with the Idle Rich*). For more than thirty years, Veblen's books exercised enormous influence; in the 1930s, for example, *The Theory of the Leisure Class* headed a list of "books that have changed our minds," and Veblen scored higher than many scientists and philosophers whose names are today more generally familiar than his own. Veblen was influential among economists but had more influence among journalists, intellectuals and historians who were delighted with the acerbic social criticism he delivered in witty, satirical prose clearly intended to reach an audience beyond the specialists in his field. In selecting Veblen as his graduate teacher, Leacock chose an outspoken man who can be seen as a model for many aspects of Leacock's own later career, especially his use of humor and literary powers to reach the general public, rather than only the specialist, with social criticism and iconoclastic economic views.

Canadian students of economics usually went to Great Britain; Leacock and a handful of others are recognized by historians of education in Canada as being controversial importers of a new, "scientific" approach to economics from the

United States. Veblen's was not the science of the later twentieth century, but as an "institutional economist" he analyzed and commented on the actual circumstances of economic structures and behavior in his own time. He departed from the theoretical principles of the nineteenth century to seek a ground in careful observation of fact for his judgments on finance and business. Leacock's years in Chicago were the first and only time he lived in the United States. There was a good deal of traffic between Canada and the United States at the end of the nineteenth century, much of it draining population away from Canada. One million people went south in the 1880s, another half-million in the 1890s. Some of them were immigrants who decided to try their luck in more developed areas in the United States, after testing the Canadian prairies. Others were authors looking for audiences and markets. Inventors and businessmen also went south seeking capital and equipment: Alexander Graham Bell moved from his father's home in the southern Ontario to the eastern United States, where he patented his invention, the telephone, in the 1870s. Several of Leacock's brothers and sisters lived in the United States at various times. Although Leacock later wrote for United States audiences and toured there, he did not find any reason to adopt the country for his own after studying in Chicago.

In order to begin his graduate studies, Leacock had to borrow money from his mother and brothers and sisters. An indenture dated November 22, 1899, permitted the trust that supported her to advance him $1,500. The seven children, besides Stephen, who were of age had to sign the document as parties of the fourth part. Not only were they future legatees of Agnes' estate, but they would be responsible for repaying the money to the trust if Stephen proved unable to observe his repayment schedule, which provided for him to pay six per cent annual interest on the loan. Stephen was well aware of Agnes' financial situation, for in the spring of 1882 he had become one of her trustees, along with G.M. Rae and his life-long friend and lawyer, Goldwin Larratt Smith, when the aging English trustees had asked to withdraw. He knew that her assets were the stocks and cash given to her in trust upon her marriage to his father. These had generated the $80 per month upon which she was living in the 1880s; they consisted originally of £700 stock in the Great Indian Peninsular Railway, £1,773 in three per cent Consolidated Bank Annuities, and £1,173 in cash, but were now somewhat depleted by her necessity at times to draw on the capital. However, by the late 1890s new stocks and some new cash had enriched the trust as a result of bequests to Agnes from the uncle who had so befriended her in England, the Rev. Charles Butler. The principal addition this had made to the trust was approximately £3,000 in three and three-and-a-half per cent stock. By 1899, Leacock felt he could safely borrow enough to supplement his own savings and pay for his studies toward a doctorate, and a career in university teaching.

During his first year at the University of Chicago, Leacock completed six courses and received marks high enough to earn a fellowship in "political economy." When he went back to Chicago in the fall of 1900, he had Beatrix with him. In August, 1900 they were married quietly at the Little Church Around the Corner in the theater district in New York, where Beatrix had been working. Their first home together was a small apartment near the University of Chicago, but they had only been settled a few months when they moved to Montreal, where Leacock began work as a part-time lecturer in political science and history. Despite his fellowship, Leacock evidently felt he could no longer afford to be without a job. He tried first at the University of Toronto, but Professor Mavor, head of the economics department by this time, refused to consider him. Backed by warm recommendations from Upper Canada College principal George Parkin, Leacock was able to obtain an appointment at McGill. McGill principal William Peterson wrote Parkin later that he had been impressed with Leacock from their first meeting. From 1901 through 1903, Leacock spent only one quarter of each year in Chicago and devoted the rest of his time to teaching at McGill.

At the time of his marriage, Leacock had just turned thirty-one. He was straight and slender, and gave the impression of being taller than his height of five feet ten inches. He had added a certain amount of maturity to his face by growing a fashionable Edwardian mustache: combined with the square massiveness of his chin, it could help make him seem, at times, solid and respectable. Generally, however, he looked as young as or younger than his age. He often wore stylish and well-fitted clothes, and his untroubled if sometimes serious face was dominated by a striking head of dark, glossy and usually well-combed hair. However, the few informal photographs of him from this period leave no doubt that, away from the portrait camera, the rumpled and tousled Leacock of later years was developing.

In the fall of 1900, Leacock was one of a small number of graduate students in political economy whose work was directed by Veblen. In *My Discovery of the West*, published seven years after his professor's death in 1929, Leacock wrote fondly and appreciatively of Veblen's theoretical powers but less positively about his writing style or classroom technique.

> Veblen had a beautiful and thoughtful mind, free from anger and dispute, and heedless of all money motive. As a lecturer, he had no manner, but sat mumbling into his lap, scarcely intelligible. But the words which thus fell into his lap were priceless. . . . His writings, brilliant though they are, are too abstruse for popular reading, and not abstruse enough to be unintelligible and rank as gospel, like the Social Credit of Major Douglas.

Leacock also devotes a paragraph to a curious anecdote about Veblen's highly unpopular class called "Primitive Economics of the Navajo Indians," through which most students apparently slept: "After a few minutes you could hear its [the class's] deep breathing." Leacock concealed himself behind the classroom's only pillar and so escaped the fate of one student refused credit by Veblen: "He told me afterwards the man had slept in his class." But was the class worth staying awake for? "Navajo is pronounced Navaho: I got that much out of it anyway." Leacock's judgment that Veblen was "too abstruse for popular reading" should be weighed against the wide acknowledgment of the economist's work in intellectual circles and the high praise it received as a text of great verbal skill as well as profound thought. *The Theory of the Leisure Class* merits reading by all those interested in observing the formation of Leacock's thought on social issues. In it, Veblen establishes several key points and then applies them in various fields of human experience, often with an incisive overturning of accepted social values. The key points, as outlined by Leacock in *My Discovery of the West*, are these:

> The ideas of the lectures were gathered later into Veblen's books. The central point of his thought is that human industry is not carried on to satisfy human wants but in order to make money. The two motives do not work, thinks Veblen, to a single end as Adam Smith and John Stuart Mill had thought they do. They fall apart. Hence a lot of people get too much money. These have to find ways of spending it in "conspicuous consumption." This is the "leisure class", a sort of flower on a manure heap.
>
> Contrasted with the "money makers" are the "engineers", that is men who make *things* not money, — the "real boys", so to speak. They could satisfy all our reasonable wants if they guided industrial society. But they don't. The money getters, with their leisure class women and their "honorific expenditure", have entrenched themselves as "Vested Interests", — and there you are! What did Veblen propose to do about it? Nothing, so far as I remember.

There is a striving after simplicity in Leacock's presentation that verges on the flippant, especially in his concluding description of Veblen's suggestions for solving the problems he so uncompromisingly insisted were to blame for the difficulties of his contemporaries. But Veblen was, in fact, little concerned with solutions, and Leacock's summary does justice to Veblen's quarrel with capitalism. Veblen attacked the work ethic, which justified the possession of wealth, by arguing that money was accumulated not by the honest effort to produce valuable objects (work) but rather in a barbaric attempt to prove superiority over other men through the possession of the most valuable goods. Money, once acquired, did not improve life for the community at large, as some economists argued, but effectively discouraged social improvements because the wealthy spent money only to drive home the point of their superiority. Veblen wrote:

> The institution of a leisure class hinders cultural development immediately (1) by the inertia proper to the class itself, (2) through its prescriptive example of conspicuous waste and of conservatism,

and (3) indirectly through that system of unequal distribution of wealth and sustenance on which the institution itself rests.

Veblen argued that even activities one might suppose to be useful are undertaken because they demonstrate the leisured person's absolute freedom from any necessity:

> So, for instance, in our time there is the knowledge of the dead languages and the occult sciences; of correct spelling; of syntax and prosody; of the varied forms of domestic music and other household art; of the latest proprieties of dress, furniture, and equipage; of games, sports and fancy-bred animals, such as dogs and race-horses. In all these branches of knowledge the initial motive from which their acquisition proceeded at the outset, and through which they first came into vogue, may have been something quite different from the wish to show that one's time had not been spent in industrial employment; but unless these accomplishments had approved themselves as serviceable evidence of an unproductive expenditure of time, they would not have survived and held their place as conventional accomplishments of the leisure class.

The Theory of the Leisure Class, finally, draws repeated attention to the questionable value of the status of women in the leisure class. Men expect women to enjoy their position as recipients of leisure and wealth given them by their husbands, without admitting that their demands reduce women to "chattels" and "unfree servants." A wife busies herself with a round of social engagements and household duties that "prove on analysis to serve little or no ulterior end beyond showing that she does not occupy herself with anything that is gainful or that is of substantial use."

In 1904 Veblen published another book, *The Theory of Business Enterprise,* which considered the intricacies of money management rather than the social impact of "conspicuous consumption" by the wealthy leisure class. Shortly after the publication of the second book, however, he was asked to leave the University of Chicago; Leacock says only that "they 'let him out' of Chicago University," but the specific quarrel that led to his dismissal is well-known. Veblen was discharged because he traveled openly with a woman companion, his secretary, on an Atlantic crossing; at the time, he was estranged from his wife, who eventually divorced him. One might have supposed that the same university officials who admired Veblen for his outspoken attacks on his society's treatment of women would have expected unconventional personal behavior from the economist. Apparently, they were prepared to endure his endless campaign against university regulations with regard to his classroom methods but could not accept the breach of marital propriety. From Chicago, Veblen went on to teach at Stanford and later in the midwest at a small college; after a second discharge for reasons similar to those that forced him to leave Chicago, he became a recluse and died alone in 1929.

Leacock demonstrated his admiration for Veblen's theories by incorporating many of his teacher's complaints against society in his own work. He treated Veblen somewhat as he did Marx and socialist thinkers, drawing heavily on their criticism of *laissez faire* capitalism but rejecting their reconstructive suggestions and developing his own. Certain texts by Leacock display a rather direct use of Veblen's teachings. It is interesting to consider whether Veblen's highly individual personal style, too, might have had any influence on Leacock's later life; there seems little parallel between Veblen and Leacock on the question of women, either in their theoretical discussions of women in society or in the conduct of their personal lives. Leacock was a faithful, devoted husband to Beatrix until her death in 1925; no scandal attached to his name throughout his many years as a widower, despite the busy public life he led. How did the newlywed Leacocks' react to the outrageous conduct of Stephen's famous, respected teacher? On this point Leacock is silent, although it seems unlikely that he could have spent three years working closely under Veblen without hearing the stories about his personal life. When University of Chicago chancellor William Rainey Harper challenged Veblen regarding the possible impact of his conduct on the "moral health" of other professors' wives, Veblen is supposed to have replied, "I've tried them all. They are no good." Although Leacock separated himself privately and professionally from Veblen's attitudes towards women, he seems to have been tempted to imitate some of Veblen's iconoclastic attacks on university regulations. Veblen refused to take attendance in class; students absent when he read the roll were not reported. Similar stories of Leacock's dislike of McGill's introduction of compulsory class attendance abound from later years. Veblen disliked the university's requirement that teachers wear an academic gown and was notoriously careless about his dress; Leacock's admirers outdo themselves in describing his tattered gown and generally untidy appearance. Veblen disliked keeping office hours and refused to take trouble over grading his students. Leacock on occasion is recorded as speaking quite cavalierly about assigning final marks. Still, there are differences that perhaps outweigh all these similarities. By Leacock's account, and general agreement among other former students, Veblen had a poor classroom technique. Leacock, on the other hand, was remembered universally by his students as a commanding, if not always humorous, speaker in class. More important, Leacock was concerned always to encourage change only by setting the values he found in tradition against current abuses; it is this that made him deeply suspicious of the radical criticisms and remedies found in work such as Veblen's.

Leacock's doctoral thesis was a historical study, "The Doctrine of Laissez Faire," an indication that even in work submitted to Veblen, Leacock pursued his personal, more traditional interests along with his teacher's revolutionary ones. At his final oral examination, he was asked to discuss the tax system of the State of Illinois. Leacock refused, saying he knew nothing about it. He offered instead to speak on the theory of value. A fundamental philosophical concept for nineteenth-century political economy, the theory of value deals with the idea of the valuable or the good; it was used to analyze the relationship between a fair price and the inherent worth of manufactured objects or services. Leacock spoke learnedly on this subject and was passed by the committee of examiners. In May, 1903 he received his doctorate in political economy from the University of Chicago *magna cum laude*.

Throughout his life, Leacock maintained a friendly acquaintance with the University of Chicago and with the city, where he was always much in demand as a speaker, both by civic groups and by Chicago-based lecture bureaus that

served the midwest. As an alumnus of the university's graduate school, he recommended outstanding McGill undergraduates to the University of Chicago in not a few cases. A
letter to his old department, which Leacock wrote on behalf of
a female student in 1915, brough him this response from J.
Lawrence Laughlin, who had been one of his favorite professors:

> It was a great satisfaction to get your personal note in your letter
> of recommendation for Miss Going. In fact, I had been on the point
> of writing you for a long time because your name and your books
> had become a household word with us. Mrs. Laughlin has had no
> end of pleasure and merriment out of your books; and her pleasure
> has been shared by my son. . . . Of course, I claim that all this suc-
> cess has been due to the work you did in my economics seminar!

Aside from Thorstein Veblen, it had been Laughlin, Henry
Pratt Judson and Caspar Miller who, among the University of
Chicago's faculty members, had most attracted Leacock to the
school. The students he met there remembered him just as
vividly as did his teachers, and they too sometimes contacted
him, directly or indirectly. One letter he received fifteen years
after he had left the university provides a brief glimpse of his
student days. Charles Starrett of the Chicago *Daily News*
wrote to him:

> My friend and associate of the News, Mr. Leroy T. Binion, dis-
> covered me, recently, chuckling over the Nonsense Novels, and
> demanded to look at the volume. Thereupon he discovered that the
> author was one Stephen Leacock, with whom, he asserted, he had
> "gone to school" — that is, at the University of Chicago. Then he
> unfolded a number of anecdotes of the period, describing how the
> political economy class frequently became a debate between Lea-
> cock and the professor, in which the professor was as likely to be
> worsted as Mr. Leacock.

Immediately after Leacock had received his doctorate, he was
hired by McGill as a full-time lecturer in the department of
economics and political science at a salary, with extra night-
class duties, of two thousand dollars per year. During the summer of 1903, Stephen and Beatrix took a brief honeymoon trip

to England and France; it was the first time Leacock had been in his native country since his emigration in 1876. The opening of the fall term found them back in Montreal, established comfortably in a small flat near the university. They had spent much of every year in the city since 1901, but this time they were settling down permanently. Stories abound about Leacock at McGill, in the classroom and out; not too surprisingly, relatively few of the first-person accounts of his antics date from these very early days. But even in his very first class, the one that began his life at McGill on the day before Queen Victoria's death, 21 January, 1901, Leacock managed to make a memorable impression. The students of McGill's first-ever class in political science privately petitioned Peterson, the principal, to continue to keep Leacock on the staff because they had appreciated his teaching and technique as lecturer. It was not an era in which student evaluations were relied on as a measure of teacher performance, and Peterson evidently made no mention of the student support to Leacock at the time. Leacock learned of it many years later from some of the students of the class.

Until 1903, Leacock had taught history and political science. Once he had his doctorate in economics, he wanted to teach his specialty as well. A dispute arose between Leacock and the chairman of the department, Doctor A.W. Flux, when Leacock introduced courses in economics into the McGill curriculum without receiving the chairman's approval in advance. Flux challenged Leacock's methods in letters to Peterson, and certainly Leacock seems to have been forcing his ideas through without attention to university procedure. More serious, though, were the charges Flux raised as to Leacock's competence to teach economics. Flux reported to Peterson on inquiries he had made to Thorstein Veblen at the University of Chicago; Flux claimed that Veblen had replied in "curiously vague terms" and had shown a "hesitancy to praise;" he did not, however, produce the letter for others to evaluate. Despite his registered doubts as to Leacock's ability, Flux surrendered the point and allowed his junior faculty member to begin teaching economics. This incident is the first challenge to Leacock as an economist from the McGill community; it is interesting as well because Flux tried to use the

words of Veblen against Leacock. From what we have seen of
Veblen, we might be allowed to dismiss the evidence of his
apparent lack of interest; after all, Leacock had just graduated
under his direction with excellent marks. Veblen may well
have been too preoccupied with his own growing troubles or
simply uninterested in the squabbling of another university's
faculty. If Flux had been able to gain any support, surely he
could have stopped one of his subordinates from tampering
with the school's curriculum. Perhaps trouble arose simply
because Flux saw that his newest faculty member would be
difficult to handle, or because the chairman needed a political-
science teacher and was not interested in an economist. Perhaps, though, Leacock was proving to be more controversial
on economic issues than he was on history and political
science and, therefore, challenged the department's established views.

In the meantime, Leacock was writing again. As we have
seen, political science was still a comparatively new university subject, and he felt that there was a real need for a sound
textbook on all aspects of the discipline. He worked on his
manuscript for almost three years; in 1906, an American company, Houghton Mifflin, released Leacock's first book, *Elements of Political Science*. It proved to be Leacock's biggest
money-maker among all his books, including the many
volumes of humor he wrote. *Elements of Political Science* was
soon required reading at thirty-six American universities and
many others throughout the British empire. It was translated
into eighteen languages and enjoyed lasting popularity as far
afield as China and Africa. Reviews of the book were generally approving: "a useful textbook of the subject, brought well
up-to-date," "clear-cut, well written, logically arranged, and
convincing." Edward E. Hill, writing in *School Review*, worried that, "It is almost too strong to be taken clear by the
young student of political science, but will make an excellent
diet when properly diluted with class-room discussion." The
most serious objection raised was that Leacock offered "conventional" opinions, especially on issues related to the British
empire.

Elements of Political Science was reissued in 1913 and revised in 1921. In a very volatile era and a changing discipline,

it proved to be an enduring success. For readers hoping to find either wit or impassioned social criticism in its pages, *Elements of Political Science* may be something of a disappointment. It is thoroughly a textbook, moving clearly and slowly through the topics one might expect: the nature of political science, the nature of the state, forms of government around the world, recent changes in political organizations and so on. We have seen already something of the book in Leacock's explanation of the differences between political economy and political science. A further example shows Leacock's approach, which is impartial while at the same time presenting clearly stated value judgments:

> Entirely opposed to the individualistic conception of government are the doctrines known as socialism, collectivism, communism, and which, subject to later distinction, may be spoken of together as the socialistic theory of the state. No socialistic state has actually existed on any except a small and experimental scale. Socialism is therefore mainly an ideal rather than an actuality. But the doctrines it embodies have appealed so strongly to so many minds, have exercised such an important influence on actual legislation and practical politics, and contain in spite of their fallacious nature so much that is of use and inspiration, as to merit a special treatment.

Books by Karl Marx are listed among the chapter's recommended outside reading, and Leacock balances his initial judgment as to the "fallacious" nature of socialist theory by presenting a very thorough summary of it. He disapproves of socialism for two reasons. First, he does not accept Marx's contention that a capitalistic economy must inevitably collapse due to its own wasteful politics. Second, he does not approve of the socialist remedy to the failings of capitalism, that is, the substitution of government ownership for private enterprise. In the light of what we observed about his studies with Veblen, Leacock's principal point of agreement with socialism is perhaps not too surprising: he agrees with much of its criticism about the failings of the present economic system and welcomes any help in bringing about reform.

On more valid grounds the socialists draw attention to the

wastefulness of the individualistic method of production and distribution. A vast amount of work is performed under it that has no social utility; a great deal of work is duplicated and even done several times over with no general advantage. . . . From what has been said it will be easily seen that the critical or destructive side of socialistic theory contains a great deal that is true and extremely useful in indicating the proper direction of measures of social reform.

Thus Leacock welcomes the help of socialists but strongly disapproves of the direction of reform they propose.

Elements of Political Science devotes considerable attention to the development of the British empire; this may be attributed as much to the current-events situation at the turn of the century as to Leacock's own famed reverence for Great Britain. Complaints that his opinions are "conventional" and outdated almost certainly stem from his analysis of imperial politics in the early 1900s. Leacock argues that the growth of a movement for complete independence of British dominions has given way to a resurgence of interest in imperial unity. But the unity he is proposing is not a return to colonial dependence for countries like his own. He envisions full voting rights within the empire for every imperial citizen.

The new wave of imperialism that has affected public opinion in all the great states of the world has fascinated the national ambitions of all the British subjects with the possibility of the future power of their colossal empire. The smaller destiny of isolated independence is set aside in favor of participating in the plenitude of power possible in union. The combined efforts of Britain and the colonies called forth by the Transvaal War have done much to strengthen this feeling. But with the acceptance of this new point of view, the troubled question of interimperial relations again looms large upon the horizon. . . . If independence is no longer to be the future ideal of the colonies, and since geographical reasons forbid a complete amalgamation, it looks as if the manifest destiny of the colonial system must now be sought in imperial federation. . . . It does not seem possible that another generation can go by and find Canada and Australia still outside of the imperial councils; it hardly seems possible that the group of ministers who control the foreign policy of the empire can permanently remain the appointees of the electorate of the British Isles, to the exclusion of the British dominions beyond the seas.

103

Leacock wanted an imperial parliament elected by all the citizens of the empire, which would then make policy for the empire.

With *Elements of Political Science*, Leacock established a wide readership among college students around the world. His lectures and the book also gained him another audience. In 1905, a year before *Elements of Political Science* was published, Leacock began public-speaking engagements in Canada. His subject was Canada in the British empire, and he was popular enough to be invited, in 1907, to make a world tour as a spokesman for imperial policies. We have seen something of his particular views on the subject from his book, and the tour provides a good opportunity to consider in detail the precise character of Leacock's "imperialism." Now, more than eighty years after the tour, Leacock's reputation as a supporter of the empire is usually mentioned as a self-evident failing of his political thought. To be an imperialist is bad enough, but to be a supporter of the British empire seems to remove him altogether to the curio cupboard. A review of the events of the tour and an examination of Leacock's actual remarks lead towards a different judgment. Just as his economic theory can be shown to be, for his time, innovative and sensitive to the cause of social reform, so too his support of the empire was grounded as much in his conviction of what was best for his own country as in an idea of what was best for Great Britain.

Chapter Six

Our British Empire

L*ITERARY LAPSES* was only four years away when Leacock published *Elements of Political Science*, but there was little indication between 1906 and 1910 that he anticipated, or was interested in, success as a humorist. Increasingly busy outside his McGill classroom, Leacock made speeches and wrote for magazines and newspapers on financial and political subjects, especially the future of the British empire. Although he was noted for the humorous asides with which he relieved the seriousness of his themes, Leacock was no longer producing the lighthearted jibes at the customs of the day that he had published in the 1890s. For the first time, he was not chafing for a better job, but the determination to improve himself had not been laid to rest altogether by his success at McGill. He eagerly accepted opportunities to speak outside his classroom, and offered himself to the community at large as an expert on contemporary politics and economic affairs. Throughout his life, Leacock devoted much time to popular writing on issues of government, education and social changes, a practice he began in the years before *Literary Lapses* established him as a popular humorist. Although his many articles and books on politics and economics receive little attention now, and although they were overshadowed relatively early in his career by the great success of his humor, Leacock continued to speak out about current events.

His first public success came as a social commentator. Encouraged by this success, Leacock determined to make the experiment with humor. The two areas of his writing, humor and economics, are closely linked, because in his serious writing Leacock discusses many of the same subjects and displays the same attitudes found in his humor pieces. In his most ambitious works of humor, *Sunshine Sketches of a Little Town* and *Arcadian Adventures with the Idle Rich*, his social vision is an integral part of his satirical analysis of small towns and big cities. Leacock did not struggle between his social criticism as a professor and his social satire as a humorist. Especially in the early years of the century, he drew confidence and material from his university studies, which made his humor possible. The articles and speeches on politics from the years before 1910 are very different in tone and development from his early humor pieces, but the two types of writing are closely linked because both spring from Leacock's search for ways to make the world aware of the vision of the good he held clearly in his own mind. Leacock perhaps was too optimistic in thinking that he could publish both types of work without creating some confusion and even hostility in his readers. As years passed and the proof accumulated that his serious writing on social questions was receiving little attention, the careful demarcation between the two styles blurred and Leacock began to rely on the tools of the humorist's trade, and on his reputation as a humorist, to supply the persuasion behind his opinions on politics. But before 1910, Leacock was moving gradually outward from the one position of authority he held, his professorship at McGill. He did not expect his audiences to be convinced by wit or entertained only by jokes and quips; rather, he was working hard for the causes in which he believed.

The 1980s have actors-turned-activists or politicians, while retired politicians regularly write books, deliver lectures and occupy the sofas on late-night talk shows. Early in the century, there was also considerable interchange between journalism, including humorous writing, and government. About the time Leacock was starting his high-school teaching, an Ontario native, Sir Gilbert Parker, left Canada for a journalism career in Australia. Soon after, Parker emerged in London society as a popular novelist of the Canadian frontier; eventually, he served several terms in the British Parliament and was part of the welcoming committee that met Leacock during his triumphant tour of Great Britain in 1921. G.K. Chesterton and Hilaire Belloc both stood for Parliament, and Belloc was elected to a seat for one term. Even popular writers with no desire to become politicians frequently divided their time between social satire and more serious social commentary. Chesterton, a close contemporary of Leacock's and one of the most prominent journalist-humorists of the years between 1900 and 1910, certainly straddles the line between humorist and political analyst. Jerome K. Jerome too became a serious social commentator in many of his later essays. Because Leacock is best-known for his humor writing, the rest of his life's work as author and teacher sometimes is dismissed as the sort of presumptuous or pointless meddling into affairs beyond his talents that the political journalism of Chesterton, for example, is now judged by some. In the 1870s, Mark Twain, who had begun his journalism career as a muck-raking reporter, found himself warned off repeatedly when he attempted any serious remarks on political affairs. One letter writer said of Twain in a New York newspaper, "No thinking man would attach any value to the view of a humorist," whom he classed with "actors and clowns, who make it a business to cater to our amusement in jest and burlesque." Twain hated the lecture platform because he felt that the success he had there was a threat to his more serious literary reputation. But Twain had come from the stage, the scene of his early success, to his more mature novels and stories. Leacock, on the other hand, began as a public figure representing education and expertise in challenging disciplines, politics and economics. His ideal of the university, stated first in this period through essays on education, stressed the formation of liberally trained persons competent to make judgments and provide leadership in many fields. The very fact that the university's role in society was changing away from this ideal in his time made Leacock more insistent that he believed in the training of such people and more determined to be one himself. Friends constantly mention that he was a man who liked to see all things done well, from sailing to writing a treatise on economics. The value he placed on university training made him feel that, in comparison to many other prominent commentators of the age, he was particularly well-qualified to speak.

Leacock might be pardoned for thinking that he was justified in his initial optimism because, for several years following his appointment at McGill, he met only success: with his students, with his lecture audiences, with other writers and with his readers and publishers, if sales are any proof. He became so successful that he began to wish to guard himself from the demands of public life. In 1908, he purchased the land on Lake Couchiching near Orillia where he would build his famous summer house. It was like going home, because his mother lived in the Lake Simcoe area and his brothers and sisters either visited regularly or lived there also. About the same time, he acquired another "home," the University Club in Montreal, a private club for McGill students, faculty and graduates. The club epitomizes the city side of Leacock's life, which was overshadowed later in his career when he retired from the university and spent more time in Orillia. His reputation as a country sage is based in part on *Sunshine Sketches of a Little Town*, an early book, but it rested also on the images of him gathered from his last years. But of all the homes he had, the University Club was the one at which Leacock felt most completely accepted for what he wished to be. In comparison to literary figures who spent their years in London or New York, Leacock lived in relative isolation, especially early in his career, from other writers. But Leacock drew powerful support from, and enjoyed the refreshing atmosphere of, the teachers and businessmen he met at the University Club; his friends at the club, as much as the family group at Orillia, must be credited with nurturing Leacock's efforts as a writer. However, literary associations were not altogether lacking for Leacock. Soon after his arrival in the city he joined the Montreal Pen and Pencil Club, where he was closely associated with Andrew (later Sir Andrew) Macphail, physician, historian of science and man of letters. An essayist in the best manner of the eighteenth and nineteenth centuries, Macphail was Leacock's chief literary mentor and confidant throughout his life. Much of Leacock's work was eventually done in the tradition to which Macphail belonged — that of Dr. Johnson, Hume, Macauley and Arnold. In Leacock, of course, the mixture was different and essentially lighter; to the list of his antecedents as an essayist we would have to add his favorite humorists and Addison, Charles Lamb, perhaps Stevenson. At the Pen and Pencil Club, Leacock knew many Montreal authors and literary amateurs of the time, most of them now forgotten. Among their number, however, were MacPhail's close friend, John McCrae, later famous as the author of "In Flanders Fields," and the painter Robert Harris, who was also a poet and memoirist.

Even before the publication of *Elements of Political Science*, Leacock was gaining popularity as a public speaker. In 1905, he gave a series of six lectures on the British empire in Ottawa; he was sponsored by the May Court Club. In 1906, he gave a lecture called "The Imperial Crisis" at the Canadian Club in Toronto. A former student, Dacres Cameron, persuaded the Canadian Manufacturers' Association to invite Leacock to its Montreal meeting; Cameron, secretary of the organization, reassured the doubtful businessmen that Leacock could be witty as well as informative. The Montreal meeting was so successful that Leacock soon after addressed a larger annual gathering in Toronto. In the spring of 1907, his many lecture successes reached their high point when Earl Grey, governor-general of Canada since 1904, approached Leacock about making a world tour on behalf of imperial unity. Grey had heard Leacock speak in Ottawa and was aware that the recently formed Cecil Rhodes Trust was looking for a lecturer to promote the cause of the British empire. On 26 March, Leacock responded to the suggestion in a letter outlining a route for the tour, the title of his lecture — "Imperial Development and Organization" — and a salary proposal of five hundred pounds per year. The major problem in the way of the trip was Leacock's work at McGill. Grey wrote Peterson asking for a leave of absence of two years for Leacock. "I think you will be doing a service to Canada and the Empire if you can see your way to allow him to do this work, for which he is by nature so admirably fitted," the governor-general explained. He also enlisted the help of Leacock's former principal at Upper Canada College, Sir George Parkin, in recommending that Leacock go on the tour. Parkin had left Upper Canada College in 1902 to take a position with the Cecil Rhodes Trust; he was organizing the famous Rhodes Scholarship Program to bring students from British colonies, past and present, to study at Oxford University. Parkin, who had written strong letters of recommendation in support of Leacock's appointment to McGill, again praised his former colleague; the board of governors at McGill approved a one-year leave of absence and agreed to pay the expenses of the trip. The Rhodes Trust made a cash contribution, and Earl Grey offered to make up any difference between the budget and the actual cost of the tour.

It was a great age for touring. After European travelers had for years been sizing up the Americas, Mark Twain had restored the balance richly with *Innocents Abroad* and several highly successful world trips on which he lectured and read from his novels and stories. In the summer of 1907, as Leacock was engaged in his tour, Twain made his last trip across the Atlantic, to receive, along with Rodin, Saint-Säens and Rudyard Kipling, an honorary doctor's degree from Oxford University. Leacock's tour differed from the famous Twain tours of the turn of the century because Leacock had no international reputation to assure him audiences. Rather, he was chosen by a private foundation and assisted by recommendations from government and university to be the official spokesman for a cause. He was not an employee of government or an elected official, but he was clearly expected to represent, in some measure, a position acceptable to governments in the empire. The clearest precedent for the trip was a tour made by Sir George Parkin himself, five years before he became principal of Upper Canada College, on behalf of the Imperial Federation League. The league was founded in 1884 by members from British colonies and from Great Britain, who were convinced that the best course for the empire was the type of unity Leacock outlined in *Elements of Political Science*. Parkin, a New Brunswick native, was a charter member of the league and, in 1889, accepted an invitation to tour Australia and New Zealand as a representative of the organization. Often finding himself without any audience to address, Parkin nevertheless gave interviews and met with private citizens and government officials to present his cause. At the end of the trip, he returned to England and there worked without pause as a lecturer and journalist on behalf of imperial unity, even after the Imperial Federation League collapsed due to internal difficulties in 1893. The League had been organized to counter a threat that had, in some measure, disappeared by the mid-1890s because a renewed spirit of imperial unity had grown up due to British activities in India, the Sudan and southern Africa. Beginning in 1868, the year after Canada's confederation, Great Britain under Gladstone's first administration was being led firmly in the direction of freeing the former colonies, on the ground that they were merely distractions from the work of reforming the home country. The Imperial Federation League sought to counter this belief, in large measure because the former colonies or continuing possessions feared that they could not survive independently. But by the end of the century, rivalries between Great Britain and other European powers for control of trade and shipping around the world had made the empire of renewed importance to London.

Perhaps the key event in the years between Parkin's tour and Leacock's trip was the Boer War (1899 to 1902). In the fighting to control the southern tip of Africa, Great Britain relied on its former colonies — Canada, New Zealand and Australia — to supply troops and military equipment. Leacock spoke warmly, in *Elements of Political Science*, of the proof of imperial unity shown by the successful British war effort in South Africa. For the first time, the colonies were not a drain on the home country's resources but rather were a help in protecting Britain's interests. Alliances among other European countries had isolated Great Britain increasingly from its closest neighbors; without the far-reaching network of bases and supply points provided by the old colonies, there seemed little to bolster British security. The Boer War received strong support in Great Britain. There were few dissenting voices raised against the campaign to protect the rights of English nationals living in the Boer states; one of the few belonged to G.K. Chesterton, who emerged as a popular journalist through his writings on the war. Chesterton objected to the war because he felt the empire was not in the best interests of the people living in Great Britain; he had humanitarian objections, as well, to the British use of military force against the Boers. In Canada, the cause was not met with universal approval, especially in Quebec, but Prime Minister Wilfrid Laurier agreed to send several thousand troops. Leacock's comments on the war in *Elements of Political Science* suggest approval both of imperial co-operation during the fighting and of the peace terms that brought a united group of British and Boer settlements into the empire as the Union of South Africa.

In a later work, *Our British Empire: Its Structure, Its Unity, Its Strength*, Leacock expressed strong regret at the military conflict and praised the Boers as "unsurpassed in the world's record of patriotic heroism." But he regretted the war because he felt diplomacy would have achieved the proper end — that is, the admission of the area into the empire — much better.

> The tragedy of it is, as seen by many of us, that all that was ever gained by the war would have come naturally enough anyway, with patience and a lapse of time. People cannot, not even Dutch farmers, live forever on memories of Great Treks and kraals and assegais. Life must go on, and would have, and Dutch and British union under the Empire would have come as easy and welcome destiny. It came another way.

Leacock felt the result of the war was desirable because it brought another piece of the world into strong unity with Great Britain and the rest of the empire.

There was more to Leacock's imperialism, particularly in 1907, than gratitude for British heritage and pride in Canada's contributions to the empire's needs. Already in *Elements of Political Science* he had demanded equal representation for all imperial citizens in an imperial legislative assembly. In 1907, before leaving for the lecture tour, he published an essay, "Greater Canada: An Appeal," on the occasion of the Imperial Conference, which that spring was drawing government leaders from dominions and colonies around the world to London. He called for a "wider citizenship" for Canadians in the empire, the one measure he felt would bring "the realization of a Greater Canada."

> Shall we still whine in our poverty, still draw imaginary pictures of our thin herds shivering in the cold blasts of the North, their shepherds huddled for shelter in the log cabins of Montreal and Toronto? . . . Or, shall we say to the people of England, "The time has come; we know and realize our country. We will be your colony no longer. Make us one with you in an Empire, Permanent and Indivisible."

Praising "the inevitable greatness of Canada," Leacock warned that, without imperial membership of an order beyond colonial status, Canada would at best be trapped in "stagnation" and at worst be drawn into "the strife of races" within its boundaries and lost through the attraction of annexation with the United States. The warning he gave was timely enough: disturbed by Britian's demands for military support and its concessessions to the United States in the Alaska boundary dispute in 1903, Prime Minister Wilfrid Laurier was moving steadily away from his former steadfast support of the imperial connection towards closer ties with the United States. In 1910, he concluded a trade treaty with United States President William Howard Taft, which was not enacted because of Laurier's defeat in the 1911 election. But Leacock tended to blame Great Britain only for failure to use its opportunities in Canada, not for spoiling the goodwill of Canadians through mismanagement of its role as maker of foreign policy for the dominion. Rather, he accused Canadians of failing to insist strongly enough that they would give up the comforts of living as "peasant pensioners" on the imperial bounty. He called on his countrymen to demand the wider role he envisioned they should have.

On 27 April, 1907, Leacock and Beatrix embarked from Halifax on board the S.S. *Victorian*. He was thirty-seven, just eight years older than when he borrowed money to begin his doctoral studies in Chicago. His first lectures were in London, where he addressed the Royal Colonial Institute and the Victoria League. At Oxford he addressed a group of Rhodes scholars and dined at All Souls College. Leacock wrote,

> I saw a great many people in London . . . went to lunch with Mr. Balfour [former prime minister], stayed in the country with Rudyard Kipling and saw . . . Fabian Ware (Editor, Morning Post) and Amery of the Times.

Reports of the tour came to Canada from around the world as Leacock made his year-long progress from Europe to Australia and New Zealand, then to South Africa and, finally, home across the Pacific for lectures in the major Canadian cities from Vancouver to Montreal. He was greeted with special warmth at the University of Capetown and was sought out by government officials in all the dominions. Everywhere his audiences were enthusiastic: Leacock seemingly had solved some problems that caused his tour to get off to a rough start.

Another tour of this type was never made by Leacock, although he remained faithful throughout his life to the ideal of imperial unity. It seems that Leacock felt himself ill-suited to the role of official spokesman. Although his cause was one being championed around the world by the governments within the empire, Leacock stirred critical comment by his particular manner of championing imperialism. Before leaving for England, he was warned by Earl Grey that he was too negative in his comments about the United States (a country toward which Leacock grew warmer and warmer thoughout his life). "It is quite possible to crow & flap one's wings without treading on one's neighbour's corns," Grey wrote. The tour began with perhaps its most controversial incident: Leacock published in London's *Morning Post* an article called "John Bull, Farmer," in which he criticized the Imperial Conference (just ended) for not taking positive steps towards unity among the dominions. The article, written in American dialect, concluded with the prophecy that antiquated ideas would be swept aside by the former colonies and Great Britain would find itself in a subordinate position or excluded altogether:

> The old man's got old and he don't know it; can't kick him off the place; but I reckon that the next time we come together to talk things over the boys have got to step right in and manage the whole farm.

Leacock was widely criticized by the British and Canadian press. Peterson wrote to warn him against any further outburst: "Much of your offense consisted in rushing in where, by tacit compact, the genuine Canadian is afraid to tread." Winston Churchill referred to the article as "offensive twaddle." In later years, despite his long record of writings on political subjects, Leacock still carried the label, in some official circles, of being not "quite safe" enough to trust with dutiful expression of the established government position. Although Earl Grey had obviously envisioned for his protegé a career as imperial apologist similar to that followed by Parkin after his tour, Leacock did not pursue his opportunity. In later years, he participated actively in political campaigning but steadfastly refused to run for office. The tour had helped teach him that repeating the party line, even with the special flourishes his rhetoric could bring to it, was not his way.

"Greater Canada: An Appeal," along with press accounts of Leacock's performances during the tour, provides an insight into the style he had developed for conveying his political ideas. Relying little on humor, he wrote and spoke in elaborate, flowing phrases rich in images and descriptions.

> And of all this take only our two new provinces, twin giants of the future, Alberta and Saskatchewan. Three decades ago this was the "great lone land," the frozen west, with its herds of bison and its Indian tepees, known to you only in the pictured desolation of its unending snow. . . .

"Greater Canada" was one of Leacock's platform addresses; it was published as a pamphlet and also appeared in McGill's *University Magazine*. In it, Leacock displayed a strong command of the political style of the day, flowery, emotional, inspirational and dramatic. He struggled to embody in this style a very personal approach to the political crises of the time. Above all, he was attempting to find a way to be both honorably Canadian and honorably British. Imperialism, Leacock said in "Greater Canada," was for many "a tainted word." So it is today. For modern Canadian commentators, Leacock's devotion to imperialism is immediately suspect, sometimes cause enough to dismiss parts of his work as brutal rather than funny, bigoted rather than humane. On one point the verdict of history is clear: Leacock overestimated the influence the British empire, as an organized political entity, could have for peace and civilization during the twentieth century. As the century progressed, he could see that the empire was dissolving and becoming weaker. He was realistic about this, but never ceased to propose ways in which the process could be reversed or the remainder of the empire could be strengthened and renovated. At the time of his death, the spectacle of the Commonwealth countries' performance in World War II had reconfirmed him in his faith that the empire, though its appearance might be changed, was a real force for good — an "inspiration, not a formula," as he once said. Writing in the first decade of the century as a controversialist rather than as a scholar, Leacock championed the empire on the grounds that it was the best hope of the world. World War I confirmed him in his judgment and, if anything, reinforced his conviction that his faith was better put in the empire, with its strongly protective defense of its own customs and traditions, than in international organizations like the League of Nations. The imperial hopes of rival European powers, particularly Germany, at the end of the nineteenth century justified to some extent the sort of insularity Leacock believed in.

It is unfortunate that Leacock saw the empire solely as an organization of Anglo-Saxon nations, and assumed that these nations would always want to have as little to do as possible with the original populations of the lands they inhabited. The native residents of India or New Zealand were not to be thought of as true parts of the empire, and certainly not as autonomous or semi-autonomous parts with a right to influence and to representation for their opinions. It is more than unfortunate, it is perhaps disturbing, that Leacock further founded some of his praise of the British empire on the idea of the superiority of the Anglo-Saxon peoples and, in general, the "white races."

In *Our British Empire*, for example, he said, "The rigor of the cold and the stimulus of effort bred the 'white races,' whose superiority no one must doubt." He drew a strong distinction between colonies like Canada, where British immigrants produced a population of mostly European origin — such colonies were capable of self-rule, he said — and colonies in which non-white native populations remained under British authority.

> Still less could federation include the black subjects of the Queen now multiplying in Africa. These must remain as sleeping partners in the Empire, dreaming of their future heritage, and blessed at least with decent government and fair play.

Leacock was not alone in adopting positions of this sort. The British Ministry of Education used *Our British Empire* as a morale-building tool, and none of the changes in the text the

Ministry requested dealt with the passages on race. In a writer beloved for the kindliness of his laughter, the presence of this deliberate belittling of some human beings as inherently inferior is most unattractive. In these attitudes he was a man of his time, but one can expect a writer of Leacock's stature to transcend such ideas. When Leacock remained strongly within the boundaries of his own community, he seemed little inclined to make this type of comparison. The assertion of the authority of British civilization over any other with which the empire came in contact became more strident as the empire granted independent status to former colonies in Africa and Asia. Early in his career, Leacock did not express the prejudices he later voiced frequently in the context of supporting the cause of British imperialism.

Leacock returned from the tour to his familiar McGill routine. He had been promoted to assistant professor, with a raise of five hundred dollars per year, soon after the publication of *Elements of Political Science*. After the tour he became a full professor, with a seat on the faculty of arts, and was named the William K. Dow professor of political economy. His salary was raised to four thousand dollars per year; he was also appointed temporary chairman of the department of economics and political science. Although the appointment was not confirmed until 1933, Leacock served from 1908 until his retirement in 1936 as chairman. As department head, he was in charge of determining which classes would be held each term. He required each of his teachers to submit to him before the term began a page-long summary of new courses and those already offered. In addition to his administrative duties as chairman, Leacock continued to publish for scholarly magazines and conferences. In 1907, he contributed to the Makers of Canada series a study of early Canadian politics, *Baldwin, LaFontaine, and Hincks: Responsible Government*; Leacock's friend, Pelham Edgar, was editor of the series. In 1908, he addressed the American Political Science Association on "The Limitations of Federal Government." Articles based on the Makers of Canada study also appeared in *American Political Science Review* and *Addresses Delivered Before the Canadian Club of Ottawa, 1903-9*. He became involved in university publications through a student, W.E. Gladstone Murray, later head of the Canadian Broadcasting Corporation in the 1930s. Leacock loaned Murray ten dollars when they met one day in 1909 in the student union, and Murray complained that he would be forced to leave school if he did not find work. Leacock later encouraged him to start *The McGill Daily* and regularly contributed to the paper. Murray played billiards with Leacock regularly, although he experienced "periodic humiliation" due to Leacock's "superior skill."

> In 1911, after a game one evening, Dr. Leacock remarked that he was tired of these "unrelated and insignificant encounters." Whereupon he challenged me to 20,000-up, which he estimated we could finish in 20 years. . . . The games took place in widely varying environments — clubs, private homes, grand hotels, but mostly in good old down-to-earth pubs. Actually the game ran for thirty years and was never finished, the final score being 18,975 for Dr. Leacock and 17,793 for me.

Another favorite billiards haunt was the University Club, which opened on Dorchester Street in the spring of 1908; before leaving for his world tour, Leacock had attended a meeting to organize the new facility.

McGill supplied many of Leacock's closest friends. Andrew Macphail was the university's professor of the history of medicine. He encouraged Leacock to publish essays on social and political issues in the *University Magazine*, which Macphail founded in 1907. Macphail was a native of Prince Edward Island who came to Montreal to study medicine in 1884. A widower since 1902, Macphail devoted himself increasingly to the world of literature. The great literary passion of his life was Louis Hémon's novel of rural Québec, *Maria Chapdelaine*, for which Macphail published the first English translation in 1921. It was superseded later in the same year by the translation of William Hume Blake, but Macphail remained devoted to writing, especially essays. He edited a posthumous collection of poems by John McCrae, and wrote a memoir about life in Prince Edward Island called *The Master's Wife*, which was published posthumously in 1939. Macphail and Leacock were inseparable friends at the University Club, at Macphail's lonely mansion, which he maintained in high Victorian decor, and at Leacock's convivial dinner parties. They shared a commitment to the British empire; Macphail voiced the same excesses of white supremacy as grounds for excluding full citizenship to native people in the empire that Leacock expressed late in life.

Between 1907 and 1910, Leacock published several pieces in the *University Magazine*, including "Literature and Education in America" and "The Apology of a Professor: An Essay on Modern Learning," which bear similarities to one of the most famous pieces Leacock ever produced: "Oxford As I See It," fruit of his 1921 tour. Many of the same themes he expressed there are present in these early publications, although little of the whimsical humor of Leacock's later style is evident in these impassioned pleas for a reform of the university system. After struggling for many years to attain the rank of university professor, Leacock found that the title did not carry the sort of authority he had expected it would (his example was the educational system of the late nineteenth century). In part he blamed the schools, whose passion for the methods of science had reduced the training of humanities students to an overspecialization that made them of little use to society.

> The pretentious claim made by so many of our universities that the thesis presented for the doctor's degree must present a distinct contribution to human knowledge will not stand examination. . . . Our American process of research has led to an absurd admiration of the mere collection of facts, extremely useful things in their way but in point of literary eminence standing in the same class as the Twelfth Census of the United States or the Statistical Abstract of the United Kingdom.

In the past, the university had "aimed at a wide and humane culture of the intellect." Now the doctorate was earned by writing "a useless little pamphlet called [a] thesis which is new in the sense that nobody ever wrote it before, and erudite in the sense that nobody will ever read it." While the universities corrupted the value of the professor by making him suited only to the very narrow bounds of his own specialty, society at large was confused in its search for authoritative information by the abundance of self-proclaimed "professors" of the banjo, of swimming and of patent medicines. In the debate over what a university should be, Leacock wholeheartedly joined the side arguing for an institution based on the liberal arts and humanities and higher sciences, rather than one providing professional or technical training of any kind. This spirited debate continues to the present time, and today Leacock would be viewed as a partisan of the "elitist university" concept, as opposed to the university that is part of a system of mass public education. He was sensitive to the problem of elitism, however, and tried to propose ways in which even elitist universities could find students by applying standards of ability rather than of parentage or class. He remains one of the most effective champions of a university based on the idea of intellectual merit and devoted to training generalist thinkers rather than professional practitioners or experts. His thought on this problem has a breadth that went beyond the question of university aims and structures, because he saw how social changes were affecting education. He felt that society's growing bias toward commercialism and materialism had made publicity the most prized method of communication, to the extent that most people now had little capacity for — and little interest in — exact knowledge of nature, society or human experience. "The only missionary we care for is an advertiser," he wrote, "and even the undertaker must send us a Christmas calendar if he desires to retain our custom."

Both in his thought on the university, and in the totality of his career as a writer, Leacock was drawn to two opposing poles, both of them representing elements of truth that must, somehow, be maintained together. He felt that education was being watered down dangerously to make it available to all. Still, every member of a democratic society must be well educated, or the society would be at the mercy of an uninformed, uncritical electorate's decisions and opinions. How were these two, seemingly opposed goals to be reconciled? Presumably he expected the university to supply an elite educated group that would in turn guide the rest of society. Within the man Leacock, the same dual goal existed. He aspired to be the kind of person that he thought the universities should produce. On the other hand, he was drawn to the popular press and the lecture stage as means of influencing a broad segment of the public. In general, he was successful in expressing his thoughts in a way that made them intelligible and forceful for a wide audience. His work almost never shows any of the condescension seen in the writings of many intellectuals who stoop to communicate to the masses. This is because Leacock's experience gave him true solidarity with both the common man and the inhabitants of the academy. He had real respect for any person who performed with honor in his own station and walk of life, but he did not believe that this form of merit suited a person to a university education and the tasks it trained one to do. He satirizes the pretensions and failings of workmen, professional people, academics, divines, government and business leaders — but his most acid criticisms are always reserved for the influential, those who guide society, who have been to university but have misunderstood and misused — simply ignored — what they learned there.

In fact, if Leacock displays any imbalance in his handling of this question, it is that he sometimes thoughtlessly sides with boorish philistines in order to make his points against the abuses of intellectuals and artists. He goes overboard in demonstrating that he is one of the "common" people, indulging their prejudices when, for the sake of effect, he makes sweeping attacks on intellectual fads and fashions. He sometimes found himself accused of despising literature, education, even his own profession. For example, in 1906, Leacock published "The Passing of the Poet," one of the few strictly humorous pieces he produced between the 1890s and 1910. In it, he pokes fun at the excesses of Romantic verse.

> The undue access of emotion frequently assumed a pathological character. The sight of a daisy, of a withered leaf or an up-turned sod, seemed to disturb the poet's mental equipoise. Spring unnerved him. The lambs distressed him. The flowers made him cry. The daffodils made him laugh. Day dazzled him. Night frightened him.

Leacock claimed to applaud the day that would substitute Huxley's *Physiology* for Grey's "Elegy in a Country Churchyard," or the police news of the Dumfries *Chronicle* for the verse of Robert Burns. The difficulty of the jest is that Leacock attempted to score against poetry and also against the decayed styles of informative writing being practiced in his time; for at least one reader, Susan R. Cameron, Leacock's article was not acceptable. In a later issue of the magazine that had published Leacock's piece, she criticized him for dismissing poets "as futile creatures, tolerated in earlier, sillier generations than ours, and destined to become extinct as the race becomes full grown." Cameron was disappointed to think that Leacock, "an academic person of distinction," would be so mistaken about the value of poetry. Yet Leacock shared with her the disappointment of living in an age that, in his opinion, did not have writing as great as the writing of the past. Similar confusions arose in later years, especially when Leacock attempted to combine humor with a discussion of literature and the humanities.

During his world tour, Leacock had written to his sister Daisy about helping him to purchase "a small place on Lake Couchiching," and in another letter had waxed lyrical over the home he would build there. Even before contacting Daisy, Leacock contacted his mother, and through her his brother Charlie, and got them to act as his agents in making the purchase. The letter was written on the day of his departure from France for Australia and New Zealand aboard the *Macedonia*. After lecturing in England, Leacock and Beatrix took ten days in Paris and then traveled to Marseilles in time to embark on 30 May. The letter he wrote to Agnes on that day shows that he had been considering a purchase of Lake Couchiching property for some time past. It also shows that a certain homesickness was increasing his desire for what he called "a place of my own" in Canada:

> Tell Charlie to get a *place*: if the little point is not too wet I'd like it. If it is not obtainable then the Hughes point. On either of those, he may, subject to ratification by me, make an offer. And I'd like him to do something about it this summer so that I can take up the place next spring. The more I see of foreign parts, the less I think of them compared to Canada. And I want a place of my own.

He was ever after to maintain that Simcoe's waters are superior in beauty to the Aegean's. As it turned out, the little point was available. In 1908, with brother Charlie's help, he purchased thirty-three acres for sixteen hundred dollars. He christened the site "Old Brewery Bay." (Apparently there had once been a brewery located near the site.) A one-room shack was built during the first summer and became the nucleus for the first house Leacock built on the property; the present building, now the Leacock Memorial Home, was begun in 1926, after the death of Beatrix. Writing to Daisy, Leacock spoke of a return to the Lake Simcoe area as "coming home." Although he had fled the farm, Leacock had spent his summers around the lake for many years, and his mother and brothers and sisters either lived in the area or visited frequently. Ties to the area were reinforced by Leacock's marriage: Beatrix, too, had family settled in the Lake Simcoe region. Still, the purchase of Old Brewery Bay marked a new age in Leacock's life. The trip around the world had convinced him that he was no party man, and that he would not give up Canada for the opportunities available to him in England. In 1909, securely established in the university community, and rerooted in the soil of his Canadian boyhood by the establishment of Old Brewery Bay, Leacock found in his family support for a new endeavor, a return to the writing of humor. This encouragement led in the following year to the publication of *Literary Lapses*.

Chapter Seven

Lapsing into Literature

I N THE SPRING of 1909, Stephen Leacock signed a three-year lease for a house at 165 Côte-des-Neiges Road in Montreal. The agreement with owner William George Slack provided the option for an additional three-year lease. Located on the east side of the busy Montreal street, the semi-detached brick house later was purchased by Leacock and remained his city home until shortly before his death in 1944. There were three stories; the third floor had been servants' quarters. (The house was later renumbered 3869 and, in the 1950s, was torn down to make room for adding a new wing to Montreal General Hospital.) Many memorable parties were held in the dining room, where Leacock entertained McGill friends like Andrew Macphail and visiting friends like Douglas Fairbanks and Mary Pickford. Leacock delighted in reading fresh sketches as after-dinner entertainment, but, however delightful, parties ended early for him. He went to bed by ten o'clock because his habit year-round, in Orillia in the summer and Montreal in the winter, was to rise early to write and study. The fresh sketches for after-dinner reading often were conceived in the hours between five o'clock and the family breakfast, when Leacock was at work in his upstairs study. Attached to the study was a porch where Leacock spent the nights on a small couch. During his 1921 British tour, it should be recalled, he extolled the virtues of sleeping outside. True, he nearly froze once when he was locked out on a particularly cold night, and he frequently had to wear his raccoon coat to a bed from which he had swept the snow. Curious as it seems, however, Leacock was not alone in the practice of sleeping outdoors during the harsh Canadian winters. In fact, he was part of a turn-of-the-century health fad; as a Halifax teenager, Hugh MacLennan had slept outside. Nellie McClung, who was bringing up a growing family in a Manitoba town,

Leacock photographed at Ryde on the Isle of Wight, probably in 1875.
PUBLIC ARCHIVES CANADA/C-31959

Agnes Leacock (née Butler), Stephen Leacock's mother, photographed about 1855, twelve years before her marriage to Walter Peter Leacock.
PUBLIC ARCHIVES CANADA/C-31913

The Leacock family photographed on the Isle of Wight, about 1870. From left: Thomas Murdock Leacock, Edward Philip (''E.P.'') Leacock, Walter Peter Leacock, Stephen's older brothers Jim and Dick, and Agnes holding Stephen.
PUBLIC ARCHIVES CANADA/C-31928

Leacock's grandfather, Thomas
Murdock Leacock.
PUBLIC ARCHIVES CANADA/C-22898

Leacock's father, Walter Peter
Leacock, photographed at Sutton,
Ontario, on 15 July, 1877.
PUBLIC ARCHIVES CANADA/C-22899

Edward Philip ("E.P.") Leacock
as a Member of Legislative Assembly, Manitoba, 1878.
PUBLIC ARCHIVES CANADA/C-31963

The Leacock farmhouse at Egypt, Ontario; the building is now gone.
PUBLIC ARCHIVES CANADA/C-25716

The Leacock family as it was at the farm in Egypt, Ontario, after the departure of the father, Walter Peter Leacock. Left to right: Teddy with Gyp the dog, Charlie, Stephen, Dot, Carrie, Agnes, Daisy, Jim, Maymie, Missie, George.
PUBLIC ARCHIVES CANADA/C-31954

Leacock upon his graduation from
Upper Canada College in 1887.
PUBLIC ARCHIVES CANADA/C-31965

Leacock at seventeen: a photograph
taken in October, 1887.
PUBLIC ARCHIVES CANADA/C-33111

This group portrait of the 1891 staff of the University of Toronto *Varsity* includes Leacock,
standing at far right and wearing his mortarboard.
PUBLIC ARCHIVES CANADA/C-31952

Beatrix Leacock: undated photograph, probably from before her
marriage.
PUBLIC ARCHIVES CANADA/C-33110

Beatrix Leacock, photographed
about 1900.
PUBLIC ARCHIVES CANADA/C-31937

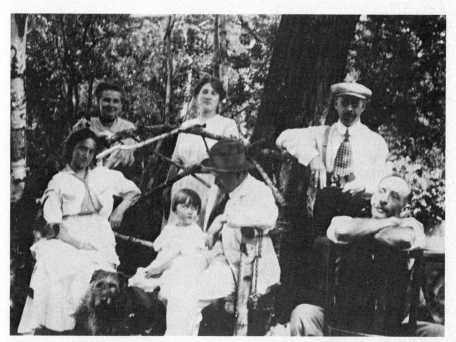

This picture, taken about 1913 at Old Brewery Bay, shows Beatrix (seated left) with her mother, Mrs. Kate Hamilton (standing left).

Leacock (in wheelbarrow) and friends in Bieners (center with two unidentified women, at Old Brewery Bay in 1908. Behind Leacock is the ''cookhouse'' from which his first Old Brewery Bay home evolved.
PUBLIC ARCHIVES CANADA/C-31930

Leacock's first home at Old Brewery Bay, which grew by progressive additions from the original ''cookhouse'' that Leacock and his brother Charlie built in 1908. This house was demolished when Leacock's new home was built in 1928.
PUBLIC ARCHIVES CANADA/C-33107

also spent years sleeping in backyard tents because of the reputed health benefits the nights outdoors provided.

The Côte-des-Neiges house was the final element of a success story Leacock had been putting together for ten years. From his first doubtful step, leaving the faculty of Upper Canada College in 1899, he went on to achievement after achievement. Rising from the position of temporary lecturer to the position of chairman of the department of economics and political science in only seven years, Leacock also secured a public platform for his views on the several fields he had identified as particularly his own: Canadian history, imperial economic structures and the impact of government policies on social development. He had seen his mother through the difficult years of economic hardship that followed his father's desertion and could visit her happily in her Lake Simcoe home where she was surrounded, especially in the summer, by a successful family of grown children and a growing flock of grandchildren. A healthy, active man in his fortieth year who had taxed himself heavily since high-school graduation with double duty as teacher and student, teacher and writer, teacher and lecturer, Leacock might have been expected to be satisfied with the chance his new Orillia home gave him to indulge his fondness for sailing, fishing and gardening.

Instead, he began to discuss with his family and friends the possibility of collecting his humorous sketches into a book. Leacock had copies on file of the many pieces he had written before 1900 while he was working at Upper Canada College. These would form the bulk of his manuscript, but he also had available a handful of more recent humorous pieces; they had been written for Macphail's *University Magazine*. It has been suggested that Leacock considered the book as a money-making venture to meet the increased expenses in Orillia. With not one but two households to maintain, he certainly must have felt the need of money. Not long before, he had asked for a salary increase at McGill, explaining that he was plagued by debts. Leacock's early pieces were not protected by copyright; he knew they were popular, for they continued to be reprinted, but for these reprintings he received no payment. By collecting them in a book Leacock would hold the copyright to them, and thus earn money. There are several indications, however, that Leacock was hoping for something more than a profitable collection of previously published work. Behind the struggle for his first humor publication lies not only Leacock's eager search for a new source of income but also the determination to distinguish himself in a type of writing that had interested him for many years.

Perhaps the best indication of this is Leacock's persistence, despite the obstacles he met, in trying to get his humor pieces, which he called *Literary Lapses*, published in book form. Beatrix and Marion Sandwell (née Street), who in 1908 had married Leacock's former student Bernard K. Sandwell, compiled a selection of sketches from Leacock's files. Then Leacock discovered that Sandwell, a drama critic for the *Montreal Herald* at the time, was opposed to their publication. He was worried that Leacock would damage his growing reputation as an economist and political commentator by publishing a collection of recreational humor. The writing of occasional humorous essays between serious projects was acceptable, Sandwell thought, but he warned that the new manuscript would clash with, rather than reinforce, Leacock's authority. (The disagreement did not harm their relationship. Sandwell later was instrumental in arranging for the writing of the newspaper series that, in 1912, would be collected as *Sunshine Sketches of a Little Town*, and remained a close associate of Leacock's in several other projects.) Leacock may not have found Sandwell's zeal for his professional standing difficult to accept, particularly because it indicated that his friend was certain the manuscript must be accepted. As it turned out, however, they both were wrong. Leacock submitted his manuscript to the New York publisher of *Elements of Political Science*, Houghton Mifflin, which returned it without encouragement.

Leacock always gave his brother George credit for keeping the project alive after the first rejection. George was Stephen's closest friend among his many brothers. The first Leacock child born in Canada, George was eight years younger than Stephen. A man with little taste for education, George was highly regarded in the family as a wit and storyteller. Leacock often credited George as a source of his stories. In *Too Much College*, Leacock offers a lighthearted analysis of the art of humor with help from "one such story I can quote from memory, not actually of my own but of my brother George." The story, drawn from George's experience with an Ontario electrical company, was given by Leacock in its bare outline in a discussion of different methods of humorous delivery. A workman is electrocuted while attempting to install a delicate new piece of apparatus. A team of inspectors from the company arrives to discover how the accident occurred. One bright fellow comes forward and offers to explain. He places his hands on the equipment, just as the dead man had done, tells the inspectors to turn on the power, and is electrocuted. Leacock said of the anecdote that he was always happy to end the story by revealing that the second man was only knocked unconscious, not really killed. "But when my brother George, who is a real storyteller, tells this story, he not only kills the second man but the chief of police — who undertook to explain it to the mayor of the town, and then the mayor and half of the town council. Nothing like Art for Art's sake." It is often said that the charm of Leacock's humor derives from the success he has in recreating the rhythm of spoken language. In this art, apparently, George was especially gifted; family members agree that if George had only been able to spell, he too would have been famous as a humorist. George had a summer home in the small town of Aurora, not far from Lake Simcoe. In addition to his work as an electrical engineer, leading eventually to presidency of the Moloney Electrical Company of Toronto, he was an accomplished horse breeder. On a visit to Montreal, he heard the news of Stephen's rejected manuscript and asked to read it. When George told his brother the work was good and deserved to be published, Leacock agreed to keep trying.

George had a hand, too, in deciding how the manuscript would get into print. He proposed that he and Leacock publish the book themselves and share the profits. The first contact with a Montreal printer, the Gazette Publishing Company, was made by George, who also provided a fifty-dollar deposit towards the costs. The plan was to make an inexpensive edition for sale on railway station newsstands. The brothers expected to earn seven cents per copy, with five cents going to George and two cents to Stephen. Before making final arrangements for the book's printing, however, Stephen returned the fifty dollars George had contributed and undertook arrangements for the book on his own. There is no record of why Leacock decided to do this. It seems unlikely that he did so to cheat his brother, as some have suggested. At most the profit of the first edition they planned would be a little more than two hundred dollars, of which George's share would have been only a little more than one hundred forty dollars. Against that, George would have been expected to pay the larger portion of the more than four hundred fifty dollars it would cost to produce the edition. George himself was untroubled that he did not share in the small financial success of the first edition; on the contrary, he remained an enthusiastic supporter of his brother's career and an ungrudging source of great stories.

The Gazette Publishing Company agreed to print an edition of three thousand copies of *Literary Lapses*, for which Leacock would be charged 15 ⅓ ¢ per copy payable three months after delivery. He arranged for the book's distribution with the Montreal News Company, which would sell the text for 35¢ and return to Leacock 23¢ per copy. Leacock was to supply two hundred paper signs and a hundred cardboard placards to advertise *Literary Lapses*, and he also agreed to pay for any copies returned to him unsold. Thus, he was risking $461 plus the cost of the advertising posters for a possible net profit of $229 (his yearly income at this time was no more than $3,500). This seems a strong indication that Leacock was looking beyond this first edition towards future humor projects, which would make his initial risk worthwhile. *Literary Lapses* appeared on Montreal newsstands in the summer of 1910. The book was one hundred twenty-five pages long; it contained twenty-six pieces and was bound in green boards with a green buckram spine. The title appeared on a label glued to the cover. The book contained no biographical information about the author, but a brief preface acknowledged several magazines in which his sketches had appeared. These included *Truth*, where the bulk of his early work was presented under the editorship of fellow Canadian Peter McArthur; *Life*, in which "My Financial Career" appeared; *Saturday Night*, the Toronto magazine (within a year, *Saturday Night* published

Leacock's "Novels in Nutshells," collected in 1911 as *Nonsense Novels)*; and several English periodicals, among them *Punch, Puck* and *Lancet*. Sales were excellent. The first edition sold out over the summer. Leacock's agreement with the Montreal News Company provided for the possibility of further editions, but the next appearance of *Literary Lapses* turned out to be a transaction of an entirely different sort. Leacock found himself launched as a humorist in the international marketplace without having to risk another cent.

One of the buyers of the Montreal edition of *Literary Lapses* was John Lane, publisher of the Bodley Head in London. Lane was a frequent visitor to Canada and regularly stopped in Montreal in search of rare steel engravings for his collection. In 1895, he published the first book by Ontario Mohawk poet Pauline Johnson, *The White Wampum*. (Johnson had visited his London offices.) Recently, Lane had been quick to see the promise of the Yukon balladeer Robert Service, and had acquired Service's first books for British publication. His most famous North American author was Mark Twain, whose death in April, 1910 undoubtedly sharpened Lane's eye for a likely successor. He returned to England and sent Leacock a telegram offering to print a British edition of *Literary Lapses*. Years later, Leacock recalled this first contact with Lane. "I cabled back, 'I accept with thanks.' Later on at a banquet Mr. Lane said he realised from the cable that I was the kind of man who would spend two shillings to say thank you." Leacock made a brief trip to England before the beginning of the 1910 school year and was hailed as the "Canadian Mark Twain," where just three years before, on the Rhodes Tour, he had been a serious authority on imperial economics. Lane's edition of *Literary Lapses* included fourteen new pieces and appeared late in 1910. It was Leacock's introduction to readers around the world. It went through thirty-five popular editions and is still in print as an inexpensive paperback in Canada. Many of the pieces are included in anthologies of Leacock's best work.

It was an amazing sequence of events, and all crowded into one summer. Perhaps biographers have been justified in supposing that Leacock was not expecting to build a career on a modest venture like his privately financed first edition of

Literary Lapses. But other writers had done precisely that. For example, Robert Service's meteoric rise to prominence had taken place just two years before. Early in 1907, Service had been working as a bank teller in Whitehorse, Yukon Territory, and had sent the manuscript of his first book, *Songs of a Sourdough*, to Ryerson Press in Toronto. He intended the book to be a self-publication, which he planned to distribute to friends who had praised his recitations at parties in Whitehorse and Dawson City. Before submitting his book to Ryerson, Service had published only a few poems in the Whitehorse *Star*. Ryerson editor William Briggs told Service that the manuscript had proved popular among the typesetters, to whom it had gone as a commercial printing job. Briggs had become interested in the book and was prepared to undertake the publication himself and to pay Service a royalty. Ryerson salesmen found that the book was as popular among readers across the country as it had been in the composing room. By 1909, Service had produced two more volumes of his northern ballads and was receiving royalties from American and British as well as Canadian editions. He had become an internationally famous author.

His poetry took Service away from his teller's cage, but other popular Canadian authors of the period achieved international success without changing their lives. This was an important consideration for Leacock, who was interested in accommodating success as a humorist in his already busy schedule. In 1908, *Anne of Green Gables* was published in Boston and brought popularity to Lucy Maude Montgomery, who was a native and resident of Prince Edward Island. Montgomery's success, like Service's, came as a result of a long and obscure apprenticeship. Unlike Service, however, Montgomery never abandoned her domestic routine: she cared for her grandmother and, later, became the energetic wife of an Ontario minister. If Leacock needed more precedents for success, he had one in a fellow University of Toronto graduate, the Reverend Charles Gordon. Under the pen name "Ralph Connor," Gordon wrote a series of moral adventure novels, set in the Canadian northwest, that were popular in the United States and Great Britain, as well as Canada, at the turn of the century. Gordon's career as a novelist began with a serial on his mission experiences in the west written for a Presbyterian magazine, *The Westminster*, in Toronto. The serial was expanded into *Black Rock: A Tale of the Selkirks*, published in 1898. Thereafter, while serving at his parish in Winnipeg and playing an active role in social reform movements in the city, he published annually for fourteen years an edifying story in time for the Christmas market. All of these Canadian examples, which shared a great return on a small beginning, were in the air around 1910 and would have done much to convince Leacock that he could try for international success without being forced to leave his life in Canada.

If Leacock did not have success in mind when he started, he certainly scented it by the fall of 1910, when he made arrangements to supply a Toronto magazine, *Saturday Night*, with a ten-week series of literary parodies he called "Novels in Nutshells." The series, collected as *Nonsense Novels* in 1911, marked the real beginning of his career as a humorist. *Literary Lapses*, especially the first Montreal edition, contained material that was twenty years old. With *Nonsense Novels*, Leacock proved he could produce sufficient new material for a book in only a few months. Furthermore, after an absence of more than a decade from active humor writing, he returned to it with a greater skill and creativity than he had yet shown. The series began to appear in *Saturday Night* on 10 December, 1910, with "Gertrude the Governess." The editors said of Leacock, "Everybody loves good clean humor. Everybody is attracted by it, for the real humorist is a rare bird, and it is rarer still that one is captured on the nest right here at home." *Nonsense Novels* proved to be the most successful of all of Leacock's humor collections; translated into many languages, it has had more than three dozen editions and reprintings. With it, Leacock established a tradition that he maintained almost every year for the next thirty years: he published a selection of the pieces he had produced for periodicals as an autumn book. *Nonsense Novels* possessed a unity of theme that, with notable exceptions including *Sunshine Sketches* and *My Discovery of England*, Leacock's later collections did not provide. Many of them more resembled *Literary Lapses* in the wide variety of subjects and forms they brought together. The success of his first two books provided

Leacock with a publisher for his books; as well, many periodical editors were eager for material. The *Saturday Night* arrangement was only the first of many profitable publications by Leacock in newspapers and magazines. Immediately after the appearance of John Lane's edition of *Literary Lapses*, Leacock had received an invitation to publish in the prestigious *Harper's Magazine*, and from then until his death he always possessed easy access to the best New York periodicals. Leacock is so often praised for his skill as a public speaker that it may be forgotten that essentially he was a humorist for the print media. This was the way he began in the 1890s, and it was the route to his first success in book publication. Lecturing grew out of his readers' desire to meet a favorite author. Periodical publications gave Leacock opportunities to offer rapid, concise responses to current events. A few of his pieces resemble the work of a newspaper columnist rather than the creation of a comic novelist or short-story writer. Leacock drew material from newspapers and magazines, which provided information and entertainment for his society. He laughed at the expense of news stories and advice columns, scientific reports and formula fictions of many types from melodrama to romance. Periodical markets meant a valuable double income from his pieces, which could appear once in a magazine and again in the annual collection.

Without the magazines, Leacock might not have become a humorist. His continued reliance on them as a market for his material had some disadvantages for his collections. The more specific and local his cause for writing, the more likely that his finished sketch would go out of date. Some of Leacock's early pieces contain less than a thousand words and read like humorous fillers: a snatch of conversation, a witty twist to a recent news story, an evocation of the excesses of ancient poets or modern slang. Their references to current events and their slight comic development limit their audience to Leacock's contemporaries. This difficulty is apparent especially in *Literary Lapses*, in which Leacock first attempts to manufacture something enduring out of a passing humorous insight. Even there, several pieces demonstrate that Leacock's keen sense of the ridiculous fed on his attentive study of his society, a necessary starting point for the creation of a humorous sketch whose insights would far outlive him. "My Financial Career" is steeped in the particulars of the banking establishments of Leacock's time; for some readers, the details prove a stumbling block to appreciating the insight Leacock brings to the story. True, a modern person might wish to see the conflict Leacock describes take place between a man and a banking machine, but the character Leacock creates — the simple individual who wishes to preserve his dignity in a situation out of his control — has not become dated. The literary parodies in *Nonsense Novels* also depend on Leacock's command of the popular tastes and interests of his contemporary readers. The advance of style lay not in abandoning the close ties to current tastes, but in finding forms for his humorous responses that touch on enduring human concerns revealed by the particular situations Leacock used for inspiration.

Many reviewers liked *Literary Lapses*: "uproariously funny," "the form of these sketches is excellent," "the book is full of smiles." Some noticed, though, that the pieces were not all of the same quality. Some of the work was imitative, they said, and "written with a rapid pen." Leacock alluded to some doubtful praises of the first book in a brief preface to *Nonsense Novels*. He said some reviewers had characterized him as "a young man from the most westerly part of the Western States, to whom many things might be pardoned as due to the exuberant animal spirits of youth." The reviewers hoped that the author's work might improve as he grew older and better educated. As a matter of fact, this deduction from *Literary Lapses* was not far off the mark, although Leacock would not admit it: many of the pieces show a potentially brilliant writer who had not yet stretched himself or practiced his craft very much. Leacock ignored this point and instead turned to the question of his future productions, warning that nothing more in the way of education could be expected from him. "All that education could do in this case has been tried and has failed. As a Professor of Political Economy in a great university, the author admits that he ought to know better."

There were also some reservations about *Nonsense Novels*. While most commentators could only praise the skill and genius of Leacock's humor, others complained that parody could not permit "the sounding of the heights of ideal humor."

The *New York Times* and the *Nation* agreed that Leacock suffered from a lack of restraint. Had he curbed it, the pieces plagued by "facetiousness or horseplay" might have been shaped into something quite good, said the *Nation*. The *Times* opined, "If the skits are sometimes quite funny they are more often little better than noisy horseplay with words — a performance distinctly of the same class as that given by the circus clown." Even certain fans of the book hoped for humor of "subtler qualities" in future efforts.

The charges were aimed not at the sometimes ephemeral character of Leacock's jests, a concern for readers today, but at his lack of self-restraint and self-criticism. These two "faults" are often lumped together. However, the extreme imaginative exuberance of some of his humor, displayed throughout *Nonsense Novels*, is one of his great strengths, *pace* the *Nation* and *Times*. The complaint he was unself-critical was a constant one throughout his career and has been a theme of criticism since his death. Tastes in humor vary greatly, but even die-hard champions of Leacock fault him for sometimes pursuing a quick laugh at the expense of the unity of a piece. They object to the uneven quality of the pieces he culled from his periodical work for book publication. Given a second chance to judge his work, free of the deadlines of magazines and papers, Leacock rarely rewrote for his books and on occasion seemed content to fill out a volume with pieces of uncertain merit. Many readers have been disappointed with miscellaneous collections because they lack the uniformity of theme shown in a book like *Sunshine Sketches*, and because the pieces in them are uneven in concept, style and quality.

The book was never Leacock's principal form, as disappointing as that might have been to all those who waited for him to produce a novel. For Leacock, most of his humor books were simply ways to present the brief pieces he found himself drawn to write. He seldom conceived his collections as unified works, and thus a book that preserves a few gems perhaps deserves to be called a success. *Literary Lapses* contains several highly regarded pieces: "My Financial Career," "Boarding House Geometry," "A,B,C" and "The Awful Fate of Melpomenus Jones." More of the pieces in *Nonsense Novels* are memorable. Certain classic parodies from the book are repeatedly reprinted, but the whole volume can be read with pleasure.

Although only a few pieces from *Literary Lapses* rank among Leacock's best, many of the selections that are limited remain of interest — if only as early forms of themes that Leacock returned to, in a more mature voice, in later books. Perhaps the most flawed are two lengthy pieces, "Number Fifty-Six" and "An Experiment with Policeman Hogan." These stories contain too much sentiment and too little of Leacock's always bracing wit. Many of the very brief pieces, such as "A Model Dialogue," admirably capture a familiar frustration and suggest a remedy almost too good to be true. A person offering to perform a card trick is driven to distraction by the willing, but obtuse, assistance of his victim.

"Well, let me see, I'll — pick — the — ace — of — spades."
"Great Caesar! I mean you are to pull a card out of the pack."
"Oh, to pull it out of the pack! Now I understand. Hand me the pack. All right — I've got it."
"Have you picked one?"
"Yes, it's the three of hearts. Did you know it?"
"Hang it! Don't tell me like that. You spoil the thing. Here, try again. Pick a card."

Leacock gives a similar antidote to the heckler in the crowd in "A Conjurer's Revenge." He is sarcastic in "Hints to Travellers" and is only a little less long-winded than the long-windedness he tries to burlesque in "Getting the Thread of It." On occasion, a promising joke seems to reach too far for a punch line, as in "The New Food," when a hapless child of a future age is blown to bits by eating several pill-sized Christmas dinners and then drinking a glass of water. In "How to Avoid Getting Married," Leacock captures the tone of letters to advice columns and attempts a clever role reversal: a beleaguered young man seeks masculine help to solve the dilemma of his forward girl friend. Leacock has difficulty in delivering a conclusion worthy of his premise: "If a girl desires to woo you, before allowing her to press her suit, ask her if she knows how to press yours. If she can, let her woo; if not, tell her to whoa."

In *Literary Lapses*, Leacock is defining his territory: the plight of the little man troubled by technological changes, as in "Reflections on Riding" or by social conventions to which he is an uneasy adherent, as in "The Awful Fate of Melpomenus Jones;" the pomposities of the rich ("Self-Made Men"), the learned ("The Poet Answered"), the enthusiastic ("Back to the Bush") and the upper classes ("Aristocratic Education"). Parody is included in "Lord Oxhead's Secret," which approaches the level of the *Nonsense Novels*; of Gwendolyn, the heroine, Leacock says, "She bore herself with that sweet simplicity which was her greatest charm. She was probably more simple than any girl of her age for miles around."

A forerunner to Leacock's many essays and sketches on education, "A Manual of Education" is one of the most successful pieces in *Literary Lapses*. The sketch displays a compact organization and simple delivery that captures Leacock's humorous wonderment at the process of learning. "My book is intended to embody in concise form these remnants of early instruction," he explains, and promises in future a simple ten-sheet summary, suitable for carrying in the hip pocket, of the entire content of six years of college. (He later made good this promise with the superb "The Outlines of Everything" in *Winnowed Wisdom*.) On astronomy, Leacock's "Manual" provides these insights:

> Astronomy teaches the correct use of the sun and the planets. These may be put on a frame of little sticks and turned around. This causes the tides. Those at the ends of the sticks are enormously far away. From time to time a diligent search of the sticks reveals new planets. The orbit of a planet is the distance the stick goes round in going round. Astronomy is intensely interesting. It should be done at night, in a high tower in Spitzbergen. This is to avoid the astronomy being interrupted. A really good astronomer can tell when a comet is coming too near him by the warning buzz of the revolving sticks.

The perils of knowing are also examined in "The Force of Statistics," "Saloonio" and "Half-Hours with the Poets."

For all its faults, the book identifies Leacock as an astute human observer with the gift of summoning up in his readers the therapeutic response of laughter. More than that, Leacock demonstrates that his times and these times have a great deal in common. His worries about the deterioration of education or the unhelpful learning served up in the popular press or the evil example given society by its leaders — the rich, the celebrities, the powerful — hit home because he balances them always by the sympathetic sharing in the lives of individuals, like his "John Smith."

> In the boy's choice of a profession there was not seen that keen longing for a life-work that we find in the celebrities. He didn't want to be a lawyer, because you have to know law. He didn't want to be a doctor, because you have to know medicine. He didn't want to be a businessman, because you have to know business; and he didn't want to be a school-teacher, because he had seen too many of them. As far as he had any choice, it lay between being Robinson Crusoe and being the Prince of Wales.

Leacock insists that the simple things that perplex people are important, interesting and worth caring about: how to change trains, how to say good-bye to your host, how to discourage a friend who insists on taking you on camping trips.

One thing is missing: the mature voice of Leacock, the friendly sound that is worth listening to for its humanity even when it seems to be conveying little that is new. Leacock makes use of the first person frequently in *Literary Lapses*, but the timorous aspirant in "My Financial Career" is not the same person as the acerbic critic of the rich who speaks in "How to Make a Million Dollars." Understandably, the early pieces are not working to establish a single comic voice, because Leacock wrote them for many different occasions and many different periodicals. As his work became well known, however, he gradually brought more of himself — his interests, his work, his opinions — into the narrative voice used in his first-person works.

This comic voice did not appear either in his second humor book, *Nonsense Novels*, which presents ten different voices. American short-story writer Bret Harte had published his parodies of popular fiction, *Condensed Novels*, in 1867; the book was reissued in 1902. Leacock mined an established vein with great individuality. Some critics worried that he frequently descended too low in search of his quips, but the book sold and American president Theodore Roosevelt incorporated a line from "Gertrude the Governess" into a speech with due credit to Leacock. (The line Roosevelt borrowed is now famous: "Lord Ronald said nothing; he flung himself from the room, flung himself upon his horse and rode madly off in all directions.") In the book, Leacock presented parodies of ten distinct types of stories. "Maddened by Mystery: or The Defective Detective" is only the first of many treatments Leacock did of the follies of mystery fiction. "'Q.' A Psychic Pstory of the Psupernatural" introduces another theme, the distrust of spiritualism. (In other books, Leacock directly attacked spiritualism.) "Guido the Gimlet of Ghent: A Romance of Chivalry" follows the long-distance romance of the hero and Isolde the Slender, for whom Guido regularly performed feats of daring, including killing a Saracen, "quite a large one;" Leacock's hero, Mark Twain, had parodied the "medieval" novel and had even blamed civilization's present decay on Sir Walter Scott. "Gertrude the Governess: or Simple Seventeen" is a sentimental romance among the noble classes, which overturns the tradition of love conquering money, a trick Leacock would return to in future stories of young love. "A Hero in Homespun: or The Life Struggle of Hezekiah Hayloft" follows a naive young man to the city and admiringly traces his route to social distinction through a life of crime. Other targets are the emotional memoir, the sea story, the Christmas tale, the science-fiction allegory and, one of his very best, "Hannah of the Highlands: or The Laird of Loch Aucherlocherty," a hilarious account of love's impact on an ancient Scottish feud.

In all the "novels," Leacock drew together plot and character devices that faithfully mirrored the type of tale he wished to parody. At every point, the unlikeliness of situation and the excesses of expression in his originals are suggested by the variations he offers on the familiar elements. Hannah, the beautiful Highland lass, is first seen "gathering lobsters in the burn that ran through the Glen." As she sings, "the birds seemed to pause to listen, and as they listened to the simple words of the Gaelic folk song, fell off the bough with a thud on the grass." Some fatal chance brings the new laird, Ian McWhinus, to the glen, where he offers a sixpence for one of the lobsters. It is love at first sight. But Hannah is a

McShamus, and no member of her family has spoken to a McWhinus for nearly two centuries because of an ancient feud begun in a dispute about religion.

> Shamus McShamus, an embittered Calvinist, half crazed perhaps with liquor, had maintained that damnation could be achieved only by faith. Whimper McWhinus had held that damnation could be achieved also by good works.

Heedless of the quarrel, Hannah determines to pledge her love to Ian. But she discovers that he is married to an American woman; in fact, he bought the lobster for her. With this revelation, the story moves rapidly to its inevitable climax.

One of the great charms of the *Nonsense Novels* is that Leacock manages to turn a new twist at every story's end. The final blow to the conventions of the fiction he is satirizing comes with an overturning of its cherished expectations, usually of tragic death or miraculous rescue. *Nonsense Novels* displays a great advance over the early work collected in *Literary Lapses*. The pieces are longer, more consistent in quality, more complex in structure and character than most of the early sketches. They form a bridge to Leacock's next project, one of his most ambitious and memorable books, *Sunshine Sketches of a Little Town*, in which he came close to writing a novel of his own.

Chapter Eight

The Train to Mariposa

T HE YEARS 1912 to 1914 were, in many ways, Leacock's most productive. At the beginning and end of this creative moment in his life stand *Sunshine Sketches of a Little Town* and *Arcadian Adventures with the Idle Rich*, books in which he explored the two environments — small town and mercantile metropolis — he now inhabited. In 1913, between these two works, appeared one of Leacock's most interesting annual miscellanies of humorous essays, *Behind the Beyond*. The history of *Sunshine Sketches*, written and published in 1912, goes back at least to 1911, when Leacock participated in the national election portrayed in the book's last two chapters, "The Great Election in Missinaba County" and "The Candidacy of Mr. Smith." More probably, the history goes back to the summer of 1908, when he acquired property on Lake Couchiching on Orillia's eastern outskirts, named it Old Brewery Bay and built his first cottage, called the "cook house," with his brother Charlie's help. Leacock's financial difficulties had prevented him from building the house he wanted in 1909, and the "cook house" remained little more than a summer cottage until after World War I. By 1908 Leacock had arrived as a landowner and householder, a permanent resident in Orillia, even if he did occupy his property only seasonally. In *Sunshine Sketches*, Orillia, called "Mariposa," is viewed from the perspective of an established resident, a community member, through this citizen in the book feels a certain distance, at times, between himself and the town. The book reveals intimate knowledge of Orillia, affectionate and critical insights into small-town existence, exemplified by Mariposa, that had certainly been gathering in Leacock since his childhood. But the book does not convey primarily a child's vision remembered in adulthood or an adolescent experience of summer holidays filled with sport and romance, though these play their parts. Prominent in the book is the complex attitude of a grown man, a citizen, who is somewhat distanced from his fellows by his insight into society and human motives but who nevertheless chooses to belong, even to the point of sometimes closing one eye to folly and ranging himself with those he satirizes.

Leacock prepared himself for his two most unified books of humor, *Sunshine Sketches* and *Arcadian Adventures*, by publishing *Nonsense Novels*, which he had started during the summer of 1910 in Old Brewery Bay; it was the first of his many works written there. In 1911, Leacock's increased prominence was attracting to him opportunities in several spheres of life. Early in the year he accepted an invitation to become a member of the Fleming Electoral Reform Commission of Quebec. Not much later, the country's political passions, compounded by French-English tensions and debates about the economy and Canada's relations to the British empire, came to a boiling point in the famous, and acrimonious, "reciprocity" campaign that resulted in Liberal Prime Minister Wilfrid Laurier's defeat on 21 September by Conservative Robert Borden.

Leacock spoke publicly during the election as a Conservative, which meant speaking against the Liberal party's free-trade economic position, even though he himself had taught the benefits of a limited free-trade policy to his McGill students. A free-trade agreement between Canada and the United States had been negotiated in 1854 by Lord Elgin (governor-general of Canada from 1847 to 1854); it was abrogated in 1866. In 1910, political factors made United States president William Howard Taft amenable to a restoration of limited free trade. Laurier believed in trade reciprocity both in principal and as a remedy to existing political and economic pressures, and in 1911 he negotiated a reciprocal lowering of tariffs between the two countries on many farm and resource products and some manufactured items. The move proved to be Laurier's greatest political blunder. It alientated the business community, which was used to the benefits of protective tariffs, and it aggravated deep-seated conflicts in both French and English Canada about the country's relationship to the British empire. English Canadians were concerned about Laurier's action for practical and emotional reasons. Some feared the move would offend Britain, still Canada's major market for most goods; others saw Laurier's reciprocity agreement as a flouting of the "Mother Country," a step away from the empire, even a move towards union with the United States. To a great degree, such fears were aroused and exaggerated by the anti-reciprocity Conservatives, with whom Leacock was allied, although he parodied their inflated rhetoric in *Sunshine Sketches*: "it was a huge election and . . . on it turned issues of the most tremendous importance, such as whether or not Mariposa should become part of the United States, and whether the flag that had waved over the school house at Tecumseh Township for ten centuries should be trampled under the hoof of an alien invader, and whether Britons should be slaves, and whether Canadians should be Britons, and whether the farming class would prove themselves Canadians. . . ." Laurier's defeat in English Canada proved that the organized farmers, who had pressured him for reciprocity, were no political match for the manufacturing interests that desired protective tariffs. The issue of continued strong ties to the renewed empire, first announced and promoted by Benjamin Disraeli in the 1880s, seemed closely enough linked to the reciprocity issue that a vast majority of English Canadians voted for the Conservative party out of a combination of loyal sentiment and their understanding of the economic merits of the case.

Leacock had spoken and published as both a free-trader and a champion of a reorganized, federated empire, so this election represented a conflict for him. He was true to his deepest nature in choosing the Tory, imperial camp over the Liberal side, which championed an economic policy much closer to his own ideas, for Leacock believed most surely not in any analytical or technical concept, but in the inherited forms of political life, culture and civility. In his view the empire — the embodiment of Canada's link to British civilization — was among the most important of these inherited forms. His view was not a simple clinging to the status quo out of jingoism, fear of change, or mere class solidarity. His writings show that he understood, from boyhood up, that the British system of society and government was to a great degree unfair and ponderous; it often benefited the undeserving, excluded the able and impeded the establishment of the justice that was its own *raison d'etre*. On the other hand, he thought modern economic, industrial and political systems entrapped people in ways that were still worse — the systems were devoid of humane and civilizing values or goals, and were open only to change that occurred for mechanical, inhuman reasons. Once Leacock decided to enter the political arena, he would logically be guided to the Tory camp not only by his upbringing as a son of old England but by half a lifetime of personal effort to develop ideas and a literary sensibility that would give depth to the beliefs first imparted to him in childhood. It is clear that he chose his political side primarily to be where he felt he truly belonged and not because he opposed reciprocal tariff reductions on principle.

Leacock's satirical view of the election may have emerged in the hindsight of 1912, when he was at work on *Sunshine Sketches*. If it existed during the campaign, it did not prevent him from vigorously supporting all the Conservative positions in speeches in Montreal and Simcoe County. His public advocacy of an anti-reciprocity stand occasioned a well-known jibe against Leacock, made by Doctor J.C. Hemmeon, his colleague in the department of economics and political science. Hemmeon stated in class that economists are all free-trade advocates, and a student objected that Leacock was a protectionist. "I repeat," Hemmeon replied, "all economists are free-traders." This sarcasm has been construed as a slight to Leacock's professional ability, but it seems more likely to have been aimed at his participation in politics, which caused him to oppose what Hemmeon knew he had taught. In Montreal, Leacock participated in the election at the local level and the national level, for he had been persuaded to assist the Conservatives' national publicity effort by the rising politician Richard Bedford (later Viscount) Bennett, who was to become Canada's tenth prime minister (7 August, 1930 to 23 October, 1935). Leacock, with the help of an acquaintance who had once worked in England for the Westminster *Gazette*, wrote full-page newspaper advertisements, published nationally, that played up the claim that Laurier's reciprocity agreement meant "selling out" to the United States. Leacock worked in a Montreal riding on behalf of a lawyer, John

Hackette, QC, the only Conservative member of parliament elected that year from Quebec. (In that province, Laurier's smashing defeat was at the hands of the Nationalistes.) In his home riding of East Simcoe, Leacock supported another winner, Conservative candidate L.B. Bennett, who defeated Liberal Manley Chew of Midland. Leacock played an important role in East Simcoe. In August, 1911, he delivered a major political address at the Orillia Opera House (built in 1896 and still standing downtown at Mississauga and West streets). Known locally ever since as "the reciprocity address," Leacock's speech made an impression on many local residents. In the audience was Leslie M. Frost, later a premier of Ontario, who recalled that Leacock "made a very devastating attack on the whole reciprocity idea" and that the people of Orillia felt the speech "had considerable to do with the election of an anti-reciprocity Conservative." Leacock was serious about the 1911 election, and his speeches of the time were packed with factual material, convincing arguments and even, it appears, emotional rhetoric. Although he seldom if ever used it again, he had a talent for the oratorical style of the day, which was highly partisan, florid and bombastic, and aimed at overwhelming its less educated hearers with a torrent of euphony and cultured diction. The Orillia *Packet*, the town's Conservative newspaper, reported Leacock's speech at the Opera House thus: "Professor Leacock discussed the question on the highest plane and the audience hung on his glowing periods for nearly an hour." On the other hand, the Liberal organ, the Orillia *Times*, paraphrased his remarks in a way that may have influenced his own parody of political speech-making in *Sunshine Sketches*: "the foundations of the British Empire will be shaken [by a Liberal victory] . . . Canadians will become hewers of wood and drawers of water for the Yankees . . . will be their bond slaves and their hired men."

The last two chapters in *Sunshine Sketches* deride political positions, rhetoric and even the methods used by the Conservatives (although the Liberals are not passed over). Leacock satirizes the use of economic arguments and statistics; he portrays speakers who have no idea what they are talking about and listeners who claim, out of pure vanity or party prejudice, to follow and be convinced by purely nonsensical lines of thought. In the end, the fictional election is won through the pure cunning of the hotel keeper, Josh Smith, who has no political ideas and runs as a Conservative only because there is already a Liberal candidate. Smith wins because he uses the telegraph and newspapers to convince the townsmen that there is a Conservative landslide and that, to be on the winning and influential side, they must vote for him. In September, 1911, there was, in reality, a national landslide for the Conservatives; one sees in this satire Leacock's likely assessment of what really swayed the election in Orillia, and how much the various opinions on reciprocity, his own and others', really counted.

The end of the campaign and election coincided rather neatly with the opening of the 1911 fall term at McGill. The most important thing that happened to Leacock that fall was the arrival of a request from the *Montreal Star* that he should provide it with a series of articles. According to Bernard K. Sandwell, the idea originated with Sandwell's friend Edward Beck, the *Star*'s managing editor, who wished to persuade the humorist to provide something particularly Canadian. The official request to Leacock came after the project was approved by Sir Hugh Graham. (The owner and publisher of the *Star*, Graham, made Lord Atholstan in 1917, had cofounded the newspaper in 1869 with another humorist, George T. Lanigan, author of the comic poem "The Ahkoond of Swat: A Threnody.") Sandwell introduced Leacock to Beck, and the three men decided that the work would take the form of a serial rather than a set of unconnected pieces and that it would have a Canadian setting. In Sandwell's belief, this agreement represented, at the time, "the only really large-scale commission ever received for a fictional job to be done for a purely Canadian audience." Leacock filled this bare format with the life and charm of the little town of Mariposa, thus creating his *Sunshine Sketches*.

It is possible that a basic concept was a part of Leacock's contribution to the early meetings with Beck and Sandwell. There exist two pages of his notes, dated 7 January 1912. The first gives the general concept of *Sunshine Sketches* and the second outlines the story that became "The Speculations of Jefferson Thorpe." These notes are headed "Plan and Ideas for a series of sketches about a little country town and the people in it: Each sketch about 4000 words: General title — SUNSHINE SKETCHES OF A LITTLE TOWN." Leacock records the titles for "sketches up to date" (those already conceived): "The Hostelry of Mr. Smith," "The Speculations of Calverly Short" and "The Tidal Wave of Local Option." The last of these was never written, although its subject, prohibition, was to serve Leacock in future essays. Later in his notes, he says to himself, "For Calverly try *Madison* Short" and, on the second page, not satisfied with either name, he uses the heading "The Speculations of Jefferson." He used the first name of his own barber in Orillia, Jefferson Short. Only the first name satisfied him; sometime between 7 January and the appearance of the sketch in the *Star* on 2 March, he changed the surname.

These notes of Leacock's support the oft-repeated claim that the characters in his book are based closely upon his Orillia friends and acquaintances, for in them he names several of his models: "Jim Smith, Lach Johnson, McCosh, Canon Greene, Jeff Short" and several others. Leacock did know the people who are portrayed, recognizably if with exaggerations and other changes, in *Sunshine Sketches*. He counted several of them among his close friends and sporting companions; he frequented their businesses and used their services. The fact that he maintained these associations just as warmly after the book was published as before, together with what testimony can be still gathered from Leacock's Orillia friends and their descendants, indicates that the story of the town's high dudgeon over the book is mainly legendary. Towards the end of his life, Leacock would write that, in 1912, he had received a letter from his friend Mel Tudhope, an Orillia lawyer and judge, threatening, tongue in cheek, to sue for libel on behalf of some of the people portrayed. This, Leacock said, "led the publisher to think it wiser to alter the names so in the book edition they are changed." A different account comes from Charles H. Hale who, with his brother Russell, published the *Orillia Packet and Times*; the brothers were combined to form the Mariposa journalist Hussell, and their newspaper became the Mariposa *Newspacket*. On information derived from Hale, J.V. McAree of the Toronto *Globe and Mail* wrote in 1958:

Mr. Leacock consulted Mr. Hale who advised him to be a little less precise in his description of the various people at whom he poked gentle fun. This he did. In a preface, he also said that the fictional characters were really fictional and that the setting might be any small Canadian community. This did not satisfy all of them and there were mutterings about libel suits. These died down, however.

Charles Hale was an intimate friend of Leacock's; it is possible Hale advised the author in these terms. Leacock never mentioned having heard any serious indication that libel actions were considered; he stated that the letter from Tudhope had been "in fun." The addition of a preface to the book, possibly as a result of grumblings from Orillia citizens and Hale's advice, was a much more substantial change than any of the actual alterations in characters' names; as to alterations in characters' descriptions, there are none. Only two important names were changed. Judge Pepperleigh (in the book) had been police magistrate McGaw (in the *Star* serial); he was based on John McCosh, who was mayor of Orillia in 1886, 1903 and 1904 and was later appointed the town's police magistrate. George Mullins of the Mariposa Exchange Bank (in the book) had been George Popley (in the *Star*); his original was George Rapley, manager of the Traders Bank, which stood at 82 Mississaga Street East and which employed John Stephens, the model of Peter Pupkin, suitor of Judge Pepperleigh's daughter, Zena. Perhaps there is some significance to the fact that Leacock changed the names only of such pillars of the community as a bank manager and a prominent local politician. Other changes between the original serial and the book version are negligible. Transitional summaries, needed to remind newspaper readers where the story left off, were eliminated or shortened, and a few other slight changes were made. (For example, the name of the township was changed from Medonte — a township just west of Orillia — to Tecumseh, which lies far to the south.)

Josh Smith, the wily and gargantuan hotelier, one of the chief unifying presences of *Sunshine Sketches*, had his original in Jim Smith, proprietor of the Daly House. The real Smith, who weighed more than three hundred pounds and had a wife who weighed less than one hundred, loaned even his physical characteristics to the fictional Smith; the Daly

House, on which Smith's Hotel was based, stood at the corner of Matchedash and Mississaga Streets until it was destroyed by fire in 1949. Jefferson Thorpe, the speculating barber, was, as we have seen, Jefferson Short, Leacock's barber; his shop was at 152 Mississaga Street East. In 1977 his barber's pole, mentioned by Leacock, was found in the basement of a building on this site; it was being used to support crossbeam. Like the barber in Leacock's story, Short had a daughter named Myra who was known locally as an aspiring actress. Golgotha Gingham, the Mariposa undertaker, was based on Horace Bingham, an Orillia undertaker; the Liberal MP John Henry Bagshaw on Judge R.D. Gunn; Netley's Butcher Shop on Hatley's; McCarthy's office block on Mulcahy's; Missinabi Street on Mississaga Street, and so on. John McCosh, the original of Judge Pepperleigh, had a son, Percy, who, like Neil Pepperleigh, went to the Boer War in South Africa. The model of Zena Pepperleigh, the judge's daughter and Peter Pupkin's light-of-love, was Ovida McCosh. The McCosh home, now the Mundell Funeral Home, still stands at 79 West Street North.

Leacock borrowed characters directly from Orillia and he drew on incidents as well. The burning of Dean Drone's Church of England Church in his chapter "The Beacon on the Hill" was based on the burning of Saint James Anglican, whose incumbent, the Reverend Richard Green (rector of Saint James from 1888 to 1911), was the model of the "Rural Dean" himself. Leacock's fire broke out late one night in April, and the citizens of Mariposa desperately fought to keep it from spreading through the wooden town. The fire that destroyed Saint James broke out just after nine o'clock in the morning on Sunday, 19 March, 1905, and, like the fictional fire, it left the church "nothing but a ragged group of walls with a sodden heap of bricks and blackened wood. . . ." Even the financial situation surrounding the fire provided elements for Leacock's fictional situation, in which the dean, hard-pressed to meet the mortgage payments for the needlessly elaborate church, is rescued as by providence from his financial quandary when the overinsured building burns. Although the insurance on Saint James did not cover the rebuilding costs, it did exceed the value of the mortgage, as the Orillia *Times* noted:

St. James church was erected in 1890, at a cost of over $18,000. The organ was a $3,000 instrument, and it is doubtful if both could be replaced to-day for less than $25,000. There is a mortgage of $7,100 on the building. The building and organ were insured for $12,300. . . .

Leacock added and embellished, but the basis of his fiction was fact.

Perhaps the best known of his chapters, "The Marine Excursion of the Knights of Pythias," was also based on fact. Leacock narrates the hilariously ill-fated excursion of the *Mariposa Belle*; he suggests that its "sinking" is a customary event. Such incidents seem to have been not uncommon among the steamers that plied lakes Simcoe and Couchiching in Leacock's days in Orillia as a student summer vacationer and, later, as a new householder. Professor Arthur Lower has traced the origin of "The Marine Excursion" to the sinking of the lake steamer *Enterprise* at its dock in Barrie in August, 1902. Professor Ralph Curry, on the other hand, points out that the steamer *Islay* sank while skirting the Couchiching shore in a manner similar to that of the *Mariposa Belle*. While the *Enterprise* is probably the physical model of Leacock's steamer, the third of the three boats that served Lake Couchiching around the turn of the century, the *Longford*, has perhaps the strongest claim of all to being the humorist's inspiration. It did not sink; it ran aground on a sandbar during a businessmen's outing on the lake one warm afternoon in October, 1898. At the wheel was Captain Laughlin ("Lockie") Johnson, the original of Leacock's Captain Christie Johnson. The details of this incident — and the mixture of affable deadpan description and wisecracks with which an unnamed Orillia *Times* reporter recorded it — are so incipiently Leacockian that the *Longford*'s misadventure, too, must have gone into the saga of the *Mariposa Belle*. Here is that story, from the Orillia *Times* of 27 October, 1898:

The annual outing of the business men of the town, on the steamer Longford, has come to be as much a feature as Thanksgiving Day, and neither Messrs. Thomson or their guests would feel that the boating season had been properly closed if the event did not take place. Thursday last was a beautiful day, nearly as warm and bright as July, and when Mr. Geo. Thomson appeared on Main Street, and announced that the Longford would leave at 11 o'clock, everybody who could, put aside business and started for the dock.

Crossing Lake Couchiching, the boat called at Longford, where Mr. Wm. Thomson was taken on board, and after a short time spent at Geneva Park, steamed down to the Portage, where the Longford Co.'s herd of cattle was inspected and lunch partaken of. The day being so delightful, Mr. Thomson suggested a run down to Beaverton, and everyone being willing, the Longford was headed for the Narrows. When east of Ship Island, and within a short distance off Horse Shoe, a sudden jar was felt, and the party found themselves stranded on Sanson's shoal.

Captain Johnson had miscalculated the course, or had failed to allow for the low water, as ten feet further east would have cleared the shoal nicely.

The life boat was lowered and the anchor taken out a short distance, with a cable attached to the winch. All hands manned the capstan, but were unable to draw the boat off.

Mr. Dean happened along with his steam yacht Dolly, and took Mr. Geo. Thomson and a crew to Longford, where they rigged up the Curlew, and proceeded to take the crowd home to Orillia. With all hands on board, the Curlew was just getting nicely underway when she, too, bumped on the shoal and came to a standstill. The life boat from the Longford was put in commission, and the schooner, lightened of her human freight, floated free. The party got aboard again and sailed into Orillia without further mishap.

The only loss was the loss of the P.M.'s head-gear which went overboard and sank. Police Magistrate Lafferty may be strong on points of law but he is decidedly weak on a capstan.

Capt. Johnston [sic] was heard renaming the shoal. As he did so in Gaelic, the reporter was unable to catch the title, but it sounded like "Howingehennadididothat." Capt. Johnston has been sailing these lakes for over thirty years, and this is the first shoal he has discovered.

How the Longford got out of the course is a mystery but it is supposed that the electricity generated by the heated discussions of the voters' list court deranged the compass and drew the needle in that direction.

With the first shock there was a general rush for life preservers. Commodore Haywood never goes to sea without one of his own. As he reached for his hip pocket, he had several offers to assist him "Blow" it, but as the preserver would not go around, he was forced to decline. Moral . . ."Consider the lilies."

The abundant laughter of *Sunshine Sketches* comes from the strength of Leacock's imagination, which was able to combine many forms of humor — wit, satire, verbal play, caricature and exaggeration, understatement, nonsense in plot and in dialogue — to a degree that very few writers have achieved. And yet, the book's characteristic tone springs from something more fundamental than its humor, something that supports the humor. This is Leacock's comic view of the world, which suffuses his portrait of Mariposa with a kindly but somewhat melancholy light in which everything is clear yet subtly muted, softened and distanced. His perfected style here — simple yet ever varied, supple, intimate, preserving the accent of speech with his own distinctive version of the essay's sophisticated literacy — has become the ideal means of expressing a vision of an apparently changeless world that is slowly changing and passing, of a benign existence that is only an island always threatened, from within and without, by the less pleasant realities of the great world and of human nature. When Leacock was writing, the small-town Canada he described was in full vigor; he adhered to a real model, yet there is a sense of a lost parardise, of times remembered, in his depiction of Mariposa.

Like classic comedic writing, *Sunshine Sketches* shows us a world in which crises are not of ultimate seriousness, a world that renews itself through the always-repeated rituals of life and the loves and marriages of the younger generation. Yet the marriage of Peter Pupkin and Zena Pepperleigh does not have a central, symbolic role; it is not the climax of the main plot. Leacock was disappointed by his failure to make *Sunshine Sketches* a unified novel; he thought this failure stemmed from his inability to make the Pupkin-Pepperleigh romance a thread that ran through the entire book. In fact, the book seems to indicate that Leacock could not create such a unity because he did not believe in it. The minor importance of the romance is in tune with his constant emphasis, both in this book and throughout his writings, on the motives of covetousness and status-seeking that underlie romantic sentiments. Zena, like many of his heroines, protests a love-inspired asceticism, but when she learns of Pupkin's family wealth, "she bore up as bravely as so fine a girl as Zena would,

151

and when he spoke of diamonds she said she would wear them for his sake." Leacock looks at such motivations, such workings of the human mind, mildly but clearly; his attitude is not condemnatory, but he realizes that such weakness to temptation, such ready abandonment of avowed principles, is what ultimately destroys the human happiness — here represented by Mariposa — that people miraculously manage to find for themselves. Zena's attitude, magnified, is exactly that of the plutocrat who, in the final essay in the book, "L'Envoi: The Train to Mariposa," sits in the Mausoleum Club in the great city and dreams of going back to his home town, although he never will; it is this attitude that has exiled him and that keeps him in exile.

Leacock's narrator sits next to this plutocrat in the Mausoleum Club and stage-manages the empty dream of returning. This is only one of many occasions in *Sunshine Sketches* on which the narrator, who generally distances himself from the foibles under examination, identifies with what he satirizes. In life, Leacock had one foot in Mariposa and one on Plutoria Avenue. He lived a myth of small-town Arcadia and made it more than a myth; at the same time he hungered for, and to a large measure achieved, the success in the climate of the larger "outside" world that is everything to the millionaires, academics and divines of the city in *Arcadian Adventures with the Idle Rich*. He presents both worlds as flawed and limited, although it is the city that comes in for more bitter, more pointed criticism. Leacock could not be content with the retired, unknown life of a cracker-barrel philosopher. When we read of Peter Pupkin's father, the Maritime millionaire with forestry and real-estate interests and a hand in government and law, we may recall that it was Leacock, of all those on the Orillia scene, who was related by marriage to a similar figure, Sir Henry Pellatt, owner of a magnificent summer estate in Orillia.

It is fitting and effective that *Sunshine Sketches* reaches its climax not in a marriage but in politics. In the election, the falseness of the outside world intrudes most seriously upon Mariposa; the election reveals how prone the people of Mariposa are to be governed by their own foibles. Once this tempest has been stilled into amusing inconsequentiality, the magic power of Mariposa is dramatically confirmed. At the same time, this power is revealed, even more clearly than in earlier chapters, to consist of nothing but the town's smallness and harmlessness. The people of Mariposa resemble, in all respects, the people and forces of the outside world. But in them everything that is dangerous has been reduced in scale and placed in an arena where it does not seem to matter. The melancholy of Leacock's tone comes from the subtly expressed fact that, despite this seeming, it does too matter. Influences tending towards a more ruthless world do pass into Mariposa — and perhaps they change it, but at the least they drive some people out of it, and it is lost to such people, perhaps forever. Even if Mariposa remains always present, always possible, it may move somehow beyond our reach, beyond our ability to live in it any more. This is why the narrator, at the end, is not in Mariposa, but is seated with the plutocrat in the Mausoleum Club, dreaming of "the little Town in the Sunshine" but dominated by the attraction of the city that he will explore in *Arcadian Adventures with the Idle Rich.*

Sunshine Sketches was written at Leacock's Côte-des-Neiges house. He had made his first notes for the project on 7 January and the first completed sketch appeared on 17 February. This piece, "Mariposa and its People," with the second, "The Glorious Victory of Mr. Smith" (24 February), constituted the opening chapter of the book, "The Hostelry of Mr. Smith." Thereafter the installments appeared at intervals of one to two weeks, until the series was completed on 22 June. B.K. Sandwell wrote that "The stories were shaped out at the dinner table" of Leacock's home, where the humorist would tell the story ideas he had developed during his early-morning working sessions, thus testing and improving them before committing a final version to paper. His chair was customarily placed well back from the head of the table so he could leap up at will and move about the room, enacting his stories, when the spirit moved him.

The stories appeared in book form in August, so it is likely that Leacock made final revisions and read proofs during the summer in Old Brewery Bay, surrounded by the people and scenes of which he had written. (To spend as much time as possible each year in Orillia, he used to leave McGill as soon as he could, seldom staying in Montreal late enough to attend graduation ceremonies.) Despite the jocular warnings of Mel Tudhope, Horace Bingham's complaint that Golgotha Gingham has been too obsessed with his business and barber Jeff Short's protests — "I never thought he was going to put in a book what I told him" — Leacock continued to participate normally in the social life of the town. Tudhope and the Hale brothers, especially Charles, with whom Leacock played cricket, were among his closest friends, as was Doctor Edward Ardagh, his billiard companion and the model for Doctor Gallagher of *Sunshine Sketches*. In Orillia, Leacock pursued his devotion to fishing, often employing Orillia's famous world-champion oarsman, Jake Gaudaur, as a guide. It became clear to his neighbors that this seasonal resident was someone more distinguished and more widely known than the average professional man with a summer cottage, and people involved in city politics began to ask Leacock to speak at city events. Over the years he spoke at the opening of the bridge over the narrows connecting lakes Simcoe and Couchiching and at the dedication of Orillia's monument to Champlain, who in 1615 had spent nearly a year at the Huron capital, Cahiague, just west of the city's site, and had fished at the narrows. In the preface to *Here Are My Lectures* (1937), Leacock recalled that he was once introduced at an Orillia function as "one of the foremost humorists of East Simcoe."

At McGill, in the fall of 1912, he was engaged in expanding his department, an effort authorized by McGill's principal Sir William Peterson, as part of an overall upgrading of the faculty of arts. Leacock's methods as chairman featured careful selection of professors, complete loyalty to his staff and scrutiny of the department's offerings. During the 1912 academic year he made a trip to New York to consult with the American representatives of his British publisher; he made a hit in New York as a speaker at the Lotus Club when he extemporaneously filled in for a guest of honor who never arrived. In 1913, when the University Club moved into a new building (which it still occupies, at 183 rue Mansfield), Leacock provided an analysis of moving costs that proved it would be cheaper to drink the bar's stock and buy again than to move the bottles; the membership did not accept his logic.

During the year Leacock published two scholarly articles, "The University and Business" and "The Canadian Senate and the Naval Bill." (He published seven scholarly essays between 1910 and 1912.) He also wrote many of the pieces later collected in *Behind the Beyond.* "Behind the Beyond," "The Dentist and the Gas," "With the Photographer," "Making a Magazine," "My Unknown Friend" and "Under the Barber's Knife" all appeared in *American Mercury*, and "Homer and Humbug" appeared in *Century.* When the book appeared in the fall of 1913l, it was Leacock's fourth consecutive bestseller and raised his annual income to more than ten thousand dollars for the first time. His reputation was making it easy for him to place his pieces and was bringing him requests from editors and fan mail from other writers. In 1915 an article by Douglas Bush, then a University of Toronto undergraduate, praised Leacock as a humorist superior to Mark Twain and elicited from Leacock a letter of thanks and a gift copy of *The Adventures of Huckleberry Finn* in refutation of the idea. Other letters he received about this time came from Faith Baldwin (1913), F. Scott Fitzgerald (1916) and Kenneth Roberts (1917). On 5 December, 1913 he received a request from British humorist E.V. Lucas to contribute to a humor anthology, and soon his mail was bringing him other requests for articles, a query from a publisher seeking to lure him onto its list of authors and suggestions from playwrights and theater companies about dramatizing some of his sketches. Another important event of the 1912 academic year was the arrival of Professor René du Roure, who would soon become one of Leacock's best friends. The physical antithesis of Leacock, du Roure was a slight, short and impeccably turned-out Frenchman who had immigrated in 1909 to teach at the Université Laval in Quebec City. After three years there, he joined McGill's department of romance languages.

Although four of the five short essays grouped under the title "Familiar Incidents" are weak (the exception is "My Unknown Friend"), *Behind the Beyond* maintains a generally high level of humor and style. It shows Leacock in many of his different moods and manners. The title piece, "Behind the Beyond: A Modern Problem Play," is only one of the essays and stories in the book that is linked to the ideas Leacock was developing in *Sunshine Sketches* and *Arcadian Adventures*. Like some of the essays in *Literary Lapses* and all of the parodies in *Nonsense Novels*, "Behind the Beyond" shows how people are easily swayed by the ridiculous attitudes disseminated through what we would now call "popular culture." A constant in Leacock's work, this theme is especially strong in his earlier books. It is a noteworthy thread in *Sunshine Sketches*, for instance. The romance of Zena Pepperleigh and Peter Pupkin definitely has elements of *Don Quixote*; the romantic maiden shapes her notions according to novels of chivalry she reads when her fierce father is not present to keep her attention fixed on *The Pioneers of Tecumseh Township*. When her shy suitor can do no more than whiz by her porch on his bicycle every evening, she sees "a sort of dim parallel between the passing of the bicycle and the ride of Tancred the Inconsolable along the banks of the Danube." In "Behind the Beyond," Leacock incorporates both the literature and its audience into his story. The theatergoers in "Behind the Beyond" hang spellbound upon the play, despite the patent foolishness of plot and characters, and the shoddy stage business that emphasizes the transparent artificiality of it all. The door is obviously cardboard, the valet enters before the bell sounds for him, Sir John "reads" letters without looking at them and announces that it is eight o'clock when the stage clock tells another time altogether. Nevertheless, the audience is deeply impressed, although it clings to the pretense of disparaging the play. Leacock displays the watchers' gullibility by treating them as a huge chorus that goes through synchronized stages of feeling; there seems to be no individual with a divergent opinion. When Jack Harding, who is "meant to typify weakness," promises to carry off Lady Cicely to a romantic port of her dreams (she mentions Para Noia), the audience is with him: "Any man in the audience would do as much. They'd take her to Honolulu." The men are so absorbed in the play that they become Jack Harding, except that their idea of a romantic destination is amusingly mundane next to the fictional playwright's flight of geographical nonsense. The audience's judgment that it is a "perfectly rotten play, but very strong" shows how theatergoers adopt attitudes they profess to analyze and judge. (In the same way, the citizens of Mariposa ape — while deprecating — the notions that come to them from the city and from books and magazines.)

The five acerbic travel essays, linked under the title "Parisian Pastimes," look forward to *Arcadian Adventures*, especially in their stinging depiction of the follies of wealth and fashion and the foolishness of those who seek them out. Other aspects of Leacock's art can be seen in even comparatively weak sketches, such as "Under the Barber's Knife." In this story Leacock, with cinematic effects, creates a barbershop like the one that later became a staple scene of comic films and animated cartoons. The barber dominates the cowed customer, muffles him in hot towels, talks to him mercilessly while wielding a careless razor. The choleric, dictatorial editor of "Making a Magazine," a much more accomplished sketch, is Leacock's early contribution to another character that became a favorite comic type in later literature and film (where, however, he usually turned out, in the end, to have a kindly heart). These and many other early Leacock characters and situations are similar to elements of film and literature from the 1920s to the 1940s. As his era's greatest and most prominent literary humorist, an author who wrote bestsellers, a "star" whose arrival in Britain in 1921 was as noteworthy as that of Chaplin or Fairbanks and Pickford, Leacock had influences on the tone, setting and imagery of American movies in their "golden age." He was acquainted with Charlie Chaplin, who suggested he write for films, an idea Leacock entertained but never enacted; and he influenced other literary humorists who did become involved in the film industry — Robert Benchley, for example, and S.J. Perelman, who wrote for the Marx brothers. *Sunshine Sketches* is perhaps the best example of Leacock's influence or contribution to the building up of popular motifs. That contribution was also the result of a natural dove-tailing of his concerns with those of his society and time. In 1912, North America was a continent of small towns that remained, in many respects, as they had been since the late nineteenth century, and that would maintain, in many cases, their social cohesion and their appearance through the 1940s and even later. However, by World War I, American and Canadian writers were battling for the soul of the small town. Writers saw small towns as arenas of either human ennoblement or dehumanizing drudgery. Leacock presented the optimistic view in *Sunshine Sketches*; by the end of the same decade, Sinclair Lewis — a satirist but no humorist — had drawn the negative picture of cultural isolation and pettiness in his *Main Street* (1920). Leacock's vision was persuasive because it was both vivid and balanced. It presented the sunshine of the little town and also its serious foibles and touched on, if lightly, the threats posed to the town by its own faults, by various outside influences and even by the way in which its traditional farm-market economy was giving way to manufacturing and resource industries. A town much like Leacock's Mariposa but shorn of almost all the darker colors appears in the films of Frank Capra, in the Andy Hardy series and numerous others; although this town may derive more directly from Booth Tarkington and other American models, it is Leacock who gave it its most vivid and enduring expression.

In the 1913-14 academic year, Leacock was extremely busy with his writing, although the period was outwardly uneventful. He was offered the job of chairing a committee in Ottawa to study cost of living, but he rejected the post in early December. (He recommended Professor James Mavor, the man who had turned him down for a University of Toronto professorship. Leacock was not one to nurse a grudge or ignore merit for personal reasons.) In 1913 Leacock and J.C. Hemmeon founded and directed McGill's Political Economy Club. In 1914, Leacock published *Arcadian Adventures* and three popularizations of Canadian history for the "Chronicles of Canada" series: *The Dawn of Canadian History, Adventurers of the Far North* (about early exploration) and *The Mariner of St. Malo* (about Jacques Cartier). Although the three history books appeared simultaneously, Leacock had probably been preparing them for several years. *Arcadian Adventures*, on the other hand, was written during the academic year while Leacock was in the midst of the Montreal sights and sounds on which he based his city. (Elements of Toronto, New York and other cities were also used.)

Leacock's fundamentally nontechnical view of all that is comprehended in economics, political science and sociology can be clearly read in *Arcadian Adventures with the Idle Rich*. It is worth noticing that this is Leacock's most Veblenesque book. Like Veblen, Leacock uses his economic and social insights to satirize and unmask the true motives behind socio-economic classes and class behavior. This unmasking applies to the pretensions and self-conceptions of all the classes examined, and to the theories and rationalizations of economists and social observers, who claim to explain social systems accurately. While there is no doubt that Veblen is the foremost economic critic and analyst the United States has produced, the emphasis of his work seemed, to professionals in his field, to fall on social criticism rather than technical economic analyses, systems and solutions; to this day, he continues to be taken less seriously than he deserves. Leacock had even less faith than Veblen in technical and theoretical approaches to socioeconomic situations, approaches that stemmed purely from a disinterested, scientific examination of a problem and that might require the imposition of a new political or economic system on a society. Rather, as *Arcadian Adventures* and *Sunshine Sketches* clearly indicate, Leacock felt that the individual had to act from good, intelligent motives. If individuals acted well, the existing system would function properly and improve. Leacock thought that the existing system represented an order too valuable to tamper with. Between Leacock and the scientific economist there is the difference between the person who believes social change must spring from personal change of heart and one who believes it comes with change of political system. The two views seldom exclude one another absolutely; the technical view usually admits the necessity of enlisting the individual's enthusiasm, and the humanistic view will state that any change of public spirit must be made practical through effective methods. But the difference in their starting points marks them, and there was something antipathetic to modern economic science in Leacock's belief in the economic importance of the individual's attitudes, and in his conservatism, which would rule out (in a most unscientific manner) the possibility of changing certain social institutions.

Conservatism and an emphasis on the individual underlie *Arcadian Adventures* and make it an indictment of the individual greed and foolishness that burden a potentially benign world. Does Leacock regard any of the systems he depicts — capitalism and mercantilism, the modern university, organized religion, democratic government in a metropolis — as good or bad in themselves? The systems seem evil because the people who operate them seem to be inevitably and innately either foolish or greedy or hypocritical. Leacock blames the relationships among persons, not the systems those persons adapt to govern their social and economic activities. In Leacock's book, college presidents are mere promoters with no essential interest in education; financiers are ignoramuses who attribute to their own acumen the results of birth and luck; clergymen are concerned only with prestige; and all of them change their opinions as the wind blows. That is the real problem, as Leacock sees it, and much of the hilarity of *Arcadian Adventures* comes from the way in which he repeatedly drives the point home. In the first chapter, "A Little Dinner with Mr. Lucullus Fyshe," each time the financier Fyshe begins to proclaim his revolutionary socialist tendencies, something occurs to make him contradict himself and spout commands or insults at the lower classes. The very predictability of this occurrence is funny: a cleverly exaggerated representation of Fyshe's complete inability to be honest with himself, to see what he is doing and saying. Leacock implies that if Fyshe would act on what he claims to understand, there would be no labor unrest and no revolutionary socialism because there would be none of the social conditions that cause them. Throughout the book, the reader sees that the "Idle Rich" have become so wholly pragmatic, so cynically intent on their own advantage, so willing to change with the opportunities of the day and the moment, that they no longer realize they are being dishonest. It has become impossible for them to change, or even — except perhaps in rare moments of nostalgia or emptiness — to recognize what they are. For Leacock, then, the humanistic belief that the individual's attitudes determine society does not amount to faith that the individual can be converted and society thereby improved.

In the story of the inadvertent multimillionaire from Cahoga Country, told in "The Wizard of Finance" and "The

Arrested Philanthropy of Mr. Tomlinson," Tomlinson is saved from the corrupt city (where his sudden wealth places him) only by a complete lack of comprehension. And this lack of comprehension comes from the fact that the healthier rural attitudes of his native region on the banks of Lake Erie are embedded in Tomlinson, just as corrupt and trivial attitudes are embedded in the financiers and lawyers who prey on him. Leacock portrays a world in which there is little opening for change, and in which this very changelessness makes the vicious and stupid actions of the rich humorously inconsequential. Life goes on much the same, no matter what they do. Months after Tomlinson's fortune has vanished, the debits and credits of his empire neatly resolving themselves into a nought, President Boomer and Lucullus Fysche are still involved in their heedless money-grubbing and their hypocritical efforts to seem impressive; Tomlinson is back on his Lake Erie hillside, where he now sees "nothing but the land sloping to the lake and the creek murmuring again to the willows." However, in Leacock's world there is a slow change occurring, although it is nearly unobservable and all seems comfortingly stable. There is evidence of change in the decay of the university under Boomer's control, and in a subtle fact that is almost buried near the end of the tale: "the development capital had disappeared." Those who seeded gold in Tomlinson's creek, where only fool's gold was to be found in the rocks, managed to get what they wanted out of the ten-days'-wonder of the nonexistent gold field. Leacock's emphasis is on the way in which the "Idle Rich" act, but there are indications here and there of the effects they have, too.

At the outset of *Arcadian Adventures*, Leacock justifies the title of his book by comparing the "Idle Rich" to shepherds and shepherdesses. They live in an Arcadia of their own imaginations, as did the courtiers during those ages that produced pastoral literature with its decorative landscapes and rural characters. Such literature was sometimes artificial and foolish. At its best, however, it was used to create an ideal country world to criticize the shortcomings of the sophisticated court and city. *Sunshine Sketches* created a true, and a fascinating, Arcadia, ineffably pleasant and yet far from perfect, and shows up the fallaciousness of the worldy atti-

161

tudes that intrude, the vices of the Mariposa people and their vulnerability to all that could harm them. *Arcadian Adventures* concentrates more on the satirical side of the pastoral, emphasizing the corruption of the city dweller, which becomes very apparent whenever the "Idle Rich" congratulate themselves on their goodness and simplicity or whenever a real shepherd from the environs of Mariposa — such as Tomlinson — wanders among them. Both books are idylls: they present an almost timeless world that appears to absorb human folly without too much ill effect. Together, they portray very winningly a North American version of La Belle Epoque, the golden calm before the storm of World War I.

Chapter Nine

Some Just Complaints About the War

I N EARLY 1914, Stephen Leacock was enjoying the fruits of the success achieved by his first books. These had already established him — in the minds of the most perceptive onlookers — as the leading English-language humorist and as the man who was redirecting and reinvigorating literary humor in the twentieth century. In January he received a letter from Frederick Eckstein of Doubleday Page & Company, of New York, attempting to lure him away from his use of John Lane's New York office as his American publisher. Eckstein offered Leacock a leather-bound edition of his works, similar to editions Doubleday had made for Kipling, Conrad and O. Henry. The editor wrote that "now nearly everyone here has the Leacock 'bug.' We have been through various stages of the Kipling 'bug,' the O. Henry and the Conrad ditto, but of all we seem to have the first in the most virulent form." Leacock remained with Lane. Doubleday's sporadic courtship of him over a long period finally bore fruit when, in the 1940s, he gave the firm several of his nonhumorous books at the prompting of editor Thomas B. Costain, a fellow Canadian. Since the publication of *Behind the Beyond*, Leacock's acuteness as an observer of the drama and his potential as a playwright had been commented upon; on 2 February, 1914, James L. Ford wrote him to report on an amateur production of the book's title sketch that was held in a private New York home for a high-society audience. In early 1914 Leacock's mail was bringing him many requests to provide material to the most prestigious, widely circulated periodicals in England and the United States, and was providing another reflection of his popularity in the form of fan letters. One from a New Orleans architect perceptively touched on the many roles and points of view Leacock had adopted in various works. The writer asked, "But are you an optimist or a pessimist? Your writings show the melancholy cynicism of Bernard Shaw, the good-natured banter of Gil Blas, the hoping-for-better satire of Aristophanes. Are you a Proteus?" As the fateful August drew nearer, he even received tribute from Germany. On 22 May, Claire Hellwig wrote from Munich to ask for the rights to translate *Nonsense Novels* into German; she had already secured the consent of a far-off Leacock admirer, the novelist Gustave Meyrink, to provide an introduction and find a German publisher for the translation. Leacock has been translated into German, but this particular initiative was lost in the bitterness of the moment. War was declared on Germany on 4 August; the first Canadian contingent, 33,000 troops, arrived in Plymouth, England on 16 October.

Stephen Leacock was five months away from his forty-fifth birthday when, on 4 August, 1914, Canada entered World War I. For the next four years, many aspects of his life went on almost unaffected by the fighting: winters in the classroom, summers in Orillia, year-round writing for a continuing series of humor books and articles. He enjoyed expanded responsibilities at McGill, and he published his first collection of serious essays. After fifteen years of marriage, the Leacocks became parents for the first and only time; their son, Stephen Lushington Leacock, was born on 19 August, 1915. The first boy born to one of Agnes Leacock's many sons, Stephen was welcomed lovingly into the large extended family presided over by his grandmother from her home in Sutton.

Still, the war brought some changes. At the request of the Canadian government, Leacock devoted much of his time to lecturing on behalf of the Belgian Relief Fund. His periodical writing was devoted to pieces of straightforward propaganda urging continued citizen support in Canada and entry into the war by the United States. He did not enter military service, but the McGill community he loved was changed by the war as volunteers from the faculty and student body formed several troop divisions sent overseas. His closest friend spent three years as a prisoner of war in Germany after being wounded in combat. While convinced that the British cause was just and must triumph, Leacock chronicled with dissatisfaction the changes in society brought by the war. Some of the changes would disappear with the end of fighting, but others — women's suffrage, prohibition, public-morality campaigns led by fundamentalist religions — promised to be permanent features of postwar Canada.

In 1914 Leacock was still experimenting with humor. From first to last, he was a master of a wide range of short prose forms. He regularly parodied fiction and drama but also wrote many other types of prose: news stories, textbooks, scholarly articles, serious essays. He also parodied many verbal patterns: lectures, speakers' introductory remarks, political harangues, conversation, entertainers' patter. With *Sunshine Sketches* and *Arcadian Adventures*, Leacock demonstrated his mastery in a longer, more complex form — a series of linked stories — and moved beyond his earlier pieces by blending comic observation with astute social criticism. When these books encouraged his readers and critics to hope for a novel, Leacock excused himself; he could conceive the characters, he said, but he could not "make things happen to them." The level of sustained organization achieved in *Sunshine Sketches* and *Arcadian Adventures* was not attempted again. In future books, Leacock occasionally collected a group of formally similar pieces, in the manner of *Nonsense Novels*, and there was a strong thematic unity in *My Discovery of England* (1922), the book produced from his successful 1921 tour. In general, however, the collections resembled *Behind the Beyond* in their variety.

Leacock's experiences during World War I may have contributed to the direction of his work in two ways. First, he devoted much of his time for four years to a single social issue: winning the war. His attention turned, for the first time, outside his own community to consider that community's enemies, who became the object of more destructive attacks than he had ever launched at the foolish or greedy or unkind close to him. In his own society, he criticized only groups whose faults were tied directly to the war effort. After the war, he never entirely shed the role of a champion of Anglo-Saxon civilization in a hostile world. Second, when Leacock could turn his attention away from his cause to the question of the world's future health in peacetime, he discovered that the world had changed forever from the settled structures whose weaknesses and strengths he had defined so well before the war. He felt at odds with his society in ways that he had not four years before. Embattled by changes in the community, which touched very close to home, Leacock set out with the old vigor to convince people that traditional ways should be maintained. For many years, Leacock was struggling to strike a rewarding relationship with his new world.

The war drew Canada away from its closest neighbor, the United States. As a member of the British empire, Canada was automatically at war with Germany when Great Britain declared war. The United States remained neutral until 1917. In the years immediately before 1914, Canada had made a strong choice for continued close ties with Great Britain and the empire in the 1911 election depicted by Leacock in *Sunshine Sketches*. In *Arcadian Adventures*, Leacock reinforced his conviction that the materialism of United States society was a dangerous influence for Canada. While working for stronger Canadian power within the empire, Leacock distrusted close association with the United States. He felt the United States might absorb Canada, which would destroy much that he found valuable in the country. Although the course of the war brought changes to Canada's relationship with Great Britain, Leacock never expressed regret that the imperial ties had drawn the country into the costly fighting. On the contrary, he urged the cause on the United States as a battle for the preservation of civilization. Canadians shared Leacock's support of the British war effort, especially in the early phases of the fighting. Although the outbreak of violence in the summer of 1914 caught many by surprise, Leacock had warned for years in his classes that German militarism posed a threat to world peace. Leacock's language training had included German (he was one of three McGill faculty members called on to review doctoral theses written in German). During his student days in Chicago, Leacock had frequented German neighborhoods to practice the language and had met a nationalistic spirit, which he feared would inspire military conflict. A British view dating from the same period may be seen in Jerome K. Jerome's *Three Men on the Bummel*, in which Jerome mixed his wit at the expense of foreign travelers with satirical attacks on the regimentation he found in Germany. In "The Devil and the Deep Sea: A Discussion of Modern Morality," a 1901 essay that first appeared in book form during the war, Leacock attributed to German philosophy a large measure of the breakdown he saw in society. In the essay, the lessons taught by religion have been repudiated by humanity, which "has called itself a Superman, and headed straight for the cliff over which is the deep sea." In later work, he would apply the same terminology to the German leaders and theoreticians of the war effort, as in "Sidelights on the Supermen. An Interview with General Bernhardi," which appeared in *Moonbeams from a Larger Lunacy* in 1915. Leacock wrote, during World War II, that the seeds of both conflicts had been sown by Germany when it urged the Boers into conflict with Great Britain in 1899.

It was a general conviction, according to Leacock, that the war would last only a short time because the world's industries could not produce sufficient weaponry quickly enough to sustain the fighting, whatever the desire of the combatants to continue. One of the reasons the prediction did not come true was that Canada, which began the war years supplying agricultural products, created a new industrial base provided by factories built for war materials. Canada also provided more than six hundred thousand men, including four army divisions; the vast majority were volunteers. Conscription, which proved one of the most divisive questions raised by the war, was not instituted until 1917. McGill's soldiers made up six infantry companies and provided a siege battery and a five-hundred bed army hospital. Doctor John McCrae, author of "In Flanders Fields," was a member of the hospital staff. Before the war, Leacock was busy with campus activities like the founding of the Political Economy Club. With the war underway, Leacock busied himself more with writing news and opinion pieces for student publications. The sketch on General Bernhardi appeared in a special supplement on the war produced by the *McGill Daily*. Leacock's circle of friends was altered considerably by the departure of student soldiers. Gladstone Murray, who started the *McGill Daily* with Leacock's help, became a flying ace. Another friend was not so fortunate. Leacock and French-born teacher René du Roure had found a community of interests that made them constant companions, especially at the University Club, where their billiards games, like Leacock's with Gladstone Murray, were a memorable attraction. Du Roure had worked in the French diplomatic service before coming to Canada; he returned home to enlist soon after the war began. Wounded in his first battle, he spent three years in German hospitals as a prisoner of war.

Moonbeams from the Larger Lunacy, Leacock's humor collection for 1915, was received warmly by critics and readers, who bought it out through eight reprintings. The author was called "the court jester of the day." Many of the seventeen pieces in the book appeared in magazines, especially one called *American Mercury*, before the war began; this was the same publication in which the stories of *Arcadian Adventures of the Idle Rich* had appeared during 1914. Many of the pieces are parodies, including "Who Is Also Who. A Companion Volume to Who's Who," "Aristocratic Anecdotes: or, Little Stories of Great People" and "Spoof: A Thousand-Guinea Novel. New! Fascinating! Perplexing!" The publishing business and, more generally, the world of celebrities, link much of this work from before the war. (In the book's preface, Leacock disarmingly pokes fun at himself as well: "The wise child, after the lemonade jug is empty, takes the lemons from the bottom of it and squeezes them into a still brew. So does the sagacious author, after having sold his material to magazines and been paid for it, clap it into book-covers and give it another squeeze.") "Spoof" burlesques the clichés of romantic fiction and the publishers who produce it: "Readers are requested to note that this novel has taken our special prize of a cheque for a thousand guineas. This alone guarantees for all intelligent readers a palpitating interest in every line of it." In "The Reading Public: A Book-Store Study," a clerk cunningly sells several copies of the same book "as a sea story, a land story, a story of the jungle, and a story of the mountains," as the tastes of each prospective customer require. Leacock, who had written light verse since his student days, also included some samples in the collection. An admirer of the poetry of W.S. Gilbert and Lewis Carroll, Leacock was more accomplished in prose than in verse, but he wrote some good "bad poetry" to exemplify the work of a character he called "Ram Spudd" in the story "Ram Spudd: The New-World Singer. Is He Divinely Inspired? Or Is He Not? At Any Rate We Discovered Him."

Pieces directly related to the war include "Sidelights on the Supermen," "In the Good Time after the War" and a number of the brief conversational vignettes from "Afternoon Adventures at the Club." In this last genial grouping of scenes from club life, which includes the much anthologized "Hallucination of Mr. Butt," Leacock depicts war-induced instances of vanity and ignorance in much the same way that he customarily mocks the extravagances of businessmen or outdoorsmen. "In the Good Time After the War" pictures a friendly session of the British parliament in which strong brotherly feeling created by co-operation in the war effort defuses permanently the issue of Irish Home Rule. Leacock's hope that the war might make some real difference in the question seems, at best, a poor prophecy and, at worst, a careless dismissal of the issues lying behind the Irish campaign for independence. Leacock's "Sidelights on the Supermen," written originally for a student audience, makes good use of the two sides of his career; the story allows a confusion to develop between his works of economics and humor. General Bernhardi visits Leacock late one night at his office. When asked how he managed to get by the janitor acting as a doorman, Bernhardi replies, "I killed him. . . . His resistance was very slight. Apparently in this country your janitors are unarmed." The general has come to praise Leacock's humor as it is displayed, for example, in *Elements of Political Science* and to bemoan the failure of the English-speaking public to understand solid German humor, as in Bernhardi's text: "A surprise attack, in order to be justified, must be made only on the armed forces of the state and not on its peaceful inhabitants. Otherwise the attack becomes a treacherous crime." Catching the flavor of the game, Leacock reduces Bernhardi to a deflated bag of wind by citing to him from the same German text: "In the event of war the loosely-joined British Empire will break into pieces, and the colonies will consult their own interests." What begins as a witty exchange ends with the patriotic but routine notion of the braggart revealed in his true insignificance; in this case, the impressive uniform of Bernhardi is punctured by the stilletto top of his helmet and shrinks "into a tattered heap." In sum, Leacock's early pieces on the war are filled with pride and optimism;

while he never lost the pride, the lessons of the war did temper his jauntiness. By the time the fighting ended he was bitter.

In January 1915, the Leacocks learned that Beatrix, thirty-six, was pregnant. The couple had been married for almost fifteen years and had begun to think that their hope for a child would never be realized. Preparations for the birth did not alter the family routine, however, until very shortly before the event, when Stephen and Beatrix hurried back from Orillia to Montreal, where Stephen Lushington Leacock was born on 19 August. Leacock happily wrote to Agnes to invite her to the city.

My Dear Mother —
Young Stephen was born at a quarter to three this afternoon. He is a fine young boy, in fact a regular corker, and weighs eight and a quarter pounds. Beatrix had made an error about the date of his birth, but thank heaven, we left Orillia in time or the journey might have been too much for her. He had a close run for his life as he had decided to throw himself into the world wrong end first. We had the three best men in Montreal and four nurses. Peters told me that without those *seven* people working at it, there would have been no chance. Beatrix was taken ill at 6 this morning and I drove her over to the maternity hospital. She had a bad time but it is over now & she is resting & doing fine. The baby looks just like Barbara and little Stephen and me and all the rest. Beatrix was awfully well right up to the end except that she had a bad fall two days ago. But Peters says the baby is not a premature baby being if anything over developed. Beatrix will have to stay where she is for some time, I don't know how long, two weeks I should think. How soon can you come down? We must take up the arrangements for the christening right away. I want my friend Mr. Symonds the rector of the cathedral to do it.

I sent a wire to George today. Will you please tell Charlie and the rest. Teddy is probably still with you. . . . I gave the telegraph company a dollar to take the message from Sutton to the Grange. So don't let them charge you for it. . . . I could only stay with Beatrix for a little while this afternoon as they wanted her to sleep but I am going over after dinner and we'll see the baby together. I never yet saw a baby that looked so complete, so all there, so little like a red monkey as Stephen does: indeed he seems to me a most remarkable child. Please write and tell Carrie that her present hit it just right because it arrived at the very hour that he was born. I'd write to her myself but I have no address. Beatrix won't be able to write for some days. Be sure to let me know right away just how soon you can come, and come as soon as you can.

Your loving son
(Old) Stephen Leacock

P.S. Tomorrow I am going to make my will and appoint trustees, guardians and a staff of godfathers, godmothers, proxies, and assistants. We have decided that from the boy's birth there shall be no extravagance on him. We got from Eatons a plain basket for him to sleep in, — there — I guess this is as much as it is fair to inflict in one dose.

George, Charlie and Teddy, are, of course, his brothers, and Carrie is one of his sisters, Mrs. Jan Ulrichsen, the mother of Barbara and of "little Stephen," who was Leacock's godson and namesake. Another family member was heard from when on 26 August Dr. Rosamond Leacock — Dot — wrote from Calgary agreeing to be the new baby's godmother.

An entry from Agnes's diary carries the story forward a few weeks, to 5 September, when she wrote, at her home in Sutton:

It is a long time since I have written anything but letters, and a great event has taken place. My first Leacock grandchild was born on the 19th of August, Stephen's boy. He and Beatrix have been married a long time and this longed for child has taken up all my thoughts of late. I hope very soon to see him; at present he and his mother are in the maternity hospital, and it's not much use for me to go to Montreal till they get him home to Cote des Neiges, as one can see so little of people in hospital, but Stephen writes often of the boy and he's a chip off the old block I'm sure — like Stephen and my father. He is to be called Stephen Lushington.

Stephen honored his mother's family by giving his son a family name, Lushington. Leacock's happiness was eventually darkened by health problems that become apparent in his "most remarkable child," but in the fall of 1915 his only concern was for Beatrix's recovery from the difficult delivery. When she returned home well and busy with the new baby, it seemed that family life at the Leacock home was changed for the better.

The war had entered its second year and the Canadian First

Division had distinguished itself in April, 1915 at the battle of Ypres. The pattern of trench warfare along the western front, which would last until 1918, was already well-established. The war Leacock once had thought must end in months became a nightmare of casualties and destruction. The Canadian government approached Leacock to help raise money for the Belgian Relief Fund, a cause that occupied him periodically until the war ended. Touring for the fund was one of Leacock's first experiences as a humorous lecturer. He had spoken humorously on only a handful of casual occasions before the war. Most of his lecturing and public speaking had been done as an economist or a campaigner for the Conservative party, although the sprinkling of humor he sometimes had brought to these appearances had helped make him a sought-after speaker. Leacock developed, during the fund-raising appearances, the format he would use on his British tour in 1921. In the guise of a lecturer on popular literature or drama, Leacock would weave together parodies of fiction with wry comments on its shortcomings. His lecture was called "Frenzied Fiction." (Leacock borrowed the title for a humor collection in 1917, but that book is not a record of his experiences on the tour or of the texts of his speeches.) The best account of Leacock's adventures along the way is the essay "We Have With Us To-Night," which appeared in *My Discovery of England*. There, Leacock described the woes of his early years as a lecturer. One experience in particular he identified as coming from the war tours.

> I recall in this same connection the chairman of a meeting at a certain town in Vermont. He represents the type of chairman who turns up so late in the evening that the committee have no time to explain to him properly what the meeting is about or who the speaker is. I noticed on this occasion that he introduced me very guardedly by name (from a little card) and said nothing about the Belgians, and nothing about my being (supposed to be) a humorist. This last was a great error. The audience, for want of guidance, remained very silent and decorous, and well behaved during my talk. Then, somehow, at the end, while someone was moving a vote of thanks, the chairman discovered his error. So he tried to make it good. Just as the audience were getting up to put on their wraps, he rose, knocked on his desk and said:

"Just a minute, please, ladies and gentlemen, just a minute. I have just found out — I should have known it sooner, but I was late in coming to this meeting — that the speaker who has just addressed you has done so in behalf of the Belgian Relief Fund. I understand that he is a well-known Canadian humorist (ha! ha!) and I am sure that we have all been immensely amused (ha! ha!). He is giving his delightful talk (ha! ha!) — though I didn't know this until just this minute — for the Belgian Relief Fund, and he is giving his services for nothing. I am sure when we realize this, we shall all feel that it has been well worth while to come. I am only sorry that we didn't have a better turn-out tonight. But I can assure the speaker that if he will come again, we shall guarantee him a capacity audience."

As this passage suggests, Leacock took no pay for the appearances, which were scheduled in Canada and the United States. The money raised went primarily to refugees housed at Nantes during the war. The flavor of Leacock's speeches, some of which were published late in his life in the volume *Here Are My Lectures*, is suggested by a popular piece in *Further Foolishness* (1916). "The Snoopopaths; or, Fifty Stories in One" combined scenes and dialogue from the type of story Leacock designates as "snoopopathic" with commentary by Leacock. The commentary makes the sketch "not so much a story as a sort of essay." The main characters in Leacock's parody romance are "A MAN" and "A WOMAN." He explains, "I put these words in capitals to indicate that they have got to stick out of the story with the crudity of a drawing done by a child with a burnt stick." The mock drama rises suspensefully to a surprise ending while the author pokes fun, in every sentence, at the excesses of description such stories commonly included.

Leacock was now setting himself an extraordinary taxing schedule of activities that included humorous and scholarly writing, teaching, administrative duties as department chairman, and the Belgian Relief Fund lectures. In addition, he continued to appear at literary functions to which he was invited, many of them in New York. Writing to Pelham Edgar in February, 1916 (to turn down a request to speak in Toronto), Leacock said that he was about to spend a week making Belgian Relief Fund appearances in eastern Ontario, then speak at two cities in the southwestern part of the province, then fulfill an engagement of his own to speak at a New York literary banquet and, finally, give more Relief Fund lectures in Baltimore, Pittsburgh, Buffalo and Wellesley, Massachusetts. At the same time, his social life among Montreal business leaders, writers and artists remained a full one. He provides a glimpse of his activities, and his wry way of looking at the world around him, in his comments to Edgar:

Funny damned thing here the other night: — a banquet was arranged for Brymner the artist in congratulations on his C.M.G. [William Brymner, a painter, had received the honor in 1910]. Mr Baker of the C.P.R. kindly placed the C.P.R. station dining room at the disposal of the committee... It was the first time the Railway dining room had ever been so used & hence all the staff from the chef down were on their mettle. They wanted to show that when it came to *banquets* the C.P.R. could break all records. But of course being a *station dining room*, their one idea of efficiency was *high speed*. Time was everything. Oysters and soup flew through the air. Dish succeeded dish like lightning & the poor little banquet, never a very costly one or elaborate even as planned, was over in thirty-five minutes. Over its corpse, three or four speeches were made. But as it turned out that all of the speakers were men of few words, each relying on other people to do the talk, the whole banquet which began at 8:30 was over at a quarter to ten. The gay revellers were out on the street at ten o'clock, and the dining room cleaned up . . . and closed tight within five minutes of their leaving. The whole thing is felt by the Railway to be a triumph of management. They think, with a little more practice, that they'll be able to run a banquet through in about twenty-five minutes.

Despite his unflagging energy and keenness for all he encountered, Leacock could now sometimes feel a tiredness that was compounded of his heavy demands upon his energy, a sense that he was aging, and the realization that the war was ending forever the world he had known in his childhood and his prime. Around this time he begins to express directly the melancholy attitude that is embodied implicitly in *Sunshine Sketches* and *Arcadian Adventures*: ultimately no human effort or accomplishment is of importance. He shares with other English essayists concerned for moral issues — and notably with Samuel Johnson — a sense that the task of life is to fill up, honorably and with as much goodness as possible, the expanse of time that stretches toward death. Like Charles II (who crops up in a book Leacock published in 1916), he had become one of the rare persons able to understand that "nothing really matters very much." In his February, 1916 letter to Edgar, after narrating the uproarious incident of the C.P.R.'s speed banquet, he turns aside to muse,

> I am also getting old. Are you. I had expected to stay young for ever and always felt as if I had not *begun* yet and was still planning what I would do when I grew up. Now I find, almost suddenly, that it is nearly over.
> I feel like the indignant miller at the ballot box, who said, — "Is *that* all, boss, is *that* all you do?" — And so with life: one asks, "Is *that* all, boss?"

To Leacock, such reflections were never a cause for disappointed lethargy but rather a spur to redoubled effort and kindliness on behalf of his fellows.

In his war work, Leacock asked for American dollars to help refugees, but he also hoped to see the United States enter the war. Another story from *Further Foolishness*, "The White House from Without In," criticizes the neutrality policies of President Woodrow Wilson by means of fictional extracts from the president's diary. Leacock is scornful of the way the president dealt with German submarine attacks on United States shipping, the issue that eventually drew the United States into the war, and the military operations in Central America, which occupied United States attention from 1914 to 1917. Leacock attributes to Wilson a naive eagerness to believe German protestations of innocence in relation to the submarine attacks. "Cables from Germany. Chancellor now positive as to *Torpid*. Sworn evidence that she was sunk by some one throwing a rock." In several of the pieces in *Frenzied Fiction*, United States foreign policy with regard to Europe and Central America is mentioned often. The book, published late in 1917, included Leacock's congratulatory essay, "Father Knickerbocker: A Fantasy," which concludes, "And I knew that a great nation had cast aside the bonds of sloth and luxury, and was girding itself to join in the fight for the free democracy of all mankind." Theodore Roosevelt, who had supported the entry of the United States into the war, wrote Leacock in 1919 to invite him to dinner in New York. Roosevelt sent along an article he had written praising the part played by Canada in the fighting.

Although Leacock continued to write about the war, he worked on a variety of other projects as well. In 1915, he provided a group of verses for a gift book illustrated by A.H. Fish, who had done the stylish drawings for *Behind the Beyond*. Leacock wrote the verses as a favor to Fish and to his London publisher, John Lane, who produced the gift book, which was called *The Marionettes' Calendar*. Another enterprise based in London was a dramatization, by Charles Hawtrey and Basil Macdonald Hastings, of the story "Q" from *Nonsense Novels*. The play opened on 29 November, 1915 at the London Coliseum to good notices. Leacock shared the royalties for the work. (During the 1920s and 1930s, several other plays based on his humor articles were produced, and Leacock investigated the possibility of writing for the stage and the movies.) *Essays and Literary Studies*, published in 1916, was a selection of Leacock's articles on education, social issues and literature. The earliest, "A Rehabilitation of Charles II," originally appeared in 1906, but several pieces from the war years, including "The Woman Question," which originally appeared in *Maclean's* in 1915, were also chosen. "The Apology of a Professor," "The Devil and the Deep Sea" and "Literature and Education in America" were written in 1909 and 1910 for Andrew Macphail's *University Magazine*. After seven well-received books of humor, Leacock was guaranteed attention for this departure in style. In general, reviews were positive, although one critic questioned whether the seriousness of the subjects addressed was matched by the author's avowed reliance on "the half-truth." (Leacock concluded one essay with the explanation, "The half-truth is to me a kind of mellow moonlight in which I love to dwell. One sees better in it.")

In *Essays and Literary Studies*, Leacock expanded his efforts as a popular author. Although he never again published a volume devoted entirely to his essays on literature and social issues, several of his humor collections featured at least one article of a distinctively serious subject and tone. A well known example is "Oxford as I See It" from *My Discovery of England*. The division between Leacock the serious writer and Leacock the humorist almost disappears in many of his essays; there is simply Leacock, the human observer who commands satire, persuasion, argumentation and the knowledge that his subject requires. The development of a mature style as an essayist brought to many of his later works a softer, more thoughtful approach to his humorous pieces as well; the surface glitter of exaggerations and absurdities became sometimes secondary to the sympathetic penetration of very human and very simple scenes — a man fishing or gardening or just growing old. The master of first-person narration began to use the style to reveal an engaging self rather than to display imaginative virtuosity. In his earliest essays, though, Leacock was not yet writing about himself, and the blending of humor and persuasion varies greatly from piece to piece in tone and in effectiveness. In general, the works collected in *Essays and Literary Studies* are some of the most thoroughly serious Leacock published. In the memorable last piece in the book, "A Rehabilitation of Charles II," Leacock sets out to rehabilitate the reputation of one of England's less savory monarchs. He explains:

> Thus it is that we live in an age of historical surprises. We know now that Rome was not founded by Romulus, that the apple shot by William Tell was not lying on his son's head at the immediate time of the shooting, and that America was not in the true sense of the term discovered by Christopher Columbus, who had spent eighteen years of tearful persuasion in trying to prove that there was no such continent.

Leacock's busy search through the career of Charles II for commendable achievements is conducted with an admirable display of historical knowledge, although the best attributes Leacock can find are negative: Charles did not really care about his religion and he was not overly interested in politics. In sum, "He had grasped as few men have done the great truth that nothing really matters very much."

Two humor collections, *Further Foolishness* (1916) and

Frenzied Fiction (1917), were well received. *Frenzied Fiction* was welcomed as "better than others of his recent books." The pieces are long and well developed and there is a pleasant range of tones, from the sentimental "Merry Christmas" to the hilarity of "My Revelations as a Spy." The war appears in several pieces, but the book is weighted strongly in the direction of other subjects, including prohibition, health fads and spiritualism. *Further Foolishness* includes a group of five pieces called "Peace, War, and Politics" (the group contains "The White House from Without In"). Limited somewhat by the very specific wartime issues Leacock satirizes, they are nevertheless well-paced and often incisive in their criticism of foreign policy in Germany, Turkey and Mexico. Several of the articles in both books are parodies of newspaper features and popular fiction.

Both *Further Foolishness* and *Essays and Literary Studies* contain theoretical discussions of humor, the first of many Leacock wrote over the years. As his own career became a more prominent subject in his writing and in his public appearances, he darted back and forth over the line that separates the comic and the critic, especially the critic who analyzes comic performance. In *Essays and Literary Studies*, he included appreciations of Dickens, O. Henry and a general subject, "American Humour." Leacock states his general principle that the best humor must be kindly:

> The short comings of our existence, the sad contrast of our aims and our achievements, the little fretted aspiration of the day that fades into the nothingness of tomorrow, kindle in the mellowed mind a sense of gentle amusement from which all selfish exultation has been chastened by the realisation of our common lot of sorrow.

The same theme is repeated, with many comic illustrations, in "Humor as I See It," the concluding entry of *Further Foolishness*. "Humour as I See It" contains many phrases associated with Leacock, including the definition that "it is a prime condition of humor that it must be without harm or malice, nor should it convey incidentally any real picture of sorrow or suffering or death." One spur to these reflections on humor was a review in which a critic had said, "What is there, after all, in Professor Leacock's humour but a rather ingenious mixture of hyperbole and myosis?" Leacock replied, "The man was right. How he stumbled upon this trade secret I do not know." He explained that it was his custom to go into the cellar and mix half a gallon of myosis with a pint of hyperbole, with an occasional admixture of paresis.

Leacock did not publish a book in 1918, the last year of the war, because of the demands of his lecture work for the Belgian Relief Fund. He turned happily to favorite interests as soon as the fighting ended. With Beatrix, he began planning an addition to his house in Orillia; they also planned a boathouse, whose second story served as his office for many years. René du Roure returned to Montreal and his friendship with Leacock. They shared teaching duties for a new program on French government and culture established at McGill. Du Roure was the most frequent guest of the Leacocks in Orillia in the summers, and a popular dinner companion at the house on Côte-des-Neiges Road. In 1919, Leacock encouraged the establishment of the *McGill News* and was the paper's first editorial-board chairman. He also began teaching courses in the university's new sociology department. The end of the war brought Leacock four honorary degrees, the first in 1919 from Queen's University in Kingston and three others, in 1920, from Dartmouth, Brown and the University of Toronto. Leacock continued in demand as a lecturer after his work for the Belgian Relief Fund ended; although no extensive tour was arranged until 1921, he visited the United States frequently on speaking engagements in 1919 and 1920.

Another pleasant addition to his life that came with the end of the war was the friendship of American humorist Robert Benchley, with whom Leacock began to correspond in 1919. Throughout his life, Benchley was a loyal admirer and professed imitator of Leacock's. The friendship began after Leacock lectured at Benchley's alma mater, Harvard University. Benchley was told by a friend that Leacock had praised Benchley's work and suggested he publish a book. An early letter from Leacock to Benchley reveals that he provided the younger writer with practical advice and encouragement in developing his work. Leacock sent along an advertising flyer from an etiquette instructor who promised customers absolutely reliable tips on meeting royalty. Leacock wrote:

> It doesn't quite become me as a loyal subject to get too funny about kingship. But I wonder if your nimble wit couldn't do something about this new coming of the King to America . . . . Some hotels will have notices (*Kings not admitted*), others will cater to the king trade. — I see a title like *Kings Wanted* or *What Shall We do with our Kings* . . . . Possible openings ought to supply you with plenty of ideas. Go to it.

Leacock provided the preface for Benchley's first book, *Of All Things*, in 1922. Benchley sent a copy to Leacock with the inscription, "To Stephen Leacock, who certainly *ought* to like most of the stuff in this book as he wrote it himself first."

One of Leacock's first writing projects after the war was a six-part newspaper series for the *New York Times* entitled "The Unsolved Riddle of Social Justice." The series was sufficiently popular to be republished in book form in 1920. Critics generally responded without much enthusiasm to the essays; although there was praise for Leacock's clarity of presentation, most complained that the riddle remained unsolved at the end of his study. To understand Leacock's thought one must read the book; it is one of the few works in which he makes even oblique references to the social unrest brought to his own country by the war. An enthusiastic supporter of the empire, Leacock reserved his criticism, during the war years, for the enemy and for those outside of Canada who displayed a lack of enthusiasm for the British cause (the United States for example). He satirized only those Canadians who thought they were supporting the war effort — by fund drives or political arguments — but were, in fact, unwittingly failing to help as they should. He did not give his views on the social tensions that arose around the war's end in Canada or on the dramatic transformation taking place in Canada's relationship to the empire. In *The Unresolved Riddle*, Leacock refers to two of the most difficult problems faced in his country at the time, conscription and labor unrest. But he does not comment directly on specific Canadian events; he discusses the general questions as they relate to his examination of the world economy after the war. In 1917, Canada was divided dangerously along ethnic lines on the issue of conscription. Conservative Prime Minister Robert Borden reversed an earlier pledge that a draft would not be used to fill projected troop quotas for overseas service and called for conscription. Opposition in Parliament led to an election, which brought forth violent demonstrations against a draft, especially in the province of Quebec. A bomb destroyed a wing of the home of publisher Lord Atholstan (Leacock's sponsor for *Sunshine Sketches*) because his newspapers supported a draft. Leacock did not enter the debate, which was won by the Conservative party. Conscription is an important topic in *The Unsolved Riddle*. Leacock said any government that instituted a draft should expand social protection for its citizens. The second issue, labor unrest, centered, in Canada, on the Winnipeg General Strike of 1919. When one union went on strike, most of the city's work force joined the strike, and several demonstrators were killed by police gunfire. Borden's successor, Conservative Arthur Meighen, took harsh measures to punish the strike leaders and showed small sympathy for labor protestors and their demands for reform. Again, Leacock did not enter the public debate, but in *The Unsolved Riddle* he championed specific measures like a minimum wage as necessary to redress injustice to workers.

The Unsolved Riddle approaches the question of social justice from two perspectives: the unique historical situation created by World War I and the evolution of economic theory from the early-nineteenth-century free traders to the prominent socialist thinkers of the early twentieth century. Leacock deplored the terrible waste of the war, the loss of life and the misues of an incalculable amount of the world's wealth in the production of war machinery. But the war had taught industrial society an important lesson: that necessity could produce a level of productivity thought impossible before. In peacetime, free choice returned society to a much more haphazard and therefore inefficient mechanism of supply and demand. Leacock argued that freedom was preferable to enforced efficiency, but he also warned that a return to the old economic theories and to the inherent injustice of an unregulated capitalism would contribute to a growing disparity between the rich and the poor, which was a threat to the survival of society. Just as in *Elements of Political Science*, Leacock acknowledged that socialist thinkers had understood correctly the evil of existing economic structures in the industrialized west. He objected, however, to the socialist solution of collective ownership and shared distribution of wealth, primarily on the pragmatic grounds that such a state would produce a more terrible tyranny than was possible under the checks and balances of a democratic system. Without controls on its managers, the socialist state could only guarantee perfect equality among perfect people, according to Leacock; it was utopian and unworkable.

The proper system for restoring an equitable sharing among all citizens of a society's wealth and power would use government protection of workers to balance the economic strength of those who controlled the industries. Leacock argued that government should supply work for the able-bodied and financial support, especially medical care and education, for children, the handicapped and the aged. Leacock gave two reasons to justify this new direction for industrialized nations: first, society had to repay its debts to its citizen soldiers; second, the round of violent demonstrations would continue unless the social evils they were protesting could be removed by government intervention. Leacock warned that socialism won its adherents from those disenchanted by the inequities of the economic order in western democracies. For a traditionalist, Leacock spoke strongly on behalf of advanced causes. His reason perhaps was conservative — the pragmatic worry that the society he loved would be destroyed altogether because of the economic injustices it contained. Most conservative of all was his fear that the drive for change would sweep all away in an effort to uproot injustice. He was prepared to wait in the hopes that good changes would not displace any of the features of society he supported. Still, Leacock spoke boldly for measures not associated with the conservative philosophy of his time when he urged that the higher taxation required by the war be continued in peace as a means of financing the expansion of government social programs. Perhaps his own childhood experiences and the birth of his son had much to do with the central social measure he preached: "No society is properly organized until every child that is born into it shall have an opportunity in life."

In contrast to the careful argumentation and liberal social theory of *The Unsolved Riddle of Social Justice*, Leacock's final book of war humor was filled with a bitter triumph over his enemies. The bitterness did him little credit. *The Hohenzollerns in America*, which was published in 1919, contains a number of mildly amusing "impossibilities" about education, the movies and polite conversation. Most of the book is devoted to reflections on the war. In 1917, a poem in *Punch* praised Leacock: "And yet though so freakish and dashing,/ You are not the slave of your fun; / For there's nobody better at lashing/ The crimes and the cant of the Hun." Leacock had moved, during the war, from rather detached exposures of German pomposity to increasingly specific attacks on German war policy — diplomatic lying to the United States, bombing of neutral shipping, the use of poison gas. As the attacks grew more specific, they also centered on more specific personal targets. In the title piece of *The Hohenzollerns in America*, Leacock vented his anger at Germany by very cruel jibes at the members of the German royal family. Leacock speaks in the voice of a family member, a minor princess accompanying the deposed kaiser, his son and other relatives to a new life in the United States. The kaiser's son, "Cousin Willie," is revealed to be a drunkard; the princess notes, "what a sneaking face Cousin Willie has." Another relative, who steals furtively from the family's meager purse, is described in some new clothes: "he has got hold of a queer long overcoat with the sleeves turned up, and a little round hat, and looks exactly like a Jew." The princess tells of his "command of Yiddish" and his plans to enter the tailor business in New York. The kaiser himself is portrayed as a senile fool unable to understand his changed circumstances any better than he had understood the plight of Germany during the war: "It was pleasant to hear Uncle William talk in this way, just as quietly and rationally as at Berlin, and with the same grasp of political things."

The book was not the least popular of Leacock's collections, but it was better received in Britain than in the United States, where several reviewers criticized it harshly. According to *Saturday Review*, "We reach the conclusion that Mr. Leacock has fatally impaired his reputation by this work. Our particular quarrel with Mr. Leacock arises from his treatment of the ex-Kaiser." By the author's standards, the humor of *The Hohenzollerns in America* is not of a high quality. If the project of humor is to draw people closer through their sympathetic understanding of life's difficulties, then the project is not really humor at all. Certainly, German readers could not have drawn any sympathy from Leacock's performance. More important, Leacock was offering his usual readers the temptation to share with him a cruel glorification of the sufferings of former enemies, now defeated. Formerly, Leacock's subject had lain too close to home to permit such a thoroughgoing and unrelenting destructiveness. In the wake of the war, however, the world had changed. Perhaps the clearest difference was the realization that his country, no matter what its internal problems, was a shield against other peoples and countries that threatened to wipe out his way of life. Leacock's personal suffering showed in the bitterness with which he allowed himself to lash out in victory against the losers of the war.

There were problems within his own society, as well. The war had brought changes to Canada, many of them considered in *The Unsolved Riddle of Social Justice*. Leacock approached the problems as an expert somewhat removed from the actual conflict between industry and labor. Other changes touched him personally, especially the campaign for women's rights and the enactment of prohibition. For Leacock, both these changes could be attributed to the war, but they did not go away when the fighting ended. Comments on these two questions had already begun to appear in his books during the war; they would occupy a good deal of his time in the early 1920s as well. During his tour of Britain in 1921, Leacock said that his training as an economist had kept him from being thought of as merely a funny man. Still, the demands of his prominence began to weigh on him as he found himself involved in the difficult controversies over prohibition and women's rights. On the one hand, he was assured of a hearing; on the other hand, he found himself unable to effect the changes he most wanted to see. Leacock had begun his career as a detached observer of human folly. In the 1920s, he found himself fighting folly and not always winning.

Chapter Ten

Women and Whiskey

THE WAR was over but Leacock was not through fighting. The tenth anniversary of *Literary Lapses* found him struggling on many fronts. The cause of his country's future, which he had eagerly made his own throughout the war years, continued to occupy him. After *The Unsolved Riddle of Social Justice*, however, his interest changed from the general question of the Canadian economy to specific social issues, especially prohibition and women's rights. He promised to write for any newspaper at any time without a fee to combat the banning of alcoholic beverages, and he kept up this fight with a determination that sometimes turned to bitterness when he found how slowly his campaign progressed. The strong identification Leacock felt with his community and society had always served to soften the blow of his humorous attacks on follies and errors; as he found himself at odds with a large portion of his society, he was moved to strike out with uncharacteristic impatience. While engage in such efforts, Leacock was besieged with offers to publish and to speak. As he tried to use these opportunities to satisfy his interests and to make money, he was drawn into more commitments than he could manage. At the same time, his publisher, John Lane, warned that on both sides of the Atlantic readers were judging — based on *Further Foolishness, Frenzied Fiction* and *The Hohenzollerns in America* — that the quality of his work was dropping dangerously. Each new book was scrutinized carefully by reviewers for proof that Leacock had permitted inferior work to be published out of greed or carelessness. Although Leacock was a master of the lecture stage, to which he resorted more frequently at this time, the conditions of lecture touring left him cold, especially the process of being interviewed by local reporters. Worst of all, the income for which he was being accused of sacrificing quality was not sufficient, at the beginning of the decade, to satisfy his hopes for a new home in Orillia.

Although Leacock relied largely on a proven technique, parody, for the successful humor he wrote between 1920 and 1924, he continued to expand the range of his work as he sought for ways to take advantage of his established audience to present his serious views and, he hoped, influence the course of social development. Even in parody, he was experimenting. Leacock satirized drama in the ten nonsense plays collected in *Over the Footlights* (1923). His interest in humorous drama had been stimulated by the response of theater people to "Behind the Beyond" and by the dramatizations of it. In other work, Leacock signaled that his interest no longer lay either in sustained fiction or unified works of social theory. Instead, he cultivated the essay — his own blend of comedy, argument and astute presentation of fact and emotion — as a tool for commenting on social conditions. Particularly in *My Discovery of England* (1922) he proved himself a master at defining and arguing the fine points of a social question in a brief, entertaining piece of prose. Thus, although he found much to vex and frustrate him during the combats about public issues in the early 1920s, Leacock was developing the mature, resonant, flexible essayist's voice that would be the crowning achievement of his literary career and would provide the basis for his best writing.

The new decade began in an unpromising way. In 1920 Leacock had written a second series of "nonsense novels" for *Harper's Magazine*. Leacock sent the manuscript, called *Winsome Winnie*, to the John Lane Company office in New York and was told that the book was not accepted because it could be a financial loss to the company. Leacock knew that without the company's support his book would not be promoted properly. He wrote to the company in friendly terms. He offered to accept a royalty of fifteen percent, rather than his customary twenty percent, on all copies after five thousand; two days later the new royalty arrangement was accepted from New York, and publication of the book went ahead. There had been many considerations behind the reluctance of the John Lane Company to publish. The negative response in the United States to *The Hohenzollerns in America* may have caused fear that a new Leacock book would not be well received; the publisher's editors may have judged that the new parodies were not of the same quality as earlier ones. However, according to a letter from John Lane to Leacock in 1921, the principal issue was money. Because Leacock received a twenty-percent royalty on all copies, American editions were not profitable for the publisher. Lane added that he was hearing in New York the complaint that "you are doing too much, and there is a very general feeling, even in Canada, that you are now writing snippets for high prices, and these are too short for book form, which is a sure way of losing your hold on book buyers."

Winsome Winnie proved to be one of Leacock's most popular collections, and a hit with critics. Novelist Robertson Davies thinks it one of Leacock's very best books, superior even to the original *Nonsense Novels*. There were eventually eight reprintings of *Winsome Winnie*. The first edition of five thousand copies sold out in 1920. Three thousand more copies were sold by the end of 1921. Critics almost unanimously reported that the eight parodies were uniformly excellent. According to the *New York Times*, "Despite his delicious drolleries, Mr. Leacock's book of verbal cartoons contains an amazing amount of truthful criticism — doubly effective because its form and oblique method of delivery rob it of all malice." The few murmurs against the book were aimed at a lack of the "fresh spontaneity" of his early books. According to the London *Times Literary Supplement*, Leacock's jokes were often good for only one laugh, because they lacked real thought; they were based on "verbal surprise" or "the technical improvement in an established joke." This isolated *caveat* seems quirky, and does not really apply to *Winsome Winnie*. Leacock's parodies in *Winsome Winnie* go to the heart of the literary forms that he mocks and deal with the assumptions shared by writers and audiences; the humor is often dry and depends less on jokes than on a thorough going parody of the overall characteristics of literary genres and the attitudes underlying them. The parodies include a romance among rich families, in which the heroine, Winnie, is bankrupted by her speculating guardian; a domestic drama, in which a wife is saved from deserting her husband by the opportune arrival of a family fortune; a political melodrama, in which the fate of an empire hangs on the social gifts of a minister's wife; a murder mystery; a ghost story; a historical tale of the American Civil War; and a tale of shipwrecked lovers. One of the most charming of the lot, "The Kidnapped Plumber," is a story of the new age, in which Leacock portrays the "true" rich as highly paid tradesmen and makes them the object of the same threats, and the heroes of the same adventures, that are traditionally associated, in popular fiction, with aristocrats and business tycoons. These delightful, daring men of the kitchen sink save the police the trouble of rescuing one of their own from the grip of crime. The story begins: "But we were talking as only a group of practicing plumbers — including some of the biggest men in the profession — would talk." "Buggam Grange: A Good Old Ghost Story" is a parody that begins with consummate style as the narrator describes how night was coming on "as the vehicle in which I was contained entered upon the long and gloomy avenue that leads to Buggam Grange."

The success of *Winsome Winnie* was a bright spot in a difficult period. Leacock was hard-pressed to maintain the two sides of his writing activity, humor and serious economic essays. Demands for both — along with invitations to deliver lectures — mounted during the years immediately after the war. During the winter of 1919 and the spring of 1920, soon after the periodical versions of *The Unsolved Riddle of Social Justice* appeared in the *New York Times*, the owner of the New York *Sun*, Frank Munsey, approached the owner of *Maclean's*, Colonel J.B. Maclean, about the suitability of Leacock as a writer for his newspaper, especially on economic and social subjects. During World War I, several essays by Leacock had appeared in *Maclean's*, including "The Woman Question," "Let Us Learn to Speak Russion" (a prerevolution forecast that Russia would emerge as an important world power after the war) and "Is Permanent Peace Possible?" Colonel Maclean's first report to Munsey was mixed: "As an economist . . . he is rather flat, heavy, but I believe he would adjust himself under the tuition of men like Wardman and Mitchell to the brilliant style of the Sun." After several months of gathering information on Leacock and attempting unsuccessfully to draw the author into the discussion, Maclean wrote to Munsey: "He is not dependable in work or correspondence. We have to write and telegraph several times to get a copy of promised articles." (Existing correspondence from this period shows that Leacock had many periodical commitments. He was sometimes late in delivering his copy, and he was having great difficulty finding time to do the work necessary to accept some promising opportunities that were offered to him.) Munsey also heard from *Maclean's* regional editor in Montreal that "as an economic writer, there is a good deal of difference of opinion. Some like him; others do not. There seems a fairly general opinion that he tends to be rather dry, and if he wanders off what might be called 'strict' economics, he is inclined to be rather radical in his views." Munsey was not discouraged altogether by these reports. He had heard Leacock speak at New York City dinners. One dinner honored novelist John Galsworthy; at another, Munsey had received the Legion of Honor from the French ambassador to the United States. Munsey invited Leacock to visit him in New York at his first opportunity. Leacock agreed to do so but wrote, "I am afraid that as far as doing any writing goes, I have at present more than I can manage." Clearly Leacock was aware that he had made too many commitments. Leacock turned down the chance to become part of the *Sun*'s brilliant stable of serious, penetrating wits, which included writers such as Don Marquis, among others. In 1921 *Collier's Magazine*, one of Leacock's best outlets in the United States during the 1920s, asked him to write a series of long articles on current economic conditions. Although Leacock responded with a proposal for three features, he never submitted finished articles; two years later, the magazine's editor was still trying to get confirmation through his agent that Leacock would eventually write such a series. Although he continued to publish in *Collier's*, Leacock did not produce this series.

The success of *Winsome Winnie* did not end the distracting process of negotiating with publishers for Leacock. During the early 1920s, John Lane was attempting to sell the American branch of the Bodley Head, called the John Lane Company, and in his letters to Leacock he argued that the size of the humorist's American royalties were hurting his chances at selling.

I said that the fact that you were paid a 20% royalty in America caused the publishers I have been in negotiation with to remark that although I give such importance to your name I must be losing on every copy of your books sold, which is quite true, or was true until you arranged with Mr. Jones [J. Jefferson Jones, Lane's New York editor and a yearly summer guest in Old Brewery Bay] to accept a 15% royalty on all copies sold after 5,000 of *Winsome Winnie.*

Lane said that Leacock's audience, although strong, was somewhat elite and selective because "[Leacock's] books are not made up of sentimental trash which the great public here swallows by the million. In fact, you thrust your rapier at them all the time, and you guy all the things they stand for." The American firms that considered buying John Lane's business noticed that Leacock's recent books generally were not the best-sellers his earlier titles had been and continued to be. Finally, Lane warned that copyright protection was not perfect in the United States. This was especially true for Leacock's early books, *Literary Lapses, Nonsense Novels* and *Sunshine Sketches*, which had not been printed for sale in the United States but had been manufactured in Britain and then imported.

Although some of this trouble was smoothed over by the success of *Winsome Winnie*, Leacock began taking his own steps to improve the management of his periodical work and books in the United States and England. He engaged agents in both countries. He was soon dissatisfied with his British representative and changed to another. His American agent, Paul Reynolds, remained with him for many years, although their relationship was sometimes strained, especially at the beginning, by Leacock's occasional efforts to sell to magazines he was well acquainted with on his own. Reynolds wrote repeatedly to complain that this was damaging his work; he would call periodicals only to find that they were in direct contact with the author. In the fall of 1921, as the tour of Britain approached, Leacock was pressed from New York and London to produce a book which could be sold during the tour. He promised that the book was possible, but by the summer was forced to say that it was out of the question. As an alternative means of benefiting from the publicity of the tour, John Lane arranged to reprint six of Leacock's early books; he also prepared in England a deluxe edition of *Nonsense Novels*, illustrated by John Kettelwell. The economics of this project required Leacock to agree to a reduced royalty on the book. While Leacock was in Britain, John Lane was in New York attempting to complete the sale of his company. Leacock met several times with the Bodley Head's directors and editors while he was in London. Letters to him from the New York and London offices indicate that he had seriously begun to consider changing publishers. Writing from New York, Lane cited statistics of Leacock's poor recent sales and suggested that the quality of most of his latest work would not long maintain his reputation. But he promised continued service if Leacock would resist the temptation of large advances offered by other firms. Lane's people in London were evidently stung by Leacock's many complaints about his recent dealings with the firm. After one meeting with Leacock, director B.W. Willett wrote:

> I gathered from your general conversation and attitude at our interview that our rivals in the trade, such as literary agents and others, had been pretty busy poisoning your mind against us as a firm. Might I suggest that if you want to make enquiries about us — which, of course, you are perfectly justified in doing — you should go not to people who are prejudiced against us, either as rivals or for other reasons, but to unprejudiced people in the trade, such as booksellers. I do not believe that there is any publishing firm in England who could have worked up your books in the way that we have done in the last ten years.

Lane and his editors urged Leacock to remember that his published books would remain with Lane if Leacock changed publishers; a new firm would not be interested in promoting the old books. Lane would continue to build sales for all his books as each new one appeared. In the end, Leacock remained with John Lane's Bodley Head in England and Dodd, Mead and Company, which bought the John Lane Company. Dodd, Mead asked him for long-term contractual commitments for several books at a time, but Leacock consistently refused. He courted and entertained serious offers from such firms as

Harper Brothers and Doubleday Doran, but he did not change publishers for his humorous works.

Another disappointment for Leacock in 1921 was his inability to finance the construction of a new house in Old Brewery Bay. During the ten years from the land's purchase until the end of World War I, the original "cook house" had grown steadily, if irregularly. In 1919 Leacock and Beatrix arranged for the construction of the boathouse, the upper story of which became Leacock's sanctuary and prime writing space, and for renovations to the existing cottage, but their real goal was a new house. In July, 1921 Leacock wrote to his friend Alfred Chapman, an architect, who had already begun to plan the building, that he was forced to delay.

> I am sorry to say that I am finding far more difficulty with the financing of my house than I had expected. I knew of course the whole cost as 20,000 at least. In going over my stocks I find that owing to the depression I must sell at least 25,000 of my holdings . . . to realize this. I fear this goes back beyond housedom.

The depression to which this note referred was a widespread economic problem of the early 1920s in North America and in Europe. Leacock mentioned to Chapman that his brother George advised him that to sell the stocks would be disadvantageous because they would eventually return to full value, and that money spent at the time would buy less than the same amount spent later, under improved economic conditions. Chapman agreed, saying that the house would not be in use until the following summer in any case. When 1922 arrived, however, Leacock felt he had to decide to postpone the building again.

This was despite the fact that 1921 was his most successful year in financial terms; his income was more than twenty thousand dollars. He had been forced to refuse new projects and to leave a humor book unfinished because he spent much of the year lecturing. Lured by the promise of high fees, Leacock planned his tour of Great Britain for the fall of 1921; in the spring, he traveled extensively in the United States. As soon as the school term was over, he began a very rapid tour of the northeastern states. Each speech paid three hundred or three hundred fifty dollars. Leacock spoke in Boston and An-dover, Massachusetts; Lancaster, New Hampshire; Cleveland and Toledo, Ohio; Chicago and Evanston, Illinois; Milwaukee, Wisconsin; St. Louis, Missouri; Burlington, Iowa; and Louisville, Kentucky. The trip began with an appearance in New York at the city's Graduate Society of McGill. The tour agent was the Coit Lyceum Bureau of Boston and Cleveland, which arranged, among other appearances, a speech in Toledo for the Jewish Men's Club and one in Cleveland for the Adventuring Club. Also in 1921, the revised edition of Leacock's most successful book, *Elements of Political Science*, was published. It gave new life to the durable college text, which was due for a revision in the postwar years. Although Leacock was forced to turn down many offers for articles and speaking engagements, he wrote many articles during the years 1919 to 1921, including several for the *New York Times, Collier's* ("Is Disarmament Possible" and "Painless Tax") and *Maclean's*, despite Colonel Maclean's apparent impatience with him. In addition, he spoke on many of his school holidays at functions in the United States and Canada (for example, he spoke at New York's Pilgrim Club for the Lowell Centenary). By 1923, Leacock's earnings had reached forty thousand dollars, but work on the new Orillia house did not begin until 1928. By then, his income had gone down and would never reach the forty-thousand-dollar level again.

During the summer of 1921, Leacock was visited in Orillia by Professor William Caldwell, whose series, "Impressions of Ontario," ran in *Canadian Magazine* for several issues in 1922. Caldwell provided a delightful glimpse of Leacock in the midst of his first whirlwind year as a popular lecturer.

There was Leacock bursting into the hotel and shouting in his loud voice towards the desk: "Is Professor Caldwell here; I want him at once. His room is off, do you hear, cost or no cost, say what you like or say what he likes, he is coming out to me till over Monday and I will attend to everything." I mention all this as characteristic of the man either in his ordinary daily life or in his play, for Leacock has all the insouciance and all the impulsiveness, all the abandon of the creative artist, or the child of nature — a veritable Playboy of the Western World. Characteristic, too, was his summer get up, half covered as he was by a hastily thrown on winter overcoat over his semi-boating or semi-lounging outfit, an

193

ill-fitting and bedraggled crushed and rain-softened canvas hat and an equally sloppy clay-covered and mud-covered pair of white duck trousers that had once been new and fashionable. The whole bohemian effect was in the most delightful contrast to the fairly opulent car outside the door (no country doctor's or country minister's Ford for Leacock) earned by his own pen, and the superior, easy, commanding manner with which he bossed the whole hotel staff and hailed half a dozen people at the same time that he was shouting for me.

The year this impression was written, Leacock had bought and insured a one-year-old McLaughlin touring car. Caldwell had hoped to learn how Leacock composed; his only real conclusion was that "Leacock has simply to get worked up now and then to the boiling point, and then dash home to that upper room and work off his steam." The dashing-home part of the formula was drawn from Caldwell's personal experience at being driven at top speed along the country roads near Orillia to see Leacock's favorite fishing spots, boating areas and the homes of friends. According to Caldwell, Leacock refused to interrupt his summer holidays with lecturing or university work but wrote daily and received a constant flow of mail and visitors from the outside world, many of them "the New York and London editors who are exploiting him." Leacock's mail includes a note from J. Jefferson Jones, the Lane Company editor who had given him trouble over *Winsome Winnie*, to say regretfully that he would not be able to spend his customary holiday in Old Brewery Bay in 1921. Caldwell captured Leacock the gardener who worked "just as long as he feels like it and no longer." Much of the work was in the hands of Leacock's long-time assistant in caring for the grounds, Bill Jones, a retired army private. The charming picture of a man and his gardener provided in later years by Leacock, who portrays the man as taking credit in his conversation for the hours of shoveling, planting and harvesting done by his assistant, seems to have been drawn from life. An ardent gardener, Leacock was forever starting schemes for raising vegetables to sell at the market and always finding that other activities pulled him away from finishing the work, which was left to Jones and others, although the humorist still referred to it as his own. He took pride in the menus for the Orillia house being made up largely of the produce of the property. Caldwell concluded by wishing that Leacock "would make the effort somehow to put together the human nature that he knows so well with the political economy and the political science that he teaches at McGill." This was especially important in the postwar arena, he felt, since the world required a new social vision.

Caldwell shows Leacock in his country place. It is rarer to catch a glimpse of him at home in Montreal, but his son's pediatrician, Doctor Alton Goldbloom, wrote in his memoirs about his long-time friend, Stephen Leacock. The doctor describes him as the courtly, sophisticated presiding genius of many of the most memorable gatherings of professional and literary men he had ever attended. For Leacock, even during the casual summer months, dinner was a formal occasion, for which men were expected to wear black tie. Even if his own tie was inclined to come undone, his suit was impeccable. The maids at the Côte-des-Neiges house wore smart uniforms and spoke French. A former student tells a story of Leacock arriving late for a meeting at the Political Economy Club wearing his black tie in its customary imperfect condition. Everyone else was dressed in the formal wear that he required of them for club functions, but when Leacock removed his rain coat, he was wearing a loud check suit rather than a dinner jacket. Interrupted while dressing for the meeting, Leacock had never finished changing his clothes and had finally rushed to the meeting dressed as he was.

Another formal occasion in the fall of 1921 was a private dinner with friends Murray Gibbon, B.K. Sandwell and Pelham Edgar. Gibbon was an author and the future publicity director of the Canadian Pacific Railway. Sandwell was Leacock's friend and former student at Upper Canada College. Edgar, at this time a prominent professor of English at the University of Toronto's Victoria College, had been Leacock's colleague at Upper Canada College; in 1919, Leacock had appeared in Toronto at a fund-raising program arranged by a member of Edgar's family. The four authors were discussing a recent move to change Canadian copyright law. Some effort had been made to formulate an international copyright law that would end the piracy, common on both sides of the Atlantic, of works by popular authors in Great Britain and North America. A Canadian publisher had presented to Parliament a recommendation to change the country's law to benefit the native publishing industry. The recommendation proposed that works by Canadian authors would be protected by copyright only if they were printed in a Canadian edition. Thus, books by a Canadian author produced in New York or London could be reprinted in Canada; no payment would go to the author. This effort to foster the publishing industry hit directly at the livelihood of the country's authors, and the four friends determined to organize a meeting of the country's writers to protest the proposed legislation. The meeting was held and was the origin of the Canadian Authors' Association. Leacock was unable to attend because of his British tour. More than one hundred writers replied to their invitations to say they would come. Among those at the 7 December meeting in Montreal were novelists Frank Packard and "Ralph Connor" and poet Bliss Carman. The meeting resulted in the permanent formation of the Canadian Authors' Association, the country's first national writers' organization, which continues to operate. Gibbon was its first president and Sandwell its first secretary. The governor-general's award program was initiated by the association and Lord Tweedsmuir and was at first administered by the association. Leacock was an original subscribing member and remained active until the early 1930s. In 1937 he won the governor-general's award for *My Discovery of the West*.

The story of Leacock's triumphant British tour is told in the first chapter of this book. When he returned to Canada, the time and work pressures that had plagued him in 1921 continued. *My Discovery of England* was the first book he wrote for Dodd, Mead and Company in New York, and the editors there moved quickly from praising him as a great "adornment" to their list of authors to urging him to finish his book before public interest in his trip had died away completely. Leacock wrote back that responsibilities at the university were pressing him hard, but that he wished even more than they to have the book appear by 1 April.

In some measure, *My Discovery of England* corresponded to Professor Caldwell's hope that Leacock would combine his

196

humorous sympathy and his scholarly expertise to bring a new social vision to the world. *My Discovery of England* was at first somewhat disappointing to Dodd, Mead because it contained so many non-fiction essays on serious subjects and humorous pieces tied closely to social concerns, but the book was popular with Leacock fans. Among the many public questions addressed in the book were women's rights and prohibition, two issues that occupied a great deal of his attention throughout the 1920s. Both movements gained their first significant success in Canada during World War I, and he always associated them with the social upheaval the war had created.

Leacock wrote relatively little on the question of women's suffrage, although before the vote was given to women in Canada he published the essay, "The Woman Question," in *Maclean's* in 1915; it appeared in *Essays and Literary Studies* in 1916. Although the article begins lightly, in the manner of one of the scenes of club conversation in *Further Foolishness*, it is in fact a very serious argument on the question of the social roles proper to women. Leacock opens with a conversation he overhears; two women are agreeing that if they had the vote, there would have been no war. Doubting this claim, Leacock does not challenge seriously the right to vote. But he challenges the fundamental principle on which the extension of suffrage would rest: that men and women are equal. By 1920, women could vote in federal elections and in provincial elections except in Quebec; the first woman member of parliament, Agnes Macphail, was elected in 1921. "Women need not more freedom but less," Leacock opined, in opposition to the current of the times. "Social policy should proceed from the fundamental truth that women are and must be dependent." His principal argument was that society needed to have women in the roles of wives and mothers. He did not refrain, however, from suggesting that women were not suited to the professional activities of many important jobs: "The only trouble is that they can't do it," he explained. Just as he would later do in *The Unsolved Riddle of Social Justice*, Leacock urged that society would treat its women fairly only if it provided sufficient financial support for them without requiring them to work. This would free women to devote themselves to child-rearing. Mechanical inventions had freed women from much housework, he admitted, but inventions could not free them from their duties as mothers: "No man ever said his prayers at the knees of a vacuum cleaner." Society was criminally liable for expecting young women to support themselves before marriage in a world without jobs suitable for them, and it was "the most absurd mockery of freedom ever devised" that a widow would be left to provide for herself and young children after her husband's death. When women persisted in seeking social emancipation in education, in property ownership and even in matters of etiquette — smoking in public, for example, or frequenting bars — Leacock occasionally turned from his belief that women were seeking work unwillingly to snap that social ills were being created by these emancipated women. In *Humor: Its Theory and Technique* (1935) Leacock charges that when women turn away from their role as a sort of preserve for the purest moral principles, the result is the phenomenon of a literature filled with blasphemies and profanity.

Even more than the general question of women's place in society, the question of women's place in his classroom plagued Leacock. During World War I the numbers of women students increased sharply at McGill; when the war was over, the balance shifted slightly but women remained a large proportion of the college population. Invariably polite to his women students, Leacock continued until the end of his life to criticize what he saw as the follies of university education for women. In 1921 he wrote an article for *Collier's* called "We Are Teaching Women All Wrong," in which he said that women had been failing elementary physics at McGill for twenty-five years and it was time to take the subject away from them. He said that women could not reason or think, but they could argue. Women's strict lack of capacity for the university life was not his only complaint, or even his chief complaint. If women did have to attend school, they should study something that would be valuable to them in their future homes, such as nursing. He contended that preparation for a profession was wasted on women because eventually they married and then their training was of no use to society. Especially during the 1930s, he complained that valuable space in the country's universities should not be wasted training women who would never enter professions, while many deserving male students could find no place on campus. Co-eds came in for much of the scorn he aimed at all of the denizens, male and female alike, of the type of university developing in the early century; schools were moving away from the rigid classical curriculum of the 1800s. As well, campus activities were changing. In "Oxford as I See It" (*My Discovery of England*), Leacock confessed that the sight of female students at the august university had been upsetting to him; he worried that the male students must find it difficult to work. In many humor sketches, he portrayed his confusion at accounts of university life — many of them placed in the mouths of eager co-eds — that seemed to him proof that no valid work was being accomplished. He once addressed a McGill sorority on the subject of women college students, comparing the qualities of North American girls (who chewed tobacco) with those of British girls (who were addicted to gin) and finding little merit in either.

Leacock was fond of revealing the absurdities in the human condition; it is sometimes difficult to determine whether he is using his humor to expose an institution or group as wholly valueless or seeking to remedy flaws by exposing it to ridicule. The combination of Leacock's serious essays — like "The Women Question" and "Oxford as I See It" — and his many humorous portrayals of the empty-headed co-ed seems strong evidence that he sincerely wished to limit or end altogether higher education for women. Perhaps he was adamant precisely because he saw that a complete end was impossible, and therefore exaggerated his disapproval in an effort to secure whatever change he could. Leacock had said that he preferred "half-light" as exposing truth more clearly; in *The Garden of Folly* (1924), he said, "A half truth, like half a brick, is always more forcible as an argument than a whole one: it travels farther." His confidence that he could wield these half bricks without confusing his audience was evident, but some readers wished for something different. "When he argues about the woman question, he makes one wish that he would lay aside his facetiousness oftener," said one critic. Leacock was being asked to end the puzzlement the reader felt between serious arguments and light jibes that might or might not be intended as conveying a truth.

The question becomes even more complex when Leacock's private life is placed beside his public statements. His wife, Beatrix, devoted herself mostly to domestic concerns after marriage (although she helped Leacock with his work; for instance, she and Marion Sandwell had selected the stories in *Literary Lapses*). Beatrix was a well-educated woman who had contemplated a career. Leacock's mother was, by the standards of her age, a very well-educated woman; because of her determination Leacock received an education. But Leacock spoke of her as a hopeless teacher of her children, explaining that "she was only mother." Leacock's youngest sister, Dot (Rosamond), remained single for many years while she practiced medicince, first in Calgary and then as a distinguished pathologist at Toronto's Hospital for Sick Children. By all accounts Leacock was very close to her; he chose Dot as his son's godmother. He paid university tuition for his long-time secretary and niece, Barbara Nimmo (daughter of his sister Carrie), while she lived with him in Montreal. Barbara came to the household when his secretary Grace Reynolds left for further training. Although his own circle of professional and literary intimates admitted no women, he supported, at least on one occasion, a woman faculty member. Maude Grant, warden of the Royal College of Victoria, was fighting a proposal from Sir Edward Beatty to divert the college's endowment to other uses. Leacock approached Grant and told her, "I won't let them do anything bad to you, dear." Leacock's correspondence shows that he enthusiastically recommended at least one of his female students for admission to graduate studies in economics at the University of Chicago. Thus, he could make exceptions to his rule against education for women. But it seems that no amount of personal experience swayed him from the conviction that society's evolution was being turned in a poor direction by allowing women to study on the university level for professions of their own choosing.

Women in his classroom annoyed him, but prohibition made him furious; it made one of his favorite pastimes difficult and illegal. Prohibition was enacted in Canada as a conservation measure in the last years of World War I, but when the war ended all the provinces kept the law on the books. Even before the war, many towns had voted to be "dry," in much the way Mariposa had voted in *Sunshine Sketches*. Orillia — which was a hard-drinking town in the boom time of the lumber camps and had nineteen taverns — had become a stronghold of temperance opinion by the late nineteenth century. From World War I until the 1960s, it was one of the driest spots in Ontario. In *Sunshine Sketches* Leacock depicted the temperance campaign as a political trick to win votes. When the fictional election was over, his characters ignored the prohibition against alcohol, and eventually the law was dropped. Leacock was optimistic about the support anti-drinking campaigns could expect, but the story shows his essential approach in his long fight against prohibition. He claimed that hypocrisy and political manuevering lay behind any attempt to stop the sale of alcoholic beverages, and therefore he refused to accept the apparent judgment of his society that he should give them up. In *Further Foolishness* he staged a "temperance peace conference," and in *Frenzied Fiction* he presented a frightening vision of a dry Toronto. He depicts workers moving with dreadful efficiency from home to factories and back again; beneath the surface, however, he finds that the determination to drink succeeds despite the ban, as characters import liquor from Quebec and sell it in special brokerage firms. In *The Hohenzollerns in America* Leacock describes life in a postwar Germany beset by continuous revolutions. A principal German official, now ousted, is preparing, with delight, to return to his former job as a waiter in Toronto when Leacock tells him there is no more beer garden and no more beer. The official decides to stay in Germany and risk execution. There are worse things than death, he explains.

For the next fifteen years, Leacock's campaign continued unrelentingly in his humor collections. By 1927 all Canadian provinces except Prince Edward Island were selling alcoholic beverages in licensed stores, restaurants and taverns, but Leacock pressed the offensive until the prohibition amendment to the United States Constitution, passed in 1920, was repealed in 1933. According to a Toronto newspaper, the battle, for Leacock, was not personal but a matter of principle. In

1919 he wrote an account of the prohibition situation in North America for an English publication, the *National Review*; in 1921 he gave a lecture called "The Case Against Prohibition." He promised to "write articles against prohibition at any time for any paper for nothing." In later years, Leacock said he thought many people feared to speak out against prohibition because the forces supporting the law were attacking "the personal fortunes and political position of anyone who should dare to oppose them." The question also influenced Leacock's career as a lecturer. In 1922, Charles Schwab, the president of Bethlehem Steel, invited Leacock to speak at a dinner for Pennsylvania's two senators. Leacock had discussed the invitation with Colonel Maclean, but decided to turn down the engagement. Maclean explained to Schwab:

> It is utterly impossible for him to make an entertaining, mirth-provoking after-dinner talk to a prohibition gathering. I know that he has refused to speak at any such gathering anywhere in Canada where they have prohibition. Personally, he is a violent anti-prohibitionist.

Leacock's practice of carrying a flask of whiskey with him when he traveled led to at least two confrontations with United States customs officials. Once, he left his flask behind in his train compartment while visiting the club car. A customs officer found it and approached Leacock to say that the flask would be confiscated. Leacock replied he would not permit it and led the officer outside the train, where he took back the flask and emptied it. He was permitted to keep the flask. On another occasion, he was traveling to a lecture engagement in Buffalo, New York. Told by a border official that he could not enter the country with a flask of liquor, Leacock telegraphed the lecture's sponsors, "No hooch. No spooch." What arrangements were made to resolve the crisis is not known, but Leacock kept his appointment.

The fullest statement of his serious opposition to the prohibition movement was his 1919 article "The Tyranny of Prohibition." The vehemence of his attack on religious groups associated with the movement drew an angry response from British clergymen in letters to the public press, but Leacock persisted, in *My Discovery of England*, in praising Great Britain's opposition to prohibition. In "The Tyranny of Prohibition" he attributed the movement to hypocrites, fanatics, political opportunists and big business. Although he allowed that a handful of sincere individuals might believe that "they are doing the work of Christ on earth," he likened them to Torquemada and Philip of Spain in the damage they did in the name of good intentions. But he attributed the power of the prohibition drive to the "organized hypocrisy" practiced by politicians, who saw a cause that would win them votes, and to the unlimited dollars of business interests concerned to secure a sober, docile, reliable work force. Leacock claimed that there was no basis, in fact, for the charge that drunkenness was damaging family lives and incomes. Instead he drew a picture of "a sober industrious working man" whose evening pipe and a glass of ale turned his drudgery into a pleasant life for a brief moment. It was discrimination against the poor, he said, to prevent this single pleasure. Morality was used as an argument for prohibition, but Leacock objected that he did not need the law to tell him right and wrong. Laws against murder or robbery were used to reinforce the social conscience of the community; the law against drinking, on the contrary, left him torn between the law and his own convictions. He could not agree with the restrictions and would not obey them. He went out of his way to convey publicly that he was not abiding by prohibition laws. Once, his truck was cited for traveling without proper safety lights; Leacock paid the fine but noted on the requisite form, which inquired, "Temperate or intemperate?" that "I drink every day." This occurred in 1919, when Ontario had stringent laws on the sale and consumption of alcoholic beverages.

Was this intense propaganda truly a matter of principle? Or was it special pleading? By Leacock's own testimony and that of many friends and colleagues, he drank regularly. Visiting friends were invariably greeted with the offer of a drink to spare them the worry that the house might be "temperance." At the height of prohibition, Leacock kept his bar well-stocked; as he remarked, the flow of liquor was never completely stopped. Pharmacists did a brisk business with prescriptions for alcoholic beverages throughout the most stringent period of regulation. Everyone — rich people, criminals, and ordinary citizens — found ways to get a supply. In a popular song of the period, the stationmaster telephones a homeowner to tell him, "There's a box of books here for you, Bill, / And it's leakin' all over the station." Leacock drank beer and wine, but his favorite drink was Scotch. Drinking was a regular part of his social gatherings, club meetings and dinner parties. Stories, especially from McGill associates, are repeated of memorable occasions when Leacock performed eccentrically after drinking: the night he passed out Jehovah's Witnesses leaflets in the street; the night he unrolled a roll of toilet paper, from which he claimed to be reading a lengthy extemporized poem in free verse; the night he supposedly called out from the bushes to ask a student for an arm home because he was having difficulty walking. For all the years of his drinking, however, there is not one recorded instance of an ugly scene, public nuisance, time lost from work or other signal difficulty associated with excessive drinking. Leacock commented, in "The Tyranny of Prohibition," that he knew judges, lawyers, professors, doctors, clergymen and many other professional people who drank, but this did not translate into drunken judges on the bench or professors coming to class incapacitated by drink. He concluded that drinking did not lead inevitably to excess and was therefore a matter of private discretion. He was able to practice the moderation and control he preached. At the same time, something about the issue drew from Leacock arguments whose doubtful wisdom made his cause weaker rather than stronger. His wholesale dismissal of his opponents as fanatics and opportunists who only sought to impose temperance on others might not be totally supported by fact, but when he asserts that drunkenness was not a serious social problem, he clearly has gone far astray. His own childhood was marked by the effects of his father's drinking — his father was ineffectual and abused his mother. Perhaps the charge that people could not control their consumption of alcohol touched too close to home. Determined that he would never be like his father, Leacock refused to admit that some people were not self-disciplined. He would have been acknowledging a sad truth of his own family.

In *The Unsolved Riddle of Social Justice* (1920) Leacock

argued that society had an obligation to provide its people — able-bodied men and women alike — with meaningful work and guaranteed financial support for the medical care and education of their children. In discussing issues like the debt Canada owed to its war veterans and the elimination of poverty, Leacock could vehemently protest the plight of the working man who was forever cut off from the dignity and pleasures of life enjoyed by the rich. He could, moreover, demand worthy work for women as well as men. It is curious to contrast these broad economic and social views with his opinions expressed on the specific issues of prohibition and women's rights. When writing on women's rights, he did not offer to champion women's search for meaningful, productive work; on the contrary, he urged women to be satisfied with domestic roles. When writing about prohibition, he presented a picture of the eternally downtrodden worker to whom society owes not a better job, but the right to drink after work as the only solace for his lowly status. Leacock betrays on these two issues an unwillingness to entertain new ideas that would require him to sacrifice his habits and preferences for the good of the community. Stung by appeals to his social conscience, an area in which he might pardonably claim some distinction, Leacock could display a most unreasonable tenacity in argument to shield himself from the thought that his views on these issues might be incorrect and even harmful to others.

In 1923, Leacock published *Over the Footlights*, a group of parodies of popular drama. The pieces appeared first in *Harper's*, and were based on one of Leacock's lectures in Great Britain, "Drama as I See It." Like *Frenzied Fiction*, the lecture presented criticisms illustrated by Leacock's own satirical dramatic scenes. Negotiations for publication of *Over the Footlights* were complicated by Leacock's problems with his agents and publishers, Dodd, Mead. He was approached by several other publishers and periodical syndicates that wished to publish future work. He refused to give Dodd, Mead the three-book contract they requested, but did place *Over the Footlights* with them. The book indicates Leacock's growing interest in writing for the stage. Since the 1915 production of "Behind the Beyond," he had been concerned to obtain the dramatic and movie rights to his work in contracts. This was a point of contention with John Lane's representatives during his meetings in London. B.W. Willett, who worked for the Lane Company, claimed that Lane had left these rights available to Leacock and had even gone to the trouble, at a financial cost and with no return, of stopping illegal productions of "Behind the Beyond" in Australia and New Zealand. In later years Leacock expressed interest in writing for the stage and screen and permitting dramatic adaptations of his works by other writers. Ten of the twenty-two pieces in *Over the Footlights* are play scripts with brief introductory remarks. There are many types, for example, "Napolean at Home" (historical drama), "Cast Up by the Sea" (love on a tiny Pacific island among victims of shipwreck), and "Dead Men's Gold" (a western treasure hunt). A modern romance is called "The Soul Call," a "piffle play" in which well-to-do men and women "analyze themselves" as their souls outgrow their bodies. In the romance, Leacock makes some wry observations about the state of modern theater. "The Soul Call" is the sort of play, he said, that you hear about before you see it; its complex romantic quadrangle is the topic of heated argument at every social gathering. Should Lionel and Helga leave their spouses in pursuit of "Bergsonian illusionism"? Leacock said that the craft of acting had deteriorated to the point where directors no longer looked for skill, but were concerned only with appearance. "When they want a man to act as a butler, they don't advertise for actors — they advertise for butlers." The concept of theater as a created illusion to entertain and instruct is replaced by "realistic" revelations of personal life; the theater patrons are not audiences but peeping toms.

The twelve non-dramatic pieces in *Over the Footlights* include some charming and memorable sketches, for example, "My Affair with My Landlord," "My Lost Dollar" and "Personal Experiments with the Black Bass." In "Roughing It in the Bush," Leacock begins by criticizing the outdoor pretensions of his friends and ends by talking about his experiences. His companions for the adventure include his brother George. Against their expressed preferences, George's luxurious automobile conveys them into the wilderness; George wanted to pack in on burros and Leacock thought perhaps a wild moose might be useful. Their meals were taken at a local inn. In general, they adapted splendidly to the rugged demands of the outdoors. In a number of his articles, Leacock expresses concern that some of the most popular new features of life are making life worse rather than better. He wrote about the radio: "One more item has been added to the growing list of things I don't understand." As a youth Leacock tilted at institutions that indifferently abused unwilling victims — boarding houses, banks and so on. Now he feels a more mature sorrow that life is moving away from him. In "The Approach of the Comet," he laments that there is more information in the hands of normal people than they can possibly use; moreover, they don't understand it and aren't equipped to act on it. When a scientist informs him that a comet is on a collision course with earth, Leacock is thoroughly alarmed. Unable to interest the scientist in the humane question of mankind's survival after the event, he is reassured by another acquaintance, who explains that the collision will only be with the comet's tail. But alarm rises again when he hears a schoolchild ask his mother about the report, and she replies that the comet will destroy the world over the weekend and there is nothing to be done about it.

Over the Footlights was well received, although *Saturday Review* (which had criticized *The Hohenzollerns in America*) had harsh words for the collection: "Mr. Leacock is the contemptuous philosopher — he derides. When Mr. Leacock's vein runs thin — it does through most of *Over the Footlights* — he can provide only machine-made stuff." A second book from Leacock in 1923, *College Days*, received little critical attention, and deserved little. The book is an assemblage of occasional verses written primarily for campus events at the University of Toronto and at McGill; the verses suggest the genial occasions during his career at which Leacock had presented remarks: graduations, retirements and many others. The earliest piece in the book is from 1902 and was written for a short-lived McGill publication. Many of the verses date from the war years. Leacock said the book had "an uncommercial and ideal character," but with few exceptions the verses are too limited in reference and too slight to warrant reprinting. Perhaps Leacock believed in the quality of the work, or perhaps he simply thought it was appropriate to his life as a college professor and member of the university community that his writing for university occasions should be published. In comparison to his essays and humorous sketches on education in many other books, *College Days* is a disappointment. *Too Much College*, published in 1940, is weighted with many serious topics — the teaching of psychology, the proper instruction of a foreign language, etc. — and remains a more valuable fruit of his college experiences than this 1923 collection.

College Days appeared at nearly the same time as *Over the Footlights*. Fan mail reinforced the message of his popularity, as did the appearance of a book about him, combining biography with a brief anthology of his works, by fellow Ontario humorist Peter McArthur. Leacock was successful, but success was a mixed blessing. He welcomed many of these signs of approval and attention, but not so welcome were the prying questions of reporters or the reemergence of the criticisms made by John Lane in 1921 that he was hurting himself by working too fast and too carelessly. He apparently enjoyed his fan mail, and although more letters to him than responses from him are preserved, testimony survives to the kindliness with which he regarded his readers. In 1920 he responded to a request for a piece of manuscript from a Mr. Saunders:

> For many years I have kept manuscripts with the feeling that sooner or later a request such as yours must come. I have at present about two barrelsful. The supply far exceeds the demand. It is with great pleasure I send you a "chunk" of my writing.

What he sent was five handwritten pages of the draft of an article about the variation between English as taught in university classes and English as used by distinguished authors. The article, "English as She Is Taught at College," appeared in *College Days*. Fan letters were filled with compliments, which were often phrased in terms intended to be facetious, in honor of the author's style. A young girl from Cape Breton Island sent Leacock a watch case she had made, embroidered with a blue flower and green, yellow and pink edging, which is still preserved in his files in Old Brewery Bay; she thanked him for "a pretty Novel which I Sure Enjoyed Reading." Another fan who addressed him by letter was explorer Vilhjalmur

Stefansson, who called himself "an extravagant admirer of your humorous writings." Stefansson thanks Leacock for saying "pleasant things about my work."

Peter McArthur's book *Stephen Leacock* (1923) reprinted some of Leacock's work, and included a biographical sketch and a critical appraisal of Leacock's work. The biographical account is not especially detailed (McArthur admitted that he limited his investigations largely to what Leacock had written about his early life). McArthur did not mention that his own experiences were intertwined with Leacock's to some extent, although he recalled that University of Toronto students had appreciated Leacock's wit long before it was widely published. McArthur was briefly a student at the university during the same period as Leacock. Later — a much more important connection — he was editor of the New York magazine *Truth* when it published many of Leacock's pieces in the 1890s. These pieces formed the core of *Literary Lapses* in 1910. McArthur claimed little personal acquaintance with Leacock, however, saying that he had only been introduced to him once while Leacock was playing billiards. The distance between the two Ontario humorists may be explained by McArthur's adopting, in 1908 — just when Leacock was moving toward prominence — a retired life at his rural childhood home near Appin, from which he published his own humor, largely in Toronto newspapers. McArthur did not think Leacock was a great satirist; he lacked the fierceness and the unrelenting nature of the best social critics, and he also seemed less interested in solving problems than in analyzing them. While defending Leacock from the charge that he was a "trifler" because he was gifted with humor, McArthur worried that Leacock was moving too fast to produce for "the publishers, syndicate managers and directors of lecture bureaus." He disapproved of Leacock's production of a second volume of nonsense novels, saying that Leacock was pressured to produce the most popular kind of work rather than develop and explore his potential. Touching only lightly on the man behind the comedy, McArthur said, "Possibly he finds forgetfulness himself in his outbursts of fun-making." He did not explain precisely what he thought might lie behind Leacock's putative search for forgetfulness, although it seems possible that he was referring simply to the undertone of sadness evident in some of the writings, even in the introduction to *Sunshine Sketches* (an account of Leacock's childhood years) and the clear sense of loss and nostalgia in the book's tone. McArthur may also have been thinking of the outrage he saw in Leacock's confrontation with the features of society he found deeply objectionable.

McArthur wondered whether Leacock's popularity was destroying the quality of his writing. It was a theme on which Leacock commented, although he was talking about O. Henry. Since 1916, when Leacock had written an article on O. Henry for the *New Republic*, Leacock had been warmly praising the American's comic gifts. O. Henry's death in 1910 had brought a flood of critical writing about him. Two of the pieces in *Essays and Literary Studies* lauded O. Henry extravagantly, and Leacock persisted, throughout his London visit in 1921, to discuss O. Henry's writings with at least as much vigor as he discussed his own. The short-story writer remained something of a cause with Leacock, but the criticism of O. Henry also evidently attracted his attention. In the *New Republic* he wrote that critics were unjust in judging O. Henry by the worst of his work rather than appreciating the best. O. Henry had been seduced in his last years, Leacock said, by promises of the first real financial success he had known, to write too quickly, but this did not remove the value of most of his work. The best proof of O. Henry's value, Leacock said, was the writer's popularity with the general public. The distinguished American critic William Trowbridge Larned responded to Leacock's article and questioned judgment by popularity. "The plain people have come to be a pest," he wrote. Larned said that popularity had been known to ruin an author. "As an old and fervent admirer of Stephen Leacock's humor long before the plain people and the plain people's editors found him out, I can only hope that he will never become really popular with us." Finally, he questioned Leacock's ability to understand the flow of critical opinion in the United States, which tended to raise up idols and then destroy them quickly. Larned suggests that Leacock's Canadian background might make it impossible for him to understand the United States. In the 1920s, the question of nationality, which formerly had seemed to recommend Leacock as of equal interest to both American and British readers, began to be mentioned as a reason Leacock sometimes failed to understand either.

Popularity became an increasingly sensitive issue as the 1920s went on. On the one hand, Leacock could claim that his wide readership proved the value of his work, and this thought could buffer him against critical cavils; on the other hand, he reacted with distaste to some of the claims made upon him by his popularity, especially the voracious demand for information about him. His 1924 collection, *The Garden of Folly*, was widely reviewed and received some negative comments: "Now and again one would like to weep at the spectacle of his dragging humor around by the scruff of the neck." British reviewers wished for something a bit more suited to their audiences, and the brief remarks on humor that opened the book were dismissed as the sort of rather sententious nullities that characterized many humorists' theories of their art. Some of the articles in the book are charming — a series of romances delivered in the style of advertisements, for example, and the serious investigation into the historical importance of beards. But the principal articles are too long and too thin.

The Garden of Folly presents a brief section called "Letters to the New Rulers of the World," including one called "To a Prohibitionist" and another called "To a Spiritualist," both favorite targets of Leacock's humorous attacks. The first letter is to the League of Nations. On behalf of a small town, Leacock presents the league with congratulations on the many important diplomatic successes it has achieved. Then Leacock requests some practical help on problems faced by the town. He discounted the power of the League to solve serious international crises. Here his humor attempted to express his political and social ideas, many of which seemed increasingly ineffectual during the 1920s, when the Liberal Party reigned uninterruptedly in Ottawa.

Leacock believed that in world affairs Canada should act through the British empire. He could expect little agreement from the Canadian government of the day under Prime Minister Mackenzie King, whose Liberal party had been elected in 1920 and would remain in power, with a few interruptions, until the end of World War II. King showed little interest in following up the initiatives of Conservative Prime Minister Robert Borden and his successor, Arthur Meighen, to strengthen Canada's independent role within the changing imperial community as it had begun to develop during World War I. But King was not concerned, either, with demonstrating a nonimperial international role in the League of Nations. His government concentrated on Canada's internal economic problems and led the country into partnership with the United States, whose growing investments in Canada during the 1920s helped bring a gradual improvement from the postwar depression. Leacock found himself a rather forlorn voice on behalf of strong imperial ties, an ideal he continued to champion. General questions of politics and economics competed for time with his academic work, his humor writing and his campaign against prohibition. Worries that his career would be difficult to sustain plagued him increasingly. But the worst of the troubles of the 1920s were yet to come, as serious illness struck both his wife and his son.

Chapter Eleven

Family Sorrows

STEPHEN Leacock once said that if O. Henry's stories weren't true, they should be. In an essay about Charles Dickens entitled "Fiction and Reality," Leacock explored the borderline, in humorous writing, between fancy and fact. The Dickensian character "types" dismissed by some critics as exaggerated to the point of irrelevance were, Leacock maintained, insightful penetrations into the essence of human behavior. Dickens' selection of descriptive detail faithfully rendered the quirks and unconscious mannerisms of people, while revealing their depths. In humorists he admired, Leacock saw no clear boundary between fiction and reality; instead, he said, there was a deliberate blurring of the distinction in service of a higher truth. The humorist imaginatively alters his observations of human conduct to illuminate more faithfully the true significance of life. In addition, he draws on his own experience. Leacock was an observer, but he was also a worker, a family man and a citizen. His early humor was presented often through the voice of a first-person narrator, a sensitive young individual alive to his weaknesses and yet prone, when pressed, to strike out boldly for his own opinions against all authorities. This narrator's experiences as a boarder, a reader of popular fiction or a patron of a local laundry have some links with Leacock's experiences, but the narrator is clearly not Leacock. As the years pass and Leacock's readers identify the author with his work, Leacock is scrutinized for the secrets of his success and finds himself more and more in the public eye. As a consequence, his humor changes. The speaking voice becomes more closely Leacock's own. But when Leacock tells us most directly about himself, there are exaggerations — perhaps examples of that truthful fiction he praised in the works of O. Henry and Dickens. There are also omissions, certain territories of his life he chose not to reveal in interviews or in his writing. Perhaps if he had finished *The Boy I Left Behind Me,* Leacock would have provided information and insights on these subjects. In the chapters that were written, though, he chose to avoid many unhappy aspects of his childhood.

His family life with wife Beatrix and son Stephen (nick-named "Stevie") was perhaps the subject most closed from public view. By comparison, his brother George appears frequently as a reference point in interviews and as a character in humorous sketches; he is the moving spirit behind *Literary Lapses,* the companion of adventures in the wilderness, the source of memorable stories and an arbiter of taste in the comic art. The happy letter announcing Stevie's birth to Agnes Leacock is one of the rare documents preserved in the Leacock papers that casts a direct light on the family. Even in other sources — memoirs, accounts of friends and so on — Leacock's most intimate connections, especially Beatrix, remain in the background. Perhaps this is because so much of Leacock's life was spent outside that family circle; observers are content with the teacher, the department head, the clubman, the author and the lecturer. The reticence Leacock displayed and inspired among those who knew and wrote about him continued unbroken throughout his life. It still stands between him and anyone attempting to understand the importance of his family to him. It is especially difficult to pierce this barrier in the late 1920s, when Beatrix died and Stevie was seriously ill.

During the 1924-5 school year, Leacock made two extensive tours of the United States and several brief trips. His fee had increased, for most lectures, to five hundred dollars. During the fall, he visited several college campuses in the Connecticut River Valley area. His standard lecture at the time was called "Heroines in Literature." (A member of the audience at Smith College recalled Leacock's description of one western heroine whose cowboy protector chivalrously leaves her in her tent and goes out to sleep on the cactus.) The theme of heroines is repeated in a number of humorous sketches from his books of this period, including "Abolishing the Heroine" from *Over the Footlights* and "Hunt for a Heroine" in *Short Circuits* (1928). Leacock addressed the fiftieth-anniversary convocation of the University of Iowa; his lecture was called "Education and

Democracy." In the spring, he toured the southern United States; the trip was such a success financially that his agent, Paul Reynolds, recommended arranging another one. He used the lectures he had given during his tour of Britain and presented some new ones on his favorite humorists, Charles Dickens, O. Henry and Mark Twain. His files of the lecture texts show that Leacock was working, during the trip, to perfect outlines and passages for the new speeches. During the 1930s, he published books on Twain and Dickens; at the time of the tour, he was collecting unpublished works of O. Henry for a possible edition.

Leacock first wrote about the woes of being interviewed in *My Discovery of England.* In *Winnowed Wisdom* (1926) and *Short Circuits* he continued to complain about the experience. It wasn't only being interviewed that bothered him; he didn't like reading interviews very much, either. The essays "International Amenities" and "New Lights from New Minds" (from *Winnowed Wisdom*) question the value of reporters' eager attempts to manufacture news out of the impressions provided by visiting celebrities. In the first essay, Leacock concocts an international incident out of the escalating insults American visitors make about Great Britain and British visitors make about America. Leacock's talk to the McGill women's group about the differing merits of American and British students is the basis, in part, for "International Amenities." In "New Lights from New Minds," Leacock suggests that the whole boring process would be brightened up if celebrities commented on fields other than their own: industrialists could assess universities, sports stars could judge architecture and so on. One of the sketches in the group called "Save Me from My Friends" (*Short Circuits*) presents an exasperating encounter between Leacock the visiting lecturer and a reporter who had not been to his speech but caught up with him at the train station for a summary. With a few leading questions, the reporter is able to provide extensive coverage of the address under the headline, "Thinks Aldermen Pack of Bums." One reporter interviewed Leacock during his 1925 tour of the United States. Years later, the reporter, John Archer Carter, published the story behind his own conversation with Leacock. Archer's comments illustrate Leacock's growing reserve towards the press, and his disarming kindness in making exceptions to his rules.

Carter was a reporter for the Richmond, Virginia *News-Leader*; he approached Leacock at the Hotel Jefferson. According to Carter, Leacock did not look much like a humorist. The "big man, with a large, longish face and a mass of greying hair parted on the side," looked like a "mortician or chief mourner." Leacock handed the reporter five sheets of hotel stationery covered with handwriting. It was the interview, he explained, written while he was waiting for Carter to arrive. The Leacock text ran:

> Professor Stephen Leacock, of Montreal, head of the Department of Economics at McGill University, who is lecturing this week at the University of Richmond, had a brief chat this morning with a representative of this journal.
>
> Dr. Leacock spoke in his characteristically humorous vein of his increasing difficulty in being interviewed by the press.
>
> "I have grown to have so many friends," he said, "in so many places and of such different ways of thinking that I can't say anything at all without losing some of them. For example, I hold very strong views on the Volstead Act, but I daren't say what they are. I'd like to tell you how beautifully the Quebec system of government control works, but I mustn't. I have strong views on Evolution and Fundamentalism. In fact I truly believe that all adherents of one side are soft in the head, but I won't say which. I either think that Mussolini is the hope of the world or the death knell of democracy. People who fly across the Atlantic are either damn fools or heroes. In fact, all my opinions are too violent for friendly intercourse.
>
> "But I am here on a mission which fortunately is not controversial at all. I am giving three lectures out at the university on the relation of the great humorists of the world to social progress. The lectures are to deal with Charles Dickens and Mark Twain, and O. Henry, with a hint here and there on the side that I am doing a little good myself. That's why I don't want to give an interview. Good-bye."

When Carter asked to step into the hotel to read the "interview," Leacock agreed. They were soon talking in a friendly way. Leacock readily allowed Carter to use a few of the stories from their conversation as the basis of a story to satisfy

Carter's editor. One of the anecdotes that interested Carter concerned Leacock's efforts to collect O. Henry manuscripts. An advertisement announcing his interest in unpublished material, along with a promise to pay for any material used, brought him an unexpected flood of stories; many of them, to Leacock's disgust, were obviously frauds. He confessed to Carter that he had angrily told one lady the story she had submitted had been written by O. Henry "after his brain had been removed." Leacock said he regretted doing it, but he had been very upset by the experience of drawing so many faked stories. Carter received his interview, but Leacock remained in control of the meeting, which was a discussion of his professional rather than personal activities.

Leacock returned home to Montreal after the southern states tours to find Beatrix in ill health. Leacock took Beatrix and Stevie to Nassau in the Bahamas in late December, and left them there to spend the winter months; the trip's chief purpose, however, was to give Stevie, not Beatrix, a change of climate. When she returned to Montreal, she gave up her customary round of university and social functions, but her condition was still not considered serious enough to consult a doctor. The family spent the summer of 1925 in Orillia as usual. It was hoped that the change of air and activities would improve her health. During the fall, however, she went to her doctor with one of her closest friends, Mrs. H.T. (Fitz) Shaw. In consultation with a visiting specialist, Blair Bell of Liverpool, the doctor diagnosed her condition as breast cancer. The condition was attributed, at the time, to a severe blow from a golf ball that had hit Beatrix during the summer of 1924 in Orillia. An operation failed to treat the disease, which was pronounced incurable. During the fall 1925 term, Leacock was frequently absent from classes. He visited Beatrix daily at Ross Memorial Hospital. Leacock would not admit that his wife's case was hopeless and decided to take Beatrix to England, to Doctor Bell, although Bell did not think Beatrix's condition was treatable. (Leacock knew of Bell through a former McGill professor of pathology, Doctor George Adami, who had been appointed vice-chancellor of Liverpool University in 1919. In response to Leacock's questions, he wrote that Bell's new lead treatment for cancer was achieving very good results.) Elizabeth Kimball, Leacock's niece, wrote in her book, *The Man in the Panama Hat*, that Beatrix did not want to go to England, but preferred to accept the findings of her Montreal doctors. Nevertheless, Leacock arranged the trip. He had help from his friend Sir Edward Beatty, president of the Canadian Pacific Railway and chancellor of McGill, who arranged to have a Canadian Pacific ship, scheduled to leave in two days, outfitted with a private infirmary and a staff of two nurses to care for Beatrix. Leacock and Beatrix, with Stevie and Beatrix's mother, Mrs. Kate Hamilton, set sail. Beatrix was admitted to Doctor Bell's private hospital but was never strong enough to begin treatments. She died on 15 December 1925, only a few months after the first diagnosis of her condition.

Among the many messages of sympathy that arrived was a telegram from Sir Arthur Currie, principal of McGill: "Courage, Stephen, we are all with you." After a memorial service at Liverpool's Saint Luke's Church, conducted by Doctor Adami's father-in-law, the body was cremated and taken back to Canada where, on 31 December, Beatrix was buried in Toronto's Saint James Cemetery. Leacock intended to move his wife's body to the Leacock burial plot at Saint George's Church near Sutton, but the change was never made. The funeral took place the day after Leacock's fifty-sixth birthday. Beatrix was forty-five at the time of her death.

Leacock returned to his classroom early in 1926, but it took almost two years before he reestablished the routine of work and amusement he had followed since Beatrix had helped him to publish his first humor collection, *Literary Lapses*, in 1910. There was no book in 1925, and *Winnowed Wisdom*, which appeared in 1926, drew largely on material written for magazines before his wife's illness had been diagnosed. When he did produce a new collection, *Short Circuits*, in 1928, its themes were a determined opposition to contemporary society and a strong nostalgia for the past. Late in life, he wrote that husbands who adored their wives proved it by ignoring them, showing temper and finding out only too late how much they wished to express their love. It has been suggested that this formulation depicted some regret that he had not been appreciative enough of Beatrix. While they were married, Beatrix remained in the background, but did this reflect any neglect of her on Leacock's part? His niece Elizabeth is the only person to refer to Leacock as being drawn to other women during his marriage. She says that Beatrix "forgave him readily for his occasional philanderings," but gives no further definition of what type of unfaithfulness, if any, had been involved. The most that other witnesses to the marriage say is that Beatrix seemed content to remain in a sphere of activities separate from her husband's — as a sportswoman, member of social clubs, hostess and homemaker — and that she may have felt somewhat left behind as Leacock's success brought more and more distinguished guests to her Montreal table and to the guest rooms at Old Brewery Bay.

There is not a great deal of evidence to contradict this view of Leacock as a careless, even neglectful, husband, whose self-absorption required of Beatrix the selflessness of a martyr. Family photographs are one clue, however, that Beatrix relished her share of Stephen's life and that their relationship was easy and equal. Pictures abound of Beatrix as a smiling part of social gatherings, outings on the lake and quiet meals with her family. Photos show her with Stephen, holding the new baby, sitting on benches on the crowded porch of the "cook house" and driving with the baby in a pony cart. She was not absent from the scenes of Leacock's life. After his usual departure for bed at ten o'clock, Beatrix was left to act as hostess for their guests. Professor William Caldwell speaks of her smooth management of the busy Old Brewery Bay household, with its constant flow of celebrities, local friends and family. She was Leacock's companion during the Rhodes tour in 1907 and during the British lecture tour in 1921. Leacock's secretary, Grace Reynolds, tells of packing Beatrix's evening gowns for the 1925 trip to Liverpool; Leacock said his wife would need them when he took her to the Riviera to recuperate after her treatment. The letter announcing the baby's birth and Agnes Leacock's diary entry of the event testify to Leacock's warmth of feeling for Beatrix and for the family he was building with her. Perhaps the style of marriage he preached is not to modern tastes, but his reverence for the woman's role as wife and mother — a center of moral values through her influence in the family — is also a praise of the role Beatrix filled in his life. Both Stephen and Beatrix were children of marriages that failed, and both clung to the family ties and social circles that had been theirs as young adults. Beatrix risked a good deal to marry Leacock when he was an aspiring student economist, but her marriage asked of her only one sacrifice: she could not pursue an independent career. Everything else that had composed her life before the wedding — amateur theatricals, charitable work, social gatherings among large circles of well-to-do friends and family — remained her province after the wedding. Although his frequent meetings with celebrities are well documented, Leacock spent most of his time, by choice, as a companion to his close neighbors, his relatives and the families of professional men with whom he was associated. Beatrix, with her prominent Toronto family background, was as comfortable in such society as her husband. It is not too much to suppose that Leacock's determination to stay in Canada — first when he returned to teach at McGill and, later, when his humor writing brought him international success — was due to the rewarding family life he shared with Beatrix.

One sorrow they shared, which remained with Leacock throughout his life, was the illness of their son. Within his first few years, Stevie's parents became concerned about his rate of growth. Elizabeth Kimball remembers him as a delicate child who wore glasses from the age of two or three. Concerned over his son's physical condition, Leacock consulted friends at the McGill Medical School and selected a thirty-six-year-old specialist, Doctor Alton Goldbloom. There is no precise diagnosis given in Doctor Goldbloom's published account of the case, although it is clear that Stevie's condition involved very slow growth. Letters from Leacock to the doctor refer frequently to Leacock's fears about his son and his hopes for the treatment: "I think he's growing. But I hate to measure him." Doctor Goldbloom, however, did measure him; in 1927, Stevie, at twelve, was three feet nine inches tall and weighed forty-four pounds seven ounces. Later, Leacock wrote, "You will be very much pleased to learn that Stevie at last shows a definite and apparently rapid growth." Doctor Goldbloom reported that his treatment was successful. All accounts agree, however, that Stevie did not grow to normal height. He was never more than about four feet tall. Goldbloom's claim of success suggests that the doctor feared the child might die. Leacock once introduced the doctor to his mother as "the most fortunate doctor in the world — his patients live." It has been suggested that concern over Stevie's condition prevented the Leacocks from trying to have more children. Care for his son continued to be an absorbing worry for Leacock until the end of his life. Convinced of the need to provide his son with financial support, despite Stevie's excellent school performance, Leacock used much of his earnings to establish a large trust fund for him. This preoccupation probably accounts for at least some of the projects he undertook, for high fees, towards the end of his life.

In *The Garden of Folly*, Leacock included a brief portrait of a physician he had known in childhood, Doctor Charles Thompson Noble, whom he admired greatly for his expertise and for his compassionate care. Throughout his many books, Leacock frequently challenged the course of medical knowledge. Sometimes he mocked at the pseudoscientific pronouncements of his acquaintances, who proposed to doctor themselves with "nitrogen" and "potash." Sometimes his target was the professional medical practitioner who lacked Doctor Noble's insightful support of the whole man, and instead offered his patients complex formulas of doubtful merit. On the basis of his writings alone, Leacock might have been judged a skeptic on the value of modern medicine, but his care for his wife and son shows a different side of his personality. Impatient only with doctors who could not provide a scientific miracle, Leacock demanded of modern medicine more than he allowed others to believe it might provide. Doctor Goldbloom saw in Leacock a mixture of "sheer brilliance intermingled with naiveté and medical credulity." Just as Leacock searched beyond Montreal for help for Beatrix, he persisted in consulting other physicians about his son even after engaging Doctor Goldbloom. In Liverpool, he visited a noted pediatrician and made a special trip to New York to meet a specialist in endocrinology. His wife's death led him to donate a thousand dollars to the McGill Medical School; the money was to be used to establish the lead cancer treatment. Leacock later offered to match, dollar for dollar, any funds raised for cancer research by McGill University. For many years, he made speeches to raise money for cancer research and the cause was frequently introduced by him into other speaking engagements. At a luncheon of the New York Cancer Committee, he proposed the death penalty for anyone proved to be tricking people with fraudulent treatments for the disease.

For two summers after Beatrix's death, Leacock did not stay in Old Brewery Bay. In 1926, he accepted an invitation from friend René du Roure to stay in Montreal, where du Roure operated a French summer school. In 1927, concern for Stevie's health led Doctor Goldbloom to suggest a trip somewhere. Leacock made plans with family friends, the Shaws, to travel to the French resort, Biarritz, for the summer months. H.T. Shaw was a Montreal businessman; his wife, Fitz, was the friend of Beatrix who had accompanied her to the doctor in 1925. They brought along their daughter, Peggy, and her governess, who was to care for Stevie also. Grace Reynolds was also a member of the party. (Reynolds had been hired in 1924 as Leacock's secretary; early in 1926, Leacock invited her to move into the house to help in caring for Stevie and running the household, along with her secretarial work.) The group arrived in London early in May. Unlike his other visits to London, this trip was strictly for pleasure. Apart from an article called "On Literature" for the London *Times* and a brief visit to his publishers, Leacock spent his time with the Shaws and Grace Reynolds; they visited tourist attractions and devoted evenings to the theater. The trip to Biarritz also included a stop in Paris and a visit to northern Spain. Leacock did not prepare a book for publication in 1927. The vacation signaled the importance of his friendship with the Shaws, especially Fitz Shaw, who remained close to him until his death. In his will, he left her five hundred books from his library and the copyright of his autobiography. The precise nature of their connection is not known. Fitz Shaw separated from her husband and was frequently in Leacock's company both in Montreal and in Orillia, where she had a house very near his; during his final illness in 1944, Fitz took a room in Toronto near his hospital to be able to visit him daily. A path connected the two houses. There was no secret made of their friendship. Fitz dined frequently with Leacock in public places in Montreal, including the University Club, and she was included in the many parties and dinners in Old Brewery Bay, and sometimes accompanied him on visits to his mother at Sutton. There was a rumor in Orillia that Leacock was having an affair, although an anecdote about the gossip shows that perhaps many people thought Fitz Shaw was not the other party involved. Leacock received a telegram that said, "I will be with you tonight. René." Talk soon filled the town that the name of Leacock's lover had been revealed as René. The telegram was from René du Roure.

No evidence or testimony exists to confirm or disprove the existence of a physical relationship between Leacock and Fitz. They did not marry, nor did Leacock install Fitz in his home as an official hostess. Instead, on his return from Biarritz, he arranged with his sister Carrie that her daughter, Barbara Ulrichsen, should come to stay with him in Montreal. Barbara would replace Grace Reynolds, who was leaving to attend university. Leacock offered to provide Barbara with college tuition at McGill and general financial support if she would work as his secretary and manage the household. She became his indispensable assistant in doing his research, preparing manuscripts and conducting business. As mistress of his household, she packed his flask when he was lecturing, provided female dinner companions for the bachelor professors of the department of economics and political science when they visited and sorted Leacock's correspondence. After Leacock's death, she helped prepare the book *Last Leaves*, which contains her illuminating memoir of Leacock's final years. Leacock chose to retain in his home a family atmosphere, and he chose someone from his family to help achieve it.

During the fall of 1927, Leacock was also arranging another piece of family business, the construction of the new house in Orillia, which he had planned with Beatrix in the early 1920s. The architect, Kenneth Noxon, built the nineteen-room house during the summer of 1928. By 1 September, Leacock was writing to thank him warmly for the house, which he said would be a joy to him until the end of his life. It was described, at the time, as possessing the "long lines and steep roof of French Canadian domestic architecture." Before work began on the new house, Leacock attempted to buy adjoining property to construct a trout stream on his land; when the project fell through, he leased a stream in Oro Township, south of Orillia, and stocked it with trout at a cost of fifteen thousand dollars. The new house, which was renovated after the author's death and is now called the Stephen Leacock Memorial Home, was built on a rise of ground about one hundred yards from the shore of Lake Couchiching; it stands farther away from the water's edge than did the original house and provides a better view of the lake. A porch runs nearly the full length of the front of the house, and at the back an enclosed sun porch looks out on a garden. The house included living room, dining room, guest bedrooms and a basement billiard room; Leacock's bedroom and study were in a separate wing, at the east end of the ground floor near the library. Fireplaces in the principal rooms and the bedrooms were the primary source of heat. (Although the family came to Orillia for the Christmas holidays, Leacock found the house uncomfortable the only winter he attempted to spend there.) A tennis court was built on the grounds, and the garden contains a sundial with two inscriptions: "Grow old along with me! The best is yet to be" (Browning) and "Brevas Horas — Longos Annos," Leacock's own ambiguous coinage, expressing a mixture of hope and sorrow.

After Beatrix's death, life at home revolved in large measure around Stevie. Leacock devoted hours to his son, whom he loved deeply. A student who was spending the evening at Leacock's Montreal house to consult with the professor was distracted from his work by Stevie, who was firing a peashooter at him from the doorway of his father's study. Leacock calmly asked his son to leave, which Stevie did, only to return a few minutes later. The scene was repeated several times, until at last Leacock suggested that the boy go downstairs into the hallway, where another student was waiting, and fire at him until it was his turn to come up to read. Stevie obeyed immediately. Life in Orillia, too, was organized in large measure for the boy's amusement. Elizabeth Kimball writes of being called to Old Brewery Bay, along with other cousins spending the summer in the area, to play with Stevie. One memorable occasion was a birthday party for the child. Leacock determined to hold the party on an unoccupied farm owned by his brother Charlie. According to Kimball, the hot August day combined with the desolate landscape to make an unpleasant day for her, but father and son appeared satisfied with the gathering. Stevie was a prominent player in the amateur theatricals popular in Old Brewery Bay. A playbill from New Year's Eve, 1929, announced the production, "Beauty and the Boss, or, The Sorrows of a Stenographer." The character of Mr. Jack Jackal, "He eats Stenographers," was played by Master Stevie Leacock. Other cast members included Peggie Shaw, who had been a member of the 1927 Biarritz party, and children from many prominent Orillia families, including some who had been models for characters in *Sunshine Sketches*. Two Tudhope daughters, whose industrialist father was the chief Liberal party supporter in Orillia, were among the "bevy of stenographinettes" seeking employment in the production, which was managed by Captain René du Roure. The playbill noted that guests were to come by sleigh because cars would not be able to negotiate the road from town. A sleigh service had been arranged through Anderson's Livery in Orillia.

Many of the memories, collected over the years, of Leacock at McGill date from the 1920s. A woman student in his 1925 class regretted that Beatrix's illness had kept him away so often, but admired the way he required students to follow up questions raised in class with independent library work, on which he invariably remembered to ask for a report. Some students valued Leacock's capacity in economics or political science less than the "humanity" he conveyed in his lessons. Leacock argued forcefully for his own conservative views — "And he, before Winston Churchill, saved the British Empire every Monday, Wednesday, and Friday at three o'clock in Room 20," according to colleague John Culliton — but he was sometimes cavalier in his treatment of campus regulations. Impatient with the rule that he must take attendance, he devised many techniques to avoid marking anyone absent. He sometimes delayed attendance taking until every student was present, no matter how late in the hour this event occurred; on another occasion, he called a student's name repeatedly without answer and finally asked if the boy had any friends, inviting anyone to respond for him. Leacock's academic gown was legendary. He seems to have worn the same one throughout his entire career, although it gradually degenerated into a tattered green affair with trailing bits of cloth that reached to the floor. In the early 1920s, one class presented him with a new gown, which he wore once, but then abandoned for his old favorite. One housemaid expressed her admiration for Leacock by telling Beatrix she wished she could kiss his gown. When told, Leacock promptly tore off one of the garment's ragged ends so that the housemaid could kiss it at home whenever she wished.

Leacock was generous with money for campus activities, including the Political Economy Club. He often paid to have students' theses and papers published. For the annual class book of 1925, Leacock wrote an article suggesting that McGill needed a literary magazine. During the fall of 1925, he was interviewed by the *McGill Daily* on the topic. Leacock said that there was an urgent need "for some kind of journal which will afford to the students a proper vehicle of literary expressions and a proper training ground for learning to write." Leacock, a founder of the *Daily*, said it was "nearly useless . . . as a vehicle of culture." Several other universities, smaller and less prestigious than McGill, had outstanding literary magazines, he reported. "It is quite plain to me that in this matter of a college journal we either lead the world or else come at the tail end of the procession. I think I know which we are doing." Leacock mentioned a campus controversy over a literary supplement to the *Daily*, and said that although he did not wish to become involved in a question properly reserved for the students, he did wish to recommend a new magazine. That fall, several students founded the *McGill Fortnightly Review*, which in its two years of publication was one of the country's most influential literary magazines. A number of important writers began their careers at the *Review*. The first issue, which appeared in November, included a front-page article by Leacock. With the article Leacock sent the editors a dollar, which he said was a "more substantial testimony" of his support for their cause. The founders of the *McGill Fortnightly Review* were poets A.J.M. Smith and F.R. Scott; for managing editor they chose an eighteen-year-old sophomore, Leon Edel, later the biographer of Henry

James. Smith had been the editor of the controversial literary supplement to the *Daily* in 1921; although Smith made the literary supplement a widely acclaimed national publication, the student council of McGill withdrew funding for it after one year. Edel remembers Leacock as an inspiration to campus writers. He supported the *McGill Fortnightly Review,* and also offered living proof that literary success was as close as one of their own teachers.

Leacock published only three books in the five years between 1925 and 1929: *Winnowed Wisdom* (1926), *Short Circuits* (1928) and *The Iron Man and the Tin Woman* (1929). Of the three, only *Winnowed Wisdom,* which was composed primarily of pieces written before his wife's illness, was a critical success. "After several volumes in which the humor was spread thin, Mr. Leacock is himself again," one review reported. According to the New York *World,* however, "Those who have not read Stephen Leacock in the past . . . will derive more pleasure from *Winnowed Wisdom* than those who will be setting it up against Mr. Leacock's old books." Several of his best-known sketches are in the book, including "How My Wife and I Built a House for $4.90," "How We Kept Mother's Day," "The Give and Take of Travel," and "The Laundry Problem." A great many of the pieces are commentaries on the newspapers, including "An Advance Cable Service," "The Children's Column," "Are We Fascinated with Crime?" and "The Next War." The book returns to several forms and topics Leacock had used before, including "outlines" of scholarly subjects, transcriptions of the outrageous debating style in the British House of Commons, the conduct of public meetings with the attendant sorrows of visiting speakers and the questionable economic policies of charitable organizations. To these themes, in most instances, he brought a refreshing new twist, as in his discussion of evolution, which answers criticism of Darwin's work by offering a standard passage from the *Origin of Species*: "On the Antilles the common crow, or decapod, has two feet while in the Galapagos Islands it has a third. This third foot, however, does not appear to be used for locomotion, but merely for conversation." In "The Crossword Puzzle Craze," he uses a familiar technique: he transfers a standard vocabulary from one activity to another, with humorous consequences:

"Good morning, Short-for-Peter."
"Hullo, Diminutive-of-William. How do you experience-a-sensation in four letters this morning?"
"Worse than a word in four letters rhyming with *bell* and *tell*."

Short Circuits did not get a warm response: "The rich vein of Mr. Stephen Leacock's humor seems to have become exhausted," one reviewer said. Another commented, "Even Stephen Leacock nods now and then." Many of the articles in the collection were written at the request of Dodd, Mead editors, who asked Leacock to stretch his original manuscript for the book to fifty thousand words; the final manuscript was even longer. A smaller proportion of the pieces than usual had appeared in magazines. Leacock took some of the topics of articles he had written for magazines, including a series on the theme "Save Me from My Friends," and provided more pieces on the same subjects. Lane's complaint that Leacock had begun writing "snippets" perhaps did not apply to his work at the beginning of the 1920s so much as it did to *Short Circuits.* Leacock identified the theme of the book as "the contrast between yesterday and to-day, between to-day and to-morrow." Throughout the book, he betrayed a clear preference for the past. This theme is particularly apparent in the imitation of Gray's "Elegy in a Country Churchyard," with which the volume ends. Leacock portrays modern man living and dying in an ugly landscape of factories, stockyards, tenements and train tracks. He sadly warns of the passing of domestic animals and the loss of backyard playgrounds for children, the simple pleasures of county fairs and the security of growing up in a family home. Although the sketches share a slightness of development, which perhaps limits their value, still there is a representation of Leacock at his best even in this rather nostalgic and sad collection. Memorable pieces include "Old Junk and New Money," "A Lesson on the Links," "Softening the Stories for the Children" and "The Great Detective." *The Iron Man and the Tin Woman* is similar to *Short Circuits*: a very few fine pieces leaven a group of rather flat repetitions of old themes and techniques. "Further Specialization" follows the sound idea that overspecialization is interfering with the proper performance of jobs; the story describes the enormous staff it will take one day to give a man a shave. In "Mr. Chairman, I Beg to Move," Leacock returns to the hopeless confusion of women's-club meetings, and "The Hero of Home Week" follows a long-absent visitor whose insistence that he remembers the old days is weakened somewhat by the discovery that the old days still exist in his home town in the form of old friends, community characters and landmarks.

In all three books, Leacock's opinions on the questions of prohibition and women's rights are well represented. Satisfied as he was by the introduction of licensed liquor outlets in Canada, Leacock continued to hammer away at prohibition in the United States. In "Literature and the Eighteenth Amendment" from *Short Circuits*, he offered United States writers the use of Montreal as a setting for their stories so that traditional scenes of merriment and intrigue, featuring alcoholic beverages, could be staged legally. In *The Iron Man and the Tin Woman*, he nostalgically regretted the disappearance of "Eddie the Bar-tender" from the lives of citizens south of the Canadian border. He portrays women primarily as he seems to have met them at club meetings. (He shows very little sympathy or respect for women's clubs, which, however, provided him with a high proportion of his speaking engagements.) In his "Appeal to the Average Man," which introduces *Winnowed Wisdom*, Leacock found little to recommend either the average man or the average woman; his own goal, he said, was "to start the movement for getting above the average." Average women might be consoled by his assurance that they were, on the whole, superior to average men in Leacock's analysis, except for his few criticisms: women cannot do arithmetic beyond improper fractions, they each eat about four tons of candy in a lifetime and they read nothing but love stories. The continuing emphasis on a sharp differentiation between men and women, and their roles in society, might be explained by a Canadian controversy to which Leacock does not refer directly in his writings. After Canadian women received the vote, and women representatives were elected to the House of Commons, the legality of an appointment of a woman to the judiciary was challenged. It was argued that, under the British North America Act (the legal document that established the Dominion of Canada), only "persons" could hold such offices, and women were not persons under the law. Author Emily Murphy, whose appointment to the bench in Alberta had been challenged, took the case to court, and in 1928 the Supreme Court of Canada ruled that, in fact, women were not "persons" under the law. In 1929, the decision was reversed by the British Privy Council. (At that time the council could override the supreme court.)

In the fall of 1929, Leacock sent a new program of lectures to several bureaus in the United States. He offered a variety of subjects, ranging from literature and economics to readings from his own humorous writings. Response was so strong that he was booked for all the holidays of the school year. Between 1925 and 1929, his interest in expanding his career beyond magazines and books continued. In 1925, an adaptation of "Behind the Beyond" by V.C. Clinton-Baddeley opened in London to good reviews. It was the beginning of a long association that yielded Leacock relatively small amounts of money but enormous satisfaction as he continued to hope for the possibility of writing his own stage plays. Among the many visitors to his Montreal home at this time were friends Douglas Fairbanks and Mary Pickford, who came for dinner. The dinner was a private affair, but Leacock later told friends that he had been urged to write a screenplay in which Fairbanks and Pickford could star. His agent, Paul Reynolds, was negotiating with the Hollywood movie company, Famous Players-Lasky Corporation, on the sale of screen rights to his books. In his book *Further Foolishness*, Leacock had satirized the adaptation of traditional stories for film. During the 1920s, he frequently used the device of recasting familiar historical events or fictional episodes in terms of movie and radio techniques as a source of humor. Although he satirized their excesses and questioned sadly whether the new devices did not make people like himself obsolete before their time, he showed growing interests, in the 1930s, in the possibility of writing for radio and the movies. In 1927, Leacock also began contributing to the *Encyclopaedia Britiannica*. The articles, brief descriptions of the Canadian provinces, provide a twist on one of Leacock's most quoted lines, that he would rather have written *Alice in Wonderland* than the whole *Encyclopaedia Britannica.*

In September, 1929, Leacock was the chairman of the Upper Canada College centenary banquet, held at Toronto's Royal York Hotel. It was a memorable evening. Many distinguished alumni of the school, including provincial and national government officials, were entertained by one of the school's most famous graduates and faculty members. Only one month later, the world economy that had seemed so prosperous and stable suddenly fell apart. In Canada, the collapse began on 24 October at the Winnipeg Grain Exchange with a dramatic fall in wheat prices. Five days later the New York stock market crashed. The ensuing depression became one of Leacock's chief concerns as an economist, and also affected his personal life by cutting deeply into his earnings. He lost few, if any, of his investments, but for several years the performance of his stocks and bonds was poor, contributing to a great decrease in his income. However, he had been concerned about his income from the beginning of the decade. The many personal difficulties of the late 1920s, and the consequent changes in his practice of annual publication, had already caused a significant drop in his annual earnings from the forty thousand dollars he had achieved in 1923. His income in 1929 was only $19,000 from writing, and all of the decrease was due to loss of royalties, lecture fees and payment for syndication of articles. Thus, the troubled period before the crash had lowered Leacock's income by decreasing his productivity. The crash and the subsequent depression not only lessened his earnings from his investments but further decreased his income from writing. Negotiations with his publishers about his twenty-percent royalties became strained again, especially after the lukewarm reception his last two books received. Finally he began to accept lower percentages and smaller advances against royalties. Leacock was drawn away from humor writing by the depression, as he had been by World War I, so that much of his energy went into drafting proposals designed to restore prosperity to Canada. The struggle to be heard was a difficult one. In 1925, an English writer, C.K. Allen, had published *Oh, Mr. Leacock!*, intended as a parody of the humorist's famous style and themes. Allen displayed a tendency to take Leacock too much at his word in his exaggerated portrayals of social ills; his attempts to parody Leacock's style sounded like strong criticisms of Leacock's opinions. If there were some who took Leacock's humor too seriously, there were many more who refused to see anything serious in his writing about the depression. On the eve of the new decade, Leacock celebrated his sixtieth birthday. For the next five years, he never ceased to offer his advice on the nation's economy, although he became aware increasingly of his isolation from other theorists on the question, including the members of his own department at McGill. The struggle came to a surprising and unwelcome end in 1935, when it was announced that Stephen Leacock, with other veteran McGill faculty members, would be forced to retire due to age.

Chapter Twelve

The Saving Grace of Humour

I N THE five years between the New York stock-market crash and the announcement that he would be forced to retire from McGill, Stephen Leacock published ten books, edited or provided introductions for four others, continued a steady flow of articles and pamphlets and gave his first and only series of radio broadcasts. After the period of silence that surrounded Beatrix's death, Leacock returned, with all his former energy, to a demanding schedule of teaching and writing. He produced three new humor collections during the five years, but most of his writing was serious. The Great Depression of the 1930s was the most challenging crisis faced by Leacock as an economist. He considered it "a failure of society, and economists in particular" that the crisis had not been anticipated and avoided. Just as he had done during World War I and would do again at the outbreak of World War II in 1939, Leacock responded quickly to the national situation. In the early 1930s, he published two books and several brief works proposing directions for economic recovery. In these years Leacock was closer than ever to directly influencing Canadian government policy; indeed, he was invited twice, the second time by Prime Minister Robert Bennett himself, to run for Paliament. The depression divided Canadians, and not only along national party lines; it set union member against businessman, provincial premier against federal government and French Canadian against English Canadian. It also divided economists, and Leacock found himself at odds with many other members of his profession in his university and in the national community of experts. (This conflict emanated at least as much from Leacock and his championship of his ideas as it did from those opposed to him.) Another topic on which Leacock wrote a great deal in this period was the nature of humor. From 1916 onward, he had lectured and written on his favorite authors, especially Mark Twain,

Charles Dickens and O. Henry; he had also published occasional articles and prefaces on the general question of the humorist's art. Between 1932 and 1935 he wrote biographies of Twain and Dickens and presented their work in anthologies. In 1935 he published *Humor: Its Theory and Technique*, his most ambitious treatment of the subject. Leacock's theory met with less critical enthusiasm than did his humor, but the theory was an important expression of his personal struggle to put the proper value on the type of writing he loved to read and at which he excelled as an author. His training as a literary and linguistic scholar drew him to attempt a critical justification of humor as an art form. He was eager to prove, to himself and his readers, that humor was a respectable branch of literature and not merely ephemeral entertainment. Despite the opposition and indifference he met on this score, Leacock, in the early years of the depression, was again the earnest, active enthusiast he had been before his wife's fatal illness. Perhaps it was the fact that he had returned from adversity to his full work schedule that caused him to react so angrily to the news, in 1935, that the following spring he would be retired from the McGill faculty due to his age.

Leacock began his campaign against the depression on an old theme, Canada's participation in the British empire. The imperial harmony Leacock praised during World War I had not continued when the war was over. Conservative Prime Minister Robert Borden had demanded and won, even during the war, an independent voice for Canada in the war councils of Great Britain, and after the war had secured an independent seat for the country at the League of Nations. Perhaps continuing Conservative leadership would have made such moves towards an independent voice within British imperial decision-making a fulfillment of Leacock's hope, expressed ever since his 1907 Rhodes tour, for an imperial government that truly represented all the dominions of the empire. Under the Liberal government of Mackenzie King, however, imperial relations — and, in general, any international involvement outside the Americas — were not pursued. King refused a request from Britain for troop support in a military action in Turkey in 1922, and consistently avoided involving Canada in any general imperial defense programs during the 1920s and the last half of the 1930s. At the same time, he drew back from developing an independent international role for Canada through the League of Nations, preferring to pursue closer ties with the United States in the expectation that Canada's location in North America would protect the country from threats of war in Europe and Asia. Leacock steadily championed the importance of imperial cooperation as a safeguard for Canada and a base for economic growth. In 1924, he said in a speech in Montreal, "The silliest thing this country could do would be to cut itself loose from the help and co-operation of the British people." In 1930 he published *Economic Prosperity in the British Empire*, a book that propounded his remedy for the depression, at least as it affected the countries within the empire.

He called for the lowering of tariffs towards the goal of free trade among the dominions, and a system of imperial finance and investment to develop the still untapped resources these countries held. This book, its impact and additions to its proposals (which he made later) are all summarized accurately (if proudly) by Leacock in a blurb he wrote for another book on the same subject, *Back to Prosperity*:

Professor Leacock of McGill University published, just before the conference of 1930, a book on *Economic Prosperity in the British Empire*. His book was widely read by statesmen and economists both in England and the dominions. It is no exaggeration to say that it greatly influenced public opinion. Dr. Leacock's new volume, *The Coming Imperial Conference and the Return to Prosperity* [later retitled], deals with the work that can be achieved at the new conference of 1932. He advocates an imperial super-tariff, together with a system of 'three cornered preference'. The existing preference he admits has been largely . . . 'humbug' . . ., since Canada will not admit any imperial imports calculated to injure her manufacturers. Professor Leacock approves of this but finds the remedy in turning over to imperial, as opposed to foreign, imports the vast Canadian market for tobacco, cotton, oil, coffee, tropical fruits, rubber and things not producible in Canada. Canada receives in return the British market for wheat, and Great Britain the colonial tropical market. The three parts of the trade are carried on in 'quotas' or 'blocks' of imports at arranged prices.

Professor Leacock also urges joint action with a view to establishing inter-imperial currency, joint action to create a (limited) imperial debt, and joint action to stimulate the silver market and raise prices by increasing the monetary use of silver. . . .

Leacock also suggested a new program of immigration within the empire: settling immigrants in undeveloped regions would promote imperial prosperity. He wished to bolster the population of British descendants in the empire outside the United Kingdom. Saying that the dominions did not wish to involve their own economic survival with the other races who occupied the British empire, including the native populations of India, South Africa and New Zealand, he spoke of a conference "between nation and nation, between white men and white men." The book found eager support among pro-imperial groups; the board of trade in Orillia bought a thousand copies, which were mailed to British members of parliament and newspaper editors.

Some reviewers of *Economic Prosperity in the British Empire* sounded a note of criticism that would continue to be used against Leacock's writings by his political and economics opponents, and that echoes, from the contemporary debates down to today, in critical judgments of his political and economic work. The critics said he lacked the care for accurate statistical information and the mastery of recent economic theories necessary to solve the new economic crisis of the depression. According to the London *Times*, "Few economists will be impressed with the shortcuts the author takes 'through the jungle of statistics,' or with his pieces of 'financial magic' in which something is made out of nothing." A check of a representative sample of reviews and opinions, however, reveals that Leacock's books about imperialism — and his economic works — were reviewed, in the main, favorably or were summarized by the press respectfully and without counterargument. Newspapers and writers who entered quibbles or disagreements generally did so with regard to individual points within a discussion that was basically well-disposed to Leacock's views. Again, it is part of the myth that has grown up around Leacock, fostered by writers interested in his humor and not overly concerned for history, that he was gently accepted as a duffer in political and economic matters. In fact, Leacock's own statement that *Economic Prosperity* "was widely read by statesmen and economists" and "greatly influenced public opinion" was as precise as it was self-confident. Leacock's ideas were questioned by experts who held divergent opinions, but this was the sort of "dismissal" that Leacock himself courted and encouraged, for he wished to participate in the forum of ideas and prove that his own were beneficial and superior. As to the charge of inaccuracy, he was well aware of it and continued to hold the considered opinion that the condensations and shortcuts he took with economic statistics never affected the truth of his argument and served the useful purpose of making it more readable and therefore more influential. In 1940, when his book *Our British Empire* was read in manuscript by the British Ministry of Information, which was going to buy copies to give away, Leacock contemptuously dismissed the long list of adjusted statistics, altered dates and shades of phrasing suggested by the ministry's history expert; he rejected several "corrections" that were wrong and allowed the ministry and his publisher to satisfy themselves on the others, since none of them had any bearing on his message and none reflected an inaccuracy of any importance to the general reader.

Economists can scarcely be expected to cede influence to one of their number, except in the case of a few magisterial figures such as J.M. Keynes. But Leacock's influence as a practical economist upon politicians and working experts involved in government was real and is well documented. One example of this, relating to *Economic Prosperity*, is interesting in that it involves a fellow Canadian of the greatest influence in Great Britain. This was Max Aitken, Lord Beaverbrook, Ontario born and New Brunswick reared, who became a British newspaper magnate and later an influential politician. He was Winston Churchill's most trusted advisor during World War II. On 31 August, 1930, Aitken wrote to Leacock:

> During a yachting journey in the Channel I have been reading, for the second time, "Economic Prosperity in the British Empire".
>
> If I may be allowed to say so, I am more impressed than ever with your statement of the case for economic re-organisation. . . .

237

In the Second Part of the book, the definition of mass production and standardisation will serve to instruct many an ignorant person.

I do not agree with your policy in relation to The Argentine. I would like to buy all our Wheat imports from Canada and Australia, selling to these Dominions the imported requirements of their farming population.

The need for agricultural development in Britain is very pressing.

Very few of our economic writers know anything about it. In fact, I am very glad to get the opportunity of redressing my own viewpoint to some extent. . . .

Aitken invited Leacock to propose methods of getting the book into the hands of as many influential men as possible. Aitken's letter shows that Leacock's ideas were often developed not solely out of his debates with professional economists, but through the dialogue that his public prominence allowed him to carry on with powerful figures in government and elsewhere. Leacock modified his ideas on wheat imports along the lines indicated by Aitken in his remark on Argentina; the change was reflected in a new book on imperial economic planning published in 1932.

In 1932 Leacock again wrote on the importance of imperial economic planning in *Back to Prosperity: The Great Opportunity of the Empire Conference*, which he produced as a proposal for measures that should be taken at a conference to be held at Ottawa in July. In the United States, where there was, naturally, a hungry eagerness for any news of constructive action to relieve the depression, the North American Newspaper Alliance asked Leacock to report on the conference for its members, but he declined. In his hastily produced book, he suggested, as he had in 1930, that the dominions would find their best chance of overcoming the continuing effects of the depression through co-operation in trade and finance. Between the two books, the status of the empire had changed dramatically. In 1931, the Statute of Westminster was passed. All former dominions were acknowledged as full nation-state partners with Great Britain under the traditional British monarchy; the new partnership thus formed was called "the Commonwealth." To Leacock, the Commonwealth was a step in the wrong direction: it provided for more independent action by the dominions, but Leacock continued to campaign for cooperation among its members along the same lines he had proposed for the empire. (In *Our British Empire* [1940] he would argue that the empire, as he conceived it, still survived despite the name change.) The Imperial Conference of 1932 enacted, to some extent, the lowering of tariffs among the Commonwealth countries that Leacock had proposed. Canada shared in the agreement, which was one of a number of measures against the depression taken by the Conservative government of Richard Bennett, who came into power in 1930 in an election called by Mackenzie King. King had refused to take any action to counter the economic effects of the stock-market crash on the grounds that the separation of powers prescribed for Canada by the British North America Act left social-service programs in the hands of the provinces rather than the federal government. When King called an election for July 1930, he expected to receive a mandate to continue this policy. Instead, the Conservative party, under Bennett, a friend of Leacock's since the 1911 campaign against Sir Wilfrid Laurier, was elected. Leacock had been invited to run for Parliament as a Conservative but had declined. There is little indication that Bennett's first steps to combat the depression were influenced by Leacock, but as the years passed Bennett made increasingly clear his reliance on some of the professor's ideas and introduced programs very close to ones Leacock had proposed. In 1930 the Conservatives established a fund for social relief. The money would be distributed to the provinces, who would administer it. As well, the Conservatives set a high tariff to protect Canadian business from foreign — especially non-imperial — competition. The specific and unmistakable alignment with Leacock's views first became apparent at the 1932 Imperial Conference, when Canada participated in the lowering of tariffs among Commonwealth countries while standing by its high tariffs for other foreign nations. The close contact between Leacock, his friend Bennett and Bennett's government is witnessed by existing correspondence, press accounts, and statements of contemporaries. The evidence indicates that Leacock resisted repeated attempts by the Conservatives to increase his influence by increasing his direct involvement in the government; Leacock turned down several invitations, apparently because he preferred to maintain the freedom of his views and his impact as an impartial, academic commentator. On 2 July, 1932, just before the Imperial Conference, Bennett sent Leacock a "memorandum on monetary reconstruction," warning him to regard it as completely confidential because it was tentative and "has not yet been passed upon by the government." Bennett wrote: "It raises questions of importance, some of which are highly controversial. I shall be very glad if you can find an opportunity within the next ten days to express your opinion. . . ." Leacock refused, and returned the consultancy fee the government had sent him. In September, Bennett wrote again to offer the compliments of the Cabinet and to ask privately "to discuss with you the monetary situation."

In 1933 the depression widened its damage in Canada. At first, losses had touched primarily prairie farmers and the fishing, mining and lumber industries in the Maritime provinces; the Canadian banks were complacent because they had avoided the failures that were such a dramatic and painful aspect of the depression in the United States. By 1933, however, national unemployment had reached twenty-three percent. In 1933, Leacock published a pamphlet entitled *Stephen Leacock's Plan to Relieve the Depression in Six Days, to Remove It in Six Months, to Eradicate It in Six Years.* For the first time in his practical economic writing, he offered a plan designed solely for Canadian problems. His proposals were three: a massive government work program, including slum clearance and rebuilding projects, operated on a profit basis; a devaluation of the dollar, lessening its gold backing from twenty-three to seventeen grains, and use of the impetus from these measures to rebuild foreign trade. The devaluation of the dollar would put more money into circulation and give more buying power to working people. Leacock lectured on his proposals and sent copies of the plan to Bennett and to President Franklin Delano Roosevelt. The plan was widely discussed in the Canadian press, and to a lesser extent in the United States press and by American politicians. Newspaper accounts were generally favorable or descriptive. The most common objection was that inflation would result from lessening

the gold backing of the dollar; it is interesting that the lingering idea that Leacock was not a good economist descends, in
large part, from the arguments against him by "sounder,"
"more advanced" thinkers who believed that the gold standard could not be abandoned or weakened without disaster.
People have forgotten the issue but preserved the charge. In
fact, gold was a subject on which Leacock wrote many well-
informed and forward-looking articles during the years. He
was of his time in that he was concerned inflation would result
from an insufficiently backed dollar, but far less conservative
than many in this regard and more prepared to see that, in
fact, the gold backing of currency was not being maintained.
He took flamboyant steps to prove his economic point. The effects of the depression on the gold standard had led to the standard's collapse, and Great Britain had gone off the standard
altogether in 1931. This was not admitted immediately in
North America, however. The Canadian government strongly
maintained that the gold standard was still in effect. Leacock
withdrew ten thousand dollars from his Montreal bank and
took it to the assistant receiver general's office in the city,
demanding the equivalent in gold. The exchange was made;
the gold was given to him in coins of small denominations.
Leacock wanted to ship the gold to the United States, but the
Canadian government wrote him a letter demanding that the
gold be surrendered. When Leacock surrendered the gold, it
was accepted at face value but Leacock was charged for "loss
of weight through wear and abrasion." For the small charge
he had demonstrated publicly and dramatically that the country was no longer on the gold standard: gold would not be
given for paper currency "to the bearer on demand." Another
objection raised to Leacock's plan to end the depression was an
objection Leacock himself raised against socialism's positive
programs: it would take saints, not men, to run a massive
public-works project on a profit basis, without corruption and
profiteering, and for the good of the disadvantaged. In general,
the pamphlet was well-received; even the quibbles came in approving reviews. A few newspapers of strongly traditional
economic views disagreed entirely. One stated that the work
would find its place amid Leacock's humor. The pamphlet
strengthened Leacock's influence. Although Leacock had twit-

ted the government in public over the supposedly healthy gold standard, Bennett consulted Leacock on a measure to deal with the financial and currency problems: the formation of the Bank of Canada, which was instituted in 1934. When Roosevelt's "New Deal" programs got under way in 1932, one of the measures was a devaluation of the American dollar in a manner very close to that which Leacock had proposed for Canada. Leacock's name and ideas had been mentioned in the American discussions of the subject (Leacock used to say that "Stephen Leacock's plan" was being called "Franklin Roosevelt's plan" now that it was being put into practice.) However, reviewers of the pamphlet had drawn attention to the similarity of Leacock's basic ideas and his proposals to those of John Maynard Keynes and his followers. Although Leacock was not without influence in the United States (he was known, through a 1932 essay, as a backer of Roosevelt's principles and the broad outlines of the New Deal), in that country his voice only joined a chorus calling for the same general measures. In Canada, where neither major political party was disposed to consider a mixed economy with significant government intervention, his position was more advanced and isolated.

Leacock continued to campaign strongly for a mixed economy in which free enterprise would be balanced by government regulations and a government social-service program to support working people, dependent women and children, to educate all the young and to find jobs for the unemployed. Although it went directly against traditional Conservative-party policies, he urged the government to intervene with programs of minimum wage, civic-improvement work projects and the like. After Franklin Roosevelt's victory in 1932, Leacock praised the United States political system and electorate for creating a concensus for a mixed economy that would preserve basic individual freedoms but restrain big business and speculators and make the national government explicitly responsible for safeguarding workers and the poor. This was the direction of all future successful economies, as Leacock saw it. Indeed, the United States was then in the vanguard of developing the type of mixed economy that emerged in western countries in response to the depression, and Leacock was again prophetic. (Most industrial democracies and Commonwealth countries have since adopted a greater number of socialist economic elements than the United States has, and more than Leacock would have approved of.) In Canada, many factors inhibited the development of an American-style drive towards a mixed economy. Nevertheless, the desperate economic circumstances and the dissatisfaction of the electorate were prodding the Conservatives to do something in that direction. In 1935, Prime Minister Bennett gave a series of radio broadcasts to introduce a new program of economic-recovery measures. He offered his thoughts to the public as the basis of the new legislation he proposed to introduce. When the broadcasts were to be published, Leacock was invited to contribute a preface for one of them, and his piece was so admired by Bennett and his advisers that it was used as an introduction to the booklet as a whole. Liberal opposition leader Mackenzie King forced an election on the issue of Bennett's "New Deal" for Canada, and Bennett again wrote to Leacock and asked him to run for Parliament as a Conservative member from Orillia:

> A number of our friends are extremely anxious that you should permit your name to be placed before the Conservative convention in the constituency in which you make your summer home. I need hardly say that I am thoroughly convinced that you would render very conspicuous service to Canada in the next Parliament. Your wide knowledge, your great reputation, and your disinterested approach to problems affecting the welfare of the country could not but be of the utmost value. Won't you favorably consider this matter, and thereby give great satisfaction not only to those who know you in the community but to the thousands who have read your books with pleasure, as well as to one who subscribes himself, with high esteem and regard,
>
> R.B. Bennett

Leacock declined. He was called upon less often by the Liberal-party government of Mackenzie King, whose policies of North American isolationism and nonintervention in the economy did not suit Leacock in any way. Leacock continued to press, however, for a program of social relief such as he had outlined in *Stephen Leacock's Plan*.

Other leaders who discussed the practical economic questions of the day with Leacock included his close friends Sir Edward Beatty, president of the Canadian Pacific Railway, and General Currie, principal of McGill University. Currie encouraged Leacock, for example, to develop proposals for reconstruction in the farm industry. Leacock preserved a position of strict independence. There is a revealing exchange of letters between Beatty and Leacock from 1935, in which Leacock protested his announced retirement (Beatty was a McGill chancellor) but simultaneously chided Beatty for an attack he had made on Canada's young socialist economists. At the University of Western Ontario in London, Beatty had delivered a widely reported attack upon the theorists who had helped plan the Cooperative Commonwealth Federation's political program and had written its platform. This group of socialist intellectuals was called the League for Social Reconstruction, and among its leading figures were Frank Underhill and McGill's Frank Scott, the poet and law professor Leacock had helped seven years earlier with the *McGill Fortnightly Review*. Scott, like Leacock, was a member of the Political Science Association, Canada's national professional organization in the field. Beatty had criticized what he felt were the dangerous, erroneous ideas of the CCF (the forerunner of today's New Democratic Party), and had attributed the problem to "something wrong with the whole atmosphere of economic teaching in this country," as he restated the point to Leacock. Frank Underhill criticized Beatty's speech in an article in the *Canadian Forum*; Beatty saw Underhill's piece and wrote to Leacock. He invited Leacock (whom he knew to be opposed to socialism) to side with him publicly. At first, Leacock said only that the young economists were incapable of writing a book or a paragraph that would engage the public's attention, and that they would have no influence unless it was given to them by the ill-advised remarks of railway presidents and university chancellors. Prodded further, he had this to say:

Yes I read today [11 December, 1935] Underhill's paper in the Forum. It is written in a [word illegible] strain which will get him nowhere: I will tell him this when I get a chance. I think, if you don't mind my saying so, that in your London address and perhaps elsewhere you do not clearly enough distinguish between political economy in its real sense, and the mere polemics of Canadian politics. A great many people spend their whole lives in working on such things as economic origins and history, and theories of things that have no connection with Canada. Such great men as Thorold Rogers and William Cunningham gave their lives to the history of work & wages and the evolution of industry. Your condemnation struck a whole lot of people of whom you possibly never heard: and who are hurt but cannot answer back. You said *"with exceptions"*, but that means nothing; if I said *"With exceptions, Canadian bankers are crooks,"* how would Charles Gordon like it.

To the end of his life — as witnessed by one of his last books, *While There Is Time: The Case Against Social Catastrophe* (1944) — Leacock continued to endorse socialism's criticism of capitalism and unbridled free enterprise, and to reject its vision and specific proposals for a future society. He preferred his own improvements, which were along the lines proposed by Keynes and Roosevelt's New Deal. He was unwilling to defend the ideas of the League for Social Reconstruction, but equally unwilling to admit that the ideas were valueless.

On another important score, too, Leacock opposed Beatty. Beatty had said that professors (both Scott and Underhill were professors) should not espouse radical ideas because they might mislead students and the public. He also made this point in print, and again in an address in 1937 at Queen's University. Leacock stated uncompromisingly to him that a professor had a right to say whatever he pleased so long as he did not turn his classroom into a platform for advocating his own beliefs. Beatty was not restrained by Leacock's remarks. But B.K. Sandwell, editor of *Saturday Night*, and Eugene Forsey, both of whom had known Leacock as teacher or department chairman, joined Underhill in publicly opposing Beatty. They used the same kind of argument Leacock used to his friend in private. Sandwell wrote in his magazine on 9 November, 1935, that "if Sir Edward [Beatty] had confined himself to the general question of university men using their academic prestige to further unacademic ends, he would have made an important and much neglected point." This important, neglected point was exactly the one Leacock was interested in. In December, 1935, Leacock received a letter from someone who approved of Beatty's views, and who apparently expected Leacock to agree. Leacock wrote and carefully preserved an eloquent response:

I think I see in your letter an undercurrent of reality and I can't quite see eye to eye with you.

The idea seems to be that if a professor makes a speech outside the college, to people not connected with it, and says, "I am a socialist; capitalism is doomed", then he has shown himself unfit to teach in the college and ought to be disciplined. I don't see this. Socialism is not illegal. Its proposals are not revolutionary. They involve only parliamentary voting. Socialism is a beautiful dream, that can never be realized. But it invites the sympathy of many of the kindest and best minds in the world, (including my own) even when they cannot believe in it. In practice it is bound to fail. It is an error that dies in the sunlight. In the long run truth prevails on earth: and fools should be suffered gladly. Rich men always reach out for methods of repression and always will. But in the end righteousness wins. No professor has the right to press the propoganda of socialism on a college class; nor has he the right to press the propaganda of Christianity or of aviation or nudism or tariff protection. If he does so, he breaks his contract. But apart from that a professor ought to be as free as you are. There are and have been socialists in many of His Majesty's Cabinets in the British Empire, including the government at Westminster itself. There is no reason why a professor should not be a socialist just as he might be a ventriloquist or a prohibitionist. But he must not start ventriloquism in his class-room.

But I think the present danger at McGill is all the other way. Many people are losing sight of the fact that a University in its first and foremost meaning is a home of learning, a place of thought, a repository of the wisdom of the past and a workshop of the wisdom of the future. It is made up of its books, its classes, its students and its professors, and the writings and thoughts that it inspires. This is a university. This is, — or should be McGill, — not its finances and its accounts and its investment of money. These things are necessary, but they are only a means not an end. It is the same as in a family: the money they have represents only a means whereby family love and family happiness can be achieved. They eat meat, they don't eat the butcher's bill.

Recently one of the McGill Governors spoke to an audience of McGill students and was reported (in print in the *Daily*) as having told them that the governors were "responsible for what the professors are", — and responsible "for what they teach". Personally, I had always thought the responsibility for what we are rests with God Almighty. I know that responsibility for what we teach rests with the college Senate; if a professor were willing to teach for nothing the governors couldn't stop him. The governors for the most part do not understand the curriculum any more than we understand their business.

I have a son at McGill. I would rather have him hear fifty lectures on Socialism, than one lecture as derogatory to his father's profession as that address.

In the early 1930s Leacock's expenses were going up and his income was going down, for a variety of reasons. His interest in farming in Orillia and his projects there grew in scope. In 1930 he began planning a lodge, which was built, at great expense, in 1933 and occupied by his superintendent, John Kelly, and his housekeeper, Tina Pelletier, now man and wife. Beatrix's death had caused Leacock gradually to drop the highly successful syndication of his pieces in newspapers throughout North America, which had been accomplished for him by his agent Paul Reynolds. During the 1920s syndication had brought him between five hundred and eight hundred dollars per month for several years; it had formed the largest single source of income from his creative writing. This income was now entirely gone. Although the anthology *Laugh with Leacock* was selling well, his humor books of the 1930s were not as popular as his earlier ones had been, and they faced the additional challenge of the severely depressed book market. In 1930 and 1931, he was overburdened with college work, which kept him from humor writing and did not allow him the time to seek more income from his pieces by placing them in periodicals as well as publishing them in book form. He had added, to his teaching duties, the direction of the McGill Monographs Economic Studies Series: National Problems of Canada. He threw himself into this, acquiring and editing manuscripts, arranging publication through Macmillan of Canada, soliciting advertising from many large corporations and writing to printers. (The monographs were produced by Hale Brothers, who produced the *Orillia Packet and Times*.) Despite his efforts to save money, the series had to be discontinued for economic reasons. Because of a commitment he had made to the project, Leacock was left with responsibility for a two-hundred-seventy-dollar deficit; McGill paid this for him, and then deducted forty-five dollars a month from his salary. What time Leacock did have for writing he devoted largely to projects of supreme importance to him but of little income potential: his works on the empire and economic recovery. In addition, he lost income on *Back to Prosperity* because its British publisher failed to issue it until March, 1932, three months after it had appeared in Canada and the United States. Another project touched by Canada's economic troubles was a book he prepared for Graphic Press of Ottawa. At the invitation of the director of the press, Lawrence J. Burpee, a historian, Leacock edited and provided an intro-duction for the largely fantastical memoirs of a seventeenth-century French soldier and explorer in Canada, Louis Armand de Lom d'Acre, Baron de Lahontan. Lahontan's *Voyages* was actually on the presses, and a few copies had been printed, when Graphic Press was forced to close in 1932. Leacock was never paid for his work on the book, and apparently never acquired a copy; for years, he believed that none had been pro-duced. Leacock was shown a rare copy by a student and wrote to a Toronto bookseller in a vain attempt to purchase one for himself. He was one of several Canadian authors hurt by the collapse of Graphic. Prairie novelist Frederick Philip Grove moved to Ontario in the early 1930s in hopes of finding edi-torial work to supplement his writing income; he joined Graphic Press shortly before it closed. Grove invited Raymond Knister (who drowned in August, 1932) to submit a manu-script to a Graphic Press contest for first novels. Knister won the competition for his *White Narcissus*, but the financially hard-pressed writer received only a portion of his prize money before the press failed.

Leacock's gross income decreased sharply. In 1929 he earned $24,461.24; in 1930 he earned $17,183.36. His income continued to decline as the depression began to affect the per-formance of Leacock's stocks and bonds and as the amount and quality of his humor contined to suffer from lack of time and attention. In 1931 his gross income was $14,719.30; he derived $2,898.20 from stock dividends and bonds and

$3,466.06 from royalties, magazines fees and lectures. (In 1928 his income from dividends and bonds was $5,837.92, from literary work $14,015.99; his gross income was $26,171.13.) In early 1932 he commented in a letter to his British editor, "Like all people here I fought this hard winter low dividends and acutely unstable etc. Hence these tears."

Another disappointment in this period — although it brought in some welcome cash — came with Leacock's work for radio. In 1931 he was approached twice. First Richard Marvin of the J. Walter Thompson Company Limited, an international advertising agency, visited Leacock in his campus office and invited him to propose a program for a client. Then he was asked to quote a price for use of material from *Sunshine Sketches of a Little Town* on radio. Both projects fizzled out. In February of the same year, producer W.N. DeFoe of R.D. Broadcasting Company came to Montreal to suggest a series of programs featuring ten-minute talks by Leacock. Though Leacock responded positively, the programs never went beyond the planning stages. In 1934 Leacock did get a program on the air, but it proved a surprising letdown for all concerned. The former editor of a Toronto humor magazine, Joseph McDougall, who was working for an advertising agency, knew Leacock well and had printed several of his pieces; he approached Leacock on behalf of his agency which was planning a radio show to be sponsored by Pompeiian Hand Cream. Leacock, the agency and the sponsor settled on twenty-six broadcasts in thirteen weeks. Leacock would be paid thirteen hundred dollars for writing and delivering the series. The good humor surrounding the negotiations is suggested by an unusual clause in the contract. Leacock planned a dinner party before each broadcast and was permitted to bring his dinner guests to the studio, or, if he preferred, he could broadcast from his home. "I don't like talking to a box on a stick," he said. The initial broadcast was made from station CFCF in Montreal on 27 March, 1934. The first four shows were done in Montreal, and the last twenty-two in Orillia. According to McDougall, Leacock might have been able to make a success of the broadcasts on television. Radio audiences could not see his face and expression and seemed offended by his customary style of leading the laughter for his wit. The series was not continued after the contracted episodes. Leacock was often approached for broadcast rights to his work, and was even asked, on occasion, to broadcast them himself, but he refused all offers to return to the microphone.

Three humor collections appeared between 1930 and 1935: *Wet Wit and Dry Humor* (1930), *Afternoons in Utopia* (1932) and *The Dry Pickwick* (1932). All three were hastily produced volumes, intended to popularize his serious views through humor; none of them is among his better books. *Wet Wit and Dry Humor* and *The Dry Pickwick* are collections of pieces written for periodicals and included some material previously published in book form. *Wet Wit* was published in New York; *The Dry Pickwick*, published in England, contained some new material to replace pieces that depended, for their antiprohibition point, on the United States Volstead Act (the eighteenth amendment to the Constitution). In both books Leacock continued his campaign against the temperance movement. His target was primarily the United States, although Canada still contained towns that had voted to remain "dry" after licensed liquor outlets became legal in most Canadian provinces. Pieces in *Wet Wit* include "Confessions of a Soda Fiend" and "A Butler of the Old School." In the latter, Leacock describes a dealer in vintage water whose sources range from the Johnstown flood to ancient village pumps. A story told by a member of Leacock's academic staff shows how his published humor was interwoven with his daily life and conversation. Every year Leacock invited his professors to a dinner party to mark the opening of the new fall term. He noticed that all the men were unmarried and so asked Barbara Ulrichsen to arrange for some dinner companions for them among her friends at McGill. One of the co-eds asked for a drink of water at cocktail time. Leacock replied, "Water? Water? Ah, yes, I remember water about forty years ago. Barbara, get out that very good water we've been saving for forty years." *The Dry Pickwick* includes the title essay, in which one of Leacock's favorite Dickens characters has a nightmare of what life would be like under the restrictions of the Volstead Act. Other essays are "The Perfect Optimist," a rueful monologue on the joys of visiting the dentist, and "Ho for Happiness," in which Leacock proposes a happier sort of plot resolution than modern fiction commonly provides. *Afternoons in Utopia* was somewhat unusual among his books: he produced it in a single concerted effort without first seeking periodical publication for its contents. In December, 1931 he sent identical letters to Frank Dodd of Dodd, Mead and A. Willett of The Bodley Head:

> I plan for the spring a new book to be called Afternoons in Utopia, to be made up of a series of stories and sketches all turning on our economic future.
>
> Not *one* of the stories is written yet so there will hardly be time to get more than one or two of them in and out of magazines. But I won't wait. Life is too short. Now, — when can I have them done: I am crowded with college work and have one other book (80,000 words) to write at the same time. If I say *spring* and it's *summer* does it matter much?

The book was to be a discussion of the dangers of socialism in a form, humor, that would reach the people. Leacock always liked the book and looked upon it as a serious achievement; in his last economic book, *While There Is Time*, he cited it as one of his works on the subject of proper economic restructuring and the danger of socialism. Nevertheless, it was one of Leacock's least successful books, and never earned the one thousand dollars in royalties advanced to Leacock before publication under his Dodd, Mead contract.

Leacock's reputation as a humorist received a boost in 1930 despite the relative lack of success of his recent books. The first major anthology of his work was published on the occasion of his twentieth year as an author of humorous books, just after he had celebrated his sixtieth birthday. The collection, called *The Leacock Book* in England and *Laugh with Leacock* in North America, included thirty-four pieces from the books he had published between 1910 and 1929. The book's introduction collected words of praise from fourteen of Leacock's humorist colleagues: Irvin S. Cobb, Charles ("Chic") Sale, George Ade, Robert Benchley, Harry Leon Wilson, Homer Croy, Lawton Mackall, Christopher Morley, Ellis Parker Butler, Donald Ogden Stewart, Will Cuppy, Nunnally Johnson, George S. Chappell and Gelett Burgess. Of the group, only two, Benchley and Sale, were close friends of Leacock. Sale was a former vaudevillian from Nebraska whose best-selling book on the construction of outhouses, *The Specialist,* sold one million copies in 1929. He had visited Leacock in Montreal and in Old Brewery Bay. For *Laugh with Leacock,* Benchley repeated his early compliment to Leacock that he was greatly indebted to his work: "I have written everything that he ever wrote — anywhere from one to five years after him." Another of the group, George S. Chappell, praised Leacock as more than a humorist and mentioned "one little contact" with him at a speaking engagement, in which Leacock spoke with the same charm Chappell had found in his work. The fifteen humorists extolled Leacock for his many roles, from critic to college professor, and especially singled out his capacity to admire other humorists, to promote his art and to analyze human folly with kindliness.

Only a handful of the fifteen once-famous writers have had anything approaching the durability of Leacock for later generations of readers. Judging from Leacock's own humor anthologies, a number of the writers were favorites of his, especially Benchley and George Ade, whose historical importance in American humor is great, although the taste for his work has gone by. Many of the fifteen were Leacock's close contemporaries, including Irvin S. Cobb, "The Sage of Paducah," best known for his stories of his Kentucky hometown where he began his career as a reporter; Ade, who made his mark with the series of *Fables in Slang,* based on his column for the Chicago *Morning News,* beginning in 1897; Harry Leon Wilson, author of the once-celebrated comic novel *Ruggles of Red Gap* and a successful screenwriter; Ellis Parker Butler, remembered primarily for his 1906 story "Pigs Is Pigs"; and Gelett Burgess, who tired of the fame of his one well-remembered piece, the poem "The Purple Cow" from 1897. The younger writers acknowledged their indebtedness to Leacock's example; Cuppy called him "the real granddaddy of the best ones of the day still." These humorists were of a few types: rural newspapermen who had become known through their characterizations of their regions; college and cosmopolitan wits like Benchley and Morley; and writers for the movies, including Nunnally Johnson, who wrote, among other famous screenplays, *The Grapes of Wrath, How to Marry a Millionaire* and *The Keys of the Kingdom.* By comparison

Beatrix with Stevie, outside the Leacock's home on Côte-des-Neiges
Road, Montreal, about 1916.

Leacock and Beatrix with Stevie at their Côte-des-Neiges Road home, about 1916.
PUBLIC ARCHIVES CANADA/C-31967

Leacock holding his son at Old Brewery Bay, about 1917.
PUBLIC ARCHIVES CANADA/C-31914

Beatrix with Stevie at Old Brewery Bay,
about 1917.
PUBLIC ARCHIVES CANADA/C-31906

Stevie, about 1919.
PUBLIC ARCHIVES CANADA/C-31912

Leacock and Beatrix presiding over tea at Old Brewery Bay, about 1920. Also shown in this picture are Freddie Pellatt and Mrs. May Shaw ('Fitz'), holding Stevie.
PUBLIC ARCHIVES CANADA/C-31948

The Political Economy Club of McGill University for the academic year 1920–21. Left to right: P.H. Addy, M.J. Kern, Leacock, S.D. Pierce, H. Borden.
PUBLIC ARCHIVES CANADA/C-33106

Leacock at Old Brewery Bay with Stevie and Peggy Shaw, about 1928.
PUBLIC ARCHIVES CANADA/C-31981

The Old Brewery Bay Players in *Red Riding Hood Up-to-Date*, 14 August, 1929. Left to right, front row: Stevie as Lord Wolf, Peggy Shaw as Riding Hood. Left to right, back row: Virginia Smithers as Clarissa, Margot Castillon as Lady Hood, René du Roure, director, Jeddie Stewart as The Dowager Lady Hood, David Ulrichsen as Gaffer Gammon, Barbara Stephens as Jane.
PUBLIC ARCHIVES CANADA/C-33109

The Old. Brewery. Players in Red Riding Hood Up-to-Date August. 14. 1929.

Virginia Smithers as Clarissa
Margot Castillon as Lady Hood
Castillon Du Roure Director
Stevie Leacock as Lord Wolf
Peggy Shaw as Riding Hood
Jeddie Stewart as The Dowager Lady Hood
David Ulrichsen as Gaffer Gammon
Barbara Stephens as Jane

This photograph, taken in Montreal, shows what Leacock looked like in his oft-described costume: homburg, over-sized collar and loosened tie, suit and vest worn with gold watch chain, bulky topcoat.
PUBLIC ARCHIVES CANADA/C-7869

Agnes Leacock as she looked in the 1930s.
PUBLIC ARCHIVES CANADA/C-31958

ABOVE   Leacock inspecting an icehouse under construction at Old Brewery Bay, about 1930.
PUBLIC ARCHIVES CANADA/C-31966

BELOW   Leacock and an unidentified man building a studio at Old Brewery Bay in 1939.
PUBLIC ARCHIVES CANADA/C-31969

The boathouse at Old Brewery Bay; in its upper storey, fitted out as an office, Leacock did much of his writing.
PUBLIC ARCHIVES CANADA/C-33105

The front verandah of Leacock's house in the early 1950s, before his property was purchased by the city of Orillia and restored.
PUBLIC ARCHIVES CANADA/C-31929

Leacock's Old Brewery Bay property from the air. The author's boathouse, in the upper storey of which he did much of his writing, stood at the western tip (right foreground) of the wooded point, at the end of the long straight walk that descended from the house's front door. Leacock's farming, poultry raising and orchard activities took place on the land behind the house, at the top of the picture.
PUBLIC ARCHIVES CANADA/C-31964

with this group of his admirers, Leacock was outstandingly successful and durable, and the shape of the career that brought him to prominence was unusual. Although he could not have had his early success without writing for periodicals, he did not follow the course of most other humorists: working in regional journalism or moving to the large publishing and cultural centers. Leacock stayed at home and transcended the limits of regionalism by purposely bringing Montreal and Orillia into the great world through the universality of his literary culture, creative imagination and world presence as a social scientist. He was cosmopolitan on his own terms and in his own way, one which allowed him to meet and know many of the period's most successful writers. Leacock tells a story of entertaining William Butler Yeats at his Montreal dinner table: Yeats's distant, abstracted look prompted one of Leacock's other guests to ask him what he was thinking about. Yeats replied that he wondered whether breakfast was served on the Boston train. Another Montreal visitor, P.G. Wodehouse, met Leacock for dinner at the University Club with René du Roure. According to du Roure's account, Wodehouse and Leacock said little, seeming shy of one another, and conversation was dominated by the fourth member of the party, another member of the club. During Leacock's tour of England, he met many writers, for example Kipling and Arnold Bennett, James Barrie and G.K. Chesterton. His frequent visits to New York allowed him to meet other visiting celebrities and to remain in touch with New York friends and acquaintances. Still, the evidence indicates that Leacock did not truly live a life devoted to a community of writers. If he had any close literary associate with whom his work was discussed and developed, it was Andrew Macphail. Perhaps this influence explains the extent to which Leacock's writing gradually developed away from the nonsense sketches and pure humor of his early books to the warm, personal and more literary tone of his later essays. The literary tradition to which Leacock and MacPhail essentially belonged was not that of fiction writers or poets, but that of the consummate literary practitioner who turned his gifts to the exposition of history, philosophy, science or personal speculation.

As in his economic theory, so in his literary judgments. He

was not interested in the accepted "advanced" ideas or movements, but he was interested in influencing the present and future through his own independent and strongly held view of the best in tradition. Two of the authors he most admired were Mark Twain and Charles Dickens. Leacock published a biography of Mark Twain in 1932 and followed it in 1933 with his very successful *Charles Dickens, His Life and Work*, which was widely and enthusiastically noticed. These books, especially the one on Dickens, began to rebuild Leacock's income from popular writing by establishing him as a successful author of biography and other nonfiction books. The Dickens biography immediately began to increase his royalty income, which was assisted by the popular anthologies that resulted from the Twain and Dickens books. Leacock edited and introduced *The Greatest Pages of Charles Dickens* in 1934 and in 1935 contributed an introduction to an anthology of Twain's work. Now that Dickens is generally regarded as a literary master second only to Shakespeare, it is easy to forget that Leacock was among the first critics and scholars of stature to urge appreciation of the novelist as a great writer. Dickens had steadily lost popularity with the general public in the years after his death; among critics and writers, he carried the stigma of his Victorian preeminence and was dismissed for his old-fashioned attitudes and creation of grotesque character types. Leacock was not especially interested in Dickens as a creator of complexly structured novels; rather, he treated Dickens, like Twain, for his gifts of humor, emphasizing the novelist's power of style and imagination in presenting human life in an artfully altered, exaggerated fashion that revealed its underlying truths. During this same period, G.K. Chesterton was producing similar brief literary biographies of nineteenth-century authors, including Dickens and Browning. Chesterton's works are not regarded by present-day scholars as technically sound because of the author's greater interest in his own generalizations about his subject than in careful exposition of biographical facts and close literary analysis. Leacock and Chesterton display mastery in a common field of writing at the time: the critical biography that depended primarily upon the insights and brilliance of an outstanding writer and critic.

Leacock's interest in writing about humor continued in *Humor: Its Theory and Technique* (1935), a work he was encouraged to proceed with by the great success, in the United States, of his lectures on the technique of humor and the history of American humor. In 1936 he published *Humor and Humanity*, a similar work, and an anthology entitled *The Greatest Pages of American Humor*. The anthology was the only book that resulted from Dodd, Mead's plan to do a whole series of "Greatest Pages" books in the wake of the success of Leacock's Dickens anthology; ultimately, the publisher found that most of the proposed topics for anthologies were either not saleable enough or were impeded by the high cost of permission fees to reprint recent works. For the American humor anthology, Leacock used his personal influence and friendships to obtain, at little or no cost, his samples of contemporary humorists such as Benchley, Ade and Ring Lardner. Like his early essays on humor, Leacock's books on humor theory argued that the art should always evolve away from ridicule towards sympathy and should possess as its motive a true underlying kindness towards the victims of criticism or satire. His ideas met with little critical enthusiasm, although many reviewers and readers enjoyed the books for their stylistic adroitness, their interesting exposition of a wise man's views and the hilarious examples with which Leacock illustrated his points. Even favorable reviews, however, usually stopped to quibble with the idea of kindliness, to question Leacock's analysis of what made certain things funny and to uphold against Leacock the delights of unkindness in humor, from the scatalogical to the primitive and brutal. This reception raises the question, first posed by Peter McArthur in 1923, whether Leacock was limited in his achievement by his determination to remain kindly. For the reader who prefers pure imaginative nonsense, which Leacock practiced throughout his career, but more at its outset, this may be true. However, it is not the manner of Leacock's best and most characteristic humor, such as *Sunshine Sketches*, *Arcadian Adventures* and a host of essays. Such books, taken as examples, along with his theoretical writings, should have made his point about kindliness sufficiently clear, but it was apparently a hard one to grasp. He did not restrict himself to the innocuous to avoid giving hurt. Rather, he insisted that humor recognize the essential fragility and poignancy of human life. He hovered between a freely "religious" faith in life and a thorough agnosticism; this hovering sometimes led him to express the thought that human existence is ultimately insignificant and perhaps meaningless, that those few who (like him) were truly aware realized that nothing really mattered very much. He commented that humor and pathos are ultimately the same. He believed that a sense of the "tears of things" should soften men's hearts towards each other and lead them to use mockery, when it was called for, in the hope that it would reform — rather than dismiss and humiliate. Leacock's purpose in balancing warmth against criticism is his feeling that the power of humor lies in creating sympathy that can lead to change; even if it does not change the victim of the satire, it can change the reader and help him to avoid faults and to avoid condemning those who have them. In Leacock's view, if humor were merely to add scorn to the world, it would be increasing by one the very flaws and failings it pretended to criticize and rise above. Always, Leacock wished to hold out the hope that man can change, that moral values can be recognized and adhered to. He avoided personal invective and destructive criticism of individuals or of types, but often the point of his humor plunged very deep. He questioned the validity of the most cherished attitudes and institutions.

In 1933, the board of governors of McGill University changed Leacock's status from temporary to permanent chairman of the department of economics and political science. The change was little more than a formality. Leacock had been receiving the full chairman's salary since 1908, when he was first asked to take charge of the department temporarily. The department had grown considerably under his charge. In addition to J.C. Hemmeon, the staff included John Culliton, Eugene Forsey, J.P. Day and Carl Goldenberg. Culliton, a former student of Leacock's who joined the department in the early 1930s after study on a royal fellowship in London, shared Leacock's office and later gave him important assistance in preparing *Montreal: Seaport and City* (1942). During the 1930s, Leacock continued his regular contributions to campus periodicals. He wrote frequently for them on the themes of his professional work, such as the economic factors of the depression and the dangers of socialism. He was a campus landmark with his walking stick and ragged, bulky raccoon coat. The regularity of his schedule was something of a local institution. He was always out of bed by five o'clock and at work by five thirty. He wrote for about four morning hours each day, seven days a week. His classes were arranged so that they occupied only three afternoons a week. He would arrive at the Arts Building after his customary stroll on the mountain, and after classes he invariably went to the University Club for a game of billiards with René du Roure. On the other hand, there were decidedly irregular aspects of his conduct as well. A young reporter who visited his Arts Building office was asked to wait while Leacock finished addressing a letter. She was shocked when he calmly drew together a small pile of the correspondence he had been finishing, walked to the window and threw it out on the lawn. He explained that it saved him a trip down to the mailbox: some passerby seeing a heap of addressed letters would post them. Former students speak highly of his unfailing kindness in furthering their careers. Many pupils who studied under him became prominent in Canadian government, business, the military or literature. David Legate records the story of one student, Sydney J. Pierce, who felt that Leacock went too far in his case. Pierce was nominated by Leacock for the chair of political science at Dalhousie University, although the young man doubted his own qualifications. Leacock urged him to do some supplemental reading and to take the post; Pierce resigned after only a few months, and felt afterwards that Leacock had not properly judged his real suitability for the post. This is reminiscent of Leacock's well-meant, but unsuccessful, attempt in the 1920s to make a McGill economics professor out of B.K. Sandwell. On the other hand, Leacock could also demonstrate a strictness in maintaining the standards of his department, proof of his dedication to quality in teachers, students and level of instruction. Several students without proper credentials who applied to him for recommendations received, instead, scathing summaries of their lack of preparedness, or talent, for the positions they sought.

The death of McGill principal Sir Arthur Currie on 31 November, 1933 was one of several sad indications, in the early 1930s, that Leacock, his generation and his world could not remain proof against the effects of age. Principal since the end of World War I, Currie had grown to be one of Leacock's closest friends. Their weekly meetings gave Currie the opportunity to consult Leacock on campus and economic questions. Leacock regularly told stories about his dealings with Currie, whose adaptation of military discipline to campus life often brought delight to the humorist. On one occasion, Currie was surprised and pleased to find one of his former soldiers entering his office. He told the young man that they could enjoy a visit as soon as Currie had dealt with a discipline problem — a student Professor Leacock had complained of. The officer replied that he was the discipline problem. On another occasion, Leacock recalled, Currie was trying to help a former sergeant, now a professor, who was experiencing difficulty as a disciplinarian in his classroom. Currie suggested that the man adapt the methods he had used with his soldiers. When the sergeant said he had regularly fought with any private who defied him, Currie said he should simply threaten his students with the same. Leacock reported sadly that, whether the former sergeant ever used the threat, he could never keep order in class.

On the occasion of Currie's funeral, Leacock published a tribute in the Montreal *Herald*:

It is as a great soldier that the world at large mourns General Currie today. It is right that it should be so. His great achievement was in arms. Those who know tell us that he was one of the great generals of the war; and that if the war had continued, his record, scarcely more than begun, would have placed him among the great captains of the ages.

But there are those of us who were not privileged to know him in this wider horizon. Our memory of him is that of the thirteen years as our principal at McGill. There he sat in his college office room, ready and accessible to all of us. Beside him was his pipe with plenty of strong tobacco and plenty of strong language to keep it burning.

There was a man! I have known many college principals and presidents — a poor lot most of them, with a few brave exceptions here and there. But there was never one to match up to General Currie. College presidents, as a lot, must bow to the rich and fawn for benefactions. Not so General Currie. He thought no more of a plutocrat than of a ninepin. College presidents must be careful what they say and how they say it. Not so General Currie. He said what he thought and he said it in his own way — which was a forceful one. He knew some of the strongest words in the language. Nor was there ever such honesty as his.

For General Currie owed no responsibility to any man. For that he looked elsewhere. Never was there a man so deeply religious in the real meaning of the word. He lived, in peace as in war, with the consciousness of the imminence of death. For him life was but a pathway to something else, and he walked the path with a sense of its meaning and its end that never left him for a day. Beside him as he walked was the shadowed curtain of the infinite.

General Currie knew nothing of scholarship in the narrower sense of the term. His dusty, shabby professors were always a sort of mystery to him. He never could quite understand whether they were researching or loafing. When he first came to us, he imagined that the professors were always buried in the library, each lecture planned and prepared like Vimy Ridge.

Later on he was a little disillusioned. "Some of these gentlemen," he said, only that was not the name he used for them; he had a simple one, "don't research at all." They were like hens who wouldn't lay. But disillusioned or not he was unfailing in the devotion of his leadership.

We never had the place in his heart that he kept for his generals. Nor had we the right to it. His generals were always there in his mind, all nicknamed and labelled, as General Currie loved to name people. Indeed as time went on, we too dropped into our nicknames and labels. No one but General Currie would think of a professor of seventy as "Bill". But he had to have it so. He could not bear a world of idle dignity and pretences.

There were those of us who served under him at McGill to whom there came during his principalship those dark hours that at some time must shadow every human life. And there General Currie was beyond words, — a tenderness of sympathy, an affection for those in distress that no language can present and that no gratitude can repay.

Now it is over. We have laid him to rest. Yet we who served with him at McGill can only hope that somewhere in the sound of the martial music and the measured step of his soldiers, his soul might hear the shuffling step of his dusty professors, out of step

259

and out of breath, but following him, — as they had been wont to these thirteen years, — as best they could.

It was a frequent boast of Leacock's that he, like Aristotle, had taught a great general. Immediately after Currie's funeral, Leacock wrote to his mother that he had been with the principal the day before his last illness, at a luncheon Leacock arranged at the University Club with several of Currie's friends. Leacock and the party had gone with Currie afterward to a McGill football game. It was the last social function Currie attended, and the last time Leacock saw him.

In the same letter, Leacock told his mother that he would be coming, with Stevie, to Orillia for Christmas, and would be over to her house in Sutton on Christmas morning. Agnes was eighty-eight and would celebrate her eighty-ninth birthday just after the first of the year. She remained the center of her family as it gathered for holidays around Lake Simcoe. Since leaving the farm, she had been a close friend of the Sibbalds, the foremost pioneering family of the south shore of Lake Simcoe. She had at first lived with her younger children in a large house, probably a structure called "Rotherwood," on the Sibbald estate, which lay just east of Saint George's Anglican Church (it is now Sibbald Point Provincial Park). Later, Agnes lived with her younger daughters in Beaverton, farther east and north on the lakeshore. Beaverton remained the home of Carrie Leacock, the mother of Leacock's beloved niece and secretary, Barbara Ulrichsen. Later, Agnes lived again on the Sibbald estate, in "the Grange," a white stucco house that was her home during the 1910s: it is the address at which she received the news of Stevie's birth. Finally, Charlie built for her an attractive, somewhat eccentric house in the village of Sutton West, about four miles west of the Sibbald estate, and for the summers she had the permanent let of a cottage owned by Jack Sibbald that stood just east of Saint George's, on the brow of a sand cliff overlooking the lake and screened from the lakeshore road by a cedar hedge. Agnes's Sutton home she called "Bury Lodge," after the fondly remembered home of her English childhood. The lodge stood on the banks of the Black River. Charlie, who generally lived with his mother, built a walk down to a riverside landing stage. The house and the cottage were memorable centers of family activities, filled with souvenirs of Agnes's early life in England and the latest magazines from London, including *Punch* and the *London Illustrated News*. Of Agnes's eleven children, eight were still living; one daughter had died of heart disease in early adulthood, and one son, Dick, of accidental suffocation, according to information Leacock gave on a health record for a life-insurance policy. In early 1932, the other of Leacock's two elder brothers, Jim (Thomas James), died in Belleville, New Jersey, where he was a principal and owner of the A.M. Leacock Company. Throughout 1932, Stephen and Charlie were engaged in settling Jim's estate, eventually valued at $29,500. They also rearranged the administration and distribution of the Thomas Murdock Leacock Trust, a task necessitated by the death of the trust's principal legatee, Miss A.C. Leacock, a sister of Leacock's father.

During the summers, the other eight children and their families gathered around Agnes at Sutton and Sibbald Point, and to a somewhat lesser extent around Stephen and his Old Brewery Bay establishment. In the 1930s, as Agnes aged, her children's love for her was seconded by an urgency to give their children the experience of knowing their remarkable grandmother. All visited as often as they could, which was regularly or very frequently in the case of Stephen, George, Charlie, Daisy (Mrs. Margaret Burrows of Belleville), Carrie (Mrs. Jan Ulrichsen of Beaverton), and Maymee (Mrs. Henry Bergh of Toronto). Agnes was also visited regularly by the motherless Sheppards (five boys and a girl), the children of the deceased Missie (Mrs. Harry Sheppard). Less frequent visitors were Dot (Dr. Rosamond Leacock), whose practice was then in Calgary, and Teddy, a pharmaceutical salesman in the same city. Leacock's distinctive contribution to the visitors was a steady stream of interesting characters from the outside world, professors and journalists, writers and publishers, celebrities and agricultural scientists whom he would lure to Old Brewery Bay with the promise of trout and bass fishing; he hooked them with the relaxed, unself-conscious, slightly oddball magic of the Leacock summer land, and they returned annually.

Leacock's concern for his family shows in a large number of

ways. In 1934 he was helping the financially hard-pressed Teddy by making sure Teddy received advances on money due to him from Leacock estates (principally, by this time, that of Agnes herself). Teddy wrote to Stephen in November 1934:

> I very much appreciate what your cheques have ment to me they have relieved me of any worry as to extra expenses, possiable ment the difference of Peter keeping on at U.C.C. I enclos copy of his last report, he does not stand so well as last term, but whether he stand at the foot or top of his class I am sure the life, discipline and education he is getting will be of great value to him in his later life.

Teddy's son Peter had roomed with Stevie at Upper Canada College in 1933, and Teddy indicated that he looked forward to the boys doing so again in 1934. Throughout the 1920s and early 1930s, Leacock kept in especially close contact with his mother through letters when he could not visit her personally. She informed him of her flower gardening, which they apparently advised upon together, and discussed her paintings (such as one of lilacs she had done for Dot, who was in Calgary where lilacs did not grow), her various housekeepers and companions, the comings and goings and the health of various old friends and her reading. At various times in the late 1920s Agnes commented to her son in a way that reveals the varied intellectual life she continued to lead into her later years. Of her son's own books, the one that interested her the most seems to have been *The Unsolved Riddle of Social Justice*. She requested from him such books as the new Anglican prayer book and a life of Cardinal Newman and some of the churchman's works; after receiving them, she commented, in a letter, in some detail on the biography and on Newman's *Apologia Pro Vita Sua*. Another book that called forth some remarks from her on the relationship of men to their times was a biography of Goldwin Smith. During the early 1930s, letters show that Leacock was asking her for as much information as she could recall about her origins and childhood in England. At the time of his work on Dickens, he pumped her memory regarding a lecture appearance the novelist made in Plymouth, but she could only reply, in a letter of 25 November, 1932:

Charlie & I have hunted all through my diaries to find an account of that lecture by Dickens but 1865 is lost — all I can remember is — Fanny Bradley & I went but the hall was so packed we could not hear half he said. We were away near the door. I think we gave up trying to get nearer & went home.

Other letters show that Agnes read a letter in Latin that Stevie sent her, and replied in the same language, though she was apologetic about the rustiness of her skills in composition. For one winter, she provided board for a grandchild at her Sutton West home so the boy could attend a local high school, and she coached him in French while he was living with her. Agnes was also a frequent visitor to Leacock's home in Montreal. Leacock often told the story of her relentless attack, during a Montreal social function, on fellow guest Sir Ernest Rutherford, the Nobel Prize-winning physicist who taught at McGill until 1907. Agnes was determined, Leacock said, to argue him out of his supposed atheistic beliefs. She assumed that, because he was a scientist, he was inevitably an atheist. This is indeed typical of her. She commented, on *Unsolved Riddle*, "I enjoy it — I am glad to see by the quotations you have not forgotten your Bible."

The Christmas celebrations of 1934 proved to be the last family assembly at which Agnes presided. She died on 19 January, 1935, and was buried in the family plot at Saint George's Church. The influence she had had on her children was described by Leacock in *The Boy I Left Behind Me*. His own partnership with her in raising the youngest children after his father's departure perhaps made him the closest to her among her children, although she often snapped angrily at persons who praised only Stephen from among her children. George, she maintained, was at least as much a wit as Stephen (an opinion Stephen shared and often expressed in writing); Charlie, who lived with her, was also a special favorite. Stephen's and Agnes's partnership could be, at times, an uneasy one. If Agnes had special influence, Stephen also had a strong sense of male proprietorship over, and responsibility for, the family, which he perhaps felt he had particularly earned through his youthful sacrifices on behalf of his brothers and sisters. According to Elizabeth Kimball, one of the rare disputes ever witnessed between Stephen and his mother arose when Agnes added her voice to those who were criticizing Stephen for writing too much and too quickly. Friction was rare, however, and Agnes and Stephen co-operated closely in creating the joyful family idyll that repeated itself each summer at Lake Simcoe. Leacock's success, first as a professor and later as an author, had made possible his own home at Old Brewery Bay and the assistance he gave to his mother, the family's heart. He oversaw the trust conferred upon her at her marriage, which continued to be her main source of personal income, and stood ready to provide any other money she might need. It was Leacock, principally, who enabled the Leacock family to maintain its joyful, ever-dynamic center at Lake Simcoe, and it is not too much to say that this thriving, extended family, with its orbit of friends, was the primary motive of his work, or at least of his efforts to wring from work whatever money it could bring in. In a family, as he had said, "the money they have represents only a means whereby family love and family happiness can be achieved." Still, while it was Leacock who had been able to make that family center exist, Agnes was the center. The Leacock summer kingdom had survived diminishment in the deaths of Missie, Dick, Jim and Beatrix, but the death of Agnes meant the beginning of its dissolution. Without her presence, there was nowhere for all her children to gather with their children, no one around whom to gather. They continued to visit Stephen, and some of them continued to rent cottages in the Sutton area, to summer there, to stop in Beaverton or Aurora. But slowly, surely, the circle fell apart. Agnes' children were beginning to age as well. The grandchildren, many of them, were too old for summer play; they were marrying and going their own ways. Another factor was the demoralization caused by Agnes's death, which seems to have particularly affected one key member of the family group, Charlie, the Leacocks' last representative in Sutton. After his mother's death, he suffered increasing physical and mental difficulties, and throughout the early 1940s he was a major concern to Stephen, George and Dot, who was working at Toronto's Hospital for Sick Children. In the years after his illness of 1938, Stephen brought to the Leacock summer world a late flourishing by the pure dynamism of his own character and the resurgence of his career. But it is clear that, from the time of Agnes' death, the story is one of inexorable decline.

In one area, at least, the force of Agnes's training seems to have had no effect upon Stephen. The daughter of a minister, she had brought her children up in the Anglican Church. But, from his childhood, Stephen rebelled against the imposition of organized religion. He remembered church services of his childhood as beneficial only in providing an occasion to meet his friends at the lakeshore. In his Upper Canada College days, he used the obligatory services as a time to compose humorous stories, which he read aloud to fellow teachers as afternoon entertainment. In many works, such as *Arcadian Adventures with the Idle Rich*, Leacock satirized the practice of religion as he observed it in society. He found fault with those who sacrificed doctrine to expediency, but at the same time he questioned the wisdom of allowing doctrinal difference to stand in the way of other considerations — for instance, romance between persons of different faiths. In "The Devil and the Deep Sea," he warned that society should not abandon its traditional moral guidelines in favor of new psychological lessons for conduct. Nevertheless, he did not apply this warning to his own abandonment of organized religion, presumably the source of those traditional moral values. In his article about Arthur Currie, Leacock suggested a key to his attitude. He objected to all organized religion, but he admired Currie as a man "deeply religious in the real meaning of the word." In a short book on the American president Abraham Lincoln, *Lincoln Frees the Slaves* (1935), Leacock praised Lincoln in similar terms as a religious man, "a man who lives in the daily consciousness of the transcience of life and the imminence of death." Thus, in later years, Leacock was speaking for a form of acknowledgment of spiritual values that he did not find in any church. It is another of his links to the Victorian era — to the Victorian intelligentsia rather than to the "typical" attitudes of that period. He gives evidence of feeling, as did many Victorian intellectuals, that the moral principles of the Christian religion are one of mankind's greatest and most necessary creations, but he also indicates that the informed can accept them and shuck away their institutional and mythological trappings. The trappings must not be criticized too harshly, for the common people still need them to apprehend a morality they canot arrive at intellectually.

Leacock's worries about his own future intruded on him increasingly as his income continued to fall. His particular concern was provision for Stevie, who was performing very well at high school. Leacock's special concern at this time was his son's legacy, through his mother, from the Pellatt fortune. He wrote frequently to Mrs. R.B. Hamilton, Beatrix's mother, who under the inheritance was to have the use of Beatrix's portion to draw its interest; the capital would come to Stevie when he was of age. Leacock tried in vain to get Beatrix's mother to entrust the capital to him and let him pay her the interest. He was afraid that her brother, Sir Henry Pellatt, the builder of Casa Loma, who exercised great influence over her, would obtain the money and sink it into his bankrupt interests and his mismanaged attempts at recovery — such as a plan to turn the cavernous castle into a hotel. Although Beatrix's mother on occasion seemed ready to turn over the money to Leacock in exchange for his assurances that he would provide her an income for life, she never concluded the agreement. At her death, there was very little left of the inheritance that had been meant for Stevie. Despite the tension over this matter, Leacock frequently entertained Beatrix's mother in Old Brewery Bay.

In 1935, honors and acknowledgments of his status continued to arrive. In Great Britain, the Methuen Library of Humor published a Leacock volume, which was also marketed in the United States. On 15 January 1935, Leacock was awarded the Mark Twain Medal by the International Mark Twain Society, which cited him as "The Modern Aristophanes," a specific acknowledgment of the dimension of direct and effective social satire in his work. Earlier recipients of this award had been Guglielmo Marconi, Oliver Wendell Holmes, Rudyard Kipling, Booth Tarkington, Franklin Roosevelt and Willa Cather — but also Benito Mussolini (as a "great educator" in 1930).

As the 1934-35 academic year rolled to a close, Leacock found changes in his life. His income was down, his economic leadership was washed away by the return of the Liberal party to power in Ottawa and his latest interests in humorous writing and the theory of humor were failing to find the large audience he had enjoyed a decade before. Some of his closest friends and family members had died, and he was just beginning to feel the impact of his mother's death. In late February, 1935 he wrote to some friends:

> Very many thanks for your kind letter about Mother's death. I feel that to you & to all the Hett's her loss comes especially close: We were all so much together long ago.
>
> It was a wonderful scene at the church yard when we buried Mother: deep snow & bright, bright sun & very still & quiet in the shelter. . . .
>
> It did not seem sad at the time; it was like a gathering of the family; but now it seems so strange & sad all the time to think that she is gone.

Leacock was soon to experience another sad change. He was surprised and hurt — and defiant — to discover that the McGill board of governors had determined he must leave the university in the spring of 1936 because he had reached the age of sixty-five.

Chapter Thirteen

Mc-Guillotined

STEPHEN Leacock's teaching career of almost fifty years began at a high school in Uxbridge, Ontario in January, 1889. He gave his last lectures as a McGill professor to a group of well-wishers gathered in Montreal on 4 May, 1936. Although he became a teacher unwillingly and said that he had disliked high-school teaching from first day to last, he loved his university classroom with a passion that flared most brilliantly when he heard the news that he would have to leave it. The furor created by Leacock's enforced retirement attracted international attention and caused his admirers and friends to search for new projects, including university teaching posts, to remedy the loss he felt so deeply. English journalists suggested that he relocate in his native country, where he would be certain of an enthusiastic welcome; New York newspapers wanted to see him at a university in the United States. Proposals for extensive lecture tours came from all over the world. He was invited to speak at Harvard University and to join the staff of the University of British Columbia. Despite the battle he waged to keep his McGill post, however, Leacock refused all offers of university positions and almost all speaking engagements. Although he never relented from the conviction that he had been treated shamefully by the McGill administration, he was braced by the warmth of support from his readers around the world and announced that he would devote himself to writing. He made a final triumphant lecture tour across western Canada in the winter of 1936 and then entered "the silence which is golden." However, he redoubled his production of articles on economics, humor sketches and books. It seems likely that it was as much his strong love of familiar routine as his commitment to writing that kept Leacock in Canada. He moved from Montreal to Orillia with the changing seasons, as he had since the turn of the century.

Leacock refused, with thanks, the suggestion that he come "home" to England. After years of celebrating his British heritage, he reminded his friends that Canada had been and would continue to be home by his own choice. Still, despite the vigor of his campaign to keep his job and to perform at a pace that disproved the university's apparent conviction that he was now "useless," by the second year after his retirement Leacock was showing signs of the effects of his years and struggles. The marriage of his niece, Barbara Ulrichsen, in the summer of 1937 left him with a disarranged household. Although surrounded by faithful household staff and many friends, he found it increasingly difficult to take delight in life when one of his greatest pleasures, the companionship of intimate co-workers and family members, was being taken from him. In the spring of 1938, for the first time in a vigorous life, Leacock faced a serious illness. Such an illness might have been deeply discouraging for many, but it spurred Leacock on to a last golden period of work. The best of his humorous gifts shone through to illuminate his memories, his belief in the history and the future of his country and especially the hopefulness he felt in the experience of life itself.

Leacock's friend B.K. Sandwell had warned him, back in 1909, that the pursuit of humor might threaten his influence on serious affairs. Presumably, Sandwell feared that Leacock would not be able to get a hearing for his political and economic views, or that readers would not take his work in these fields seriously. Over the years, the paradox of the humorist-economist was raised in all manner of discussions of Leacock, from praise of his unique gifts to criticism that he refused to limit himself to what he did best. Some reviewers insulted Leacock's economic theory by saying that it must have been intended as humor — forgetting, perhaps, that Leacock had made effective use of this same witty twist as early as 1915 in "Conversations with the Supermen." Leacock might have spared himself this particular taunt had he not been a humorist; it is fair to say that because he was both a humorist and a social scientist he was prevented from producing the same body of work in either field he might have done had he concentrated on only one. The key to Leacock's rather enigmatic blend of gifts may be that he was not simply a humorist and a political economist, but rather that he was an educated man and an educator. Restless, all his life, to find new ways to channel his energy and talents, Leacock never let go of teaching. Courted by politicians and businessmen to enter more directly, during his McGill years, into the work of administering the nation's economy and government, Leacock consistently refused, so that he could remain in his classroom. In part, he hoped to school an entire generation in his views; in part, he wished to maintain the freedom to speak that his position as university professor gave him. As a professor he was unhindered by influence or the charge of special interests. Not only did he write about his special field, economics, from his vantage point in the university, but he frequently discussed education itself. Throughout his long career, Leacock approached the subject of education in many ways, as story-teller, as satirist, as critic, as apologist. Like his views on economics, his theories of education seem, at times, to lie rather to one side of twentieth-century development, neither in the vanguard of thought nor entirely opposed to it. But they remain the testimony of a man who had lived through perhaps the greatest revolution ever experienced by the modern university, as it changed from an exclusive preserve of the rich to a sort of training school required for entry into all professions. Modern troubles with universities involve new variations on the old questions of money, relevance of curricula and the proper size of the student population. Leacock made, in enduring form, some of the most cogent statements on the nature and purposes of higher education. This theme was a constant in his work; it received its most thorough treatment in a book produced after he left McGill, *Too Much College* (1939).

During the first months of 1935, Leacock was involved in Prime Minister Robert Bennett's efforts to introduce a "New Deal" package of social legislation, which led, in the summer, to a Conservative defeat in the national election forced by Liberal leader Mackenzie King. In 1935, Leacock won the Mark Twain Medal for his writing of and about humor. In Montreal, he took part in the twenty-fifth-anniversary celebration of his beloved University Club. Standing on a beer barrel in the center of the bar, Leacock presented the history of the organization as it had followed the rising and falling fortunes of its liquor budget. He also had a new concern, which he expressed in a four-page pamphlet privately printed in January. This was the financial stability of McGill University. The depression had brought severe difficulties to the school; no new direction had yet emerged because no successor had been appointed to Sir Arthur Currie. Frank Dawson Adams, a world authority on geology, was acting principal while the search for a permanent replacement was being conducted throughout Canada and in many other countries. Leacock proposed a number of budget cuts as a means of helping the university. Athletic programs could be curtailed, he said, and university posts left vacant by deaths or retirements of senior faculty members could be abolished; the income and work could be distributed to junior faculty members. "Statistics will prove that $5,000 worth of us dies each year; with luck, more." He also suggested that senior faculty be retired: "Where the senior professor is not far off pension anyway, give him one and compensate the juniors." Leacock marked the pamphlet "confidential and not for circulation" before distributing it among a small group, but he later referred to its recommendations when discussing the alignment of his department after his retirement was announced. There is no record that the board of governors used the pamphlet in its private deliberations on the financial crisis of the university in early 1935, although it is known that a financial investigation had been under way for some time.

In April 1935, Leacock wrote to a friend, the novelist J.A.T. Lloyd, that "A.E. Morgan of Hull University College is to succeed General Currie here: he will find it a hard job as the finances are in an almost hopeless state." Morgan's appointment was made in the spring; he was to take up his post in the fall for the 1935-36 school year. A letter from Leacock, written in the summer of 1935, indicates that Morgan was being consulted regarding new appointments to Leacock's department. Leacock evidently had objected to a proposed candidate, but acknowledged in a letter of 29 June that the principal must have scope to operate: "My feeling is that if the Principal, with a knowledge of the facts before him, wished Dr. Plaut to come, then I or anyone else ought to give way. This is what we would have done with General Currie." This letter makes no reference to Leacock's retirement; it is possible that he had not yet heard of it. However, the formal notice from which he apparently first received the news is dated 12 June and came to him from the treasurer of the university, A.P.S. Glassco. Glassco's announcement was little more than a form letter, which cited a recent decision by the McGill board of governors on retirement policy:

> Resolved: That all teachers and officers of the University shall automatically retire on reaching the age of 65 years, the Board, however, to reserve the right to retain the services of any officer or teacher beyond that age if it be considered in the interests of the Univeristy to do so.
>
> Pursuant to the above resolution, the Governors have instructed me to notify you that you will be retired from the University on May 31st, 1936.

There is no record of Leacock's response to this letter, or any indication in his surviving correspondence that the expectation of enforced retirement was an important issue until he returned to the campus in the fall. The policy was a new one at McGill, and it provided for exceptions. Leacock wrote to his friend Sir Edward Beatty about the question, and seems to have hoped that he might be one of the exceptions. In a letter dated 13 November, A.E. Morgan wrote to Leacock to adjust a few details of the retirement, including a small salary increase in anticipation of Leacock's pension requirements. Morgan stated that the academic year would be considered to end on 31 August rather than 31 May, as reported in Glassco's original letter. Morgan began the letter by commenting that he had understood Leacock to be aware of the new policy, which was intended to be implemented immediately. Morgan wrote, "Although it is true that the resolution of the Governors reserves to them the right in very exceptional cases to extend that period, it is the intention of the University to regard retirement at sixty-five as the normal procedure."

Clearly, Morgan intended to close the door on the possibility of making an exception for Leacock. Morgan had begun his letter with the greeting, "Dear Leacock." On 21 November, Leacock replied:

Dear Mr. Principal,

I beg to acknowledge the receipt of your letter informing me that I have been retired from the active staff of the university, and to thank you — my dear Morgan — for the personal kindliness with which you write.

S.L.

He wrote at greater length on 11 December to Beatty.

I would have written sooner but there seemed no use in it. Since I got your earlier letter I had one from the Principal definitely removing me from McGill: so that what I do or don't do, as a professor, is so nearly over that it is of no consequence. I feel deeply humiliated not at Morgan's letter, but at the thankless and unfair letter which it ratified. I am at least certain you didn't write it.

Beatty's reply, although conciliatory, determinedly refused to take up the cause, or even to understand sympathetically the complaint Leacock was making. Beatty wrote, "I do not think that you need feel the least concern about the tone of a routine letter, when you remember your long years of service to the University and the appreciation of them which you already know to be no less than world-wide." But it was precisely his long service that had led Leacock to think he should not have been addressed on the sensitive question of enforced retirement through a "routine letter." Beatty said, "For yourself, I am afraid that I have no sympathy. You have had a full life and achieved fame. Beyond that I do not see what reward any man can obtain." Beatty held out the hope that Leacock would "have many years during which your influence will be increased in some way by the fact that you are no longer an active member of the staff."

Soon after Beatty's letter, the public announcement of the retirement was made. Thirteen McGill faculty members were to be retired. They included Frank Dawson Adams, acting principal; four department chairmen; Doctor Nevil Norton Evans, who was celebrating his fiftieth year at McGill; and Doctor Charles F. Martin, senior dean and head of the medical faculty. Alone among this distinguished company, Leacock spoke publicly of his disappointment at the announcement. A reporter for the *Montreal Star* sought him out at his Arts Building office and asked for his reaction. Leacock led the way to his office, where colleague John Culliton and the reporter watched Leacock hastily write out a reply. It appeared, along with stories of his retirement, in papers around the world: "I have plenty to say about the Governors of McGill putting me out of the university. But I have all eternity to say it in. I shall shout it down to them." The *New York Times*, which frequently published Leacock's economic articles in the United States, carried an editorial in which it was urged that the retiring professor be hired by an American university "to smoke at its post-graduate students," in the manner Leacock had described admiringly in "Oxford as I See It."

Despite the local and international outcry in support of Leacock's cause, his retirement remained in force. Students and teachers disagree as to who was at fault in the matter; some put the blame on the board of governors and some blame Morgan. There is also a question as to Leacock's interpretation of his retirement. Did he believe the responsibility for it lay with the new principal or with the university's administration? Leacock's letters indicate that he understood the original decision had come from the board, not from Morgan. In the months after the retirement became public knowledge, however, he found himself at odds with the new principal over questions relating to the future of his department. The lack of courtesy that grated on Leacock when he received Morgan's letter about the retirement continued as Leacock attempted to consult with the principal. In February 1936, he sent Morgan a memorandum detailing suggestions the principal had suggested that he make about the future composition of the department. Leacock's memorandum was intended to counter a proposal that the department of economics and political science be combined with other departments. Leacock said the department's work was already too broad, and that it had "suffered greatly from the financial stringency of the past few years. It has had to forgo the services of outside examiners from other universities; it has lost various scholarships which it had from McGill and from private sources for graduate students, and, most of all, it has had to suspend the publication of the monographs on Canadian problems which were a chief feature of its work." There had also been salary cuts. Leacock's salary, for example, had decreased, in 1931, from its long-time level of fifty-five hundred dollars. Leacock emphasized that, as a Canadian institution, McGill needed a political science and economics program of a distinctive character. It is generally agreed that Morgan, a product of British universities, had begun his first year at McGill by finding fault with many of the departments because they did not correspond to British forms. Leacock recommended that his own position not be filled by a new faculty member, so that the savings from his salary could be used to aid the department. He recommended that his associate, J.C. Hemmeon, succeed him as chairman, and concluded by saying, "I am authorized by my colleagues Dr. Hemmeon and Dr. Day and Professor Culliton to say that they entirely concur in the views as to the department expressed in this letter. Mr. Forsey is ill but I have every reason to presume his acquiescence." The care and thoroughness of his suggestions, in which there was no further allusion to his personal disappointment, met with a response that infuriated him. The principal replied that Leacock had no right to submit it, "no right to ask the opinion of junior men whose opinions were not wanted; no right to make a representation in writing" on a subject Morgan wished to discuss verbally. Leacock then sent a copy of the memorandum to another retiree, Dean Charles Martin, with a request that it be given by him to the McGill senate. Leacock explained to Martin that Morgan's "manner and language were overbearing and quite unsuited to the dignity of his position or the privilege of mine." Morgan refused to consider Hemmeon as chairman, although he later relented and informed Leacock that he had invited Hemmeon to act as temporary chairman. Eventually Hemmeon did receive the post, which he held until 1945. But the exchange over the department's future shows that Leacock's dispute with Morgan lay not simply in the issue of retirement but in the manner in which the new principal was exercising his authority.

As the academic year drew to a close, the sparring between Morgan and Leacock continued. After the dispute about the department's future, they began to exchange public insults. Someone told Leacock that the board of governors had searched for Currie's successor with a fine-tooth comb. Leacock replied, "You know what you get when you resort to a fine-tooth comb." During a speaking tour, Morgan told au-

diences that his reforms had rid McGill of "university professors who prided themselves on wearing torn gowns." A
story circulated that Morgan had greeted Leacock with the
words, "Professor Leacock, I am credibly informed that, of all
the bad departments at this university, yours is one of the
worst." Leacock told friends that Morgan was running McGill
"like a boys' school." Leacock delivered his last lecture to an
audience of two hundred students, alumni and faculty
members at a dinner at the Ritz-Carleton Hotel on 4 May,
1936; Morgan did not attend. Although Leacock lost the war to
keep his job, he won his point that he deserved better treatment than Morgan had shown him. In the end, Morgan survived only one year: he was fired at the end of the 1937
academic year. When word of his dismissal became public, the
McGill Daily proposed Leacock as a likely candidate for vice-
chancellor. The board of governors chose the American
educator Lewis Williams Douglas, but they were again disappointed in their choice. Douglas left after two years because of
interests in the United States. Leacock remarked, "McGill has
established a new two-year course, leading to the degree of ex-
principal."

Leacock's attitude towards Morgan contrasts with his opinion of Sir Edward Beatty, whom he referred to as "the Chief
Justice who passed sentence on the Senility Gang." Leacock
remained close to Beatty despite the tensions created when
Beatty refused to acknowledge Leacock's right to remain at
McGill. Beatty was a prominent figure in the ceremonies that
honored Leacock in the spring of 1936. He sat next to Leacock
at the dinner at the Ritz-Carleton, and commented, "We are
all sorry to see him leave the halls of McGill." Three weeks
later Beatty presented Leacock an honorary doctor-of-laws
degree at the university convocation ceremonies. Notes for
Leacock's 4 May speech at the Ritz-Carleton are preserved
among the humorist's papers. On a sheet of stationery from
the Mount Royal Hotel, Leacock wrote out a very brief list of
topics: "My last lecture . . . old pupils / Subject . . . Paradise
lost / All retrospect . . . honour college / Tried but . . . Evening
light . . . Superself / Your gift / Paradise regained / All for today." He elaborated on this basic structure in two revisions.
The speech made little reference to the controversy over his

retirement. Leacock said, "The time came when the college said it had heard our lectures so often that it would pay us not to give any more." Calling his remarks "my last lecture," Leacock said he had saved his final appearance for his old pupils because one more talk from him could not hurt them. The paradise he was losing was the paradise of the university, and he praised "the ideal professor" as careless in his dress, gullible before the wiles of idle students but embodying "that higher idealism lifted above life." Leacock was presented with a charcoal portrait by artist Richard Jack and two leather-bound sets of his works; there were forty volumes in each set. One was given to the university library, the other to Stevie. In accepting the gifts, Leacock said,

> I am told you were in some doubt whether to let it be Shakespeare's works or my own. You have chosen wisely. I have not only written more than Shakespeare, but what I have written is worth more. Shakespeare's books can be had anywhere at fifteen cents each, while mine run from a dollar up.

It seemed, for a time, that when Leacock called this his last lecture, he was determined to make it so. Early in 1936 he sent a printed notice to lecture bureaus and publishing services throughout North America that said, "I am giving up lecturing and planning to preserve the silence which is golden." He added, "I hope never to speak publicly in Montreal again." When he returned to McGill at the end of May to receive his honorary degree, he accepted his award and waved to the crowd but declined to offer any word. The occasion was a difficult one. He was staying with his friend Sir Andrew Macphail, who had written: "For the time of your apotheosis would you think it *dignus ut intreo sub suo tecto*. There will be a chamber, a table, a stool, and a candle-stick, such as was provided in Shurem for another holy man of God." The resolution not to speak soon gave way, however, in part because of Sir Edward Beatty's encouragement. Although he had not been able, the year before, to convince Leacock to support him in his criticisms of the nation's young socialist economists, Beatty continued to encourage Leacock to remain active and provide a contrast to their views. "I still believe your powerful voice and equally powerful pen should be used to combat the inaccurate and loose thinking which the more vocal members of your profession are indulging in." Beatty's prompting was one reason why, in the fall of 1936, Leacock undertook a tour of western Canada, which took him to five provinces in two months for thirty separate speaking engagements. This was, indeed, the last lecture tour he ever made and, apart from a handful of brief appearances for special occasions, his last public speaking.

After leaving McGill, Leacock often said bitterly that he was retired "as useless." He prided himself on the volume of work he accomplished. In 1937, after the publication of *Humor and Humanity*, he wrote to a friend that it was his fifth book since the university had judged him too old to be of service. During his last year at the school, he had maintained an extremely demanding work schedule outside the classroom despite the distracting battle over his retirement. His anthology, *The Greatest Pages of American Humor*, appeared early in 1936. At the same time, his agent was attempting to place the verses planned for *Hellements of Hickonomics* with American newspapers, but found some difficulty because the poems were too long. The book, which Leacock called his "last say" about economics, appeared in the spring of 1936. Like *College Days, Hellements of Hickonomics* disappointed his admirers. The book is perhaps the most curious mixture of economics and humor Leacock ever attempted. He presented jibes at economic theories in the form of light verse. In "Oh! Mr. Malthus," he questioned the justice of the Malthusian theory that would condemn to death the people unable to support themselves by the wages provided by their capitalist employers. In January, 1936 Leacock was invited by the Toronto newspaper *The Financial Post* to write a twice-weekly column; he did not accept the offer, but often published economic and political articles in the periodical. In April, he spoke in Orillia at a ceremony marking the three-hundredth anniversary of the death of Champlain. During the spring, he wrote several papers on economics, including a series entitled "The Gathering Financial Crisis of Canada," which began to appear in the London *Morning Post* on 6 July, 1936. In the series, Leacock was critical of Canadian government policy in administering the Canadian National Railway and in combating the depression. At the same time, he expressed great confidence in the country's future, particularly through development of natural resources. (H.A. Gwynne of the *Morning Post* wrote to say, "I was taken to task by your Finance Minister, Mr. Dunning, who let it be known to me . . . that he thought that the publication of the articles the day after his arrival was intended almost as a personal affront to himself.") Another book of humor, *Funny Pieces: A Book of Random Sketches*, was published in the United States in 1936 and in England in 1937. The English edition included an answer to a request, published in London's *Daily Express*, that Leacock move to his native country. Leacock said he would not "come home" to England because he was already at home. If he moved, he would miss the close association with the United States: "they're educated just as we are and know all about kilowatts, but quit Latin at the fourth declension." Above all, he wished to stake his fortune with Canada.

We are "sitting pretty" here in Canada. East and West are two oceans faraway; we are backed up against the ice cap of the Pole; our feet rest on the fender of the American border, warm with a hundred years of friendship. The noise and tumult of Europe we scarcely hear: not for us the angers of the Balkans, the weeping of Vienna and the tumults of Berlin. Our lot lies elsewhere: shovelling up mountains, floating in the sky to look for gold, and finding still the Star of the Empire in the West.

The warmth of feeling for Canada's future was an important theme for Leacock, fresh from the experience of his triumphant western tour.

There were several reasons to make the tour. Many requests for lectures had been coming in since his announcement that he would not be making speaking engagements in the future. His friend Sir Edward Beatty wanted Leacock to counter both young socialist economists and new political movements in the Canadian west. Leacock wished to sound a note of optimism. He preached a new empire, this time a Canadian one, whose goals would be the development of natural resources and the settlement of a new immigrant population in uncultivated areas. He also hoped that his appearances could benefit

McGill financially: former students living in the west might become interested in the university's economic crisis. Leacock was also in need of fresh sources of income. His McGill pension provided him with $2,750. His 1935 income had been approximately $14,000, still substantially below what he had been earning in the 1920s. This tour was the first time he charged a fee for speaking in Canada. Leacock's choice of topics for his tour — serious discussions of current political and economic issues in Canada — was perhaps determined, in part, by the changing fortunes of his popularity. Formerly, his humor books had represented the most substantial share of his annual writing income. In July, 1936, however, royalty statements from his publishers in New York showed that Leacock was earning much more from his critical writing than he was from his new humor collections. Dodd, Mead sent him only $453.30 before taxes for six months and reported that $374.95 of the *Afternoons in Utopia* advance was still unearned. By contrast, Doubleday Doran, the publishers of *Charles Dickens: His Life and Works* and *Greatest Pages of American Humor*, sent him $2,886.53, of which $2,353.38 came from the Dickens biography. The biography sold 46,823 copies in the company's Dollar Book Club. Leacock might have hoped for a good return from a tour on economic subjects, especially with the prospect of being able to sell his speeches as articles and again in book form afterward. In addition, the disappointment of being retired might have suggested that he would gain most satisfaction by proving himself still useful in his academic discipline.

Before making the western tour, Leacock went to the eastern United States at the end of October. He spoke in Memphis, Tennessee; Amherst and Springfield, Massachusetts; and Middletown, New York. The western trip was planned to start from Montreal on 25 November. Leacock was going to travel with Stevie, a freshman at McGill; he had obtained permission to miss classes for the two months of the tour. Just before leaving, Leacock sent Dodd, Mead a proposal for a book based on the trip. He acknowledged that his subject was not commercial, but promised that his manner of presentation would make it so. He also asked for no money in advance, and offered to reduce his royalty to ten percent. During the tour, he heard back from the company that the book was not acceptable. Then Miller Services Limited of Toronto wrote to say that they wished to syndicate articles based on the trip, and would produce a book. The *Montreal Star* had already contracted for a series of twelve articles. Miller eventually sold the series — "My Discovery of the West" — to the Toronto *Globe and Mail* for $480, or $40 per article, $15 more than Leacock had suggested. Miller wrote, "I think the sale establishes a record in its total amount of any series of articles sold to an individual newspaper in Canada." Leacock kept a record of the tour in a hardbound book, in which he wrote from back to front. He noted their departure from Montreal on 25 November and the first lectures, on 27 and 28 November, at Fort William, Ontario. He addressed a dinner for McGill alumni and lectured on Canadian–United States relations to the Men and Women's Canadian Club. In Winnipeg, he turned down several offers to speak, including one from the famous Women's Press Club. (The club had spearheaded the campaign to win the vote for women in the days of World War I.) He spoke at the University Women's Club, the Men's Canadian Club and the University of Manitoba. Leacock wrote home:

> It is just like a come-to-Jesus parade. I talked at the Fort Gary Hotel and a little while before the meeting they said, "This is the record for seats except for the Queen of Rumania," and a little later, "This beats the Queen of Rumania," and later, "The Queen is nowhere."

From Winnipeg, the tour went to Regina and then to Alberta. Leacock visited his brother Teddy in Calgary and spoke five times in Edmonton, three of the speeches in one day. The trip ended in Victoria, on Vancouver Island. Leacock wrote home to Barbara that she should refuse all invitations for a time because the trip had left him tired. Still, he was triumphant on his return to Montreal in mid-January. Contracts were in place for the new book, and the success of the tour seemed a guarantee that it would have a wide audience.

In *My Discovery of the West*, Leacock wrote as a historian and a political economist. He combined analysis of contemporary economic movements, as in "The Pure Theory of Social Credit," with historical surveys of all the western provinces. His basic message was that the west would provide a source of wealth for the country as long as its resources were managed in the national interest. Although he still stressed the potential, for Canada, of the imperial relationship with Great Britain and her former dominions, he began to speak of "the empire of Canada." Leacock explored the individual potential of each province; he also proposed measures that would strengthen the country by placing more power in the hands of the federal government. These included transfer to Canada of the right to amend the British North America Act, consolidation of provincial debts into a national debt and a unified policy for the national railways (they should be government-owned or privately owned). Reviews of the book were generally positive. They praised Leacock's popular style, a selling point for audiences disinclined to venture into the serious and difficult subjects he wished to explore. His thinking was not always supported, but his ability to interest people in his viewpoint was unquestioned. "The book as a whole will not end arguments, but start them. And that, no doubt, was what Professor Leacock intended," one critic said. The blend of humor with serious subjects sometimes grated. Reviewers seemed willing to grant Leacock the right to speak on serious subjects, but some of them regretted what they saw as contrived and "unspontaneous" efforts to mix jokes with argument.

In 1937, Leacock also published *Humor and Humanity*, the second of his theoretical studies of the comic art, and *Here Are My Lectures and Stories!* As its title suggests, this third book of the year contained transcriptions of several of Leacock's popular lectures. More polished versions on similar themes had been published in other books, and reviewers seemed to wish that the lectures had not been published without reediting or revision. One of the lectures from the western tour, "How Soon Can We Start the Next War," was included, and there were several new sketches — hence the "stories" of the title. Leacock also published several articles on Canadian economic questions and a monograph entitled *What Nickel Means to the World*. The monograph was a commission from manufacturers of nickel. Leacock argued for the development of the industry and the future use of nickel coinage. This was the first of a number of writing projects undertaken by Leacock in the years after his retirement that were, to some extent, public-relations or advertising projects. It has been said that his acceptance of these commissions is proof that he unwisely subordinated his principles to his pursuit of money. He might be pardoned for searching out ways to expand his income in light of his concern about the financial security of his only son. Leacock continued to be generous with contributions to university programs and to friends and family. He helped to arrange a very popular French luncheon club with a view to providing an additional source of income for a friend's widow. He offered to underwrite any deficit between the money she earned from membership fees and the cost of operating the club, which featured conversation in French only and a program of distinguished guest speakers. Leacock had legitimate uses for the money he earned. And there was no question of mere writing for hire. The monograph on nickel was in tune with the many articles he was producing about the need to develop Canadian resources. Leacock regarded such commissions as legitimate opportunities to exercise influence as a practical economist.

Leacock was approached by his old student Gladstone Murray in June, 1937 to inquire about broadcasting again on radio. Murray, now the head of the new Canadian Broadcasting Corporation, wrote, "I have not abandoned hope that you might change your mind about the microphone some day." Murray suggested that Leacock might read from his early books. In England, the BBC presented an adaptation of *Winsome Winnie* in 1935; in 1936, negotiations were started to purchase rights to adapt "Soaked in Seaweed" for Copenhagen radio. In 1937, Leacock had a tiff with long-time collaborator, V.C. Clinton-Baddeley, when BBC television broadcast its own adaptation of "Behind the Beyond" rather than the dramatist's published one; Leacock denied Clinton-Baddeley's exclusive dramatization rights to the story. Television adaptations of other works, including "The Raft," were done in 1938. Another curiosity of his career was the publication of several stories, including "My Financial Career," in a

Russian satirical magazine published by *Pravda*. A copy of the magazine was sent to Leacock by a Montreal member of the Communist party. An introduction to the translations of Leacock's articles said, in part, that he could not be considered a left-wing writer in that "he protests against the American standard of thoughts, art and literature." Leacock wrote back to thank the sender, Louis Kon, and asked whether it might be possible to purchase additional copies. "I will gladly pay in roubles, or in the bonds of the Old Russian government, of which I still hold 8,000."

In 1935, Leacock received a doctor-of-laws degree from the University of Michigan. Other honors followed. In 1937, he was awarded the Lorne Piere Medal by the Royal Society of Canada. The resolution naming Leacock for the award noted his many honorary degrees, his stature as teacher, economist and author and his contribution "to the growing reputation of Canadian letters." Leacock won the governor-general's award for 1937, in the category of non-fiction, with *My Discovery of the West*. Equally gratifying was an invitation, in 1937, to join the faculty of the University of British Columbia. After the success of the western tour, he was invited by Lawrence Lowell, the president of Harvard University, to deliver the Lowell Institute Foundation Lectures, a series of six to eight speeches on a subject of his choice. Tours were proposed in Russia, Australia and New Zealand. For a time, Leacock considered taking the offer of a tour in Australia because he thought it might be possible to use the earnings to finance a trip around the world. Negotiations continued for some time, but eventually were abandoned. In a letter dated 1 June, 1937, Leacock mentioned to a friend in England the Lorne Pierce Medal and made light of the flood of awards he had been receiving.

> Ask them to raise me to the peerage: I have so many honorary degrees and the other day a gold medal that the peerage is all I need. Tell Eddie Peacock to tell Henry to tell Stanley Baldwin to tell Neville Chamberlain that I would accept any peerage from a Duke Sinister to a Baron Scavenger.

Peerages were certainly common enough among his close

associates at McGill, including Sir Edward Beatty and Sir Andrew Macphail.

After ten years in his household, Barbara Ulrichsen was married in the summer of 1937 to Donald Nimmo, son of one of Leacock's friends, the editor of the Detroit magazine, *Saturday Night*. The wedding was held at Old Brewery Bay, and Leacock supervised the building of special tables and trellises outdoors for the reception. He mixed drinks inside at the bar, which he said would be closed for twenty minutes to allow the ceremony to take place. Barbara Nimmo moved, with her husband, to the United States, but remained in close touch with her uncle until the end of his life, when she helped prepare an edition of his recent magazine work, *Last Leaves*. Her introductory essay is one of the very best accounts ever written of Leacock, and a source much mined by all his biographers. From her intimate association come many well-known stories about her uncle: his enthusiasm for gardening at Old Brewery Bay, his plan (abandoned finally because he could not take whiskey along) to accompany an Arctic expedition, his fondness for making elaborate household accounts and the requirement that his flask be the first item packed for a trip. She shopped for his clothes, especially his shirts, socks and ties. His suits arrived every year from a tailor on King Street, but Barbara said that, in the last seventeen years of his life, she never knew him to visit the tailor. Cloth samples were sent to the house and suits were made to old measurements designed to result in wide trousers and roomy suitcoats for comfort. He dressed for dinner in a loose-fitting dress jacket, trousers and a soft pleated shirt. Barbara witnessed his occasional outbursts of temper, some of which occurred at the end of a lecture engagement because she had forgotten to pack some essential item. Once he fired his entire Orillia staff in the midst of a house party, only to hire them back the next day. According to Barbara, he disliked lecturing and always found it difficult to eat before his performances. Afterwards, however, he enjoyed parties with friends. He would regale her and Stevie with the tale of his adventures while he shaved the next morning.

Barbara was with him during the bitter year of his retirement and testified to his fatigue at the end of the demanding western tour. She identified his life at McGill as the very heart of his experience. "He would rather have been a professor than anything else, and especially at McGill," she wrote in *Last Leaves*. Education was a pervasive part of Leacock's writing, whether he was producing a college textbook, like *The Elements of Political Science*, or a collection of humorous sketches, like *Arcadian Adventures with the Idle Rich*. He wrote only a scattering of serious essays on education, but they were among his most famous, including "Oxford as I See It" from *My Discovery of England* and "Education Eating up Life," which appeared first in the *New York Times* in 1939 and later that year in a new book, *Too Much College*. The editors at Dodd, Mead proposed the book idea after seeing the *Times* article. *Too Much College* contained nine essays on higher education, and more than twenty "Little Stories for Good Luck," which had been syndicated by Miller Services to Canadian periodicals during the early months of 1939. Many of these referred to subjects related to Leacock's years as a student and teacher.

When learning is the target of his humor, Leacock is drawn most often to laugh at the difficulty people seem to have in retaining their education. One of his favorite devices is the compact summary of knowledge, as a record of what the average person's confused memory of his schooling or as a modern "popular guide" through the labyrinth of learning. Entire subject areas are reduced to a handful of misspelled names and garbled events. He frequently satirizes the pretentious person whose claim to knowledge is exposed as folly. In "Homer and Humbug," for example, Leacock questions the sincerity of professors in their reverence for the esoteric beauties of the classics. Do they really thrill to the unique Greek periods, Leacock wondered, or is it only a sort of lodge initiation intended to set them apart from their fellows? When he jokes about learning, especially in his early books, Leacock ridicules the evaporation of knowledge and the empty pretentions of those professing to possess it. His ridicule is sometimes so extended that some question arises as to his target: is he attacking education, or is he attacking the uneducated?

In fact, Leacock wanted to do both, but in moderation. He criticized education, but not for the purpose of counseling his fellows to abandon learning; and he criticized the uneducated, but not for the purpose of directing them to enslave themselves to any particular course of study. When he poked fun at the bumblings of the pretentious, he did not always take great care to salvage the object of their pretentions. This was especially true when he wrote about the classics; he proudly retained his Greek and Latin throughout life, but always felt some impatience toward the professors of these "useless" subjects on which he had spent so many hours of his youth. Still, his primary purpose was to characterize the folly created by "a little knowledge." What he wanted most of all, as he suggested in *Winnowed Wisdom*, was for people to work beyond average attainments to something better. The type of learning that seemed most to dismay him was the pseudostudy proliferating through the popular press. He was far more disturbed by the seeming displacement of authentic study with newspaper advice columns on everything from nutrition to radio than he was by the doubtful practices of university professors.

In writing about education, Leacock displayed, from first to last, the conviction that higher learning was an essential element in society. His disapproval, over the years, of a changing university system was always grounded in the conviction that the work of professors, as researchers and as teachers, was at the heart of social progress. In *Too Much College*, he criticized new disciplines like psychology and spoke on the virtues of the study of Latin. He questioned the practice of tailoring university programs to appeal to the mass of students; he thought universities should select the brightest minds for special advancement. He attacked what he regarded as a uniquely modern determination to take the emphasis in college away from study and to place it on social and entertainment activities. Writing of his academic speciality, Leacock answered yes to the question, "Has Economics Gone to Seed?" He discussed many such questions in terms that ran far ahead of the thinking of his own time. In "Education Eating up Life," he complained that programs of study were lengthening to such an extent that a person's best productive years would be spent in the classroom rather than on the job. He doubted that the gradual elaboration of courses and degrees provided any real benefit; in fact, he said, longer courses of study really only served society's desire to slow down the entry of young people into the already overcrowded workforce. Leacock allowed that students needed time to master their subjects, but he suggested that many new disciplines did not require years of schooling. Some topics were best left to mastery through apprenticeship in a profession. His worries that the brightest students suffered unduly in a university geared to the average reflect the concerns of educators today to provide special programs for the gifted. He advised that modern languages should be taught to be spoken as well as read and written; again, he anticipated the educational theory of the later twentieth century.

In his early years, Leacock had been something of a revolutionary. He abandoned the study of languages, at which he had been a brilliant student both in high school and university, in favor of one of the new social sciences, economics. His purpose was to find a field through which he could make a definite, immediate contribution to his society. Once he entered the university community as a teacher, however, he found that society was pressuring the university to conform to its needs in ways Leacock could not approve. He objected to the alliances between business and education, which threatened to remove the traditions of thought in favor of impressive facilities and the most up-to-date theoreticians. The relevance he championed was one supplied by those shuffling, absent-minded, impractical professors he often pictured, and in whose company he wished to be counted. It was a relevance based on the pursuit of knowledge and the criticism of society from a detached and neutral vantage point.

Too Much College displays an inclination to favor traditional aspects of university curricula, for example, the study of Latin. In early essays, Leacock was inclined to dismantle traditional ways of conducting university business in his eagerness to protect the essential work of the schools. As early as 1910, however, he was the champion of the unworldly university professor against the modern "professors" who crowded the popular press. In "Oxford as I See It," he compared traditional European universities with their modern North American counterparts. Many of the features of Oxford that he praised were the same qualities he was fighting for in the essays in *Too Much College*: the retention of the classics as a basis for appreciating all modern languages and literature, the identification and fostering of gifted students, the emphasis on cultivating a life of the mind rather than developing an apparatus of regulations, examinations and schedules. Just as he had decided for himself, as a young man, to seek an unconventional field, he was prepared to be unconventional in his old age as a defender of principles that were threatened by the widespread innovations of the day. To the last, he argued that the world did not necessarily need something new in education. It needed something right, and many of those necessary right things were in the hands of educated people who were charged with the task of preserving them through the generations.

In "When Men Retire," from *Too Much College*, Leacock complained that retirement was the most dangerous threat to people in their later years. In the year after his departure from McGill, Leacock had done as much work as in any of the years he had spent as a teacher. Despite all this activity and the honors he received, however, the advance of years was telling on him. There was no work that could satisfy him as teaching had, and he found public lecturing more difficult and troublesome as he grew older. Accustomed to the pleasure of sharing his work intimately with his niece Barbara, he now had to face doing it alone. In 1937, Leacock suffered the first serious illness of his life. Remarkably, he emerged from it into a period of brilliant accomplishment, in works of humor and in works of history and social commentary.

Chapter Fourteen

While There Is Time

THE LAST six years of Stephen Leacock's life were framed by the only serious illnesses he ever suffered. The first was an enlargement of the prostate, not uncommon in elderly men. He required surgery and was hospitalized in March and April, 1938. The second was throat cancer, the cause of his death in March, 1944. Between lay a long period of concentrated and brilliant activity, in which Leacock continued the remaking of himself as a writer that had begun in the mid-1930s. He brought a renewed energy to the work. It turned out that Morgan, principal of McGill, had taken away Leacock's classroom but not his job as teacher. Leacock increasingly developed his ability to write in a way that would convey ideas, information and values, and also the personality and character of the man who was offering them. Leacock's triumph in his final years was to speak with both authority and humanity in a format that closely resembled the English personal essay. Whether he wrote of Montreal or Canada, modern educational theory or personal reminiscences, whether his subject was universal or local, he presented the subject and himself as a man. He was able to be both modest and magisterial in his later writings. He spoke with authority, but intimately, as a good teacher does, without assuming an air of superiority. In his last years, Leacock perfected his ability to make the voice, the personality that came through his writing, seem the very embodiment of the civilized values and the economic common sense for which he was arguing.

Leacock's retirement had given him more time to write and a renewed sense of the need to prove himself, to employ his great abilities and to justify himself by finding a way to be useful. It seems that this feeling was intensified by his illness of 1938. When he recovered, the Indian summer of health and vigor he experienced was filled with eager concentration upon the issues and events of the day and his dynamic reactions to them. Although the mood of his humor was sometimes nostalgic and the subjects of his serious books often historical, Leacock was not looking backward and longing for the past. If anything, his grip on the present strengthened. He was determined to bring to bear on the problems around him the traditions and values in which he believed.

In March, 1938 Leacock was admitted to Montreal's Royal Victoria Hospital for prostatic surgery, which was performed by the chief of the hospital's urology department, Doctor David W. Mackenzie. Judging by the evidence of several letters he wrote to friends, and other letters he received from his publishers, Leacock was depressed by his situation. In one note he indicated that Mackenzie had required him to stay in hospital to recuperate for a longer period than might have been strictly necessary, perhaps to make him rest and remain quiet. Leacock alluded delicately to his physical ailment, and perhaps revealed the root of his sadness: his fear of a link between the sexual and the creative prime that even such an indomitable and sensible person as himself could not help feeling:

> David Mackenzie (the best doctor in the world; I wish he could operate on all my friends) has removed my sense of humor, — he said it was inflated and must come out. I said that that might leave me a little sentimental and he said, yes, but it would do me no harm.

Leacock's publishers, Dodd, Mead and Company and The Bodley Head, had been hearing of the illness in vague terms since the beginning of March, and were keeping tabs on it because it was holding up the progress of *Model Memoirs*, Leacock's work-of-humor in progress. At the end of April he wrote that he was "better — though I am still in hospital," and in the first week of May he was finally released. The illness had kept him in Montreal longer than was his custom. Leacock left the hospital and went directly to Old Brewery Bay, where he spent the summer recuperating and finishing *Model Memoirs*. By the end of August, he had nearly completed the book; uncharacteristically, he was still referring in letters to his illness and slow recovery. In his essay "Three Score and

Ten," he would speak of an illness that was "not a tragic one
. . . but just one good flap of warning" to garrulous old men,
making them be quiet and listen more humbly to the world
around them. Leacock was feeling chastened and educated by
physical decline, the possibility of serious illness and the inevitability of death. Slowly and carefully, he felt for the
ground under his feet, and only when he had assured himself
of his new balance did he move confidently into new projects.

His basic earthiness, the part of him that combined the peasant, the gentleman farmer and the sportsman, stood him in
good stead. So, too, did his love for the town of Orillia and the
community of professional summer residents. He put his interest in practical economics to work, to build up his income.
Since the final years of Leacock's tenure at McGill, his interest in gardening had intensified. He had been preparing for
a retirement that he knew would come soon, though it had
come sooner than he had hoped, and he was ready for it. His
concern with his Old Brewery Bay property and the fields,
stream and fishing ponds in Oro Township had intensified until it was a pretense, or game, of profitable farming.
Throughout the mid-1930s he wrote often to order potato and
asparagus plants, apple and cherry trees, onion seeds, spraying equipment and several varieties of hens and turkeys. In
Old Brewery Bay he erected a windmill and a fairly large
henhouse. There was also a small barn for storing tools and
feed and grain and for sheltering an old mare for which he had
a great affection. He wrote frequently to the agricultural
department of MacDonald College in Sainte-Anne-de-Bellevue
(just west of Montreal, at the western tip of Montreal Island)
and to the Ontario Agricultural College in Guelph. He planted
an apple orchard (a few of the trees can still be seen on his
property, in the now brush-covered area south of his house).
His correspondence reveals that he was slowly learning the
most basic things about farming. Doctor D.A. Kimball, of the
Ontario Agricultural College, who accepted at least one invitation to Old Brewery Bay for trout fishing, had to explain
to him by letter that spraying was *de rigueur* to produce any
appreciable number of sound, commercial-quality apples, and
answered an anxious inquiry with the assurance that ants on
the apple trees did not mean disaster.

Raising vegetables for sale had been an interest of Leacock's before 1910, when he had first established himself in Old Brewery Bay. Some witnesses have claimed that he would trundle produce to the market in Orillia, pushing a laden wheelbarrow on the railway track for more than a mile along the Couchiching shore into Orillia. It has also been said that both grocers and customers were happy to get his produce because of its size and quality. His staff was led by gardener "Sergeant" Bill Jones. (Jones had been a private in World War I. Leacock had promoted him immediately upon hiring him in 1918.) Groundsman John Kelly later married Leacock's housekeeper, Tina Pelletier. Mrs. Kelly — Tina — was a French-Canadian from New Brunswick. It is not recorded how Leacock made the acquaintance of the Pelletiers but he valued the family highly enough that he employed many of Tina's siblings. At one period in the late 1930s he had five Pelletiers working for him, primarily on the grounds and in the garden. Lucien Pelletier was his chauffeur, and his staff also included housemaids and other inside workers. However, the farming and gardening were Leacock's chief interests. In the summer of 1937 he wrote to a friend, "fishing rotten here but season lovely & I am building, planting, ploughing, — 5 3/4 men working, — that is 5, and old Jones 1/2 & me 1/4." In 1934, his capital expenditures for Old Brewery Bay, largely for farming projects and materials, had put his overdraft account at his Montreal branch of the Bank of Montreal up to ten thousand dollars. During the academic year of 1934 Leacock had sold securities and used other sums to bring the overdraft back down to zero.

As he convalesced, Leacock occupied himself with his farming projects and with the writing of *Model Memoirs*. His attitude towards farming, which at first seems strange and contradictory, was at least in harmony with his general way of thinking. To Leacock, farming was both serious and ridiculous at once: it deserved to be done to the utmost, with care and dash, but on the other hand not too much should be expected from it, for it was, after all, very small in the scheme of things, and not likely to affect the world very much. Leacock would throw himself into each new project — including trout- and turkey-raising, asparagus growing, apple and cherry orchards, and many more — and then, after a season of two, lose interest. Basic activities such as poultry raising and the production of garden vegetables, hay and feed corn were always maintained. Leacock took pride in the fact that all the meals served at Old Brewery Bay were made up entirely of ingredients raised on the property. This was at least a slight exaggeration, for Leacock's formal, full-course meals sometimes included, for instance, canned sardines as hors d'oeuvres. On one occasion, Leacock interrupted a pleasant lunch when the soup tureen arrived filled with tinned beef consommé. He poured the soup out, reprimanded the cook and sent his guests into the garden to gather tomatoes. He waited while the tomatoes were picked and the fresh tomato soup was made. He was pleased to send broiler chickens to his relatives and friends, and (as a letter to his niece Barbara shows) kept careful tabs on the costs involved. For example, he calculated at one point that the money earned by selling eggs from laying hens offset the cost of raising and eating (or giving away) two hundred twenty-five broilers.

Many incidents illustrate Leacock's half-serious, half-jocular approach to his farming. His correspondence is filled with earnest requests to agricultural scientists, with seed catalogues and planting manuals that were carefully reviewed and filed, and with log books that meticulously traced the progress of garden, fish ponds and feed supplies. He could become overearnest, as his sometimes pestering inquiries to the Ontario Agricultural College indicate. He seems to have received a greater quantity of personally delivered information from that institution than many a farmer with hundreds of acres under cultivation. In June, 1934, he went so far as to telegraph the college in apparent panic over cutworms in his vegetable traces, and received back a telegram: "Cutworms stop Scatter poison bran mash round plants at dusk," followed by a recipe for the mash. In 1939, his correspondence shows that he had planted eight hundred asparagus roots, a considerable crop, and few or none of them had grown. Leacock blamed the failure on the seeds and demanded replacements; he considered it out of the question that planting methods or soil conditions could have had a part in the failure. Leacock's brother George, president of the Moloney Electric Company of

Toronto, was also a gentleman farmer at his home, "Meadow-lea," in Aurora, Ontario, not far from Orillia. In the spring of 1935, clearly at Leacock's request, George sent him a letter full of advice and instructions on how to plant mangels, Swede turnips and clover and timothy hay for feeding horses and cows. But Leacock was not prepared to concede superior knowledge and ability as a farmer to his brother. On 28 March, 1935, George telegraphed him in Montreal. "Planted green peas yesterday laugh that off. George D. Leacock." At the bottom of the telegram, Leacock scrawled, "Dear Kelly — We must beat this — get a warm corner somewhere & put in some peas," and mailed it to Orillia. Kelly sent a note to Leacock's niece:

> Miss Barbara
> Please tell Mr Leacock that *we* have Mr George beat we have 3 [word illegible] of peas and. . . almost 2 bags of potatoes in on the 26th march We are using some of our lettuce I have lots of plants of everything I have 250 chicks 12 days old.
> Kelly

It was just this combination of serious labor and hijinks that helped Leacock recuperate as he directed the garden's progress during the summer of 1938.

Over the summer he completed *Model Memoirs*, his book of humor for 1939, which contains such outstanding pieces as "My Victorian Girlhood," "Overworking the Alphabet," "The Dissolution of Our Dinner Club" and "All Is not Lost," a double-barreled satire that struck at the confused politics of central Europe, but more particularly at the confusing and alarmist reporting of it in the press, which served only to keep readers in a state of bewilderment and fear. During the summer and fall Leacock showed his interest in the book by picking up the pace of his correspondence with his American agent, Paul Reynolds, who was busy finding periodicals to publish the professor's humorous pieces. Some of the essays in *Model Memoirs* were completed too close to the book's scheduled publication date to be placed with magazines, but "My Victorian Girlhood" caught the fancy of *The Saturday Evening Post*. Dodd, Mead and Company held up the book's release so the *Post* issue containing the story could be published first.

That summer Leacock was also busy with friends and neighbors, helping to create an expanded version of the Old
Brewery Bay Players. The group had started with the private
theatricals he organized frequently at his home with the help
of neighboring children and adults. In the summer of 1938,
the scope of these performances was expanded mightily, under
the leadership of a now-grown playmate of Stevie's, Peggy
Shaw. Leacock and Peggy's mother, Fitz Shaw, assisted.
"Brewery Nights Entertainment" was performed on 3 August
to an audience of two hundred local people and summer residents gathered on the Couchiching lakeshore at Fitz Shaw's
home, the Old Brewery. (Just west of Leacock's property, her
house was at the site of the vanished brewery after which
Leacock had named his establishment.) "Brewery Nights
Entertainment" was presented for three consecutive years;
then the passage of time and the pressure of events scattered
the players. The second installment, in 1938, included Leacock's "The Raft: Danger and Love in One Act" and four brief
skits by young friends, among them "The Return of Champlain" and "Lady Godiva Rides By." The *Packet and Times*
reported that the weather, a combination of brief squalls and
interludes of sunshine, came to the players' aid by giving Leacock's comedy just the backdrop it required.

In mid-October he returned to Montreal. He had made
careful arrangements to accomodate some of the changes in
his life. John and Tina Kelly were given a long document
detailing their duties and compensation as his caretakers and
providing for his will to supersede the document if he should
die. They were to stay behind in Old Brewery Bay and live in
the lodge as year-round caretakers. (Tina and some of the
other indoor staff generally had gone to Montreal with him in
the past.) Leacock had decided that the house in Montreal was
too big and too expensive for only Stevie and himself. The fall
and winter of 1937 had been spent in the Mount Royal Hotel,
and now he prepared to move into a hotel permanently. He
chose the historic old Windsor Hotel on Montreal's Dominion
Square. It has been stated that Leacock maintained this arrangement to the end of his life and rented out his Montreal
home; however, during the last three winters before his death,
he wrote and received his correspondence at his Côte-des-

Neiges address. Stevie stated that the two of them were together in the house during his father's final months. Leacock did not get around to moving into the Windsor Hotel until after the New Year: he wrote Dodd, Mead of his change of address in February, 1939.

Immediately upon his return to Montreal in 1938 he had to deal with the death of one of his oldest and closest friends, Sir Andrew Macphail. Macphail had died on 23 September, just a month and a day short of his seventy-fourth birthday. Leacock had been influenced by Macphail, the author of the vigorous yet polished *Essays in Puritanism*, the glowing reminiscences of *The Master's Wife* and the uncompromising *The Medical Forces*, a controversial record and criticism of that section of the Canadian forces. Macphail contributed *The Medical Forces* to an official history of World War I. Physician, soldier and McGill's first professor of the history of medicine, Macphail resembled Leacock in many ways. He was an accomplished professional man with a passionate interest in literature. Although he had written a novel and a poetic drama, he was primarily an essayist who brought his formidable stylistic abilities to a variety of subjects, including biography, criticism and public affairs. In one letter from him that Leacock preserved, Sir Andrew encouraged his friend to develop his essay writing, telling the humorist how much he enjoyed the essays in the classic English tradition scattered through his work and how he hoped one day to see a whole volume of them. Like Leacock's, Sir Andrew's life described a yearly orbit around two centers: his childhood home in Orwell, Prince Edward Island, and Montreal. Like Leacock, he was a universal talent of great magnitude who remained determinedly rooted in the nation and regions he loved, making them the basis of his cosmopolitan achievement. A widower since early in the first decade of the century, Macphail had a dignified old-world manner that made him as much a McGill monument as Leacock. For years his home at 216 rue Peel — which he maintained in Victorian decor until his death — was a literary and intellectual center in Montreal. Macphail's friend and fellow physician John McCrae, "Jack" to intimates such as Sir Andrew and Leacock, had for years been a near neighbor at 190 rue Peel. Leacock wrote a reminiscence of Sir

Andrew for the *Queen's Quarterly* of November 1938. He was a survivor of a vanished literary era, and he bid good-bye to the man who — with the exception of himself — had been its most brilliant member.

In 1939, Leacock was still feeling the illness of the previous year; he gave it as a reason when he wrote, on 19 April, to Boston University to turn down an honorary degree; it is possible that the inconvenience of traveling to Boston, the need to spend money on the trip and the requirement that he speak at the ceremony may have affected his extremely polite refusal of the honor. In both 1938 and 1939, he was busy writing serious articles for a variety of publications, including the prestigious *Barron's*, little-known professional journals for bankers and dentists, and big-city daily newspapers. His renewed flow of humorous pieces continued to find publication in prominent magazines like *The New Yorker*. He returned to Old Brewery Bay in late spring. He was writing *Too Much College*, which had evolved out of Frank Dodd's compliment to his *New York Times* article, "Education Eating Up Life." During the summer he was occupied with the visit of King George VI and Queen Elizabeth to Canada and the United States. He wrote an article (not published until the Leacock Home Trustees released it for the 1959 visit of Queen Elizabeth II) that expressed the deep-rooted empire sentiments he developed more fully a year later in *Our British Empire*. Leacock's income continued to be low; his income-tax returns showed a gross income of $13,757.08 for 1938 and $11,717.62 for 1939. There were signs, however, that he was working steadily and successfully to regain some of his lost income. His humorous and popular non-fiction works were receiving a greater share of his attention, and he was relying upon his own economic knowledge and beliefs to invest his savings. In May, 1939 he directed his brokers to acquire 1,150 shares of East Malarctic mines, only one of several such purchases in the late 1930s and the 1940s. He sold other stocks, such as utilities, to finance his purchases of northern mining interests. He put to the practical test his own ideas that much of Canada's economic future lay in its northern mineral resources, a position he had championed at least since the 1910s, when he was one of the earliest authorities to recommend use of Canadian nickel in minting coins. Many of his articles dealt with the economics of metals (for example, "Gold Mines as Investments" in *Barron's*, 14 June, 1937). The restored performance of his stock portfolio shows that he had judged the general climate of Canadian mining and metals industries, and the particular companies in which he invested, very cannily indeed.

During the summer in Old Brewery Bay, he was involved in trying to get a Mr. Scott, an Oro Township farmer, to use the land on his fishing property as pasture in return for two tons of hay. On 9 July, Leacock and John and Tina Kelly sighted a boy, Percy Bartleman, whose canoe had capsized in Lake Couchiching near Leacock's point. The three put out in one of Leacock's boats with Kelly at the motor, but Tina became ill and they had to return to land. Leacock returned on his own and threw the boy a line. The incident made the front page of the *New York Times* the next day and was reported far and wide. In quizzical exasperation, Leacock commented to the *Toronto Daily Star* four days after the incident: "Why, the first thing you know they'll make a lifeboat station out of me. . . . You may quote me as saying that in the future I will rescue no one, not even women." In the summer of 1938, the youngest and last of Tina's brothers, Albanie, then a lad of thirteen or fourteen, had succumbed to the blandishments of his sister's beloved employer and had joined the staff. One summer day Leacock observed him rowing Stevie on the lake in one of the boats and called him ashore. Leacock strictly forbade Albanie to take the boat out again, but told him that if he would learn to swim, he could use the punt and have a gold watch as well. Albanie practiced strenuously for weeks and then triumphantly demonstrated his new ability to Leacock. True to his word, Leacock gave him the use of the punt and sent him into town with a cheque for $3.95, the price — he ascertained by telephone — of the largest gold pocket watch in the Orillia pharmacist's shop. Of the many boats Leacock owned at various times — he usually had several at once — one only was known to the venerable Sergeant Jones as "*the* boat." This was a craft designed and, after a manner of speaking, launched according to a plan by Leacock, who, as a hobbyist, had made himself a formidable expert on naval history and strategy. Jones for years sat holding his peace, drinking beer and smoking his pipe while Leacock and René du Roure discussed war and economics and literature. He was nevertheless a man who had his own opinions. During one of his last summers, Leacock drew up the plans for a new boat he had decided he must add to his fleet, a sixteen-footer made of heavy oak planks like an old Hudson Bay icebreaker. It was built keel up, as is customary with small craft, and was very heavy. Over the vigorous objections of Sergeant Jones, Leacock commanded that it be moved keel up into the water; his reading had apparently led him to believe it could be very easily turned over. The method proved disastrous. The boat plunged immediately to the bottom; because of its weight and the suction against the lakebed ooze, a team of horses was required to drag it out. Leacock was nothing abashed, and in fact seems to have immensely enjoyed the entire incident.

In 1939, he testified again to his love of sport, the region he had chosen as home and the local people in an article called "Bass Fishing with Jake Gaudaur on Lake Simcoe." Gaudaur was another favorite presence who had been removed from Leacock's world. (He died in 1937 at the age of seventy-nine.) Back in the days when single-scull rowing was one of the most popular of all sports, Gaudaur had gained the world championship by defeating Australia's James Stansbury. That was in 1896, when Gaudaur was thirty-eight and had already been competing professionally for seventeen years. (Gaudaur had defeated Stansbury in 1894 in Austin, Texas, in a time that still is unequalled, but the event was not a championship one and Stansbury was able to delay giving his Canadian challenger an official match for two years.) In 1896, Orillia welcomed Gaudaur with elaborate fireworks, a flotilla of all available craft and five hundred dollars. Gaudaur defended his title frequently and retired to Orillia in 1901, after losing the title at age forty-three. At one time he owned hotels in Toronto, Orillia and Rat Portage (now Kenora), and throughout his life he operated a fishing-guide service from his home on the narrows, not far east along the Lake Couchiching shore from Old Brewery Bay. One of Leacock's close friends, Jake Gaudaur sometimes appeared in the humorist's writing as a presiding spirit and as a character identified by name, as in the witty tale of fishing, murder and nonchalance, "Why Do We Fish?" from *My Remarkable Uncle.*

Leacock was nearing the end of his stay in Orillia for what had been a pleasant and productive summer when, unexpectedly and in tragic circumstances, he and his household suffered another crucial loss. On 6 September, his trusted superintendent John Kelly was killed when the Old Brewery Bay farm truck was struck by a Canadian Pacific Railway train at the Eady Crossing, not far from the house. Another hired man, named Hough, saved himself by leaping clear of the truck, but apparently Kelly was unable to do so, or had stayed in the vehicle to attempt to get it off the track in time. Leacock was one of the first at the scene of the accident; he provided nurses and other medical services for the stricken Tina and saw to Kelly's burial in Orillia's Roman Catholic cemetery, Saint Michael's. Much of the remainder of the summer was occupied with the sad details of arranging for compensation for the burial and the truck (which Leacock had given to Kelly some time earlier) from the railway, which agreed to pay a variety of costs although it was not at fault. In his customary fashion, Leacock drew up an elaborate memorandum outlining the financial help he was offering Tina, including the gift of a piece of his property where he had intended Kelly to build his own family house, and thinly veiling his regret that, in his circumstances at the time, he could not do more. Leacock was no longer occupying his house in Montreal so Tina could not work there; without Kelly she could not oversee Old Brewery Bay. Tina had worked for him without interruption for many years, but had to seek other housekeeping work that winter in Montreal.

One of Leacock's interests in the summer was the possibility of a film treatment of "My Financial Career," to star Robert Benchley, by Metro-Goldwyn-Mayer. Paul Reynolds wired him of the prospect in July and was still negotiating in August, but no agreement was ever concluded. Leacock had long been interested in motion pictures; he spoofed them in stories in *Further Foolishness, The Hohenzollerns in America, Over the Footlights* and *Short Circuits.* Throughout his life he was frequently approached for film rights to his works, but unfortunately none of the projected films was made. As early as

1916, a British movie company paid more than forty-four pounds for rights to consider *Sunshine Sketches* for adaptation into a scenario. During the 1920s Leacock sometimes varied the presentation of the Old Brewery Bay Players from private theatricals to a movie made with a home camera; he provided script and direction. The Leacock Home archives preserves title cards for three such productions. In attempting to negotiate with Hollywood, Leacock sometimes initiated the action, especially towards the end of his life. In the early 1940s, he asked his agent to approach Disney studios, for which his friend Robert Benchley had done some work, and proposed a screen version of *Pickwick Papers* to independent American producer David O. Selznick. It is regrettable that Selznick was not interested; since the days of the silent films, the only film from this Dickens classic was made by South African playwright-screenwriter-director Noel Langley in 1953. In early 1941, Leacock was approached again by the film industry, this time to turn into English the film *Ils Étaient Neuf Célibataires* (1939), a movie made by the celebrated French writer-director Sacha Guitry. Again, this project never proceeded beyond an exchange of letters. Finally, in 1942, "My Remarkable Uncle" drew the attention of Paramount, Warner Brothers and Twentieth Century Fox when it was published in *Reader's Digest*. Intrigued by the dramatic possibilities of the figure of the flamboyant uncle, E.P. Leacock, the companies asked Dodd, Mead for copies of the galley proofs of Leacock's humor collection, *My Remarkable Uncle*. Leacock wrote to a story editor of his fear that the sketch would not be judged suitable because it was "only a piece — not a book. I have always thought the Winnipeg boom of 1880-82 would make a good setting for a book set up with a character like my uncle as a central figure. If you thought of expanding the sketch to a story, I could be of use." In 1943, Leacock pursued the idea by writing "Boom Times" (published in *Happy Stories*, 1943), in which he developed the character of E.P. in a fictionalized setting. He sent the story immediately to Dorothy Purdell, the agent who had first approached him on behalf of Twentieth Century Fox, and she proposed it to Ernst Lubitsch and two other filmmakers and companies. Her letters to Leacock indicate that she regarded the story as an inevitable sale, but it never did

302

find a producer. Leacock was well aware of the dramatic and filmic potential of this work. He commented to would-be dramatizers that "My Financial Career" needed only to be "illustrated to become a movie" and that his "nonsense" plays could be performed on the stage with virtually no adaptation. Doctor Ralph Curry has counted, in the archives of the Leacock Home, more than one hundred fifty letters, nearly spanning Leacock's entire career as a humorist, that are related to dramatic rights, film rights and radio permissions. There are others, as well, reporting upon the successes of his dramatizedstories, from widely reviewed runs at famous London theaters to private amateur productions for New York society audiences.

Despite the persistent interest in film, it is clear that Leacock only dabbled with the industry at long-range and hoped for a lucky strike. He did not direct any consistent, concerted effort towards obtaining a film production of one of his works, and he never wrote a screenplay. During his last years, when films interested him most, there were other, more interesting and more pressing matters to occupy the foreground of his attention. In late August, 1939, the Nazi-Russia nonagression pact became known to the world. One week later, on 1 September, Hitler's Germany attacked Poland. Great Britain and France declared war on 3 September, and Canada followed suit on 10 September. In mid-October, ensconced at the Windsor Hotel in Montreal and checking the galley proofs of *Too Much College*, Leacock embarked on two works motivated by his desire to contribute his talents to the war effort. The first was a booklet prepared for Oxford University Press in Canada, *All Right, Mr. Roosevelt (Canada and the United States)*. It celebrated the peaceful relationship of the two countries as a model for, and contribution towards, peace in the world, and at the same time sought to encourage both the United States and its individual citizens to help Canada's war effort in any way possible, even by enlistment in the Canadian Armed Forces. Many Americans did enlist, thus entering World War II two years before their country did. *All Right, Mr. Roosevelt* was widely and approvingly noticed on both sides of the border. Leacock's second contribution to the war effort was *Our British Empire*. (The book was called *The*

303

British Empire in the United States.) The book combined a popular history of the empire with praise of its role in world civilization. It argued that the empire, with its essential partners, especially the United States and France, provided a model of tolerant, co-operative political and social relationship.

The war stirred many of Leacock's deepest feelings and was responsible for the form much of his writing took. Two more of his books during the 1940s attempted to foster both understanding of the British heritage and pride in it. His "belief" in progress has been mentioned as a Victorian characteristic, one that bespoke a certain complacency and may have censored the talent for scathingly satirical, and negative, social criticism that he showed in *Arcadian Adventures of the Idle Rich*. However, his attitude towards progress was related to the critical and skeptical progressive thought of the Victorian poets and thinkers, not to the rosy optimism of industrialists, go-getters and popular philosophers. Progress was possible; the historical record showed that it had been made. On the other hand, it could only be achieved by the most strenuous efforts and by constant vigilance. Lacking these, decline became inevitable. He felt that social and material progress was possible, that it was within the grasp of nations and that it was crucial to the fulfillment of individuals. But on the other hand he thought progress could be very easily lost. The war confirmed Leacock's clear sense of mankind's capacity for evil and regression. Characteristically, though, it stirred him to oppose obvious evil with a vision of what ought to prevail. There is no doubt that World War I had shaken the sense of security that allowed him to make the sweepingly acerbic social analyses implicit in *Sunshine Sketches* and explicit in *Arcadian Adventures*. Since 1918, his view of the world had remained unsettled as he had been moved about by conflicting currents: his ambition during the 1920s to use his writing for high earnings, the death of his wife and its long-lasting impact, the relative failure of his humor in the early 1930s, the blow of his forced retirement from McGill, his gradual development of other subjects for popular writing. His books on humor (*Humor: Its Theory and Technique* and *Humor and Humanity*) expressed an attitude, a philosophy that had grown slowly. Humor could assist the world's progress towards human sympathy and fulfillment by being encouraging, not lacerating. Doubtless this was not an adequate account of all great humor, even all of Leacock's great humor. But it permitted him to see a purpose for his writing, a way in which his work could assist the progress he hoped to see. Leacock never lost this vision, but his clear expression of it in his late books has significance, especially when taken together with the quantity and unity of his output at the time. *Our Heritage of Liberty* (1942), like *Our British Empire*, celebrated Anglo-American civilization, its history and its values, and at the same time attempted to show that the correct — that is, the Leacockian — interpretation of this heritage demanded an ever more strenuous effort to extend its benefits of peace, justice, freedom and a decent material existence to every individual. In *While There Is Time: The Case Against Social Catastrophe* (1944), he fell in with the feeling, certainly widespread by 1943 and before, that the war would inevitably be won. He returned his attention to the shape that must be given to the new world that would emerge from the upheavals of global depression and conflict. Once more, he interpreted the British and American past at its best as the source of the values and methods that would successfully transform the brutality and economic chaos of unrestrained free enterprise. He thought socialism was a valuable criticism of abuses, but he refused to allow it any role in positive reform; instead, he insisted upon the use of traditional institutions and traditional moral insights brought to a new pitch of social relevance.

Even in his books of humor, he is fighting the same battles, and thus his contribution to the war effort is deeper, more philosophical and lasting in nature than was his World War I propoganda, and virtually free of the offensive caricature of such works as *The Hohenzollerns in America*. An essay called "The British Soldier" (*My Remarkable Uncle*) is an example of a literary and historical essay, excellent in itself, which also manages to promote public responsibility and respect for soldiers. Leacock recalls the British soldier's tradition of courage and his historical importance to British civilization. The essay links the soldier to the poor by pointing out his poverty and low social status throughout the nineteenth century and by recalling that his occupation, poor as it often is, has long been an escape, for some, from even more dire poverty. Finally, Leacock manages to insist that it is necessary to have concrete plans, not merely ideals, for social improvement; in analyzing literature's attitudes to the soldier, he criticizes his own master, Charles Dickens, for being sentimentally opposed to poverty but having no idea how to end it. Most of Leacock's late humor is even less tightly linked to the issue of the war than is "The British Soldier," but its mingled mood of nostalgia and affirmation of Anglo-American values is in harmony with the effort to draw strength and renewal from tradition he was making in his serious books. Even *Montreal; Seaport and City* and *Canada, The Foundations of Its Future* are built upon Leacock's desire to show the historical movement of British and French civilization in building a great city and a great nation with the promise of material civilization and the broadening of freedom. They are among his best books because they unite so many of the essential components of the man: his love and knowledge of history; his imagination, which, over the years, had truly absorbed the pageant of Canada, from Cartier's departure from Saint Malo to the settlement of the northwest; his deep conviction in British values, stirred by a dire and powerful occasion; his pride in his mastery, developed over many years, as a prose stylist; and, finally, his need to contribute publicly, as a teacher, to the world's course.

In the fall of 1939, Leacock welcomed to Montreal an old friend, F. Cyril James, who had been at the London School of Economics in 1921 when Leacock urged the students to write letters to the press about one of his speeches. After a distinguished career as an economics professor, latterly at the University of Pennsylvania, James had been appointed the new principal of McGill. Leacock gave him a dinner at the University Club with René du Roure and another favorite Leacock crony, F.A. Greenshields, chief justice of the province of Quebec. During the winter, Leacock agreed to sit for Frederick B. Taylor, an artist who had graduated from McGill and had a studio near the Windsor Hotel. When Leacock finally saw the completed portrait, he exclaimed, "My God,

Taylor, that's exactly how I feel." This comment was probably the kindest one Leacock could think of; afterwards he frequently expressed dislike of the picture. Later, a group of friends persuaded Leacock to sit for the distinguished artist Edwin Holgate, who painted a good portrait in 1943. On Saturdays and Sundays Leacock went to the artist's studio in his home at Morin Heights, Quebec, a village northwest of Montreal in Argenteuil County. Holgate commented:

> He impressed me as being a philosopher with a great good humor. But first, a philosopher. He plied me with questions as if he were a small boy — and listened to the answers with an attention they did not deserve.

Holgate's picture is now in the National Gallery of Canada. A third portrait, painted by Richard Jack after the author's death, hangs in the University Club.

In January, 1940 a slight controversy began between Leacock and his brother Charlie that seemed, at first, little enough, but was the first sign of an unhappy situation. On 23 January, Leacock wrote to advance Charlie money intended to help him with some debts he had accumulated. The letter ended:

> The plain meaning of this letter is that I am advancing money to pay your debt but neither I nor my estate are to draw any profit from this. And if any doubt arises from the interpretation of this arrangement I promise, and you also promise, to accept the decision of George [Leacock] as legally binding.

He wrote also to Charlie's creditors, to say a sufficient sum was being transferred to his brother's bank. Leacock's arrangement included a monthly personal allowance for Charlie; on 22 February, Charlie returned the first payment, saying he did not need it and "Many thanks for all your trouble." In July, Leacock was concerned about Charlie's slowness in paying some of his bills, and Charlie replied testily that it had been due only to the slowness of the bank transfer of funds; he was proposing to sell one of his properties (he owned his home, "West Ridge," in Sutton, and another local house,

"Bovaire") to repay the $550 his brother had advanced. "I am again doing business & shall make more profits in this war than last, 1914-/18," he wrote on 16 July, although no one in the family seems to have known to what this referred. It may well have meant nothing. On 9 August, still concerned about Charlie's behavior but considering it nothing worse than irresponsibility, Stephen wrote, "My dear Charlie, While there is still time I wish you would try to get better control of yourself, and to make financial arrangements to carry on." A week later came Charlie's bitter reply:

> Stephen Leacock,
> Miserable man!
> I know you for what you are! . . . Leave me to my life & I'll leave you to yours.
>
> Charles Leacock

Leacock, George and their sister Dot (now a pathologist at Toronto's Hospital for Sick Children) looked more closely at Charlie. He was physically ill, a result, at least in part, of emotional or mental disturbances that made it increasingly difficult for the aging bachelor, living alone, to look after himself properly. Late in the summer he was admitted as a mental patient to the Ontario Hospital in Whitby. On 21 September, George reported by letter to Leacock that "Charlie is back at Sutton. . . . He is in fine shape mentally but looks pretty *old*." George had paid $239 in bills for Charlie, provided him an amount to live on and extended Leacock's invitation that he winter in Old Brewery Bay, where he would have the staff to help him. Charlie turned the invitation down because, he said, the house was too cold; George commented that Charlie wanted to be in his own home. However, George said, he had commanded Charlie to get at least two good meals daily in a local inn, rather than to cook for himself, which would result in a bad diet and a mess in his house. George hoped to get to Montreal to discuss Charlie's plight in person with his brother. On 18 September Charlie again was admitted to the Whitby hospital. In mid-October he addressed Leacock with childlike affection as "Stevie":

I am leaving the hospital in a day or so — as soon as Dot gets the doctor's letter to say it's O.K. for me to leave — I shall be glad to get to my farm & get some work for the winter as I like that work of fixing up.

Your affec bro
Charlie

The family drew up an agreement whereby Teddy, in Calgary, and Leacock would help to oversee Charlie's affairs. Charlie's emotional and financial difficulties continued throughout the remainder of Leacock's life. Leacock's correspondence shows that in July, 1942 the Orillia police charged him $10.50 for the service of transporting Charlie to the Whitby hospital, seventy miles distant. Charlie's debts had become unmanageable; because of his creditors, his farm, "Bovaire," was in the hands of the Ontario public trustee. The trustee declared that "the patient had no power whatsoever to deal with his estate in any way," and that Leacock's November, 1941 agreement with Teddy to answer for Charlie's debts was invalid. The agreement had been drawn up after Charlie went to the hospital; he had been allowed out on probation but never released. The agreement had been made in the knowledge that Charlie was incompetent. Charlie's mental state apparently continued to alternate between affection and anger, between docility and self-willed independence, which made it difficult for his brothers and sisters to take care of him. He occupied Leacock's thoughts throughout the humorist's final months. Six weeks before Leacock's death, Dot assured him, "Yes, I have plenty of money for Charlie — & Carrie still has a lot left of the amount you gave her in the summer — so don't worry about him." When Leacock died, Charlie was well provided for, with bequests and other income in his own name supplemented by family aid. Leacock left him his three boats and his fishing equipment, in memory of happy days with Charlie, whose love of fishing was greater than that of all his brothers.

In 1940 the Leacocks' father, Walter Peter Leacock, died in Nova Scotia at the age of ninety-two. Correspondence in Leacock's files relating to the estate of his grandfather, Thomas Murdock Leacock, shows that the humorist and his brothers — or at least George and Charlie, who co-operated with him in family business — were aware of their father's whereabouts, for they oversaw the disbursement of the estate's earnings. Although some of his brothers and sisters had visited Peter on business, Stephen never made any attempt to contact his father. On 30 April, Leacock's American publisher, Frank Dodd, wrote to propose a new anthology of his humorous work. This became *The Laugh Parade*, which appeared later in the year; it sold briskly and steadily, and with his last four humorous books — *Model Memoirs, My Remarkable Uncle, Happy Stories* and *Last Leaves* — restored his currency, and his sales figures, as a contemporary humorist. In the spring, when Leacock was already in Orillia, Stevie graduated from McGill, with honors in English, at the age of twenty-five. Leacock's friend Leslie Roberts, author of *Canada's War at Sea* (for which Leacock wrote the preface), stated on second-hand authority that Leacock missed the graduation exercises; he remained in the University Club because — to give the gist of an improbable quotation attributed to him — he felt irrelevant and out of place. Stevie taught English at McGill during the 1940-41 academic year, then began working at the publicity firm in Toronto that employed Henry Janes. Henry, the son of Leacock's friend Charlie Janes of Orillia, had been Leacock's student at McGill and recorded his memories of the famous author, who had been his friend and mentor from childhood. In the early 1940s, Stevie seemed launched on a writing career of his own. In Toronto, his main occupation became the writing of scripts for documentary films. *Guns for Victory* and *Pasture Lands* were for commercial clients, Atlas Steel and Quaker Oats respectively. *The Romance of a River* described the Hydro Electric Power Company's diversion of the Ogoki River, and *Heirs of Tomorrow* was a film for the Red Cross; it portrayed Canada's reception of displaced European children.

The summer of 1940 brought Leacock another serious loss and another mind-filling task. René du Roure died suddenly at the age of sixty. He had tried to enlist in the French armed services, as he had done in World War I, but had not been accepted because of his age. Both Leacock and McGill Principal F. Cyril James stated that du Roure's grief over the collapse of France had contributed to his death. Du Roure would never again occupy the second bedroom to the left of the staircase at Old Brewery Bay, nor would he smoke and play billiards and contribute to the education of Sergeant Jones. On 16 July, Leacock received a letter from the Gazette Printing Company of Montreal, publishers of the first edition of *Literary Lapses*. The company had been entrusted with production of a book for Distillers Corporation–Seagrams Limited. Samuel Bronfman, Seagrams' president, wished to produce a book about Canada to be distributed free, by his company, as a contribution to wartime morale and patriotism. An American literary agent hoped to visit Leacock on Bronfman's behalf. On 18 July, Leacock cabled back to the Gazette Printing Company, "Very glad to see representative here stop Please tell him to bring fishing rod." When the agent and a member of the printing company arrived, Leacock immediately conducted them out onto the lake to fish; then he gave them dinner and then, according to his custom, retired early, leaving his guests to ponder. No business had been discussed. The exasperated American, feeling that Leacock was showing his age, was prepared to leave and seek another author. The next morning, however, when the two men went to find him at the boathouse to say good-bye, Leacock came down from his study with a sheaf of writing that comprised an outline sketch of the whole project. A typed version of these notes (or possibly a later draft) is in the files of the Leacock Home. It takes the form of a report containing a précis of the book and a description of its aims. Leacock's fee was a substantial one, five thousand dollars or more, and he was to complete the book in four months. *Canada, The Foundations of Its Future* is a sweeping panorama of the country, vividly imagined and evoked in a prose that has the vigor of an exploratory voyage. Leacock handles facts easily and adds a wealth of poetic allusion, suggestion and depth. The book antedates by nearly three years the volume usually named as the first modern presentation of Canadian nationalism, Bruce Hutchison's award-winning *The Unknown Country* (1943). The books are very different in approach. Hutchison directly addresses the people and institutions of contemporary Canada and describes the landscape. Leacock evokes these things in the course of a history of a developing nation, a history that is taken to the verge of the future and looks into it. Leacock's penetration of his subject is colored by the prophetic optimism he professes for the people and land of Canada. He celebrates potential and demands a will to create. He avoids easy assumptions, such as Hutchison's that English and French Canadians were growing closer together. For many years, Leacock had been analyzing, in articles, the separatist tendencies in Canada, including the west and north. Leacock dreamed that development of the northwest could make Canada a nation comprising one hundred million people. (He published an article to this effect in *The Rotarian* in 1944.) It was, he believed, a dream based on a sober judgment of possibility, not the simplistic expectation of inevitable greatness that animated some turn-of-the-century Canadians (for instance, James W. Longley, attorney general of Nova Scotia, who told the Canadian Club of Boston in 1902, "The beginning of this century marks an epoch of phenomenal progress in British North America. The nineteenth century was the century of the United States. The twentieth century is Canada's century.") *Canada* was well-written and beautifully designed and produced by the same company that had produced the cheap red newsstand *Literary Lapses* in 1910. The book contained thirty-one illustrations by Canadian artists, such as Group of Seven member Frederick Varley. At Leacock's suggestion some art was commissioned from Charles Jefferys, the historical artist who had done cartoons, many years earlier, for Leacock's "nonsense" plays, those collected in *Over the Footlights*, when the series had had its Canadian periodical publication in *Maclean's*.

In 1940, when he returned to Montreal, Leacock lived at least part of the late fall, winter and spring in his house. (He also did this in 1941 and 1942.) In 1941, he received a suggestion that he write his autobiography. Thomas B. Costain, his editor with Doubleday Doran and Company, which had published his Dickens biography and the anthologies of Dickens and American humor, suggested that an autobiography would probably be a Book of the Month Club selection, and might sell as many as seven hundred thousand copies. Leacock did not take up the suggestion, but by 1942 he was seriously planning it as a future project, probably to be given to Dodd, Mead and Company. On a contract with Dodd, Mead dating from August, 1942, he made a marginal jotting about a projected autobiography: "I should not wish to publish this till the war is over as I think it would attract more attention in a quieter world." In December, Costain approached Leacock with another project: to write an entry about Quebec City in a series of books about North American ports that Doubleday Doran was producing. Leacock quickly answered that he would like to contribute to the series, but that his entry should be about Montreal. The result was *Montreal: Seaport and City* (1942), which he considered one of his best books. It is the book he proposed in his first letter about the idea: "a happy blend of history and geography, romance and commerce, with plenty of present day interest both for the U.S. and Canada." Among the best books ever written about a North American city, and especially notable among such books for its style, it was reissued in 1963 as *Leacock's Montreal*, with the factual matter brought up to date by Professor John Culliton, Leacock's colleague in the McGill department of economics and political science. (Culliton had helped him with research for the original edition.) Much of the book was written in the summer of 1942 in Old Brewery Bay while Leacock was also busy writing his brief book, *Our Heritage of Liberty*. This was also a historical work, one more directly related to his effort to foster pride in Anglo-American institutions as a means of contributing to wartime morale and purpose. It traced the history of democracy and argued Leacock's belief that only modern democracy could provide the social improvements the world still needed. His third book of the year was *My Remarkable Uncle*, one of his best miscellanies. While the book's humor is excellent, it reveals the figure Edwin Holgate saw when painting Leacock in 1943, "a philosopher with a great good humor. But first a philosopher." The book includes such fine pieces as "The British Soldier," "The Mathematics of the Lost Chord," "The Passing of the Kitchen," "Migration in English Literature," "Index: There Is No Index," "Why Do We Fish?" and the title piece, with its barely fictionalized portrait of Uncle E.P. Leacock, the jovial charlatan who parlayed his "ownership" of nonexistent interests into a short-lived semblance of wealth and a seat in the Manitoba Legislative Assembly. A few of the pieces contain examples of his nonsensical imagination at the top of its form, but most are deceptively relaxed and informal essays that convey serious thought through a mixture of humor, historical and literary analysis and poetic suggestion. One of the high points of the book is an essay on age, "Three Score and Ten," which the *New York Times* had printed on his seventieth birthday (30 December, 1939); it contains his moving portrayal of extreme old age as an obscure no-man's land of decisive but unknown encounters and offers his famous defiance: "Give me my stick. I'm going out on to No Man's Land. I'll face it."

In 1942 and 1943, Leacock continued to work at a remarkable pace. He produced books, serious articles, slighter newspaper and magazine pieces and humor. On 8 September, 1942, he accepted the task of directing and helping to write the revisions of all the entries about Canadian places in the *Encyclopaedia Britannica*. More than a hundred articles were involved. Some were only six lines long (entries on the smallest cities); others were substantial (entries on the provinces). The main article about Canada was more than three thousand lines. He drew up an elaborate organizational plan to guide the work and recruited qualified McGill professors and other academic acquaintances to revise or rewrite material. He kept much of the work for himself. For instance, he did a substantial portion of the article about Canada, and his correspondence is filled with information sent to him from Canadian municipal and provincial governments, who provided recent economic and social statistics. For help with the project and with a book he was writing in 1943, *Canada and the Sea*, he turned again to Barbara Ulrichsen Nimmo. From her home in Birmingham, Michigan and (after mid-1943) from Syracuse, New York, she handled much of his correspondence for the encyclopedia and typed manuscripts of articles and the draft of his book.

By July, 1943 Leacock had completed *Canada and the Sea*; he also sent the first part of the manuscript of his new humor collection, *Happy Stories*, to Dodd, Mead. This book, made uneven by the inclusion of hastily written propaganda pieces, contains some excellent material, such as "Pawn to King's Four," "Mr. McCoy Sails for Fiji" and a fictional treatment of

E.P. Leacock, "Boom Time." Leacock's work continued to bring to him many fascinating contacts with the world. In September, 1943 a Mr. H. Shave of Winnipeg wrote to him about Leacock's uncle E.P. Shave's father had arrived in the city in April 1882, and E.P. Leacock was the first man he had worked for. The elder Shave had often told how "he used to be posted at the 'Lodge' on Main Street to watch for approaching dignitaries, so that he could notify his employer before their arrival." Shave enclosed a photograph of the "old Leacock home," E.P.'s residence on the banks of the Red River, which, in 1943, was kept in good condition by its owner, the Saint Agnes Priory. Leacock was also writing a book about the art on which he had labored for so many years, *How to Write*. Published early in 1943, it was described in a February essay by Struthers Burt in *The Saturday Review*:

> This is a lovely book because it is both witty and wise. . . .The title is merely a stalking-horse for the ripe philosopher to say what he thinks of his vocation, whether he denies that noun or not — his avocation is teaching political economy, and he can even be funny about that —; and about literature in general, and life, and literary style, and above all the English language, that major instrument of beauty and common sense and civilization and articulateness.
>
> And yet it's a good text book; an excellent one. Actually a superb one. . . . He has a mind that cannot resist its own enchantment, and so he enchants other minds.

To his friend Doctor Gerhard Lomer, McGill's head librarian and the man who became Leacock's bibliographer, Leacock wrote, "This book How to Write is like a favorite child to me because I wrote it purely to suit myself with no eye on editors or sales or the public." At his death, it seemed to many that *How to Write*, *Canada* and *Montreal* would be among his most valuable books, and this judgment has merit, even though the three works, like many of his others, have since been eclipsed by the understandable interpretation of his career primarily in terms of his creative, humorous literature.

In the last half of 1943 Leacock was working on two more of the best books in his canon. One was his autobiography. (He completed only four chapters; they were published post-humously under the title *The Boy I Left Behind Me*.) The second, published after his death, was *Last Leaves*, a selection of essays of almost uniform excellence, in which humor is subordinated to a mature consideration of life, society, art — and, of course, the immediate (though now somewhat dated) concerns occasioned by the war. The collection reveals Leacock's relationship to the world. "What Can Izaak Walton Teach Us?" has wonderful things to say of Walton, fishing, life and literature; it also shows that Leacock was sublimely unaware that John Donne was no longer a dim figure remembered only because Walton had written of him. (Donne had been resurrected by T.S. Eliot, and others, as one of the most important poets of English literature.) "Common Sense and the Universe," a model of the popular scientific essay, displayed Leacock's command of the concepts and inclinations of the advanced physics of his day. "Gold" revealed that he still felt a redeemable currency should be restored in the postwar world. "Can We Beat Inflation?" intelligently addressed a problem that persists today. The essay offers Leacock's customary blend, in economic forecasting, of warnings mixed with optimism: inflation was an extremely dangerous force that could be controlled only through proper effort rigorously applied.

The last two essays, "Alice Walks in Wonderland" and "Gilbert's 'Bab' Ballads," were chapters from a book Leacock never completed, *Read It with Me*, an anthology of his favorite readings framed by his commentaries upon them. In August, 1943 he had sent Thomas B. Costain the final list of authors and works to be included in the purely personal collection and had concluded his note, "Now I must go pick beans." Among the authors on the list were Lewis Carroll, W.S. Gilbert, Jerome K. Jerome, James M. Barrie, Lady Cynthia Asquith, O. Henry, Ring Lardner, Robert Benchley, Charles Dickens, Mark Twain, Alphonse Daudet and A.A. Milne. Costain, a native of Brantford, Ontario, had become editor of *Maclean's* in 1916; he had known Leacock early in his career as a humorist and an author of serious articles for the popular press. In 1920, Costain had gone to New York as an associate editor of *The Saturday Evening Post*; there again he had dealt with Leacock's work. Finally, as an editor of Doubleday Doran and Company from 1939 to 1946, he had recruited Leacock as an author; while Costain was at Doubleday, the two men became friends. Costain became one of Leacock's summer visitors. He last saw Leacock in 1942 and gave this account of an auspicious beginning to a holiday:

> Leacock came out of the house with a letter in his hand, and he was roaring with delight. "Tom," he shouted, "you've got to see this. It's a letter from a teacher in Chicago who's compiling an anthology on absent-minded professors. And the damn fool forgot to sign his name!"

Costain began his own career as a best-selling novelist the year after Leacock's death; he wrote *The Silver Chalice* (1954), *The Tontine* (1955) and a book not unrelated to Leacock's own style of history, *The White and the Gold: The French Régime in Canada* (1954).

In the last months of Leacock's life, many of his traditional interests and causes acquired a new urgency and energy. He wrote an article about the possibility of abolishing poverty, though *Maclean's* rejected the article, as it did another proposed piece on the battle between the *Chesapeake* and the *Shannon* in the War of 1812. In May, 1943 he tried to get *Reader's Digest* to publish an article on the battle and outlined a plan that would bring the *Chesapeake's* surviving timbers (whose existence, in an old mill at Fareham, Hants, near his birthplace, he had investigated) to the United States Naval Academy as a gesture of international friendship. To *Reader's Digest* he wrote:

> When I was a boy of six (1876), about to leave England for America, my grandfather took from his desk an oblong piece of hard wood, about 8 inches by three by four. "That's a bit of the old Chesapeake," he said. Written on it in the old man's writing . . . . was, "Piece of the American Frigate Chesapeake captured by the Shannon 1913." This bit of wood . . . is on my desk as I write, the legend on it faded beyond recognition.

One morning in 1943, Henry Janes recalled, Leacock had been unable to work and had taken Janes fishing. But he had stopped at the water's edge and, pretending that Old Brewery Bay was Boston Harbor, had recounted the entire battle in all its details, tracing out of the movements of the great sailing ships with gestures of his walking stick. Perhaps it is this description, translated into literature, that appears in *The Boy I Left Behind Me*. In 1943, he was also engaged in writing *Canada and the Sea*.

Leacock's final illness struck him in late 1943 or early 1944, while he was living at his Côte-des-Neiges house and working busily and happily on several projects. It is hard to know how early he began to feel the difficulty with swallowing that was the first indication of throat cancer. In November and December he seemed to be attempting to make arrangements for everyone and everything near to him. Stevie was living with him in Montreal. On Stevie's behalf, he wrote to Harry Napier Moore, the influential editor who had taken over *Maclean's* in 1924 and was now editorial director of the Maclean-Hunter Publishing Company. He boasted of Stevie's work for his Toronto publicity firm, but stated that he would appreciate it if Moore would give Stevie the security of a steady outlet for his writing. In November and again in January, anxious for "my old mare, whose life & welfare I greatly value," he wrote to Orillia to ensure that the horse was safely stabled and fed and to find a veterinarian to repair her teeth. In January, 1944 or earlier he had apparently suffered what he believed to be an attack of influenza. He wrote in late January to his friend R. Gladstone Murray that he was

> getting better & hope soon to be out of the woods — as an aftermath of flu something went wrong with my swallowing — I believe (and please God), it is clearing up now. . . .

On 4 February, however, he wrote to Murray,

> At present I am a very sick man. With good fortune I may pass a present corner and go on for a good time yet, even years. But at present I find it very hard.

In 1947, Stevie told Nathaniel Benson that, in January, his father had said to him, "It seems to be getting terribly hard

for me to swallow. There's something terrible in my throat."
Stevie wrote:

> He knew almost from the first what it was. But he didn't tell me. I
> remember his slouching through the snow all that January from
> our home up in Côte-des-Neiges to Dr. Eddie Archibold's. One day
> the latter brought a specialist to see him. From an upper window
> he saw them arriving and he turned to me grimly and said:
> "Stevie, they're coming up here to tell me I'm finished."

Before an operation for throat cancer on 16 March, Leacock
told Stevie, "I know the death sentence is on me. Oh, if I can
only get used to the truth that I am going to die." Leacock's
attitude towards this final crisis was a mixture of faith and
agnosticism, of trust in the "Spirit" (which in *Last Leaves*
brings "Good Will on Earth") and a sense of the finality of
death. He clung with love, but perhaps also with hopelessness,
to life.

The specialist Eddie Archibold brought to see him was Doctor W.G. Turner, who confirmed Archibold's fears, made an
exact diagnosis and enlisted the aid of other specialists,
doctors Wookey, Wilkie and Pierce, in deciding how to treat
Leacock's condition. A letter to Leacock from Dot on 11
February indicates that he was already receiving regular
X-ray treatments. He was reluctant to agree to an operation,
perhaps fearing it, perhaps fearing to confirm the seriousness
of his illness or to exhaust the only remaining measure.
George wrote to him, "She [Dot] is very very strongly in favor
of the first small operation that Dr. Wookey suggests to do and
I think she is right." Apparently there was some real hope
that Leacock would survive. On 14 February Dot wrote to
him, "You certainly seem to be pulling 'out of it' wonderfully
well." She had talked to his doctors and wrote:

> they evidently *don't* feel that they must necessarily leave things
> as they are. I feel that you can be assured that at least they are go-
> ing to try to 'prolong the years' with perhaps a chance of
> altogether getting rid of the darned growth.

As comfort against the throat spasms he was suffering, Dot

said that irritation may cause them rather than a worsening of the growth. She stated that she, too, had had spasms of the esophagus and larynx for the last nine years due to "collection of fibrous tissue in those parts following the X-ray treatments I had in 1934 & 1935."

Confined to bed in his house, his speech reduced to a painful whisper, Leacock continued to work. He collected manuscripts for the book that became *Last Leaves* under a cover sheet, on which he wrote, "Barbara's Book." From December to February, the series of articles expanded from an earlier *Maclean's* piece, "What's Ahead for Canada," was appearing in the *Financial Post*; the series had been designed so that it could easily be recrafted into a book. Leacock never had the chance to write it. In March, he was taken from Montreal to Toronto's Western Hospital and on 16 March underwent an operation for cancer of the throat. At first it seemed the operation was successful and there were reports that Leacock was recovering. He soon weakened again, however. On 28 March, two hours after an exploratory X-ray of his throat, Leacock died. His last recorded words, spoken with a smile to his radiologist, were, "Did I behave pretty well? Was I a good boy?"

Leacock's body was cremated and his ashes interred on 31 March at Sibbald's Point in Saint George's churchyard, which lies at the edge of a bluff above Lake Simcoe. The funeral was small and quiet and the day blustery; a sharp wind whined in the cedar trees and swirled a few flakes of spring snow. At two-thirty that day the church held the funeral of Martin Sibbald, head of the most prominent local family, a man who had known all the Leacocks and had encouraged Leacock from his childhood; Sibbald was about twenty years the humorist's senior. Leacock's funeral followed at four o'clock. Archbishop Derwyn Owen, Anglican Primate of Canada, and Reverend P.G. Powell, the pastor, officiated at both ceremonies. Among Leacock's pallbearers and mourners were local friends, representatives of Upper Canada College, Stevie, Barbara and her husband, Donald Nimmo, George, Charlie, Teddy, Dot, Carrie and Daisy. The ashes were buried under a small umbrella elm in the family plot at the east side of the churchyard. Leacock's grave is close to the gray stone church erected on the site where, on 15 August, 1838, twenty-nine settlers had labored at an all-day bee to erect the first, wooden church, using fifteen thousand feet of timber that had been rafted down Lake Simcoe to the bluff. To this place and this people Stephen Leacock, their critic but also the voice of their spirit and their aspirations, belonged.

Chapter Fifteen

Behind the Beyond

I T IS SAID that when the elderly Mark Twain, on his last world tour, was told of American newspaper stories that he had succumbed to a fatal illness, he replied, "The reports of my death have been greatly exaggerated." Even after the worldwide notice of his passing and the ceremonies of the family funeral at Lake Simcoe, Stephen Leacock challenged the finality of death. There was writing to be published, optimism to be communicated to a world still at war, a future course for reconstruction and social justice to be recommended, laughter to be shared, plans for family and friends to be fulfilled. Two new books of his writings were published soon after his death. *Last Leaves*, his final collection of essays, was released in 1945. In 1946 the four chapters of autobiography Leacock had entrusted to his friend Fitz Shaw were published as *The Boy I Left Behind Me*. More a selection of memories and reflections than a thorough account of events, the book remains one of Leacock's most fascinating serious works, especially in its presentation of his theories of education and of his experience as a high-school teacher. Some of the articles he had placed with magazines in his last months appeared after his death; for instance, "Canada Can Support 100,000,000 People" was published in *The Rotarian* in October, 1944.

Leacock's hopes and provisions for his family were indicated in his will. Amounts were left to his brothers and sisters and to staff members, especially Sergeant Jones and Tina Kelly, who had maintained Old Brewery Bay year-round for him. His Côte-des-Neiges house in Montreal was eventually sold, then torn down to make way for an expansion of Montreal General Hospital. Leacock intended his Orillia property, Old Brewery Bay, for a permanent family legacy. It was left to Stevie, along with the other main elements of his estate, for example, a trust fund of more than $100,000 and approximately $50,000 in widely diversified, cleverly chosen securities, primarily in mining, pulp and paper and oil — the resource industries in which Leacock had seen the foundation of Canada's future. His writing continued to enrich his estate. The records of Dodd, Mead and Company show that his books for that publisher alone had earned more than $11,000 in the three years before he died; a further $1,000 came during the month after his death.

Although in 1944 the war still dominated other concerns, Leacock's death was reported and he was eulogized all over the world. In Canada his friends immediately set about to keep his name and his spirit living. The University Club arranged a Leacock corner, which today preserves his favorite chair, situated under a posthumous portrait painted by Richard Jack, whose charcoal sketch of the author was one of the gifts presented to him upon his retirement from McGill. Articles portraying his character and his quirks appeared in many publications from the pens of his oldest friends, B.K. Sandwell, Pelham Edgar and others. With the assistance of Sandwell, William Arthur Deacon and other prominent writers, a movement arose in Orillia to honor Canadian humorists with a medal in Leacock's name. The first awards banquet was held in 1947 in Orillia, and has continued an annual event; the Leacock Memorial Medal for Humor is now a major literary award. Speakers at the original banquet attempted to create again the presence of the great humorist. George Leacock and B.K. Sandwell were in fine form; Stevie did an imitation of his father and Harry Symonds, winner of the first medal for his *Ojibway Melody*, also contributed. In 1951, Leacock's old acquaintance Leslie Frost, who was from Orillia and was at that time premier of Ontario, unveiled a portrait bust of Leacock in the Orillia Public Library; the artist, noted sculptor Elizabeth Wynn Wood, was a native of the city. The library holds an outstanding collection of Leacock books and other items, especially on the subject of *Sunshine Sketches of a Little Town*, and a set of works by and about Leacock based, in part, upon copies presented by the humorist during his lifetime.

Despite all that was done to preserve a sense of Leacock's presence, the world of his relatives, friends and fellow townsmen was different without him. Stevie and George seem to have been demoralized by Leacock's death. Stevie dropped his sporadic publicity work and the writing of film scripts and devoted himself to planning literary projects that never appeared. He was financially independent because of his father's bequest and he had the Old Brewery Bay house at his disposal. But Stevie lived in the lodge rather than the main house, which stood vacant and began to deteriorate. One of the projects with which he toyed was a biography of his father. In late 1944, Thomas Costain was also considering a biography of Leacock; he consulted with Fitz Shaw and with George, who suggested that Stevie might write the book. Costain, however, demurred. Stevie began selling off the outbuildings on the property, the boathouse, the stables, the barn. Soon after the first Leacock Medal banquet was held at the main house, Stevie agreed to lease it to Henry Janes, Leacock's friend and his student at McGill in the 1920s. Janes wanted to care for the house and especially its contents. According to Leacock's will, his manuscripts were to be given to the McGill library, and Janes, with the help of a local librarian, tried to preserve the papers, many of which were strewn in disarray around the basement of the house, covered with ashes or dust and damaged by water. Other parts of the house had been disturbed. Stevie had sold off pieces of furniture; vandals had begun to make forays; in general, the house showed the effects of neglect. Janes leased the house only for the summer of the first awards banquet; he was able to interest almost no one in his dream of turning it into a shrine and a literary-arts center. Two men who were predisposed to listen were Leacock's old friend, the Orillia publisher Charles Harold Hale, and a young news reporter and local politician, J.A. (Peter) McGarvey, now a Toronto broadcaster. When Stevie offered to sell the house and its 28.8 acres for $56,000, the three men proposed the purchase to the city council. Some council members supported the purchase, but they were outvoted. One member said that, apart from the question of the expense, he refused to support any honor to Leacock, who was a reprobate. This comment prompted Stevie to tell McGarvey he would never sell the house to the city. McGarvey and Hale organized a private group to raise funds to acquire the home. The group also included out-of-town sympathizers, such as William Arthur Deacon, and several families that had known Leacock, including some that had figured in *Sunshine Sketches*: the Drinkwaters, the Tudhopes and the Ardaghs. But Stevie sold the house, and it seemed lost to the project. It had become the property of Louis Ruby, publisher of the successful scandal magazine *Flash*, who at first intended to subdivide the grounds. Then Ruby proved unexpectedly accommodating to the effort to establish it as a memorial to Leacock. McGarvey demonstrated popular support for the idea by running for Orillia council on one issue: acquiring the home. He was the top vote-getter among six candidates. Just after the election, on 10 December, 1956, the Orillia council unanimously voted to purchase the home and to provide an additional five thousand dollars to begin restoration. The Leacock Home is Canada's most elaborate and beautiful literary shrine. The city of Orillia, and the board that administers the home on the city's behalf, have given the home to the country. Over the years, the home and its grounds have been restored and — under the direction of Ralph Curry, the home's curator from 1957 to 1970 — its thousands of items, including Leacock's writing and correspondence, have been preserved and catalogued. The home's most valuable manuscript is the handwritten original of *Sunshine Sketches of a Little Town*, which was donated in 1966 by John G. McConnell, president and publisher of the *Montreal Star*. McConnell purchased the manuscript for $20,000 with the plan of presenting it to the home. Leacock's niece, Barbara Nimmo, agreed to sell the text, which had been in her possession since her uncle's death, for less than its market value because McConnell was planning to give the manuscript to the Memorial Home.

In 1956, George was seventy-nine years of age and had retired from the presidency of the Moloney Electric Company of Toronto. He lived with his wife, Mary, in Toronto near the old Woodbine (now the Greenwood) racetrack; he had attended the races almost daily for years. He continued to keep in close contact with Stevie, but neither of them had the will or desire to look after the home, although their finances would easily have allowed it. It seemed that Leacock's absence kept them at a distance. Through 1956, Stevie continued to live at the lodge, which had fallen into disrepair. He imitated his father's mannerisms, but in an erratic, painfully exaggerated fashion. He dressed sloppily and eccentrically, hired and fired servants and had himself driven everywhere in taxi cabs. Taking taxis became one of his hallmarks. In his later years, when he lived in Orillia on West Street North, in the home of his friends the Cramps (Wilbur Cramp was once a mayor of Orillia), Stevie became obsessed with the assassination of United States president John F. Kennedy. At times, he had himself driven as far as Washington, DC and New Orleans in the course of his "investigations." His unpublished manuscript on the subject supposedly exists. Loved and honored by his friends as a wit, conversationalist and convivial companion, lamented for the failed promise of his talent, Stevie died in his sleep in Orillia in 1974. All of his uncles and aunts — all of Agnes' many children — were dead, and Agnes had no direct descendant who carried the Leacock name. Many of Stevie's cousins survive, nieces and nephews, offspring of Agnes's daughters; there are descendants of other branches of the family, including the direct line of the remarkable uncle, E.P. Elizabeth Kimball, Daisy's daughter, wrote *The Man in the Panama Hat* (1970), a volume of family reminiscences.

For a creative artist, perhaps, the only real measure of immortality is the enshrinement of his books, rather than his personality. Writing seventy years after the death of Dickens, Leacock predicted that eventually the novelist he loved would be acknowledged as a genius. Leacock pointed out that the reputation of an artist frequently declines in the period immediately after his death. To some extent, this happened to Leacock. Only forty years have elapsed since his passing, and so it is impossible to argue from the evidence of history that his work will survive. Yet, of the almost thirty collections of humor he published, many are in print; his popularity remains, and he does not lack admirers among critics and scholars. New generations of admirers meet Leacock's work in many forms: one-man stage shows, a musical comedy version of *Sunshine Sketches of a Little Town*, a cartoon of "My Financial Career," and others.

Few commentators doubt that his work contains much that is memorable, but some question his claim to enduring greatness. It is said that he took the world too lightly and was too determined to be genial, or that he wrote too much and refused to refine his style to the point of excellence. In contrast to the comic authors whom he most admired himself, he wrote few humorous works that presented a unified plot and structure. If literary reputation rests for a humorist only on his longer works, Leacock should be remembered for two outstanding books, *Sunshine Sketches* and *Arcadian Adventures with the Idle Rich*. A full appreciation of Leacock's accomplishment, and enduring contribution to literature, will be based not on these books alone, but rather on the wealth of shorter pieces which place him among the most gifted essayists of the English language.

Leacock is memorable in anthologies of his work. *Laugh with Leacock*, prepared in 1930, remains in print. Other collections include *The Bodley Head Leacock*, edited in 1957 by his friend J.B. Priestly, and a recent anthology edited and introduced by novelist Robertson Davies. Since most of his own books are anthologies of short pieces, an anthology is the best way to present him. Leacock's preferred form, the essay, is no longer nearly as popular as the novel or short story, and this in part explains why Leacock is not ranked as high as those who excel in other genres. But an examination of his work shows that he belongs among the classic personal essayists, and that his best work cannot be accused of lacking either finish or imagination. Finally, the reader who turns from a Leacock anthology to the original books will soon find indispensable sketches and stories that are little known but rewarding, and will come to treasure fine passages and flights of fancy that appear abundantly even in unsuccessful pieces. Leacock was one of the first North American humorists to take humor out of the barbershop and the smoking car, and blend it with cultured writing style and a complex, satirical view of life. He was a gifted student of literature and an accomplished theoretician in the fields of economics and political science, and at his best he could infuse the insights of tradition into his humorous advice on the everyday struggle to survive in a changing world.

His world reputation may well have been limited by his decision to stay in Canada. He remained true to his own values and heritage in a way that precluded an exclusive devotion to literature and a life in literary centers. He made his success from where he was. The life's work that he set out to accomplish was to teach a useful discipline and to inculcate wisdom; humor was largely a means to this latter end. Although he expressed his own exuberant imagination through humor, he was ultimately less concerned with the creation of a fictional joke than with the humor that appeared in life. The kernel of truth in a story gave it an inherent relevance. The humorist's job was to add that element of artistic presentation and insight that revealed why a particular bit of truth should matter. He hoped that this type of sharing might really make a difference in a troubled world, but he did not wish merely to create sympathy and mutual understanding. By the end of his life he went further, and tried to foster attitudes that would lead to justices.

A man of the middle ground, he wanted to preserve traditional institutions while at the same time redressing the wrongs he found in society through vigorous programs of social action. Always he argued for change by re-interpreting inherited forms rather than radically attacking them. He wanted to contribute to beneficial change through writing, and he wanted change to come not out of fear or shame or guilt over the past, but rather out of the renewal of his culture's own highest purposes. He would not let go of the world he loved for the sake of fame for himself as an individual, and he would not give up the vital work of education that he identified with teaching at McGill. He could understand that he stood between two giants, between Great Britain and the United States, but he preferred to stay home. In all this, he differs from many other regional writers for whom nostalgia alone motivates their remembrance of traditional life and values. He also differs from many writers in that he never served the requirements of literary reputation. He would not take himself so seriously that he would give up his own beliefs in order to secure an audience. When an audience came, he was still Leacock, the Leacock who had amused himself as a high-school teacher with composing sketches during sermons, the Leacock who had relished the celebration of Christmas with his beloved younger brothers and sisters, the Leacock who had learned from his successful world tour that a home at Old Brewery Bay was the thing he most wanted.

There are many monuments to Leacock. Plaques honor him in Orillia and in Montreal; there is a historical marker in front of the Saint George's churchyard. In 1969, a Canadian stamp commemorated the centenary of his birth. But remembrances such as his home, its property and his stone in the family plot beside the old church are of another order, because they belong to Leacock's continuing presence; they exist because Leacock made himself part of the life — the spirit and intellect and sense of place — of the people among whom he lived. At McGill, a seven-story modern addition to the Arts Building, where Leacock taught, has been named after him, and a modern, controlled-environment room in the rare-book section of the McLennan Library has been designated the Leacock Room. It is furnished with the most complete existing collection of his published works and is presided over by the Frederick Taylor portrait. Yet Old Brewery Bay remains his principal shrine. There a visitor can look through his library, see his manila folder labeled "Letters from Damn Fools" and move about the unique house that Leacock's imagination created. From its many rooms, or from the lawn, or from the point of land covered with white pines and cedars and oaks, one sees placid Lake Couchiching from shifting angles and in changing moods, sparkling with summer light, reflecting the autumn woods, glowing with sunset or showing subtle tones of dun and slate under a dreary overcast. Leacock is gone; his direct line is extinct; the summer kingdom of Agnes' children and their children is broken up and dispersed. But Old Brewery Bay continues to manifest the undeniable presence of Leacock's magnetism, his *joie de vivre*, his passion for learning, his care for literary art.

Notes

WE HAVE WITH US TO-NIGHT

PG

1 rising at five o'clock — "A Master of Satire: Mr. Stephen Leacock in London," *The London Times*, 27 September, 1921, p. 12. Leacock's passion for early rising was well documented throughout his life. See below, Chapter 4, on his years at Upper Canada College, and Chapter 7 for the Côte-des-Neiges sleeping porch. "He wrote in the early morning, often (especially in Montreal) being up and at his desk in the early hours when I arrived home from a very late party," wrote Leacock's niece, Barbara Nimmo, in her preface to the original edition of *Last Leaves* (Toronto: McClelland, 1945), New Canadian Library 69, p. xix. Hereafter the book is referred to as *Last Leaves* with page numbers from the New Canadian Library edition only.

4 Charlie Chaplin — Windermere, "Leacock Lurking in the Limelight," *Toronto Star*, 29 September, 1921, p. 13.

4 *Alice in Wonderland* — "Leacock Lurking in the Limelight," p. 13. Leacock originally published his opinion on the relative importance of *Alice* and the *Britannica* in his preface to the original edition of *Sunshine Sketches of a Little Town* (London: Lane, 1912), New Canadian Library 15, third page of preface. Hereafter the book is referred to as *Sunshine Sketches* with page numbers

PG

from the New Canadian Library Edition only.

4 Successor to Mark Twain — "Stephen Leacock, Humorist," *The Morning Post*, London, 29 September, 1921, reprinted in *The Living Age*, 296 (5 November, 1921), p. 352.

5 Thomas Carlyle — "A Master of Satire," p. 12.

6 humor too uncertain — Leacock provided this information in a hand-written note to Norman H. Friedman, friend and collector of his work, dated 12 December, 1934 and preserved in an autographed first edition of *Literary Lapses* (London: Lane, 1910) in the Friedman Collection, Leacock Room, McLennan Library, McGill University.

7 teaching Latin — "A Master of Satire," p. 12.

8 London interviews — Stephen Leacock, "I Am Interviewed," *The Morning Post*, London, 9 October, 1921, p. 8. This article was reproduced with very minor revisions as "I am Interviewed by the Press" in *My Discovery of England* (New York: Dodd Mead, 1922), New Canadian Library 28, pp. 36-51. Hereafter this book is referred to as *My Discovery* with page numbers from the New Canadian Library edition only.

9 interviews counted — "Our Modest Estimators," *Punch* (London, 12 October, 1921), p. 297.

9 another interviewer — Ernest Jenkins, "Mr. Stephen Leacock: An Interview Gone Wrong," *Punch* (London, 12 October,

PG

1921), p. 294.

9 a little disillusioned — "An Interview Gone Wrong," p. 294.

11 Seaman introduction — "Mr. Stephen Leacock's Lectures," *The London Times*, 14 October, 1921, p. 8.

12 British humor — "Mr. Stephen Leacock's Tour Ended," *The London Times*, 24 December, 1921, p. 7.

12 The Snoopopaths — "The Snoopopaths; or, Fifty Stories in One," in *Further Foolishness* (London: Lane, 1916), New Canadian Library 60, p. 23. This book will be cited hereafter as *Further Foolishness* with page numbers from the New Canadian Library edition only.

12 sex-murder — "The Great Detective," in *Here Are My Lectures and Stories!* (New York: Dodd Mead, 1937), p. 8. Another version of the same theme appears under the title, "The Great Detective," in *Short Circuits* (New York: Dodd Mead, 1928), New Canadian Library 57, pp. 203-16. This book will be cited hereafter as *Short Circuits* with page numbers from the New Canadian Library edition only.

14 lecture introductions — "Mr. Stephen Leacock's Lectures," p. 8.

14 coming back — "We Have With Us To-night," *My Discovery*, p. 165.

15 G.K. Chesterton — W.E. Gladstone Murray, article in *The Telegram*, Toronto, 8 August, 1950.

15 J.M. Barrie — Stephen Leacock,

PG

"Barrie and O. Henry," *Mark Twain Quarterly* II (Fall, 1937), p. 3.

16 O. Henry — Stephen Leacock, "O. Henry and the Critics," *New Republic* IX (2 December, 1916), pp. 120-2.

17 Canadian Club — "A Canadian Club in London," *The London Times*, 12 December, 1921.

17 David M. Legate, *Stephen Leacock: A Biography* (Toronto: Doubleday Canada Limited, 1970; Macmillan of Canada, 1978, Laurentian Library 63), p. 119. This book is cited hereafter as Legate biography with page numbers from the Laurentian Library edition.

18 last prohibitionist — "Mr. Stephen Leacock on London," *The London Times*, 10 December, 1921, p. 12. Leacock published this speech, with slight revision, as "Impressions of London," in *My Discovery*, pp. 36-49.

18 House of Commons — "Mr. Stephen Leacock on London," p. 12.

18 capital reading — Positive reviews appeared in the *Boston Transcript*, 16 August, 122, p. 8; the *Saturday Review* 133 (24 June, 1922), p. 658; the *New York Tribune*, 25 June, 1922, p. 5 (Benchley was the reviewer); and *Outlook* 132 (13 September, 1922), p. 80.

19 blithe conception — Lawton Mackall, in a review for the *Nation* 115 (16 August, 1922), p. 171.

19 editor disappointed — Legate biography, p. 127, citing letter

from Dodd, Mead editors; letter on file at Leacock Home.

20 Christy & Moore — letter from Leacock to Mr. Christy, 30 December, 1921, in the Leacock Memorial Collection at Orillia Public Library, Orillia, Ontario.

21 last interview — "Mr. Stephen Leacock's Tour Ended," p. 7.

21 E.V. Lucas — Stephen Leacock, *The Boy I Left Behind Me* (New York: Dodd Mead, 1946; *The Penguin Stephen Leacock*, London, 1981), p. 349. This book is cited hereafter as *The Boy I Left* with page numbers from the Penguin edition only.

2

MY VICTORIAN BOYHOOD

23 Victorian birth — *The Boy I Left*, p. 346. Robertson Davies, introduction to *Penguin Stephen Leacock*, p. ix: "it is important for me to remember that he was a Victorian."

25 cottage was three centuries old — "Stephen Leacock," booklet prepared by the Stephen Leacock Centennial Committee, B.T. Richardson chairman, n.d., pp. 4-5.

25 Swanmore — *The Boy I Left*, pp. 346-47.

25 parents' marriage — details of the wedding, and most of the personal information about the early life of Agnes Leacock and her marriage with Peter, come from a diary dated April, 1914 by Agnes and preserved in a typewritten manuscript copy at the Stephen Leacock Memorial

Home, Orillia. See also Legate biography, p. 3.

25 first child — Agnes Leacock's diary does not make reference to any pre-marital liaison with Peter.

25 Peter Leacock's birth — Legate biography, p. 3.

26 family history — *The Boy I Left*, p. 348.

26 Peter's brothers — Elizabeth Kimball, *The Man in the Panama Hat* (Toronto: McClelland & Stewart, 1970; published with revised title, *My Uncle, Stephen Leacock*, Toronto: Goodread Biographies, 1983), p. 136. This book will be cited hereafter as Kimball with page numbers from the Goodread Biographies edition only.

26 Agnes' birthdate — Kimball, p. 16.

28 Marriage settlement — document on file at the Stephen Leacock Memorial Home (hereafter referred to as Leacock Home).

28 colonial plans — Agnes Leacock's diary, p. 10, Leacock Home.

29 birth of Thomas James — Kimball, p. 16; Leacock describes his parents' experiences in Natal very briefly in *The Boy I Left*, p. 351.

30 six children — *The Boy I Left*, p. 352.

30 asphalt contractor — Legate biography, p. 5.

30 Arthur Murdock — Kimball, p. 16.

30 Leacock baptism — Legate biography, p. 5.

30 Leacock's godmother — Agnes Leacock's diary, p. 8. Leacock

Home.

31 Leacock family — Kimball, p. 16.

31 dear Dadda — letter from Stephen Leacock to Peter Leacock, undated. Leacock Home. From the context of the letter, which announces the birth of Leacock's brother, Teddy, it can be dated 1875.

32 Canadian migration — Leacock, *Sunshine Sketches*, p. 1 of original preface.

32 uncle E.P. — Leacock, "My Remarkable Uncle," in *My Remarkable Uncle and Other Sketches* (New York: Dodd Mead, 1942), New Canadian Library 53, p. 16. This book will be cited hereafter as *My Remarkable Uncle* with page numbers from the New Canadian Library edition only.

32 farming in Hampshire — *The Boy I Left*, p. 351.

3

THE STRUGGLE TO MAKE US GENTLEMEN

40 broken heart — *The Boy I Left*, p. 366.

41 family visit — Kimball, pp. 100-11.

41 farm failure — *The Boy I Left*, p. 370.

42 Georgina Township school — *The Boy I Left*, p. 375.

42 caste and thistles — *The Boy I Left*, p. 371.

42 lost corner — Stephen Leacock, "The Old Farm and the New Frame," in *My Remarkable Uncle*, p. 21.

43 unbroken sentence — *The Boy I Left*, p. 366.

43 E.P. — *My Remarkable Uncle*, p. 14; *The Boy I Left*, pp. 386-88.

44 Peter's departure — *The Boy I Left*, p. 386.

4 father's occupation — Ralph Curry, *Stephen Leacock, Humorist and Humanist* (New York: Doubleday, 1959), p. 33. This book is cited hereafter as Curry biography.

44 Leacock children — Kimball, p. 16.

45 Agnes as teacher — *The Boy I Left*, p. 375.

45 childhood reading — *The Boy I Left*, pp. 378-81.

46 Harry Park — *The Boy I Left*, pp. 376-78.

47 Lake Simcoe — *The Boy I Left*, p. 383.

47 Charles Noble — Stephen Leacock, "Going for the Doctor," *The McGill News*, Fall 1931.

49 Leacock on the farm — Curry biography, pp. 23-24; Legate biography, pp. 12-13.

50 childhood on the farm — *The Boy I Left*, pp. 363-64.

51 both ways — *The Boy I Left*, p. 364.

52 choice of Upper Canada College — *The Boy I Left*, p. 397.

52 history of Upper Canada College — *The Boy I Left*, pp. 392-94; Richard B. Howard, *Upper Canada College 1829-1979: Colborne's Legacy* (Toronto, 1979), pp. 12-67.

53 American principles — *The Boy I Left*, pp. 375-81.

54 not a gentleman — Stephen Leacock, "The Struggle to Make Us Gentlemen," in *My Remarkable*

Uncle, pp. 28-29.

55 starting school — *The Boy I Left*, p. 401. The illness was scarlatina and, according to Curry biography, p. 34, proved a blessing in disguise, because Leacock's entry at mid-year meant that he was not getting the instruction he required, but rather being left to his own efforts to catch up with the rest of the class.

56 debating — Stephen Leacock, "Mathematics Versus Puzzles," in *Too Much College: or, Education Eating Up Life, with Kindred Essays in Education and Humor* (New York: Dodd Mead, 1939), p. 55.

56 first year grades — Curry biography, p. 36.

56 John St. house — *The Boy I Left*, p. 387.

56 family together — Kimball, p. 126.

57 game of croquet — letter from Stephen Leacock to Peter Leacock, dated 28 June, 1884. Leacock Home.

57 *College Times* — Stephen Leacock, *The College Times*, 7 April, 1887.

58 headings and dates — *The Boy I Left*, p. 409.

58 Peter leaves farm — Kimball, pp. 112-18.

59 father threatened — Curry biography, p. 41, where the source of the story is given as Stephen Leacock's older brother, George. Leacock himself alluded to his last meeting with his father in *The Boy I Left*, pp. 387-8, only by saying that, "Things went worse than ever for my father

on his return to the farm — a shadowed, tragic family life into which I need not enter."

4

EDUCATION EATING UP LIFE

60 high-school teaching — *The Boy I Left*, p. 410.

62 poverty of teachers — *The Boy I Left*, pp. 410-11.

62 professor's salary — "A Master of Satire," p. 12.

62 University of Toronto — examination performance, *University of Toronto: Class and Prize Lists*, 1888; cited in Curry biography, p. 42. Scholarship, *The Boy I Left*, p. 41.

63 first-year records — *University of Toronto: Class and Prize Lists*, 1888; cited in Curry biography, p. 43.

63 two years in one — *The Boy I Left*, p. 411. Leacock's program at Upper Canada College, coupled with his first year's success, won him third-year status, which was often granted in this way in the university system at the time. Pelham Edgar, "Stephen Leacock," *Queen's Quarterly*, LIII (May, 1946), p. 174.

63 mother's income — *The Boy I Left*, p. 411.

64 normal school — *The Boy I Left*, pp. 411-12; Robert S. Harris, *A History of Higher Education in Canada 1663-1960* (Toronto: University of Toronto Press, 1976), pp. 231-33.

65 boarding houses — *The Boy I Left*, pp. 412-13. "Boarding

PG

House Geometry," *Literary Lapses* (London: Lane, 1910), New Canadian Library 3, pp. 11-12. This book is cited hereafter as *Literary Lapses* with page numbers from the New Canadian Edition only.

65 nature of humor — *The Boy I Left*, p. 414.

66 Currie — *The Boy I Left*, p. 415.

67 Raines correspondence — Raines to Leacock, 1 February, 1936; Leacock to Raines, February, 1936. Leacock Home.

68 UCC supervisors — letter from Principal George Parkin to Principal William Peterson of McGill University, 19 January 1900, in Peterson Papers, file 70, McGill University Archives.

68 something good to say — Legate biography, p. 31.

69 junior marks — Curry biography, p. 50.

69 Christmas at Sutton — Kimball, p. 124.

70 senior marks — Curry biography, pp. 53-54.

70 ethnology examination — Bruce Murphy, "Stephen Leacock — the Greatest Living Humorist," *Ontario Library Review*, XII (February, 1928), p. 68.

71 first romance — Edgar, "Stephen Leacock," pp. 176-77.

72 humor in church — Edgar, "Stephen Leacock," pp. 178-79.

73 changes at Upper Canada College — Howard, *Upper Canada College*, pp. 124-30; Edgar, "Stephen Leacock," pp. 174-77.

74 "My Financial Career" — *Literary Lapses*, pp. 1-4.

75 American or Canadian —

76 Sara Jeannette Duncan — Dun-

PG

can praised *The College Times* under her pen name "Garth Grafton," in a March 1887 review cited by Howard, *Upper Canada College*, p. 275.

79 teaching languages — *The Boy I Left*, p. 419; "Parlez-Vous Francais?" in *Too Much College*, pp. 62-5.

79 leaving the farm — *The Boy I Left*, p. 387; Kimball, p. 138.

79 Agnes at Rotherwood — Kimball, p. 14.

80 Dot built her a house — Kimball, p. 9.

81 sporting skills — Edgar, "Stephen Leacock," pp. 173-81.

82 Lady Edgar's letter — letter from Lady Edgar to Pelham Edgar, August 1889. Leacock Home.

82 Incidents recalled by Pattison — notes by Pattison in files of Leacock Home.

84 Beatrix in New York — Curry, pp. 66-67.

84 Parkin recommendation — letter from George Parkin to William Peterson, 19 January 1900. McGill Archives.

5

HAS ECONOMICS GONE TO SEED

88 sound and insightful — Alan Bowker, editor, in his introduction to *The Social Criticism of Stephen Leacock* (Toronto: University of Toronto Press, 1973), p. ix.

89 history of economics — Stephen Leacock, "Has Economics Gone to Seed?" in *Too Much College*, pp. 109-24.

PG

89 economics in universities — Harris, *A History of Higher Education in Canada 1663-1960*, p. 217; K.W. Taylor, "Economic Scholarship in Canada," *Canadian Journal of Economics and Political Science*, 26 (1960), p. 8.

90 political economy — Stephen Leacock, *Elements of Political Science* (New York: Houghton Mifflin, 1906), pp. 8-9. The footnote cited below appears on p. 10.

91 Veblen's books exercised enormous influence — Bowker, *The Social Criticism of Stephen Leacock*, p. xi.

91 books that have changed our minds — John P. Diggins, *The Bard of Savagery: Thornstein Veblen and Modern Social Theory* (New York, 1978), p. 216.

91 controversial importers — Harris, *A History of High Education in Canada 1663-1960*, p. 321.

92 borrow money from his mother — information from a legal indenture of 22 November, 1899 advancing Leacock $1,500 from Agnes' estate. Leacock Home.

93 marriage to Beatrix — Curry biography, p. 66.

93 part-time at McGill — Curry biography, p. 59-60; Bowker, *The Social Criticism of Stephen Leacock*, p. xi.

94 work directed by Veblen — Curry biography, p. 66.

94 Veblen's classroom technique — Stephen Leacock, *My Discovery of the West* (Toronto: Allen, 1937), pp. 136-38.

95 what Veblen proposed — Leacock, *My Discovery of the West*, p. 137.

96 institution itself rests — Thorstein Veblen, *The Theory of the Leisure Class: An Economic Study of Institutions* (New York: Macmillan, 1899; rpt. New York: New American Library, 1953), p. 141 (NAL ed.).

96 leisure class — Veblen, *The Theory of the Leisure Class*, p. 47.

96 of substantial use — Veblen, *The Theory of the Leisure Class*, p. 68.

96 let him out — Leacock, *My Discovery of the West*, p. 137.

97 died a recluse — C. Wright Mills, introduction to *The Theory of the Leisure Class*, NAL ed., p. ix.

97 professors' wives — Diggins, *The Bard of Savagery*, p. 169.

98 doctoral examinations — Curry biography, p. 68, says that Leacock spoke for fifteen minutes; Legate biography, p. 35, says he spoke for several hours. Both cite only Leacock's University of Chicago "Record of Work."

99 letter from Laughlin — undated. Leacock Home.

99 letter from Starrett — 18 January, 1915. Leacock Home.

100 McGill's first-ever class — Legate biography, p. 38.

100 dispute with Flux — Flux's letters are in the McGill University Archives, Peterson Papers; cited in Legate biography, p. 42.

101 excellent marks — Veblen was a very strict grader, according to his biographer Diggins, seldom grading higher than a C; but a University of Chicago

PG

registrar's letter states Leacock never earned lower than a B.

101 reviews of *Elements* — "useful textbook," *Review of Reviews*, 34 (August, 1906), p. 253; "clear-cut," *Outlook*, 83 (28 July, 1906), p. 765; "almost too strong," Edward E. Hill, review in *School Review*, 14 (December, 1906), p. 770; "conventional," *Athenaeum*, 2 (20 October, 1906), p. 476.

102 special treatment — Leacock, *Elements of Political Science*, p. 371.

103 social reform — Leacock, *Elements of Political Science*, pp. 374-75.

103 beyond the seas — Leacock, *Elements of Political Science*, pp. 283-84.

6

OUR BRITISH EMPIRE

107 Mark Twain — Justin Kaplan, *Mr. Clemens and Mark Twain* (New York, 1966), p. 350.

109 "Imperial Crisis" — Curry biography, p. 74.

109 Leacock tour plan — Legate biography, p. 45.

109 governor-general's recommendation — letter from Grey to Peterson, 25 March, 1907. Peterson Papers, file 65, McGill Archives.

110 financing the trip — letter from grey, 25 March, 1907. Peterson Papers, file 65, McGill Archives.

111 Boer War — Leacock, *Elements of Political Science*, pp. 283-84.

112 another way — *Stephen Lea-*

PG

cock, The British Empire: Its Structure, Its Unity, Its Strength (New York: Dodd, Mead, 1940), pp. 42-43. Quotations from *Our British Empire* are cited from the U.S. edition, which substitutes "The" in the title but is otherwise identical.

112 "Greater Canada" — Stephen Leacock, "Greater Canada: An Appeal," *University Magazine*, VI (1907), p. 132; rpt. in Bowker, *The Social Criticism of Stephen Leacock*, p. 4. Passages are cited hereafter with page numbers from Bowker edition.

113 stayed with Rudyard Kipling — letter from Leacock to Peterson, 24 May, 1907. Peterson Papers, file 46, McGill Archives.

114 one's neighbour's corns — letter from Grey to Peterson, 30 January, 1906. Peterson Papers, file 65, McGill Archives.

114 the whole farm — Stephen Leacock, *The Morning Post*, London, May 1907; rpt. in the Orillia *Packet*, 30 May, 1907.

114 Winston Churchill — Bowker, *The Social Criticism of Stephen Leacock*, p. xiv.

115 "Greater Canada" — Leacock, "Greater Canada: An Appeal," p. 7.

116 not a formula — Leacock, *The British Empire*, p. 275.

116 white races — Leacock, *The British Empire*, p. 41.

116 fair play — Leacock, *The British Empire*, p. 38.

118 billiards game — Murray in conversation with David Legate, quoted in Legate biography, p. 58.

PG

119 The pretentious claim — Stephen Leacock, "Literature and Education in America," *University Magazine* VIII (1909), rpt. in Bowker, *The Social Criticism of Stephen Leacock*, p. 22.

120 retain our custom — Leacock, "Literature and Education in America," p. 25.

121 frightened him — Stephen Leacock, "The Passing of the Poet," *Canadian Magazine* (May, 1906), p. 72.

122 mistaken about poetry — Susan E. Cameron, "The Passing of the Poet: A Reply to Professor Leacock," *Canadian Magazine* (September, 1906), p. 505.

122 place of my own — letter from Leacock to Agnes, 30 May, 1907. Leacock Home.

123 coming home — letter from Leacock to Daisy, quoted by Grace Crooks, "A Taste of Humor," *Canadian Library Journal* (May-June, 1969), p. 224.

7

LAPSING INTO LITERATURE

124 Côte-des-Neiges house — copy of lease dated 14 April, 1909. Leacock Home.

126 manuscript prepared — B.K. Sandwell, "Stephen Leacock, Worst-Dressed Writer, Made Fun Respectable," *Saturday Night*, LIX (Toronto, 8 April, 1944), p. 17.

126 manuscript rejected — information from Leacock note to Norman H. Friedman in autographed copy of *Literary Lapses*.

PG

Leacock Room, McGill.

127 art's sake — Leacock, *Too Much College*, p. 210.

127 keep trying — Curry biography, pp. 79-80, based on conversation with George Leacock.

128 returned the fifty dollars to George — Curry biography, pp. 79-82, which deals with George and Stephen's plan for the publication.

128 finances of book — calculations in Leacock's hand and a copy of his letter and memorandum based on them, sent to Mr. Lasker of the Gazette Printing Co., 4 April, 1910. Leacock Home.

129 say thank you — Leacock note to Norman H. Friedman in autographed copy of *Literary Lapses*. Leacock Room, McGill.

131 here at home — introduction to first of "Novels in Nutshells," *Saturday Night*, Toronto, 10 December, 1910.

133 reviews of *Literary Lapses* — "uproariously funny," *Spectator* 105 (9 July, 1910), p. 105; "sketches excellent," *Independent* 70 (30 March, 1910), p. 670; "full of smiles," *Dial* 50 (16 February, 1911), p. 132; "rapid pen," *Dial*, p. 132.

133 know better — Stephen Leacock, in preface to *Nonsense Novels* (London: Lane, 1911), New Canadian Library 35, p. xiii. This book is cited hereafter as *Nonsense Novels*, with all page numbers from the NCL edition.

134 reviews of *Nonsense Novels* — "facetiousness," *Nation* 93 (24 August, 1911), p. 165; "noisy horseplay," *New York Times* 16

PG

(1 October, 1911), p. 591.

135 Pick a card — *Literary Lapses*, p. 118.

135 her to whoa — *Literary Lapses*, p. 29.

136 miles around — *Literary Lapses*, p. 6.

136 revolving sticks — *Literary Lapses*, p. 74.

137 Prince of Wales — *Literary Lapses*, pp. 80-81.

138 in all directions — *Nonsense Novels*, p. 54; on Roosevelt's use of the story, Legate biography, p. 55.

138 thud on the grass — *Nonsense Novels*, p. 96.

139 by good works — *Nonsense Novels*, p. 98.

8

THE TRAIN TO MARIPOSA

142 prove themselves Canadians — *Sunshine Sketches*, p. 124.

143 freetraders — Legate biography, p. 59. Another version of this anecdote exists in which Hemmeon's remark is: "All economists are socialists. This version indicates how early the idea that Leacock was not a forward-looking economist formed — among those who held it — not around an assessment of his ideas but around a general sense that he was not favorable to fashionable advanced views. The two versions together show how eager certain students and others were to enshrine in memory any apparent rebuttal to such a formidable, and beloved,

PG

counter-authority to their own views as Leacock. The "socialists" version of the anecdote is recounted by Leacock's former student David C. Monroe in E.A. Collard, ed., *The McGill You Knew: An Anthology of Memories* (Toronto: Longmans, 1975), pp. 56-57. Abundant evidence exists of the great personal regard and affection between Hemmeon and Leacock. See, for instance, Allan Anderson, *Remembering Leacock: An Oral History* (Ottawa: Deneau, 1983), p. 75, comment of Eugene Forsey (this book is hereafter cited as Anderson).

144 anti-reciprocity Conservative — Frost quoted in Legate biography, p. 60.

145 the idea originated — B.K. Sandwell, "Stephen Leacock, Worst-Dressed Writer, Made Fun Respectable,"

145 his notes — photocopy of notes dated 7 January, 1912, Leacock Home.

146 Leacock would write that — photocopy of letter, Orillia Public Library.

146- McAree — Toronto *Globe*, 26 Oc-
7 tober, 1958.

147 Josh Smith — this and subsequent information on the originals of Leacock's characters in *Sunshine Sketches* are from research of the Leacock Home staff in the Home's files and exhibits.

148- St. James fire — Orillia *Times*,
9 23 March, 1905; files of Orillia *Daily Packet and Times*.

149 Lower — Arthur Lower, "The

9

**SOME JUST COMPLAINTS
ABOUT THE WAR**

Larger Lunacy (London: Lane, 1915), New Canadian Library 43, p. ix. This book is cited hereafter as *Moonbeams* with page numbers from the New Canadian Library edition.

168 every line of it — *Moonbeams*, p. 11.

169 janitors are unarmed — *Moonbeams*, p. 114.

169 treacherous crime — *Moonbeams*, p. 116.

169 their own interests — *Moonbeams*, p. 117.

170- letter on Stevie's birth — letter
71 from Leacock to Agnes, 19 August, 1915. Leacock Home.

171 passages from diary — Agnes' diary, p. 7. Leacock Home.

172- a capacity audience — *My Dis-*
73 *covery of England*, pp. 156-57.

173 burnt stick — Stephen Leacock, "The Snoopopaths; or, Fifty Stories in One," in *Further Foolishness* (London: Lane, 1916); New Canadian Library 60, p. 23. This book is cited hereafter as *Further Foolishness* with page numbers from the New Canadian Library edition.

174 in about twenty-five minutes — letter from Leacock to Pelham Edgar, 9 February, 1916. Victoria College Library, University of Toronto.

175 is that all — letter from Leacock to Edgar, 9 February, 1916.

175 throwing a rock — *Further Foolishness*, p. 146.

176 all mankind — Stephen Leacock, "Father Knickerbocker: A Fantasy," in *Frenzied Fiction* (London: Lane, 1917), New Canadian Library 48, p. 151. This book is cited hereafter as

Frenzied Fiction with page numbers from the New Canadian Library edition.

176 Roosevelt's letter — Trent Frayne, "The Erudite Jester of McGill," *Maclean's* (1 January, 1953) quotes the letter, which reads: "I am sending you the *Metropolitan* with an article by me dealing with Canada's great record in this war. All my family, including myself, owe you much for both amusement and instruction...."

176 "Q" staged — Legate biography, p. 82.

176 the half-truth — Stephen Leacock, "The Woman Question," in *Essays and Literary Studies* (London: Lane, 1916), p. 161. This book is cited hereafter as *Essays and Studies*.

177 no such continent — "A Rehabilitation of Charles II," in *Essays and Studies*, p. 269.

177 nothing really matters — "A Rehabilitation of Charles II," in *Essays and Studies*, p. 274.

178 common lot of sorrow — "American Humour," in *Essays and Studies*, p. 445.

178 suffering or death — *Further Foolishness*, pp. 156-58.

180 Go to it — letter from Leacock to Benchley, cited in Curry biography, p. 132.

180 To Stephen Leacock — Benchley's inscription in a copy of his book, *Of All Things*. Leacock Home.

181 expand social protection — *The Unsolved Riddle of Social Justice*, p. 135.

181 minimum wage — *The Unsolved Riddle of Social Justice*, p. 142.

PG

182 advanced causes — Bowker, *The Social Criticism of Stephen Leacock*, pp. xxxvii-xxxix.

183 opportunity in life — *The Unsolved Riddle of Social Justice*, p. 140.

183 cant of the Hun — Charles L. Graves, "To Stephen Leacock," *Punch* (14 February, 1917).

183 command of Yiddish — Stephen Leacock, *The Hohenzollerns in Canada* (London: Lane, 1919), p. 31.

183 political things — *The Hohenzollerns in America*, p. 26.

10

WOMEN AND WHISKEY

186 *Winsome Winnie* not accepted — Leacock's letters to Jefferson Jones, managing editor of the John Lane Co., New York, 22 and 24 November, 1920, in files of Dodd, Mead and Co.; cited in Curry biography, pp. 136-37.

187 letter from John Lane — 4 November, 1921. Leacock Home.

187 Davies thinks it — "Introduction," in Davies, ed., *Feast of Stephen: An Anthology of Some of the Less Familiar Writings of Stephen Leacock* (Toronto: McClelland & Stewart, 1970), p. 26.

187 *New York Times* review — *New York Times*, 19 December, 1920, p. 11.

187 *Times Literary Supplement* review — *Times Literary Supplement*, London, 2 December, 1920, p. 795.

188 Maclean's first report — copy of letter from J.B. Maclean to Frank Munsey, 3 January, 1920. Leacock Home.

188 Maclean wrote to Munsey — copy of letter of 2 May, 1920. Leacock Home.

189 as an economic writer — copy of letter from H.H. Black of *Maclean's* Montreal office to J.B. Maclean. Leacock Home.

189 I am afraid that — letter from Leacock to Munsey, 17 May, 1920. Leacock Home.

189 asked him to write — letter from *Collier's*, 18 May, 1921; repeated requests from the magazine through agent Paul Reynolds, 30 November, 1921 and 7 February, 1922. Leacock Home.

190 Lane's letter — the letter of 4 November, 1921. Leacock Home.

190 Reynolds wrote repeatedly — e.g. letter to Leacock of 9 November, 1921. Leacock Home.

190- He promised...illustrated by
91 John Kettelwell — e.g. letters of 15 March and 22 April, 1921. Leacock Home.

191 Willett's letter — 3 November, 1921. Leacock Home.

191 Dodd, Mead asked him — as attested in a letter from Frank Dodd to Leacock, 6 February, 1922; on 24 January, 1923, Leacock refused to sign a three-book contract for Dodd, Mead. Leacock Home.

191 He courted — e.g. letter from Doubleday, 18 January, 1922; letter from Jefferson Jones regarding possible formation of a new publishing firm, January

PG

1922.

192 letter to Chapman — 8 July, 1921. Leacock Home.

192 Chapman agreed — Chapman's letter to Leacock, 12 July, 1921. Leacock Home.

193 forty thousand dollars — copy of Leacock's tax forms for 1923. Leacock Home.

193 delightful glimpse — William Caldwell, "Impressions of Ontario, V: A Visit to a Canadian Author," *Canadian Magazine*, 59 (May, 1922), p. 56.

194 Leacock's car — information from his accident liability policy, 7 May, 1922. Leacock Home.

194 note from Jones — 23 August, 1921. Leacock Home.

195 wrote in his memoirs — Dr. Alton Goldbloom, *Small Patients: The Autobiography of a Children's Doctor* (Toronto: Longmans, Green & Co., 1959).

195 a former student tells — Senator Eugene Forsey (who also became a professor of economics in Leacock's department), cited in Anderson, pp. 5-6.

196 editors moved quickly...Leacock wrote back — letter from B.W. Willett, 9 February, 1922; Leacock's response, 25 February, 1922. Leacock Home.

197- Women need — quotations from
98 "The Woman Question" cited from Bowker, *The Social Criticism of Stephen Leacock*, where the essay is reprinted, pp. 51-60.

198 article for *Collier's* — "We Are Teaching Women All Wrong," *Collier's*, 68 (31 December, 1921), p. 15.

199 He once addressed — Margaret

PG

Gillets, *We Walked Very Warily: A History of Women at McGill* (Montreal, 1981), p. 217.

200 incident of Maude Grant — recounted by Grant's daughter in E.A. Collard, ed., *The McGill You Knew*, p. 32.

200 one of his female students — Leacock's recommendation to the University of Chicago for this student, a Miss Going, is referred to by Professor J. Laurence Laughlin in his letter to Leacock of early 1915 (undated). Leacock Home.

201 According to a Toronto newspaper — "Professor Leacock is Opposed to Prohibition as a Matter of Principle," Toronto *World*, 4 April, 1921.

202 Maclean's letter to Schwab — 21 October, 1922, copy at Leacock Home.

202 the two flask incidents — Anderson, p. 9; the first recounted by Leacock's one-time secretary, Grace Reynolds, the second by Anderson.

202 fullest statement — "The Tyranny of Prohibition" appeared first in 1919 in the British *National Review*; cited here from its reprint in the American *Living Age*, 302 (2 August, 1919), pp. 301-306.

206 Willett claimed — letter to Leacock of 3 November, 1921. Leacock Home.

208 In 1920...A young girl — letter to Saunders; 31 January, 1920; letter from Emma McLean of West Bay, Cape Breton Island, with watch case, 24 December, 1920. Leacock Home.

208- letter from Stefansson, 22

PG

Edel tells the story of seeing Leacock on the steps of the Arts Building in Collard's *The McGill You Knew*, p. 87.

227 *Origin of Species* — Stephen Leacock, "The Outlines of Everything," *Winnowed Wisdom* (New York: Dodd, Mead, 1926), New Canadian Library 74, p. 9. This book will be cited hereafter as *Winnowed Wisdom* with page numbers from the New Canadian Library edition only.

228 bell and tell — "The Crossword Puzzle Craze," *Winnowed Wisdom*, p. 49.

229 above the average — *Winnowed Wisdom*, p. viii.

231 1929 income — financial files. Leacock Home.

231 lowered royalties — letter from Dodd, Mead to Stephen Leacock, 28 August, 1929; letter in reply, 3 September. Leacock Home.

12

THE SAVING GRACE OF HUMOUR

235 The silliest thing — Legate biography, p. 141.

235- Leacock's blurb — in Leacock's
36 hand, November, 1931. Leacock Home.

236 white men — Stephen Leacock, *Economic Prosperity in the British Empire* (London: Constable & Co. Ltd, 1930), p. 243.

236 London *Times* — review of *Economic Prosperity, Times Literary Supplement* (1923), p. 723.

237- Aitken letter — Aitken to Lea-

PG

38 cock, 31 August, 1930. Leacock Home.

238 he declined — copy of letter to North American Newspaper Alliance, 8 April, 1932. Leacock Home.

240 Bennett wrote — letter of 2 July, 1932. Leacock Home.

240 the monetary situation — letter of Bennett to Leacock, 22 September, 1932. Leacock Home.

243 Bennett's letter — letter from R.B. Bennett to Stephen Leacock, 12 July, 1935. Leacock Home.

244- exchange of letters between
45 Beatty and Leacock — letters of 7 and 12 November, 11 and 14 December, 1935. Leacock Home.

246- eloquent response — letter from
47 Stephen Leacock to unnamed correspondent, 18 December, 1935.

248- income information — informa-
49 tion from copies of Leacock's tax returns at Leacock Home.

249 Like all people here — copy of letter from Leacock, 9 January, 1932. Leacock Home.

249 Richard Marvin visit — letter of 16 November, 1931. Leacock Home.

249 DeFoe suggests programs — manuscript of article by Ralph Curry on Leacock's work for electronic media, p. 2. Leacock Home.

249 did get a program on the air — Curry biography, pp. 231-34, citing information supplied by Joseph McDougall.

249 box on a stick — Curry article on electronic media, p. 3.

13

Mc-Guillotined

PG

274 shout it down to them — *The Montreal Star*, 18 December, 1935, p. 1.

274 smoke at students — "Leacock at Leisure," *New York Times*, 21 December, 1935.

274 feature of its work — memorandum from Leacock to Morgan, 13 February, 1936. Leacock Home.

275 no right to ask — related by Leacock in letter to Dean Charles Martin, 15 February, 1936. Leacock Home. Also, following quotation.

275 fine-tooth comb — Legate biography, pp. 198-99; Anderson, p. 77.

276 wearing torn gowns — Legate biography, p. 201.

276 bad departments — Curry biography, p. 246.

276 like a boys' school — Curry biography, p. 246.

276 degree of ex-principal — Legate biography, p. 217.

276 Senility Gang — Stephen Leacock, *Funny Pieces* (New York: Dodd, Mead, 1936), p. 260.

276 halls of McGill — Legate biography, p. 210.

276 speech notes — in Leacock's hand on stationery of the Mount Royal Hotel, dated 4 May, 1936. Leacock Home.

277 a dollar up — Curry biography, p. 258.

277 I hope never — mimeographed announcement. Leacock Room, McGill.

277 Macphail letter — Macphail to Leacock, 1 May, 1936. Leacock Home.

277- I still believe — letter from
78 Beatty to Leacock, 12 Novem-

PG

ber, 1935. Leacock Home.

278 he wrote to a friend — letter to Dr. Gerhard Lomer, 19 November, 1937. Leacock Room, McGill.

279 I was taken to task — letter

284 Pravda publication — Legate biography, p. 204, citing Leacock-Kon correspondence at Leacock Room, McGill.

284 Baron Scavenger — letter from Leacock to a friend addressed only as "Frank," 1 June, 1937. Leacock Home.

285 Her introductory essay — Barbara Nimmo, "Preface" to the original edition of *Last Leaves*; pp. xiii-xxv.

14

WHILE THERE IS TIME

290 prostatic surgery — Legate biography, p. 219.

291 Mackenzie letter — Leacock to Mrs. John Drinkwater, 5 April, 1938. Leacock Room, McGill.

291 still in hospital — letter of 24 April, 1938. Leacock Home.

291 finally released — letter of 28 April, 1938 from Frank Dodd to Leacock: Dodd had heard from Leacock he would be out of hospital "next week." Leacock Home.

291 still referring — copy of a letter from Leacock, 22 August, 1938. Leacock Home.

292 Kimball — letters of 23 April and 7 June, 1934, from D.A. Kimball. Leacock Home.

293 trundle produce — Anderson, p. 144, quoting Henry Janes. Janes states that this practice,

PG

article by Taylor, "I Painted Stephen Leacock." Legate biography, pp. 230-32.

307 He impressed me — Legate biography, p. 241, quoted from Legate's correspondence with Edwin Holgate.

307 He wrote simultaneously — letter quoted and letter to bank, 23 January, 1940. Leacock Home.

309 I am leaving — this and all letters in the paragraph above relating to Charlie are in the Leacock Home files under the dates given in the text.

309 the Orillia police — letter of 21 July, 1942 to Leacock. Leacock Home.

309 in the hands of the Ontario public trustee — document dated November, 1942. Leacock Home.

309 the patient had — letter of 22 July, 1942 from Ontario public trustee. Leacock Home.

309 Dot's letter — 14 February, 1944. Leacock Home.

310 letter from Dodd — 30 April, 1940. Leacock Home.

310 out of place — Legate biography, p. 233; information given by Roberts to Legate.

310 Stevie's writing — notes of Henry Janes. Leacock Home.

311 Very glad — Leacock's telegram, 18 July, 1940, and above-mentioned letter from Gazette Printing Co., 16 July, 1940. Leacock Home.

311 came down from his study — incident recounted in tape-recording of talk given by Henry R. Mainer, 29 June, 1953 at Leacock Memorial Dinner. Orillia Public Library. Also

PG

Curry biography, pp. 310-11.

311 five thousand dollars or more — Legate biography, pp. 233-34, gives this figure, apparently basing it on a conversation with Samuel Bronfman. Mainer (see note above), and Curry biography (p. 311) following Mainer, give ten thousand dollars.

312 Longley's remark — *The Globe*, Toronto, 12 April, 1902.

312 Book of the Month Club — letter from Costain, December, 1941. Leacock Home.

313 On a contract — copy, dated August 1942. Leacock Home.

313 another project — in letters from Costain, 8 and 16 December, 1941. Leacock Home.

313 a happy blend — Leacock's words quoted back to him by Costain in letter of 16 December, 1941. Leacock Home.

314 I'll face it — *My Remarkable Uncle*, p. 179.

314 accepted the task — letter of 8 September, 1942. Leacock Home.

315 Shave's letter — 14 September, 1943. Leacock Home.

315 Burt's review — *The Saturday Review*, 6 February, 1943.

315 a favorite child — letter to Lomer, 11 January, 1943. Leacock Room, McGill.

316 pick beans — copy of note to Costain, August, 1943. Leacock Home.

317 Leacock came — Costain quoted by J.A. (Pete) McGarvey, "'Dream' That Became A Legacy," *Canadian Author & Bookman* 56, No. 3 (Spring, 1981), pp. 6-8.

317 *Maclean's* rejects two articles —

PG

15

BEHIND THE BEYOND

Bibliography

BOOKS BY LEACOCK

Adventurers of the Far North, 1914
Afternoons in Utopia, 1932
Arcadian Adventures with the Idle Rich, 1914
Back to Prosperity: The Great Opportunity of the Empire Conference, 1932
Baldwin, Lafontaine, Hincks: Responsible Government, 1907
Behind the Beyond, 1913
Boy I Left Behind Me, The, 1946
Canada and the Sea, 1944
Canada, The Foundations of Its Future, 1941
Charles Dickens, His Life and Works, 1933
College Days, 1923
Dawn of Canadian History, The, 1914
Dry Pickwick and Other Incongruities, The, 1932
Economic Prosperity in the British Empire, 1930
Elements of Political Science, 1906
Essays and Literary Studies, 1916
Frenzied Fiction, 1918
Funny Pieces, 1936
Further Foolishness, 1916
Garden of Folly, The, 1924
Gathering Financial Crisis in Canada, The
Greatest Pages of American Humor, The (selection and commentary by Leacock), 1936
Greatest Pages of Charles Dickens, The (selection and commentary by Leacock), 1934
Happy Stories, Just to Laugh At, 1943
Hellements of Hickonomics, in Hiccoughs of Verse Done in Our Social Planning Mill, 1936
Here Are My Lectures and Stories, 1937
Hohenzollerns in America, The, 1919
How to Write, 1943
Humor and Humanity, 1937
Humor, Its Theory and Technique, with Examples and Samples, 1935
Iron Man and the Tin Woman, With Other Such Futurities, The, 1929

Lahontan's Voyages (edited, introduced and annotated by
  Leacock), 1932
Last Leaves, 1945
Lincoln Frees the Slaves, 1934
Literary Lapses, 1910
Mariner of St. Malo, The, 1914
Mark Twain, 1932
*Model Memoirs and Other Sketches from Simple to
  Serious*, 1938
Montreal: Seaport and City, 1942
Moonbeams from the Larger Lunacy, 1915
My Discovery of England, 1922
My Discovery of the West, 1937
My Remarkable Uncle and Other Sketches, 1942
Nonsense Novels, 1911
Our British Empire, 1940
*Our Heritage of Liberty, Its Origin, Its Achievement,
  Its Crisis*, 1942
Over the Footlights and Other Fancies, 1923
Short Circuits, 1928
Sunshine Sketches of a Little Town, 1912
*Too Much College; or, Education Eating Up Life, with
  Kindred Essays in Education and Humor*, 1939
Unsolved Riddle of Social Justice, The, 1920
*Wet Wit and Dry Humor, Distilled from the Pages of
  Stephen Leacock*, 1931
*While There Is Time: The Case Against Social
  Catastrophe*, 1945
Winnowed Wisdom, 1926
Winsome Winnie, and Other New Nonsense Novels, 1920

PAMPHLETS AND SHORT BOOKS BY LEACOCK

*All Right, Mr. Roosevelt (Canada and the United
  States)*, 1939
*Greater Canada, an Appeal. Let Us No Longer Be a
  Colony*, 1907
The Marionette's Calendar, 1915
The Methods of Mr. Sellyer: A Book Store Study, 1914

My Memories and Miseries as a Schoolmaster, n.d.
"My Old College" 1843-1943, 1943
Other People's Money, 1944
Proper Limitations of State Interference, The, 1924
*Pursuit of Knowledge: A Discussion of Freedom and
    Compulsion in Education, The*, 1934
"Q": A Farce in One Act (with B.H. Hastings), 1915
Restoration of the Finances of McGill, The, 1935
*Stephen Leacock's Plan to Relieve the Depression in 6 Days,
    to Remove It in 6 Months, to Eradicate It in 6 Years*, 1933
What Nickel Means to the World

ANTHOLOGIES OF LEACOCK'S WORK

The Best of Leacock (Canadian title of *The Bodley
    Head Leacock*), 1957
The Bodley Head Leacock, ed. J.B. Priestley, 1957
Feast of Stephen, ed. Robertson Davies, 1970
Laugh Parade, 1940
Laugh with Leacock, 1930
The Leacock Book, ed. Ben Travers, 1930
The Leacock Roundabout, 1946
The Penguin Stephen Leacock, ed. Robertson Davies, 1981
The Unicorn Leacock, ed. James Reeves, 1960

BOOKS ABOUT LEACOCK

Cameron, D.A., *Faces of Leacock: An Appreciation*, 1967
Curry, Ralph L. *Stephen Leacock, Humorist and Humanist*,
    1959
Davies, Robertson, *Stephen Leacock*, 1970
Kimball, Elizabeth, *The Man in the Panama Hat*, 1970
Legate, David M., *Stephen Leacock*, 1970
Lomer, Gerhard R., *Stephen Leacock: A Check-List and
    Index of His Writings*, 1954
Masson, T.L., in *Our American Humorists* (pp. 209-29), 1931
Mikes, George, in *Eight Humorists* (pp. 41-65), 1954
Phelps, Arthur L., in *Canadian Writers* (pp. 70-76), 1951

Index

Index

Acknowledgments

The authors thank all those whose assistance was crucial to the writing of this book and who generously offered their time and help.

First we would like to mention the present director and the secretary of the Stephen Leacock Memorial Home, Jay Cody and Doris Medlock. Any students of Leacock inevitably benefit from the work of Dr. Ralph Curry, first curator of the Leacock Home and first biographer of Leacock. All those who have supported the Leacock Home — officials and citizens of Orillia and other friends of Leacock — have provided the humorist's admirers with an opportunity to work in his continuing presence. Leacock's niece, Barbara Nimmo, and McClelland & Stewart Ltd. have granted permission to quote from Leacock's copyrighted works. We also have received friendly assistance from the staffs of the Orillia Public Library, the MacLennan Library of McGill University and the Public Archives of Canada. The University of Toronto Press has allowed us to quote passages from materials under its copyright in Alan Bowker's *The Social Criticism of Stephen Leacock*.

We must also extend general thanks to the many writers of biographical studies and essays, memoirs, reminiscences and anecdotes who have done so much to enshrine the memory of Leacock, often preserving the testimony of persons now dead.